HANDBOOK OF METHODS
FOR DETECTING TEST BIAS

Other books edited by Ronald A. Berk

Criterion-Referenced Measurement: The State of the Art
Educational Evaluation Methodology: The State of the Art

HANDBOOK OF METHODS FOR DETECTING TEST BIAS

EDITED BY RONALD A. BERK

The Johns Hopkins University Press • Baltimore and London

The Johns Hopkins University Press, Baltimore, Maryland 21218
The Johns Hopkins Press Ltd., London

Library of Congress Cataloging in Publication Data
Main entry under title:

Handbook of methods for detecting test bias.

  Based on papers presented at the 3rd annual
Johns Hopkins University National Symposium on
Educational Research (NSER) held in Washington,
D.C., in Nov. 1980.
  Includes index.
  1. Test bias—Congresses. I. Berk, Ronald A.
II. Johns Hopkins University National Symposium on
Educational Research (3rd: 1980: Washington, D.C.)
LB3060.62.H36   371.2´6´013   81-48190
ISBN 0-8018-2662-4   AACR2

To Corinne

CONTENTS

PREFACE

THIS BOOK PROVIDES a state-of-the-art assessment of the methods for detecting test bias. It is a product of the third annual Johns Hopkins University National Symposium on Educational Research (NSER), held in Washington, D.C. in November 1980.

THE SYMPOSIUM

The idea for a symposium was first suggested to me by Gilbert B. Schiffman. The state-of-the-art concept applied to the symposium was stimulated by the divisional state-of-the-art addresses presented at the 1978 American Educational Research Association Conference. The need for a "research symposium" with a practical orientation became obvious as I observed that much of the research generated year after year did not seem to be reflected in classroom and school district practices. Consequently, despite the sophisticated research dissemination methods available, a gap between research findings and their implementation in practice was evident. The symposium was seen as one possible vehicle to bridge the gap.

Purposes

The symposium was conceived as a mechanism for assembling research scholars on a topic of national concern to educational researchers and practitioners. The scholars selected to participate in the third symposium have contributed substantially to the advancement and understanding of test bias methodology through their publications and through their leadership in studying bias in standardized achievement, aptitude, and intelligence tests. Their task was to synthesize the research on the topic that has accumulated over the past decade and translate the results into guidelines that practitioners can use and problems that researchers can investigate.

The presentations provided a state-of-the-art assessment of bias methodology in terms of what has been done, what should be done, and what still needs to be done. The symposium dealt only with bias methods for two reasons: (1) the more than a dozen methods that have been proposed for use with achievement, aptitude, and intelligence tests have created much confusion in the field, to the extent that it has become excessively difficult to choose a "best" method or combination of methods for a given application, and (2) the different interpretations and incomparability of previous studies of test bias often stem, in part, from the design and statistical analyses employed.

Advisory Board

The annual theme and invited speakers for the symposium are chosen according to the recommendations of the NSER Advisory Board. I gratefully acknowledge the useful contributions of the 1980 board members: Robert L. Brennan, Lois E. Burrill, Carmen J. Finley, Lorraine R. Gay, Ronald K. Hambleton, Freda M. Holley, David J. Kleinke, James M. McPartland, William B. Michael, and Lorrie A. Shepard. Drs. Brennan and Burrill's suggestions for structuring the symposium were particularly valuable.

Audience

The symposium was designed to attract researchers from universities, private corporations, and R & D laboratories, and test makers and test users at the federal, state, and local levels. The response to the 1980 NSER was enthusiastic. More than 180 distinguished educators from 33 states, Canada, Bermuda, and The Netherlands attended the symposium.

ACKNOWLEDGMENTS

The symposium and this book represent the culmination of a tremendous amount of work by several individuals. I am delighted to mention the contributions of a few who deserve special credit. First, I extend my deepest appreciation to the 16 authors and to Nancy S. Cole (University of Pittsburgh), Lawrence M. Rudner (National Institute of Education), and William R. Merz (California State University, Sacramento), who served as discussants at the symposium, for sharing their expertise and exhibiting remarkable patience and cooperation. The administrative support given by Dean Roman J. Verhaalen and Elaine C. Davis of the Evening College and the financial support of Keith E. Glancy and the Office of Continuing Education of The Johns Hopkins University made it all possible. Lynn E. Wilkinson and Sharon D. Custis coordinated the symposium effectively and efficiently. Henry Tom, social sciences editor, and Miriam K. Tillman, manuscript editor, of The Johns Hopkins University Press, provided useful suggestions and valuable editorial assistance throughout the publication process. Finally, I want to thank my secretary, Ann W. Hall, and the numerous typists from Kelly Services of Baltimore who completed the necessary manuscript format changes and retyping of the references.

INTRODUCTION
RONALD A. BERK

TESTS AND TESTING practices have been the objects of close, thorough scrutiny in recent years. This is demonstrated by the consistently increasing public and professional criticisms of tests (Brim, 1965; Cronbach, 1975; Kamin, 1975; Nairn et al., 1980), the state legislative mandates of testing practices (e.g., truth-in-testing in New York), and the federal laws designating fair uses of tests (e.g., Education for All Handicapped Children Act of 1975, Vocational Rehabilitation Act of 1973). Viewed in terms of a general antitesting sentiment, no single type of criticism has been as vexing and thorny to test users and test makers as the criticisms that pertain to sex, racial, and ethnic test bias. A charge of bias can be directed against any available measurement device quite easily. What is not quite so easy is to obtain incontrovertible evidence to substantiate or to refute that charge. The need for dense arguments from logical, theoretical, and empirical perspectives can be best illustrated by the unscientific character of the plaintiffs' and defendants' arguments in the major legal cases on bias to date, for example, the *Larry P.* case (*Larry P., et al.* v. *Wilson Riles, et al.,* 1972, 1979).

The term *bias* has become socially volatile. It can evoke emotional reactions akin to the words *discrimination* and *racism.* The considerable controversy over bias in testing which has emerged in the past decade has added numerous negative overtones and connotations to its meaning. Possibly the only positive outgrowth of the polemics surrounding bias has been its galvanizing effect on the measurement community. In the late 1960s and early 1970s psychometricians hastened to provide definitions of bias in terms of objective criteria, to develop rigorous and precise methods for studying bias, and to conduct empirical investigations of test bias. The subsequent proliferation of methods to detect bias and studies to determine whether or not specific tests are biased has not yet abated.

A UNIFIED CONCEPTUALIZATION OF BIAS

A framework is needed to review bias methodology and to sort out the individual contributions to this volume in the context of the literature. The few

1

schemes that have been recommended previously are based largely on the traditional trinary conceptualization of validity (Jensen, 1980; Reynolds, 1982): content, criterion-related, and construct.* On the surface, this classification appears to be convenient and meaningful since most charges of bias, such as inappropriate content, differential predictive validity, and measurement of different constructs, can be defined as potential sources of invalidity. In other words, the three types of validity can be translated into three types of bias: content bias, predictive bias, and construct bias.

This trinary conceptualization of bias, however, is problematic. First, the categories overlap and, in some instances, it may be difficult to squeeze a particular bias issue (e.g., examiner bias, inequitable social consequences) into a single slot. Certain sources of bias such as race of the examiner have been labeled situational biases since they result from factors in the external testing situation rather than from the test itself (see Jensen, 1980, chap. 12, for a detailed explanation). It is clearly unnecessary to label the type of bias in order to gather evidence to prove it does or does not exist. Second, a compartmentalized thinking of bias could foster the notion that there are alternative approaches and a test maker need only pick one of them. This could lead to an incorrect conclusion, for example, that because there is no evidence of content bias, the test is completely unbiased in relation to all score uses. Finally, the three categories are inadequate for classifying the diverse forms of bias that may be suspected in terms of possible test score interpretations, uses, and inferences.

The recent trend toward a unified conceptualization of validity (Cronbach, 1980; Guion, 1977, 1980; Linn, 1980; Messick, 1979; Tenopyr, 1977) seems to suggest a more useful framework. Such a conceptualization of bias would de-emphasize the types of bias and instead emphasize the data-gathering process and the methods to obtain the kinds of evidence essential to answer the charges. The test maker would concentrate on the inferences to be made with the scores and the sources of bias that could invalidate those inferences. Subsequently, evidence would be accumulated to ascertain the presence or absence of bias. If internal modifications can remove the detected bias, then the final test might be considered "debiased" for the intended score inferences. If the total test is found to be biased, however, score inferences related to that source of bias would be inappropriate.

---

*Jensen (1980, p. 377) partitions validity into predictive, internal construct, and external construct. Internal construct validity criteria would include content validity; however, since he defines the assessment of bias as "a purely objective, empirical, statistical and quantitative matter entirely independent of subjective value judgments ..." (p. 375), the judgmental procedures associated with the determination of content validity and, in this case, content bias are ignored (see discussion of "culture bound fallacy," pp. 371–372). Instead, "internal" criteria of bias are considered only in terms of how particular statistical properties of a test differ significantly in any two populations (p. 429).

FOCUS ON ITEM BIAS METHODOLOGY

The primary focus of this book is item bias methods. The justification for this orientation can be explicated in terms of the preceding conceptualization. Initially, the content or behaviors that a test measures is an integral part of all score inferences. Since the item is the most fundamental level of content analysis and the foundation for these inferences, item bias studies are necessary for all tests. However, they are not sufficient for all test score inferences and uses. For example, additional studies would be required if the scores were used to make predictions about future performance. Second, charges of bias from numerous sources frequently include a citation of specific items that are claimed to be biased against a minority population. These sources can be public or professional organizations such as Parents in Action on Special Education (PACE), the National Education Association, and the Association of Black Psychologists (Jackson, 1975; Williams, 1970, 1971), or individual citizens and organizations as plaintiffs (e.g., *Armstead, et al.* v. *Starkville Mississippi Municipal Separate School District*, 1972; *Larry P., et al.* v. *Wilson Riles, et al.*, 1972; *PASE, et al.* v. *Joseph P. Hannon, et al.*, 1980). Third, the results of bias studies at the subtest and total test levels do not preclude the presence of bias at the item level. For example, a predictive bias study that does not reject the null hypothesis of no sex bias does not rule out the possibility that specific items on the test may be biased against females.

Other reasons for concentrating on item bias methods include the following: (1) item bias studies can be incorporated into the early stages of test construction and item analysis to minimize the chances of bias accusations arising later; (2) the elimination of item bias may decrease the likelihood of test bias, although research evidence is needed to verify this relationship; and (3) the regression and factor analytic methods employed in test bias studies of predictive and construct bias questions, respectively, are not particularly troublesome compared to proposed item bias methods.

Despite the importance attached' to item bias methods, a state-of-the-art volume on bias methodology would be incomplete without a comprehensive treatment of test bias methods. Such methods are essential to answer the varied charges of bias that may occur. Therefore, an exhaustive survey of methods germane to that topic has been included (see chapter 8).

A Philosophical Perspective

Two philosophical positions on item bias underlie the structure of this book. The first pertains to how item bias is perceived. That is, an item that is biased will favor or disfavor one particular population compared to other populations. In some cases, item biases may tend to cancel one another when viewed in terms of subtest or total test scores. Even if the individual item biases balance out across the test or the bias effect accounts for only a minute proportion of the total variance, the test should still be regarded as biased. Biases of any kind are socially and psychometrically undesirable, and every effort should be expended to minimize if not completely eliminate bias (cf. Jensen, 1980, p. 455).

The second position relates to the types of method that should be employed to identify bias. Judgmental procedures involving a panel of minority judges, for example, sometimes referred to as "armchair analyses," should be used in conjunction with selected statistical methods. An investigation of bias should include the following: (1) *judgmental review* to detect stereotypic, culture-specific, and offensive language and to assure fair representation in the work roles and life styles of sex, racial, and ethnic groups; (2) *statistical analysis* based on an appropriate experimental or quasi-experimental design to detect performance discrepancies in relation to item, construct, and/or predictive bias; and (3) *a posteriori analysis* of the statistical results to discern whether true item or test bias is present and, if it is, to deduce explanations for why it occurred and consider procedures for eliminating it. In essence, a study should begin with judgment and end with judgment. While the research comparing the data from judgmental and statistical methods has found almost irreconcilable differences between the methods (see Cotter & Berk, 1981; Plake, 1980; Sandoval & Miille, 1980), a more perceptive interpretation might be that the two methods are tapping different kinds of bias. Consequently, one should integrate the information from both types of analysis in order to gain as much insight as possible into the various forms of bias that could be identified. This seems necessary given the philosophical, political, social, educational, and psychological implications of bias. Furthermore, a dual strategy is usually required to satisfactorily address all claims of bias and produce credible results.

PURPOSES OF THE BOOK

This book attempts to determine the state of the art of bias methodology. Its contribution to the literature will depend largely on how well it accomplishes the following purposes: (1) to clarify the term *bias* and related terminology; (2) to synthesize the research that has been amassed on the topic over the past decade; (3) to translate the research findings into forms meaningful and useful to practitioners and researchers; (4) to bring into sharp focus the major issues in bias methodology that have been resolved and those that need resolution.

Specifically, the book is intended to provide test makers and test users with an understanding of the rationale, procedures, and interpretations associated with the different bias methods and to evaluate the attributes of those methods with the prospect of deducing which methods are "best." By furnishing practitioners with these particular research tools, it is expected that they will be able to scientifically and dispassionately appraise the quality of the bias studies that have accumulated and determine for themselves whether a preponderance of evidence exists regarding bias in individual tests. Where the findings are inconclusive or nonexistent, the test maker should be able to design, execute, and interpret an appropriate study of bias. It is especially important in this research domain that studies be conducted with scrupulous impartiality and objectivity.

Probably any volume that claims to present a state-of-the-art assessment of any research domain is doomed to the flaw of some omission. The methods chosen for review in this book have been deemed essential to the attainment of the aforestated purposes. One topic that often falls under the rubric of bias, commonly referred to as "bias in selection," has been omitted, because it is not a characteristic of a test or its component items. The problem of selection relates to how a test (biased or unbiased) is used to select persons from a given pool of applicants. The consequences of a selection strategy or model* are contingent upon the selection philosophy (see Hunter & Schmidt, 1976) and whether or not the test is biased, usually from the standpoint of predictive validity criteria. Test users interested in the various models for fair selection should consult the special issue of the *Journal of Educational Measurement* (Spring 1976) devoted exclusively to that topic, particularly the Petersen and Novick (1976) review, and Jensen's (1980, pp. 391–420) extensive description of a dozen different models. (Also see the brief discussions by Shepard, chapter 1, and Reynolds, chapter 8.)

ORGANIZATION OF THE BOOK

The book is divided into nine chapters. The topics covered are arranged sequentially according to the key steps in troubleshooting test bias. These steps and the corresponding chapters (1 through 8) are listed in Table I.1. Inasmuch as the research and discourse on bias are organized in terms of "validity issues," the troubleshooting steps and the substance of a few of the chapters unavoidably reflect the traditional validity scheme. This, after all, is the state-of-the-art organization of the domain. It is hoped that eventually, once bias methodologies have been thoroughly assimilated and widely applied by professional test makers, this organization will yield to a more unified conceptualization of the problem, as advocated previously.

Chapter 9, which is the final as well as the most lengthy chapter in the book, identifies the bias methods employed by six different publishers of most major standardized achievement, aptitude, and intelligence tests. These

---

*A variety of models for fair selection have been proposed. They include equal risk regression, proportional representation, constant ratio, conditional probability, equal probability, and expected utility.

TABLE I.1. Step-By-Step Procedure for Troubleshooting Test Bias, with Corresponding Chapter References

Step[a]	Chapter
1. Define bias based on charge and/or intended score use(s)	1
2. Specify level(s) of analysis—item, subtest, test, or combination—necessary to gather evidence[b]	1
3. Select a panel of reviewers according to the sex and ethnic composition of the target population	2
4. Devise procedures and instruments (e.g., checklist) for judgmental analysis	2
5. Conduct judgmental analysis	2
6. Use an experimental design to study bias effect or develop a quasi-experimental design (e.g., matched groups or pseudogroups) before using the delta plot or a similar bias method	3
7. Choose an appropriate item bias method	4, 5, & 6
8. Conduct statistical analysis	4 & 5
9. Identify "biased" items as a result of steps 5 and 8	4 & 5
10. Conduct a posteriori analyses to assess which items are truly biased and why they are biased	7
11. Make appropriate modifications to correct biases	7
12. Subject final collection of items to construct validation study	8
13. Choose an appropriate method for determining the factorial similarity of subtests or total test across groups	8
14. Conduct construct bias analysis	8
15. Identify an external criterion measure to evaluate predictive bias	8
16. Choose an appropriate method for determining differential predictive validity of subtests or total test	8
17. Conduct predictive bias analysis	8
18. Analyze the results of steps 14 and 17 to decide which subtests or whether the total test should be used with the target populations	8

[a]Ideally, these steps should be incorporated into the test construction process; however, they can
also be applied post hoc. These steps designate procedures for detecting most types of bias.
[b]The first two steps will delimit which of the succeeding 16 steps are essential. Steps 3 through
11 deal with judgmental and statistical item bias analyses; steps 12 through 18 indicate construct
and predictive bias procedures.

publishers are CTB/McGraw-Hill, Riverside Publishing Company/Houghton
Mifflin, The Psychological Corporation, Science Research Associates, The
American College Testing Program, and Educational Testing Service. This
chapter can serve as a reference and starting point for a bias study of any one
of the 27 tests reviewed.

For ease of use by practitioners and researchers, chapters 2 through 8
dealing with specific bias methods have the same quadripartite structure: (1)
"Introduction," (2) "Review of Methods," (3) "Recommendations for Test
Developers and Test Users," and (4) "References." Within this framework
all of the authors have made a deliberate effort to proffer a lucid, step-by-
step presentation of bias methods and to critique the methods in terms of
their relative strengths and weaknesses, including some recommendations
for a "best" method or strategy for attacking the problem.

The organization of chapter 9 is similar to the above, except that part 3 is
titled "Future Research on Bias" and the structure is repeated six times, one

for each test publisher. The perspective and contents also differ completely from the earlier chapters. The intent is to convey each publisher's policy on bias, the methods that have been employed with the most popular tests, and the type of bias research on these tests planned for the future.

INTENDED USES OF THE BOOK

As the title suggests and the structure and contents indicate, this volume should be used as a handbook for the following audiences: (1) all test users who encounter problems of sex, racial, and/or ethnic bias in the tests they administer and the scores they interpret, (2) all test developers at the school district, state, and national levels and test publishers who have the professional obligation to utilize the methods presented in the succeeding chapters to produce instruments that are unbiased and valid for the populations with which they are to be used, (3) researchers who are interested in investigating bias methodology issues and bias in particular tests, (4) graduate students in education, psychology, and sociology who are studying measurement theory and practices and the implications of test bias, and (5) professionals in related fields and laymen who desire a greater understanding of test bias and the burgeoning literature on the topic. Given the diversity of backgrounds of these groups, the exposition of the methods is primarily didactic. Even so, the technical material in chapters 3 through 8 presumes that readers have had basic coursework in measurement, statistics, and research methods. Readers who wish to acquire more than a conceptual understanding of the methods and do not possess a working knowledge in these areas will probably have difficulty with those chapters.

REFERENCES

Armstead, et al. v. *Starkville Mississippi Municipal Separate School District,* No. EC 70-51-5 (N.D. Miss., 1972).

Brim, O. G., Jr. American attitudes towards intelligence tests. *American Psychologist,* 1965, *20,* 125–130.

Cotter, D. E., & Berk, R. A. *Item bias in the WISC-R using black, white, and Hispanic learning disabled children.* Paper presented at the annual meeting of the American Educational Research Association, Los Angeles, April 1981.

Cronbach, L. J. Five decades of public controversy over mental testing. *American Psychologist,* 1975, *30,* 1–14.

Cronbach, L. J. Validity on parole: How can we go straight? In W. B. Schrader (Ed.), *New directions for testing and measurement* (No. 5)—*Measuring achievement: Progress over a decade.* San Francisco: Jossey-Bass, 1980. Pp. 99–108.

Guion, R. M. Content validity—The source of my discontent. *Applied Psychological Measurement,* 1977, *1,* 1–10.

Guion, R. M. On trinitarian doctrines of validity. *Professional Psychology*, 1980, *11*, 385–398.

Hunter, J. E., & Schmidt, F. L. A critical analysis of the statistical and ethical implications of various definitions of "test bias." *Psychological Bulletin*, 1976, *83*, 1053–1071.

Jackson, C. D. On the report of the Ad Hoc Committee on Educational Uses of Tests with Disadvantaged Students: Another psychological view from the Association of Black Psychologists. *American Psychologist*, 1975, *30*, 86–90.

Jensen, A. R. *Bias in mental testing*. New York: Free Press, 1980.

Kamin, L. J. Social and legal consequences of IQ tests as classification instruments: Some warnings from our past. *Journal of School Psychology*, 1975, *13*, 317–323.

Larry P., et al. v. *Wilson Riles, Superintendent of Public Instruction for the State of California, et al.* 343 F. Supp. 1306, (N.D. Cal., 1972); Aff'd 502 F. 2d 963 (9th Cir., 1974).

Larry P., et al. v. *Wilson Riles, Superintendent of Public Instruction for the State of California, et al.*, No. C-71-2270 (N.D. Cal., Oct. 11, 1979).

Linn, R. L. Issues of validity for criterion-referenced measures. *Applied Psychological Measurement*, 1980, *4*, 547–561.

Messick, S. *Test validity and the ethics of assessment*. Paper presented at the annual meeting of the American Psychological Association, New York, September 1979.

Nairn, A., & Associates. *The reign of ETS: The corporation that makes up minds.* Washington, D.C.: Author, 1980.

Parents in Action on Special Education (PASE), et al. v. *Joseph P. Hannon, General Superintendent of Schools in Chicago, et al.*, No. 74 C 3586 (N.D. Ill., July 7, 1980).

Petersen, N. S., & Novick, M. R. An evaluation of some models for culture-fair selection. *Journal of Educational Measurement*, 1976, *13*, 3–29.

Plake, B. S. A comparison of a statistical and subjective procedure to ascertain item validity: One step in the test validation process. *Educational and Psychological Measurement*, 1980, *40*, 397–404.

Reynolds, C. R. The problem of bias in psychological assessment. In C. R. Reynolds & T. B. Gutkin (Eds.), *The handbook of school psychology*. New York: Wiley, 1982. Pp. 178–208.

Sandoval, J., & Miille, M. P. W. Accuracy of judgments of WISC-R item difficulty for minority groups. *Journal of Consulting and Clinical Psychology*, 1980, *48*, 249–253.

Tenopyr, M. L. Content-construct confusion. *Personnel Psychology*, 1977, *30*, 47–54.

Williams, R. L. Danger: Testing and dehumanizing Black children. *Clinical Child Psychology Newsletter*, 1970, *9*, 5–6.

Williams, R. L. Abuses and misuses in testing black children. *Counseling Psychologist*, 1971, *2*, 62–77.

1 DEFINITIONS OF BIAS
LORRIE A. SHEPARD

INTRODUCTION

THE PURPOSE OF this chapter is to provide a conceptual definition of item bias. To do this, I first review two closely related topics: the larger issue of culture-fair testing and bias in selection. Together, these provide a context for understanding what is meant by bias in individual test items.

An overview of these areas of study serves two purposes. First, it highlights a continuum of distinctions about whether bias is *in* a test or in the way a test is *used*. Second, the relevant bodies of literature illustrate the difficulties that may arise when researchers simplify a complex concept and tailor it to a particular application. This often precludes common or compatible meanings for shared terms. Both of these points require elaboration.

The second point is broached first because it is more general and because it explains the style of the remainder of the chapter. In a recent lecture Scriven (1980) admonished educational researchers to learn how to do conceptual analysis. He debunked operational definitions because they trade simplicity and clarity for accuracy by trying to represent too simply and concretely the original more complex and more important concepts. Because operational definitions are simplifications, Scriven asserts, they lack realistic "embeddedness." They capture some, but not all, of the intended meaning of the concept. For this reason operational definitions may be adequate substitutes for the original concept in one application, but fail in other contexts. This criticism can certainly be leveled at the several one-sentence definitions that characterize the literature on test bias. It explains why these definitions remind one of reports from blind men who have encountered an elephant.

This chapter is not a conceptual analysis. It would be overly ambitious to survey here the several aspects of test bias and also to undertake the kind of in-depth analysis necessary to map accurately the meaning of the more general concepts of test bias. The chapter does, however, reflect the benefits of several lessons derived from Scriven. Explicit definitions, that is, strings of

9

words that are intended as all-purpose substitutes for much richer concepts, are avoided. Instead, examples are used to try to elaborate the richness of meaning in the concept of test bias. Multiple attempts will be made to say what that concept is and what it is not. For the narrower task of defining item bias, rather than test bias, a beginning is made toward a conceptual analysis.

The literature on test bias provides a context for discussing item bias; it especially helps to document a continuum of differences in the extent to which bias might inhere in the way a test is *used* rather than in the test itself. This continuum is used to organize the review portion of the chapter.

Bias versus Unfairness

Many authors who discuss test bias (Jensen, 1980; Reynolds, 1982) distinguish between fairness in testing as opposed to unbiased tests. Merz (1974) and Green (1975), for example, discussed how biased tests could be used fairly or unfairly. They suggested that "unfairness is not in the nature of the test, but *bias* is" (Green, 1975, p. 33; italics added). This distinction is problematic for two reasons. First, everyday understandings of the two key terms do not unequivocally convey the intended difference. To be biased is to be unfair, unjust, prejudiced. Calling your test "biased" conveys very nearly the same message as a placard calling an employer "unfair." When we get to the point of choosing methods for detecting biased items, we must be sure either that the methods are faithful to the full flavor of these terms, or that it is clearly understood what narrow feature of the term the chosen methods address.

The distinction between bias that is somehow *in* the test and unfairness that is in the *use* of the test is also an awkward distinction for psychometricians to have made. Most authors define bias as a type of invalidity (Green, 1975; Reynolds, 1982). Bias, however, is now being taken as an inherent feature of a test, while its opposite, validity, has always been considered to be a property of test use, not of the test itself. The test standards (APA/AERA/NCME, 1974) and Cronbach's (1971) comprehensive chapter on test validation both make it clear that validity is ascribed to the accuracy of test score interpretations; validity will change with different purposes. The difference between fairness and unbiasedness is further confused by the bias-in-selection literature (see Petersen & Novick, 1976), which clearly pertains to the use of tests but poses different models of predictive validity as indicators of bias. There, bias is defined as a particular kind of invalidity that is *outside* of the test.

Despite the muddle that results from expecting the terms *unfairness* and *bias* always to have a consistent meaning from one author to the next, it is worthwhile to try to preserve the distinction made by some authors. The difference between bias in a test and unfair test use is fundamental to an understanding of the purpose served by different methods for detecting bias. It is possible to be faithful to the rule that validity must always pertain to the particular inferences made from a test, yet still admit different degrees of externality through which bias may be more or less closely associated with the *use* of a test, rather than its internal characteristics. There is a validity continuum, anchored at one end by unbiased tests that measure what they were designed to measure and do so equally well for all groups. Further along the continuum are tests that provide equal predictive validity in particular contexts. At the farthest end of the continuum are tests for which validity is established by resolving issues of social justice and values, as well as scientific arguments over what statistical model of fairness to apply and what the criterion will be.

The following examples are contrived to illustrate different instances of bias that represent the extremes of the continuum from unfairness in the uses of tests to bias in the test itself:

Imagine a test designed to select employees in a private corporation. The test is deemed unbiased because it has the same internal structural properties for both majority and minority groups and because the content is highly relevant to subsequent job demands as determined by task analysis. Moreover, the predictive validity coefficients are very nearly the same for both groups despite a substantial difference in mean performances. Now, imagine that you are the corporation president and someone claims that a two-week on-the-job orientation would alter the pattern of prediction differentially for minority and majority groups. What if this claim were substantiated? Would it be fair to use the test that selects a disproportionately small number of minority applicants without providing the two-week orientation? Would your answer be different if the required training took six months or if the employer were a public institution?

Suppose, in another situation, a test of reasoning ability is again being used to select employees. Assume for the moment that the test is internally unbiased and has equal predictive validity for minority and majority groups. At the same time that reasoning ability was identified as an important prerequisite for job success, it was also agreed that motivation and social skills had been important characteristics of previously successful employees. But no tests or indicators were developed for these traits because the first efforts had poor reliability and validity. If the unbiased reasoning test produces a large difference between minority and majority group means, is it fair to use the test without measures of the other two traits? In particular, would it be fair if you have reason to believe that the validity coefficients for these latter indicators would be smaller than for the reasoning test (though not zero), and that the difference between group means would be less than on the reasoning test?

These questions go beyond either the internal or the predictive validity of the test. Justice and validity for the use of the test will be determined in conjunction with other pieces of information and value positions.

At the other extreme of the continuum, consider the following examples of *internally biased tests:*

On a math computations test, the largest difference between blacks and whites is on the word-problem subtest. When items are presented orally, the differential difficulty disappears.

A verbal analogies test is used to compare the reasoning ability of German and Italian immigrants to the United States (matched on English fluency). Eighty percent of the test items are based on words with Latin origins.

On an auditory discrimination test for kindergartners, Chicano children score relatively much lower than white children when the next-most attractive answer choice comes before the correct answer than when it comes after.

Obviously each example involves the way the test was used. As soon as an inference is made about the ability reflected in the test score, the test is "used." In this way *validity* always applies to the *use* of a test. It should also be clear, however, that these examples involve errors in the tests themselves, errors that prevent the items from reflecting what was intended to be measured.

One goal of this chapter is to present a conceptual understanding of item bias and of the methods for detecting its presence, a topic treated in the final section, "Bias in Test Items." Prior to that, two different levels of bias or unfairness in test use are summarized in "The Larger Social Context of Test Use" and "Bias in Selection."

THE LARGER SOCIAL CONTEXT OF TEST USE

It is important to discuss the larger social issue of whether tests are fair to all groups not only to provide a context for understanding item bias, but also, as a matter of conscience, to acknowledge what a small part of the total issue we are actually tackling. The question of test bias, especially bias in tests of school achievement and academic aptitude, is so prominent because some people believe that tests are the instruments of a racist society (Williams, 1970, 1974). To a lesser degree there is concern that tests give an unfair advantage to males and to members of the middle class. Techniques for finding biased items, of course, do not fully resolve questions of racism: first, because they do not address more external aspects of the uses of tests, and second, because they involve subjective judgments as well as the application of statistical rules. If one does not trust the motives of the test developer, one is not likely to believe the developer's claim that the test is unbiased. The best we can do is to make explicit how much can be determined by purely mechanical rules and where values enter the process. In addition, the issues discussed in the remainder of this section are acknowledged as entirely beyond the scope of item bias investigations.

One reason that bias in mental testing is so volatile an issue is that it invokes the specter of biological determinism, i.e., whether there is a large difference in intelligence (1σ) between black and white Americans that can be attributed largely to inherited differences (Jensen, 1969). Ongoing concerns about bias in intelligence tests (e.g., Eells et al., 1951) escaled sharply in the 1970s in response to Jensen's conclusions about racial differences in IQ.

Some critics claimed that the difference did not exist and could be explained entirely by bias in the measures. An a priori assumption of equivalent group means, however, has been rejected by most scholars who believe that the existence of a difference between groups is not automatically a sign of bias (Cleary, 1968; Guion, 1966; Jensen, 1976, 1980; Linn, 1973; Thorndike, 1971). A more reasonable position is to assert that some small or large part of the difference may be due to bias and that methods of detecting bias will uncover and reduce this source of invalidity.

Ultimately, the more serious proposition in Jensen's thesis is that racial differences in IQ are inherited and, therefore, largely fixed, explaining the failure of large-scale educational programs for the disadvantaged. This latter issue is, of course, not addressed by bias studies, but its philosophical implications overshadow them.

Many scientists agree that a significant genetic component accounts for individual differences in what we call IQ. They disagree, however, as to its magnitude, the permanence of this magnitude, and the import of heritability coefficients for public policy (Bereiter, 1969; Cronbach, 1969; Crow, 1969; Elkind, 1969). For example, Cronbach (1969) questioned the social policy implications of Jensen's research, emphasizing two points: (1) that a changing society will require multiple talents and learning abilities beyond those captured in Jensen's conceptualization of intelligence (p. 194) (the measurement issue); and (2) that heritability indices are misleading because they specify only the genetic contribution for a trait given a certain range of environments (p. 194) (the heritability issue). In other words, the large heritability coefficient of .80 could be sharply different, say .50, if a change in environment were profound.

It is interesting that ten years later the philosopher David Hawkins (1980) made nearly the same points in a review of Jensen's new book, *Bias in Mental Testing* (1980). Jensen's book is an exhaustive treatment of bias in ability tests in which much evidence from research is assembled to establish whether racial and sex differences are real. The book does not address the issue of whether such differences are inherited. Nonetheless, Hawkins says that the question of bias cannot be disentangled from the question of inherent racial differences in mental ability, so he gives the least attention to the issue of bias, essentially accepting Jensen's conclusions.

The present-day average test-score differences between blacks and whites are then mostly real, they will not completely go away merely through imaginative conscientious efforts to reduce testing biases. If this were not true, if African genesis, followed by a long and brutal enslavement and its historical aftermath, had left no marks of profound and continuing differences in the soil and subsoil of American life, in the direction and development of talents and abilities, both our problems and our opportunities would be less challenging than they are. In a wider conception of culture and cultural differences than Jensen acknowledges it is not the tests per se which are at stake but a whole complexion of social life, with which the tests are indeed somewhat congruent. (Hawkins, 1980, p. 3)

Instead, Hawkins challenges what he believes are the ultimate conclusions of Jensen's research. He thinks that a pessimistic view has been taken regarding the mutability of group differences, a view based on a static picture of likely interventions. There are rare examples, he says, of dramatic changes in IQ due to extraordinary interventions. Both Cronbach and Hawkins urge that the discovery of these interventions and their match with individual strengths should direct future inquiry. It is obvious that this line of inquiry will ultimately be much more significant in determining human potential. Clearly, values and one's world view govern enthusiasm for these endeavors.

That a purportedly technical investigation of the matter of bias should elicit this kind of response illustrates that our scholarly techniques cannot capture but also cannot ignore the larger issues. Of course, we are much better off to learn that negatively worded items disadvantage blacks (Scheuneman, 1979) or that word knowledge tests should not be mistaken for measures of intelligence (Green, 1975). It also helps, however, to be somewhat humble about the limitations of internal studies or statistical decision rules in the absence of an explication of the values that impinge on the use of tests. The heritability of IQ debate is just one of the issues larger than the substance of the test.

In a recent address intended to update our understanding of validity, Cronbach (1980) called for a more comprehensive and unified conceptualization of validity. He argued that it is not strictly a technical matter and posed the following questions that exemplify the nonpsychometric arguments needed to defend the use of a test:

A validity coefficient supports an argument from only one corner. The other guy wires are responses to challenges such as these: (1) What justifies this criterion? What biases does it have? (Wild and Dwyer, 1980). (2) Does a steep regression imply that the ability measured is necessary for the course of study? Or could instructors adapt so as to help the low scorer master the work? High predictive validity implies bad instruction, says the egalitarian critic. (3) Among the applicants who meet a reasonable standard, all of whom will probably be adequate students, what justifies creaming off the ones who scored highest? (Lerner, 1978). (4) Present selection practices concentrate high scores in prestige schools. Is this better for the nation than some mechanism that would distribute qualified law students more evenly over schools? (p. 103)

The larger social context for the meaning of bias requires that we consider not only how well we measure, but also whether it is appropriate and fair to test for the intended trait. The authors of the present volume have obviously been influenced by the call from Cronbach and others (see Berk, Introduction) for a more unified conceptualization of validity. Perhaps the most respectful way of responding to these insights is to acknowledge that even a broadened view of what constitutes unbiasedness in test items provides only one or two of the pieces in the complete picture of fair testing. As Berk notes, item bias studies serve a practical purpose, and "are necessary for all tests

. . . [but] they are not sufficient for all test score inferences and uses" (Introduction).

BIAS IN SELECTION

The bias-in-selection literature is reviewed here briefly. This body of research is important because it reflects the unfolding of psychometricians' thinking about the bias issue before much attention was paid to the internal properties of tests. It also represents an intermediate stage on the continuum from bias in the test to unfairness in the total context of test use.

The complexity of the literature on bias in selection makes it impossible to treat it adequately on the way to a discussion of item bias. Only a few key references are cited to try to convey how bias is viewed within this framework. The discussion consists of three parts: differential predictive validity, the criterion problem, and the actuarial problem.

Differential Predictive Validity

Choosing applicants for educational or employment positions is the most extensive practical use of tests. Tests related to the final "criterion" performance are used to identify the most qualified candidates. Bias in this context is conceived of as differential predictive validity. Since the relationship between test and criterion performance is operationalized by regression equations, test bias was first defined as unequal regressions. This definition as articulated by Cleary (1968) has been widely adopted in the methodological literature (Anastasi, 1976; Bartlett & O'Leary, 1969; Einhorn & Bass, 1971; Guion, 1966; Linn & Werts, 1971); it is also the definition usually relied upon in empirical studies of group differences in validity (Centra, Linn, & Parry, 1970; Jensen, 1980; Kallingal, 1971; Stanley, 1971; Stanley & Porter, 1967; Temp, 1971).

A test is biased for members of a subgroup of the population if, in the prediction of a criterion for which the test was designed, consistent nonzero errors of prediction are made for members of the subgroup. In other words, the test is biased if the criterion score predicted from the common regression line is consistently too high or too low for members of the subgroup. With this definition of bias, there may be a connotation of "unfair," particularly if the use of the test produces a prediction that is too low. (Cleary, 1968, p. 115)

The regression model guarantees unbiasedness when the test is a perfect predictor of the criterion and seems like a reasonable way to handle imperfect predictions fairly. Of course, a perfectly valid predictor never occurs in practice. In addition, two other particular circumstances frequently occur in reality, especially when the groups of interest are majority and minority ethnic groups: unequal group means on the test and smaller differences between group means on the criterion than on the test. This is the first sign that something is amiss with the equal regressions definition of fairness. If the minority group is not as far behind the majority group on the criterion as on the test (in standard score units), then they are disadvantaged by the test. Thorndike (1971) was perhaps the first to recognize the conundrum that the selection rule "which is 'fair' to individual members of the group scoring lower on the test, is 'unfair' to the lower (scoring) group as a whole in the sense that the proportion qualified on the test will be smaller, relative to the higher-scoring group, than the proportion that will reach any specified level of criterion performance" (p. 63). Thorndike proposed instead that different cutoff scores on the test should be set so that the proportion of applicants selected from each group would correspond to their proportion of successful performances on the criterion. For example, in college selection, if 20% of the minority group would "succeed," i.e., earn a C average or better, and 50% of the majority group would meet this criterion, then 20% of the minority and 50% of the majority applicants should be accepted (rather than the smaller percentage of minority applicants likely to be accepted with a single cutoff and typical patterns of group differences). The differences between the Cleary and Thorndike definitions of fairness have been very thoroughly explained by Linn (1973), Schmidt and Hunter (1974), Petersen and Novick (1976), and Jensen (1980).

The reader who is new to this area of study is likely to accept the Thorndike model with some satisfaction, since apparently an error in the definition has been discovered and rectified. It has the additional appeal of typically admitting more minority candidates. The Thorndike model, however, did not become the new and widely accepted definition of fairness. Instead, what followed were several more definitions (Cole, 1973; Darlington, 1971; Einhorn & Bass, 1971; Linn, 1973), each proposing different rules for what quantities should be equalized in the prediction paradigm. For example, the Thorndike rule would equalize marginal probabilities. The Cole (1973) proposal would equalize conditional probabilities; that is, majority and minority members who succeed on the criterion should have the same probability of being selected.

One important reference on bias in selection is a special issue of the *Journal of Educational Measurement* devoted to that topic (1976, *13*, 1–99). The lead article by Petersen and Novick (1976) is a comprehensive treatment of the various selection models. They explain the distinctions between the definitions and also the internal contradictions within the models. For example, it is not possible to follow Thorndike's rule and accept applicants in proportion to each group's success rate on the criterion without violating its logical converse, which is to reject in proportion to each group's failure rate.

Petersen and Novick conclude that none of the models is technically or mathematically more defensible than another. The advice they give to an employer or admissions officer trying to select among them is to adopt a decision-theoretic approach and explicitly consider the utilities assigned for each group to each decision and outcome. As Jensen (1980) emphasizes, "assigning utilities is a wholly subjective matter. But at least the Expected Utility Model forces an explicit evaluation of the utilities assigned to every possible outcome of the selection process for every single person involved" (p. 410).

Even with adjustments for "utilities," however, there is a gap between psychometric models of unbiasedness and moral conceptions of fairness. Ellett (1980), a philosopher, analyzed fairness in selection. He concluded that none of the psychometric definitions of fairness provide sufficient conditions for fairness in a moral sense. Specifically, he found the decision-theoretic approach inadequate because the theory "cannot distinguish between the deliberations of a knave or a fool and the deliberations of a good and wise man" (p. 66). Moreover, "social utility is logically distinct from the principle of justice. The principle of utility is an aggregate principle, but the principle of justice is a distributive principle" (p. 67), i.e., how good and bad are distributed to individuals in the society (Frankena, 1962, p. 4). Ellett (1980) proposed a model for fair selection that would reserve some percentage of the opportunities (e.g., 25%) for those in a "middle group" who meet minimum requirements but whose probabilities of success are not as great as those in the high group. This reflects a compromise of maximum efficiency in selection to achieve greater fairness.

The literature on bias in selection does not produce a universally applicable definition of test fairness even within the limited conceptualization of predictive validity. The role of values in choosing a formulation of unbiased selection is clear and inescapable. There is not a statistical solution unless one proposes that the only goal of selection is to maximize the criterion performance of the selected group. This, however, is itself a value position, which Ellett (1980) suggests must be scrutinized using the method of moral debate.

The Criterion Problem

A standard caveat appears with every model of predictive fairness: selection is unbiased (by any given definition) only if the criterion is unbiased. As Petersen and Novick (1976) summarized:

This selection strategy presupposes that an acceptable criterion variable is available. Inappropriateness of the criterion variable will not be treated in this paper, although this may be the most important problem. Thus, the following discussion of selection fairness will be based on the premise that the available criterion score is a relevant, reliable and unbiased measure of performance for applicants in each subpopulation. All previous contributions in this area have implicitly made these assumptions. (p. 4)

If the criterion that the test predicts is, for instance, the employer's ratings of job performance, and if the employers are sometimes bigots or chauvinists, then corresponding biases in the tests will not be revealed by the prediction fairness models. Subtler cultural biases that are not relevant to criterion performance, but that pervade both the test and task, will add to the appearance of predictive validity rather than detracting from it.

Attention is paid to this issue in a separate and often nonpsychometric literature addressed to the question of test relevance. In *Griggs, et al.* v. *Duke Power Co.* (1971) the court ruled that, on the basis of Title VII of the Civil Rights Act of 1964, an employer must show that any requirement for selection or promotion have "a manifest relationship to the employment in question." Jensen (1980) notes that there are several interpretations possible for "manifest relationship." It could refer simply to a predictive validity correlation, or it could mean the test items should bear close resemblance to the job demands (p. 35). The Equal Employment Opportunity Commission (1970) guidelines were less ambiguous, specifically using the word relevance: "any differential rejection rates that may exist, based on a test, must be relevant to performance on the jobs in question" (Section 1607.4). The more recent guidelines (EEOC, 1977), however, lack this umbrella statement and actually clarify the several paths to validity cited by Jensen. By these regulations one could show unbiasedness by means of content validation, *or* by predictive validation, *or* by construct validation. The specifications for predictive validity do require, however, that the test's content be logically related to a task analysis of critical work behavior.

The Actuarial Problem

Because the literature on bias in selection arose in response to a very pressing concern about the practical use of tests, there has been a very patchwork approach to the conceptualization of test bias. Energy has been largely focused on fairness in the regression equations used to set cutoff scores. Despite the caveats, much less attention was given either to logical evidence of validity or to more elaborate empirical evidence of construct validity. Only more recently have measurement specialists brought out their full bag of tricks and begun to assert for the bias question that the same rules apply that have always governed validity. Validity is multifaceted and cannot possibly be confirmed by a single correlation coefficient. Linn (personal communication, 1980) contended that although the operational definitions of unbiased selection fell short of the full concepts, they served the useful purpose of clarifying thinking and identifying shortcomings in the models. As a result, it was found that knowledge of over- or under-prediction was not sufficient and that value choices could not be avoided. The consideration of explicit alternative definitions, however, paved the way for a broader conceptualization of validity that might otherwise have been dismissed as "fuzzy-headedness."

Excessive devotion to a predictive validity definition of fairness strengthened the view that validity was an actuarial problem. This view allows for statistical evidence of bias, e.g., significant differences in regression slopes (see Reynolds, chapter 8), but not for logical evidence of bias. As was noted previously, this is not *the* technically recommended position, but only one of several value positions. Hunter and Schmidt (1976) have identified three different value positions that subsume all of the fairness models: unqualified individualism, qualified individualism, and quotas. *Unqualified individualism* is the actuarial position; the goal of achieving the highest criterion performance in the selected group is furthered by use of whatever variables enhance the predictive correlation, including race and sex (see McNemar, 1975). *Qualified individualism* seeks to maximize predictive validity, except by using group membership as a predictor variable. *Quotas* argue for some loss in predictive validity to accomplish trade-offs of other socially or morally important ends. In the extreme, quotas would ignore predictive validity and select applicants from each group in proportion to their percentages in the population.

Jensen (1980, p. 420) has concluded, however, that because those who support qualified individualism are, when faced with a biased test, willing to sacrifice overall predictive validity (and fairness to individuals) to achieve fairness to groups, theirs is also a quota philosophy. In other words, there is only one position that is entirely sound from a psychometric view, plus or minus some adjustments for other beliefs about fairness. This elimination of the middle ground, however, presumes that predictive validity is the end-all of psychometric validity. If, however, we recast the question in the framework of construct validity, the predictive coefficient between the test and any one variable is only one term in a network of relations that all reflect on the validity of the test interpretation. Although we have asserted all along that values influence definitions of fairness, it is also true that there might be good psychometric reasons to omit variables that would maximize the predictive correlation. As Jensen himself explains, those who support qualified individualism are willing to allow only those predictors that show some functional relation to the criterion performance; they eschew variables that may correlate with the criterion only because of their mutual correlation with some third variable. This is defensible on psychometric grounds; it just requires a more elaborate theoretical model. If we apply the insights of construct validation, it would permit us to use testable evidence about casual links to answer questions about what the test measures as well as its actuarial relation to the criterion.

In another context Jensen (1980) aptly summarizes the principles of construct validation.

And so the process of construct validation is round-about, consisting mainly of showing in more and more different ways that the test scores behave as should be expected if, in fact, the test measures the construct in question. Thus, construct validity rests on a growing network of theoretically expected and empirically substantiated correlations and outcomes of specially designed experiments to test the construct validity of the measuring instrument. (p. 422)

This is exactly right and should be applied to tests used for employment and educational selections as well as to measures of psychological constructs. Predictive validity correlations constitute just one small piece of the comprehensive validity picture. Predictive validity is not a separate form of validation coequal to construct validation. Jensen (1980) implies the opposite by the organization of his book and the presumption that construct validation is called for only in the absence of a "single clear-cut external criterion" (p. 420).

As an example of the kinds of influences that explanatory evidence would have in making decisions in predictive situations, consider the example already given where two groups are further apart on the test than on the criterion. There are at least two hypotheses about why this could occur. One is that the criterion is less reliable than the test; the other is that the criterion performance is explained by a third variable, not captured in the test, on which group differences are smaller. These hypotheses are testable, of course, in the difficult and tentative manner of construct validation and correlational research. The important point is that evidence supporting the third variable hypothesis would be a technical reason for reducing the importance of the test in the selection decision. However, if we find that the criterion is less reliable than the test, then it is a matter of values whether the full predictive strengths of the test should be used or if groups are entitled to at least the same gamble in the test which they face in the criterion.

Increasingly, measurement experts are calling for a more comprehensive view of validity to defend the inferences made from a test (Cronbach, 1980; Linn, 1980). All along, construct validity has been the more inclusive "branch" of validity that addresses most accurately the traditional slogan for validity, "Does this test measure what it is intended to measure?" Strong actuarial correlations do not, by themselves, answer this question; they only strengthen the understanding of what is measured by confirming patterns of relationship. This is the more complete view of validity and unbiasedness with which we should approach the topic of bias in test items.

BIAS IN TEST ITEMS

Item bias and test bias methodologies are superficially different but should not imply different conceptualizations of bias. The methodologies appear to be different because of practical considerations, e.g., one often has many items but not many tests. More significantly, they seem to rest on different definitions because the test bias literature has been so heavily invested in the predictive validity question.

If we adopt the more inclusive approach to test bias, which is consonant with construct validity, then the parallel between unbiased tests and unbiased items can be drawn more easily. As was discussed in the previous section, a coherent pattern of empirical results that confirms logical relations is necessary to validate the inferences made from test results. Likewise, unbiasedness in test items is best conceptualized as equal construct validity across groups and must be confirmed by verifying expected patterns of relationships. The discussion of item-bias detection methods follows the model of construct validity and is organized into two parts: logical analyses and empirical analyses.

Logical Analyses

The construct validation method (see Cronbach & Meehl, 1955) is essentially the scientific method. Hypotheses, which are tentative theories, lead to expectations about how actual data will behave. When results are consistent with predictions from the theory, the theory gathers strength. The deductive step, from theory to expected observables, is a logical step. Also in construct validation, logical analysis or conceptual analysis (see Scriven, 1980) remains the only means for formally elaborating what is to be measured and how this trait is expected to relate to other variables. Of course, logical analyses are not sufficient by themselves nor, as Cronbach (1971) explains, are they sufficient to "disprove a validity claim. The analysis puts forth a counter hypothesis whose pertinence can be verified only empirically" (p. 475).

In a recent review, Reynolds (1982) questioned "the armchair or expert minority panel approach to determining biased items" (p. 190). He summarized several studies (Jensen, 1977; Plake, 1980; Sandoval & Miille, 1980) that have found dismal evidence for the effectiveness of such reviews in finding biased test items. When asked to subjectively review items, judges were consistently unable to identify items that were relatively more difficult for black or Chicano children than for white children. Given the purpose, however, for logical analysis envisioned in this chapter, i.e., to assure the appropriateness of the test questions for the intended construct, it is worth noting that the Sandoval and Miille (1980) study did not use judges who could be considered experts on the construct in question, i.e., intelligence. The judges were black, Mexican-American, and white university students, presumably undergraduates. The Jensen (1977) study had the same finding with black and white psychologists. Nevertheless, it should be emphasized that the kind of logical analysis needed to advance construct validity requires a thorough understanding of the concept under investigation. Logical analysis recapitulates the test development process whereby items are developed to reflect the intended construct. In the case of analysis for bias, the expert judges are asking the more specialized question, Will the match of the item to the construct be the same across groups? To establish hypotheses and counter-hypotheses about what test items measure, it can be argued that the judges have to have the same substantive expertise as the test developers. These analyses have a scholarly, not a political, purpose.

Minority review panels also serve important political and social justice goals. For these purposes it is more appropriate that members of the panel represent constituencies pertinent to the use of the test rather than be experts on the trait measured by the test. For example, see Jaeger (1978) and Shepard (1979a) for a discussion of the relevant audiences to involve in the setting of standards for minimum competency testing programs.

Regardless of the poor validity of subjective reviews, important reasons still remain for seeking such counsel. First, any aspect of the test format that is offensive to members of any group should be eliminated whether or not it explains any decrement in performance. Stereotyped portrayals are objectionable as a matter of principle even though disadvantaged groups may be thoroughly aware of expected right answers. Second, empirical methods for detecting bias are insensitive to any delayed or pervasive reduction in performance caused by perceived unfairness in the questions. Apart from the issue of bias, ambiguous items conceivably could frustrate examinees enough to lessen their scores on subsequent items. Similarly, one can imagine that offensive items or items entirely foreign to an examinee's experience could harm motivation and attention on later test questions. Finally, subjective reviews of test items are valuable when they generate hypotheses about the nature of bias. As we will see, there is no foolproof statistical bias detection method. Item bias techniques themselves require validation (see Shepard, Camilli, & Averill, 1980). Despite the apparently large dross rate, studying the items jointly confirmed as biased should improve our understanding of both subjective and empirical methods. (See Tittle, chapter 2, for a more extensive discussion of judgmental review procedures.)

A final distinction may help clarify the role of logical analysis. Logical analysis is not identical to the process of content validation. It goes beyond content specification and includes explication of the inferences made when a test is used to represent a trait. It can be argued that the greater the inference made in trying to operationalize a psychological construct, the more opportunity there is for the test to be biased. For instance, ability tests have greater potential for bias than achievement tests (Shepard, 1979b) because ability items rely on the developer's conjecture about how the trait will manifest itself, while achievement test items are a direct sample of the intended domain. Flaugher (1978), for example, expects that achievement tests should be much less vulnerable to the charge of bias unless they are mistakenly interpreted as measures of "capacity." Then the inappropriateness of the inference produces the bias.

Usually, achievement tests have only needed content validation rather than construct validation. Content validity is established by expert judgment and involves explicating the content domain and verifying that items are representative of it. The developments in criterion-referenced and domain-referenced testing have ensured that this can be done with much greater care and insight (Popham, 1980; Roid & Haladyna, 1980). Measurement experts are beginning to suggest, however, that even criterion-referenced achievement tests require construct validation (Hambleton, 1980; Hambleton et al., 1978; Linn, 1979, 1980; Messick, 1975). Empirical support is needed for the logical arguments about what the test measures. For the purpose of preventing bias, logically appropriate content must be tested for irrelevant difficulties that are not obvious to subjective scrutiny.

Empirical Analyses

Statistical techniques for finding biased items are internal methods designed to ensure that the meaning, which individual items contribute to the total test, is the same for all groups. It should be noted that there are other internal methods for studying bias in tests which are not covered in this discussion. For example, factor analysis has been used to see if the internal structure of a test is consistent across groups (Humphreys & Taber, 1973; Jensen, 1977; see Reynolds, chapter 8). It provides a test of the within-construct portion of the nomological network; these relationships are just as important to the defense of test inferences as are the external patterns of relationship discussed previously. The techniques we are interested in do not differ in kind from the factor analytic approach but have a particular practical feature. Violations of anticipated patterns, which could be evidence of bias, can be pinpointed in individual test items.

Numerous empirical methods have been proposed for operationalizing item bias. These include differential differences in item difficulty (Angoff & Ford, 1973), group differences in item discriminations (Green & Draper, 1972), comparisons of item characteristic curves (Durovic, 1975; Lord, 1977; Wright, Mead & Draba, 1976) and chi-square approximations of the latent trait methods (Camilli, 1979; Scheuneman, 1979). Recent developments are thoroughly reviewed in chapters 4 and 5.

A consistent strategy used by these methods involves adjusting somehow for differences in overall group means and then considering additional differences as a sign of bias. A couple of operational definitions give the flavor of how these techniques work.

A test item can be considered to be unbiased if all individuals having the same underlying ability level have an equal probability of correctly answering the item, regardless of their subgroup membership. (Pine, 1977, p. 38)

An item is unbiased if, for all individuals having the same score on a homogeneous subtest containing the item, the proportion of individuals getting the item correct is the same for each population group being considered. (Scheuneman, 1975, p. 2)

These methods are intended to distinguish between real group differences in performance and those created by irrelevant difficulty in the wording of the questions or differential validity in what the item is assumed to represent.

Just as a standard warning exists in the bias-in-selection literature regarding the problem of a biased criterion, the obligatory caveat for item bias methods is that they cannot detect pervasive bias because they lack an external criterion. As explained by Shepard et al. (1980), "a major limitation of all of the bias detection approaches employed in the research to date is that they are all based on a criterion internal to the test in question. They cannot escape the circularity inherent in using total score on the test or the average item to identify individuals of equal ability and hence specify the standard of unbiasedness" (p. 6) (see also Petersen, 1977). These are really two faces of the same problem. An external criterion will not help salvage item bias methods if it is contaminated by the same type of bias that affects the items. The only solution in both cases is an extended study of relations that collectively justify the inferences made from the test.

Another sense of how item bias methods work, however, does not require an apology for the absence of an external criterion. These methods should not be thought of as impoverished substitutes for predictive validity methods. They answer a different question, more fundamental to an improved understanding of what a test measures. The predictive validity paradigm is a limited model to emulate, because it focuses on only one element in a more demanding schema of validity and does not, by itself, enlighten us about the meaning of obtained correlations.

Item bias methods detect items that are anomalous. Whatever it is that the rest of the items measure, the biased item behaves differently. We see this because the group differences are not the same for this item as for other items. As discussed by Shepard et al., (1980),

Bias cannot be identified in an isolated test item. Test questions designed to measure the same construct must be studied together; bias is discovered when an item does not fit the pattern established by others in the set. Bias is a contextual property; it depends on the characteristics of the items comprising the test that are used to measure the 'ability' in the definition of item bias. Thus, the 'bias' assessed by these techniques is 'anomaly in a context of other items'; it is not bias in the sense of unfairness. (pp. 3–4)

If a test of spatial reasoning inadvertently included several vocabulary items, they would be biased indicators of the trait. The same items in a test comprised of many more items like them would probably not be biased and would not be flagged by the detection methods. This example makes it obvious why logical analyses must accompany and control the use of statistical techniques. In a test composed equally of two types of item, reflecting very different ways of representing a construct (or perhaps two different constructs), it will be a dead heat to decide statistically which set defines the test trait and which set becomes a biased measure of it. In chapter 4, Angoff proposes that item bias methods instead be called *item discrepancy methods*. This term better emphasizes that the statistical techniques signal deviations from the regular pattern established by other items in the test. They do not address the appropriateness of the test purpose or moral questions of fairness.

In some ways this discrepancy or "anomaly" characterization of item bias is a *post hoc* conceptualization. It is not the understanding that was held and then operationalized in the various methods. It is, however, a feature that pervades the methods and simply restates the implications of using an internal criterion. From the above examples, it should be clear that the assumption of unidimensionality underlying all of the methods (see especially, Hunter, 1975) is not merely a statistical prerequisite but is central to the way in which item bias is defined.

The unidimensionality requirement, or the anomaly conceptualization of item bias, has important implications for how tests are developed. Tests or item sets that we wish to examine for bias must be homogeneous with respect to the construct they intend to represent. Tests cannot consist of an assortment of different content or constructs, *even if the separate pieces are all relevant to an external criterion.* If several traits are needed to explain criterion performance, measures of each should be developed separately and then pooled in the prediction application. In essence, these methods force us to "purify" our measures of a single trait, by casting out items that measure tangential or irrelevant traits to the disadvantage of some groups. This line of reasoning should not, of course, be pursued to the point of absurd reductionism, but it conveys the general idea of how item bias methods work. In the case where there is only one predictor trait, it is conceivable that "homogenizing" a test—by removing items with differential internal validity—could actually reduce predictive correlations (by reducing variability in the test scores). Such a sacrifice in predictive validity, however, purchases much greater clarity about what is actually being measured and how it relates to the criterion. The lost predictive correlation can be regained only if a second trait, relevant to the criterion, can be identified in the anomalous items. Then, a second predictor can be explicitly defined.

Empirical item bias detection methods test our understanding of the construct being measured. When faulty conceptualizations of a trait produce different implicit inferences for different groups, statistical techniques can reveal the error missed by logical analysis. Both empirical and logical evidence are required to verify that test items measure what is inferred to be measured for all groups.

CONCLUSION

In keeping with Scriven's earlier advice regarding the loss of meaning in operational definitions, a simplistic, concrete definition of item bias has not been offered. Instead, an understanding of bias—as psychometric features that somehow misrepresent the abilities of one group—is expected to guide the detection of bias in particular instances. In the absence of a concrete, stipulative definition, applicable in all situations, the authors of this book have agreed on practical strategies for identifying bias. The consensus is that judgmental and statistical methods should be used in combination. Logical analysis must be used to establish the relevance of items to the implied trait. Statistical techniques are used to find aberrant items in what were believed to be homogeneous sets of items, thus detecting flaws in the original logic and inference. Finally, judgmental analyses should be reapplied to look for patterns in the statistically biased items and to further refine the understanding of the trait.

Items are not fundamentally different from tests; therefore, the entire process of establishing that sets of items are unbiased is the same as the process of construct validation for the test. For tests or items, this requirement is larger than strictly actuarial or statistical validity. The demands for logical validity include not only verification of the match between items and constructs but also a coherent theory regarding relations among variables, especially between the test and criterion performance. Logically deduced patterns must then be confirmed empirically, in the first case by internal item bias methods and in the second by external relationships. Still, this expanded view of psychometric unbiasedness omits consideration of social justice issues in the use of tests.

Cronbach (1980) has offered us a more inclusive understanding of validity in which technical evidence is just one of the arguments that interplay to justify a test interpretation. He summarized by saying, "We might once have identified validation with a single question, what does the instrument measure? That question will not have an objective, universal answer. A yet more judgmental question now takes on equal importance: And why should *that* be measured?" (p. 107).

Test and item bias are conceptualized as invalidity, something that distorts the meaning of test results for some groups. Cronbach's advice about validity is prescriptive for the study of bias. From this broader perspective, the methods for detecting biased test items are not sufficient. They provide one essential element in a rationale for fair use of tests. The logical analyses involved in the construct validation of test items partially consider, "Why should this trait be measured?" But there are larger social issues, discussed in the first section of this chapter that are outside the ken of psychometric methods. These issues that govern the full meaning of bias and unfairness must also be considered before the use of a test can be called fair.

REFERENCES

APA/AERA/NCME Committee. *Standards for educational and psychological tests* (rev. ed.). Washington, D.C.: American Psychological Association, 1974.
Anastasi, A. *Psychological testing* (4th ed.). New York: Macmillan, 1976.
Angoff, W. H., & Ford, S. F. Item-race interaction on a test of scholastic aptitude. *Journal of Educational Measurement,* 1973, *10,* 95–105.

Bartlett, C. J., & O'Leary, B. S. A differential prediction model to moderate the effects of heterogeneous grounds in personnel selection and classification. *Personnel Psychology,* 1969, *22,* 1–17.

Bereiter, C. The future of individual differences. *Harvard Educational Review,* 1969, *2,* 162–170.

Camilli, G. A critique of the chi-square method for assessing item bias. Unpublished paper, Laboratory of Educational Research, University of Colorado, Boulder, 1979.

Centra, J. A., Linn, R. L., & Parry, M. E. Academic growth in predominantly Negro and predominantly white colleges. *American Educational Research Journal,* 1970, *1,* 83–98.

Cleary, T. A. Test bias: Prediction of grades of Negro and white students in integrated colleges. *Journal of Educational Measurement,* 1968, *5,* 115–124.

Cole, N. S. Bias in selection. *Journal of Educational Measurement,* 1973, *10,* 237–255.

Cronbach, L. J. Heredity, environment, and educational policy. *Harvard Educational Review,* 1969, *2,* 162–170.

Cronbach, L. J. Test validation. In R. L. Thorndike (Ed.), *Educational measurement* (2nd ed.). Washington, D.C.: American Council on Education, 1971. Pp. 443–507.

Cronbach, L. J. Validity on parole: How can we go straight? W. B. Schrader (Ed.), *New directions for testing and measurement* (No. 5)—*Measuring achievement: Progress over a decade.* San Francisco: Jossey-Bass, 1980. Pp. 99–108.

Cronbach, L. J., & Meehl, P. E. Construct validity in psychological tests. *Psychological Bulletin,* 1955, *52,* 281–302.

Crow, J. F. Genetic theories and influences: Comments on the value of diversity. *Harvard Educational Review,* 1969, *2,* 153–161.

Darlington, R. B. Another look at "cultural fairness." *Journal of Educational Measurement,* 1971, *8,* 71–82.

Durovic, J. J. *Definitions of test bias: A taxonomy and an illustration of an alternative model.* Unpublished doctoral dissertation, State University of New York at Albany, 1975.

Eells, K., Davis, A., Havighurst, R. J., Herrick, V. E., & Tyler, R. W. *Intelligence and cultural differences.* Chicago: University of Chicago Press, 1951.

Einhorn, J. J., & Bass, A. R. Methodological considerations relevant to discrimination in employment testing. *Psychological Bulletin,* 1971, *75,* 261–269.

Elkind, D. Piagetian and psychometric conceptions of intelligence. *Harvard Educational Review,* 1969, *2,* 171–189.

Ellett, F. S. *Fairness and the predictors.* Paper presented at the annual meeting of the American Educational Research Association, Boston, April 1980.

Equal Employment Opportunity Commission (EEOC). Guidelines on employee selection procedures. *Federal Register,* 1970, *35* (149), 12333–12336.

Equal Employment Opportunity Commission (EEOC). Uniform guidelines on employee selection procedures. *Federal Register,* 1977, *42* (251), 65542–65552.

Flaugher, R. L. The many definitions of test bias. *American Psychologist,* 1978, *33,* 671–679.

Frankena, W. K. The concept of social justice. In R. B. Brandt (Ed.) *Social justice.* Englewood Cliffs, N.J.: Prentice-Hall, 1962. Pp. 1–29.

Green, D. R. What does it mean to say a test is biased? *Education and Urban Society,* 1975, *8,* 33–52.

28   LORRIE A. SHEPARD

Green, D. R., & Draper, J. F. *Exploratory studies of bias in achievement tests.* Paper presented at the annual meeting of the American Psychological Association, Honolulu, September, 1972. (ERIC Document Reproduction Service No. ED 070 794)

Griggs, et al. v. *Duke Power Company,* U.S. Supreme Court, No. 124, October term, 1970 (March 8, 1971).

Guion, R. M. Employment tests and discriminatory hiring. *Industrial Relations,* 1966, *5,* 20-37.

Hambleton, R. K. Test score validity and standard setting-methods. In R. A. Berk (Ed.), *Criterion-referenced measurement: The state of the art.* Baltimore: Johns Hopkins University Press, 1980. Pp. 80-123.

Hambleton, R. K., Swaminathan, H., Algina, J., & Coulson, D. B. Criterion-referenced testing and measurement: A review of technical issues and developments. *Review of Educational Research,* 1978, *48,* 1-47.

Hawkins, D. (Review of *Bias in mental testing* by Arthur R. Jensen). Unpublished, University of Colorado, Boulder, 1980.

Humphreys, L. G., & Taher, T. Ability factors as a function of advantaged and disadvantaged groups. *Journal of Educational Measurement,* 1973, *10,* 107-115.

Hunter, J. E. *A critical analysis of the use of item means and item-test correlations to determine the presence or absence of content bias in achievement test items.* Paper presented at the National Institute of Education Conference on Test Bias, Annapolis, Md., December 1975.

Hunter, J. E., & Schmidt, F. L. A critical analysis of the statistical and ethical implications of various definitions of "test bias." *Psychological Bulletin,* 1976, *83,* 1053-1071.

Jaeger, R. M. *A proposal for setting a standard on the North Carolina High School Competency Test.* Paper presented at the Spring meeting of the North Carolina Association for Research in Education, Chapel Hill, 1978.

Jensen, A. R. How much can we boost IQ and scholastic achievement? *Harvard Educational Review,* 1969, *39,* 1-123.

Jensen, A. R. Test bias and construct validity. *Phi Delta Kappan,* 1976, *58,* 340-346.

Jensen, A. R. An examination of cultural bias in the Wonderlic Personnel Test. *Intelligence,* 1977, *1,* 51-64.

Jensen, A. R. *Bias in mental testing.* New York: Free Press, 1980.

Kallingal, A. The prediction of grades for black and white students of Michigan State University. *Journal of Educational Measurement,* 1971, *8,* 263-265.

Lerner, B. Equal protection and external screening: Davis, De Funis, and Bakke. In *Proceedings of the ETS Invitational Conference on Testing Problems.* Princeton, N.J.: Educational Testing Service, 1978. Pp. 3-27.

Linn, R. L. Fair test use in selection. *Review of Educational Research,* 1973, *43,* 139-161.

Linn, R. L. Issues of validity in measurement for competency-based programs. In M. S. Bunda & J. R. Sanders (Eds.), *Practices and problems in competency-based education.* Washington, D.C.: National Council on Measurement in Education, 1979. Pp. 108-123.

Linn, R. L. Issues of validity for criterion-referenced measures. *Applied Psychological Measurement,* 1980, *4,* 547-561.

Linn, R. L., & Werts, C. E. Considerations for studies of test bias. *Journal of Educational Measurement,* 1971, *8,* 1-4.

Lord, F. M. A study of item bias, using item characteristic curves theory. In Y. H.

Poortinga (Ed.), *Basic problems in cross-cultural psychology.* Amsterdam: Swets and Zeitlinger, 1977. Pp. 19–29.

McNemar, Q. On so-called test bias. *American Psychologist,* 1975, *30,* 848–851.

Merz, W. R. *A biased test may be fair, but what does that really mean?* Paper presented at the meeting of the California Educational Research Association, San Francisco, 1974.

Messick, S. The standard problem: Meaning and values in measurement and evaluation. *American Psychologist,* 1975, *30,* 955–966.

Petersen, N. S. *Bias in the selection rule: Bias in the test.* Paper presented at the Third International Symposium on Educational Testing, University of Leyden, Netherlands, June 1977.

Petersen, N. S., & Novick, M. R. An evaluation of some models for culture-fair selection. *Journal of Educational Measurement,* 1976, *13,* 3–29.

Pine, S. M. Applications of item characteristic curve theory to the problem of test bias. In D. J. Weiss (Ed.), *Applications of computerized adaptive testing* (RR 77-1). Minneapolis: Department of Psychology, Psychometric Methods Program, University of Minnesota, March 1977. Pp. 37–43.

Plake, B. S. A comparison of a statistical and subjective procedure to ascertain item validity: One step in the test validation process. *Educational and Psychological Measurement,* 1980, *40,* 397–404.

Popham, W. J. Domain specification strategies. In R. A. Berk (Ed.), *Criterion-referenced measurement: The state of the art.* Baltimore: Johns Hopkins University Press, 1980. Pp. 15–31.

Reynolds, C. R. The problem of bias in psychological assessment. In C. R. Reynolds & T. B. Gutkin (Eds.), *The handbook of school psychology.* New York: Wiley, 1982. Pp. 178–208.

Roid, G. H., & Haladyna, T. M. The emergence of an item-writing technology. *Review of Educational Research,* 1980, *50,* 293–314.

Sandoval, J., & Miille, M. P. W. Accuracy of judgments of WISC-R item difficulty for minority groups. *Journal of Consulting and Clinical Psychology,* 1980, *48,* 249–253.

Scheuneman, J. D. *A new method of assessing bias in test items.* Paper presented at the annual meeting of the American Educational Research Association, Washington, D.C., April 1975. (ERIC Document Reproduction Service No. ED 106 359)

Scheuneman, J. D. A method of assessing bias in test items. *Journal of Educational Measurement,* 1979, *16,* 143–152.

Schmidt, F. L., & Hunter, J. E. Racial and ethnic bias in psychological tests: Divergent implications of two definitions of test bias. *American Psychologist,* 1974, *29,* 1–8.

Scriven, M. Method of inquiry in the philosophy of education. In R. M. Jaeger (Ed.), *Alternative methodologies in educational research.* Washington, D.C.: American Educational Research Cassette Series, 1980..

Shepard, L. A. Setting standards. In M. A. Bunda & J. R. Sanders (Eds.), *Practices and problems in competency-based measurement.* Washington, D.C.: National Council on Measurement in Education, 1979. Pp. 59–71. (a)

Shepard, L. A. *Validity of tests used to diagnose learning disabilities.* Paper prepared for the Office of Evaluation and Pupil Services, Boulder Valley School District, Boulder, Colo., August 1979. (b)

Shepard, L. A., Camilli, G., & Averill, M. *Comparison of six procedures for detecting test item bias using both internal and external ability criteria.* Paper presented at the annual meeting of the National Council on Measurement in Education, Boston, April 1980.

Stanley, J. C. Predicting college success of the educationally disadvantaged. *Science,* 1971, *171,* 640–647.

Stanley, J. C., & Porter, A. C. Correlation of Scholastic Aptitude Test scores with college grades for Negroes versus whites. *Journal of Educational Measurement,* 1967, *4,* 199–218.

Temp, G. Test bias: Validity of the SAT for blacks and whites in thirteen integrated institutions. *Journal of Educational Measurement,* 1971, *8,* 245–251.

Thorndike, R. L. Concepts of culture-fairness. *Journal of Educational Measurement,* 1971, *8,* 63–70.

Wild, C. L., & Dwyer, C. A. Sex bias in selection. In L.J.T. van der Kamp, D.N.M. de Gruijter, & W. F. Langerak (Eds.), *Psychometrics for educational debates.* New York: Wiley, 1980.

Williams, R. L. Danger: Testing dehumanizing black children. *Clinical Child Psychology Newsletter,* 1970, *9,* 5–6.

Williams, R. L. From dehumanization to Black intellectual genocide: A rejoinder. In G. J. Williams & S. Gordon (Eds.), *Clinical child psychology: Current practices and future perspectives.* New York: Behavioral Publications, 1974.

Wright, B. D., Mead, R. J., & Draba, R. *Detecting and correcting test item bias with a logistic response model* (Research Memorandum No. 22). Chicago: Statistical Laboratory, Department of Education, University of Chicago, 1976.

2 USE OF JUDGMENTAL METHODS IN ITEM BIAS STUDIES
CAROL KEHR TITTLE

INTRODUCTION

JUDGMENTAL METHODS have always been applied to items, to item tryout forms, and to the selection of items for final forms of educational and psychological tests. What is new is the attention being paid to whom the judges are, the focus of the judgments, and the systemization (formalizing) of judgments. This chapter includes a general introduction to describe why these methods are becoming prominent, a review of the substantive focus of the judgments as well as when they should occur in the test development process, and a series of recommendations for the test developer and the test user both in applying (and seeking the results of the application of) judgmental processes in test development and test use.

The substantive focus of the judgments includes two areas that may be said to deal with the face validity of the instrument, stereotyping and fair representation of women and minorities. A third area includes both face and content validity: equal familiarity or experience of subgroups with the nominal content of items. A fourth area is concerned with content and construct validity: the opportunity to learn item content and processes, that is, the match or overlap of items with the instructional process.

It has long been recognized that we obtain no more from analyses of research and evaluation data than the measuring instruments can provide. The renewal of interest in item bias, or the fairness of tests used in evaluation and research, has placed the focus of studies on the most important part of the evaluation research process, and that is the instrument upon which inferences are based. While there has been intermittent attention given to the problems that measuring instruments may pose in evaluation design (e.g., Boruch & Gomez, 1977), the current attention to judgmental item bias studies stems from several sources. These sources are the criticisms by minorities and women of educational and psychological tests for stereotyping

31

and differential familiarity with context and content of items, and the attempts to develop program-sensitive measures of achievement.

The limitations of norm-referenced achievement tests as program-sensitive measures for evaluation are becoming more widely publicized (see Cole & Nitko, 1981). Linn (1980), for example, has summarized these dissatisfactions based on the need for content theory. Tyler (1977) has drawn attention to their limitations in the evaluation of programs of compensatory education, and writers such as Cervantes (1974), Samuda (1975), and Williams, Mosby, and Hinson (1977) have discussed the testing of American minorities more generally. McKenna (1977) has presented the views of the National Education Association. His criticisms of standardized testing (norm-referenced), for example, include lack of relationship to local instructional objectives and curricula, emphasis on recall, and culture and linguistic bias as exemplified by the use of vocabulary and illustrations most familiar to white, middle-class students. In some inner city schools, teachers point to the lack of fit between what they are teaching and what tests measure, and label the tests as biased against their pupils. These criticisms emphasize the need for closer attention to the construct validity of tests used in evaluation. Judgmental methods have a role in establishing construct validity and responding to the criticisms of bias.

These criticisms themselves can be seen as a reaction to the much broader sociopolitical context of the use of tests in program evaluations, as a response to an expansion of public programs and an effort to "account" for the responsible use of such funds. The rapid extension of educational funding was carried out initially in a time of economic expansion and the civil rights efforts. The funding has slowed, but the push for equal opportunities in education and educational outcomes has not. American schools have moved in the last 50 years from a situation in which educational opportunity was rationed, to the present effort to expand opportunity to all children and youth and to provide universal education within a democratic educational system (Tyler, 1980).

A move toward litigation over the use of tests in business, governmental, and educational settings attests to a continued period of examination of tests, the test development process, and the use of test scores. Cronbach (1980) has noted the fundamental nature of present trends.

The public intends to judge specific test uses for itself, directly or through courts and legislatures. . . . Our task is not to judge *for* nonprofessionals but to clarify, so that in their judgments they can use their power perceptively.

The politicization of testing ought not be surprising. Test data influence the fortunes of individuals and the support given to human service programs. Quite properly tests are subject to supervision by the polity, and open to pressure from anyone seeking to better his [or her] lot or the lot of constituents and dependents. This process of counter-pressures and negotiation and ultimate mutual accommodation gives the American system its unique virtues as well as its defects.

We might once have identified validation with a single question, What does the instrument measure? That question will not have an objective, universal answer. A yet more judgmental question now takes on equal importance: And why should *that* be measured? (pp. 100, 107)

The response to the politicization of testing has been one of accommodation by test publishers, test developers, and evaluators, as described later in this chapter and in subsequent chapters. The accommodation has taken the form of reviews of tests for stereotyping of minorities and women, efforts to examine the balance or representation of women and minorities in tests, and the use of statistical methods to detect items on which subgroups perform differently, as well as to identify the match between the instruction and the test in evaluation. The reviews and judgments are more or less formalized and vary in terms of who the judges are and what form the review takes, as do the applications of statistical methods. Yet, these accommodations begin to form a new set of procedures, or, in Kuhn's (1977) terms, "concrete problem solutions that the profession has come to accept as paradigms" (p. xix).

These paradigms are in their initial stage of formulation and may yet result in a set of procedures that will be analogous to that of the legal system in a particular sense, that of the definition of *pure procedural justice* (Rawls, 1971): the situation in which there is a correct or fair procedure such that the outcome is similarly judged to be correct or fair, whatever it is, provided that the procedure has been properly followed. This is a definition of justice in the situation where there is no independent criterion for the correct outcome and is similar to the situation of measuring educational attainment. In the test development setting there needs to be a closer examination and agreement on the test development process, the judgmental and statistical data that are to be developed and reported, and the decision rules used as the basis to identify the final set of test items. Such agreement would permit both users and developers to reach a conclusion as to whether a test is "fair" for a particular subgroup, e.g., minorities or women (Tittle, 1975). The involvement of groups of judges, both internal and external to the test development setting, and the *documentation* of their judgments, should permit the focus to shift from explaining any subgroup score differences based on characteristics (such as sex, SES, or racial/ethnic status) to whether in fact the test was "fair" for a particular subgroup. If the test is perceived as fair, it should be possible to move on to the instructional implications of the outcomes for programmatic change and individual learning.

In the legal setting, the use of trials is based upon the idea of a jury of peers to result in a "fair" judgment. The definition of "peer" has changed with the addition of constitutional amendments to guarantee the rights of individuals regardless of their race, religion, or sex. Similarly the principles of justice as fairness applied to item fairness means the inclusion in the judgment process of the least advantaged groups, those with the least authority and income, or unequal basic rights because of fixed natural characteristics, e.g., racial, ethnic, and sex groups. It means as well the representation of these groups in the test content (using ideas analogous to those proposed by Rawls, 1971). With this legal and philosophical underpinning of concepts of equity, we are not concerned with whether or not the implementation of these ideas "causes" minorities or women to attain higher scores on particular tests or affects performance in any way.* The procedures are carried out because they are both just and fair, and the resulting test may be perceived by the various constituent groups to be a fair test. Jones (1980) has made the same point about competency tests, "A competency test must not only be fair; it must be perceived to be fair" (p. 66).

Thus the judgmental methods arise from a different, nonstatistical ground. In examining fairness or bias primarily on statistical grounds, we may again be witnessing a technical solution to a problem that is broader than the technical issues. As Breland and Ironson (1976) demonstrated in the use of tests in selection, none of the technical solutions reflected the values of a law school selection process, as evidenced by the admission of a greater number of minority students than indicated by the technical solutions. Our present situation may indeed be similar. The perceived fairness of the tests used in evaluation and research is based on diverse values and experiences, and our task is to represent these values in the test development process, and in research and evaluation more generally (Perloff, Padgett, & Brock, 1980).

In the next section, the judgmental methods in use in several areas are examined. As the review indicates, the general areas for judgment are being clarified, and there are issues for users to consider in applying the judgmental methods.

REVIEW OF JUDGMENTAL METHODS

The stages in the development of a test, from setting the test specification through a review of the final test ready for administration, provide the framework within which judgmental methods are used. These stages are identified below, followed by a review of the guidelines and procedures for

---

*While it is not argued here that judgmental reviews identify items on which there will be group differences in performance, it should be noted that there is some research literature that supports this relationship. For example, see Coffman (1961) and Donlon (1971) for judges' identification of SAT items as easier for men or women; Medley and Quirk's (1974) use of items familiar to black candidates on the "general culture section" of the National Teacher Examination; Milton (1958) on the influence of context on problem solving; McCarthy's (1975) study of ratings of context familiarity of SAT-type items for high school boys and girls and differences in item indices; and Donlon, Ekstrom, and Lockheed's (1979) study of sex bias in achievement batteries. Dwyer (1979) has speculated on the history of sex differences on the SAT-V and M, as well as reviewing the general role of tests in producing sex-related differences in performance. The findings are not all consistent, however.

judgments. We should note at the outset that these methods are useful for item writers for multiple-choice tests, for those selecting items from item pools, for those using any of the item writing technologies (Roid & Haladyna, 1980), or for those setting domain specifications. The methods described below have been applied to the development of tests that are norm-referenced, criterion- or objectives-referenced, or domain-referenced. As Nitko (1974) noted, the ambiguities inherent in traditional item writing are generally inherent in criterion-referenced item writing.

The applications of judgments to stereotyping, representation and familiarity are described below, as well as the use of judgments in determining the overlap between tests, curriculum, and instruction. The review also identifies some of the issues arising from the use of judgmental methods to date.

The Test Development Process: Stages for Application of Judgmental Methods

The test development process can be divided into several stages: test planning, item writing and review, item tryout, selection of the final items, and development of norms and scaling.

Test planning. Judgments of the categories to use in planning the test, i.e., defining test specifications, set the stage for item writing and reviewing. These judgments are of concern in terms of the perceptions of fairness of the nominal content (stereotyping and familiarity) and the positive representation of minorities and women. Similarly, the categories defined here become important to later analysis of the overlap between instruction, curriculum, and the test. In this initial stage it is important to identify judges who can review test specifications and item or domain specifications from several perspectives:

1. Do the specifications include the positive representation of the various minority or least advantaged groups who will take the final test?
2. Do the specifications include the need to balance or provide for the use of passages (particularly for reading tests) likely to be equally familiar or equally unfamiliar to subgroups who will take the test?

Studies by Schmeiser (1979; 1980; also chapter 3) appear to support the notion that including representation of blacks, for example, in the content of the *American College Testing Program's (ACT)* social studies tests does not differentially affect the test performance of blacks and whites, females or males. However, some of the earlier achievement research suggests that the use of "diverse cultural content" should distinguish between situations in which the cultural content serves as a vehicle to test cognitive skills that are clearly passage dependent (and the context is equally unfamiliar to all groups) and those that can be answered independently of passages or are differentially familiar.

3. Do the specifications caution against the use of item forms that may affect
    group performance differentially?

Sherman (1976) examined the use of the "I don't know" alternative in the
National Assessment of Educational Progress. For science questions, groups
using the response more frequently than the national average and who were
correct less often included Southeastern adults, 17-year-olds, adult females,
black adults, and rural adults. This response alternative apparently functions to tap an aspect of uncertainty related to response style of particular
groups.

4. Do the specifications include a level of detail in analysis which will permit
    the categorization of content, curriculum materials, and instruction on
    such aspects as the format in which items are set, their subject matter
    content, and the skill or cognitive process the item is designed to elicit?

Additional judgments might incorporate the concepts of whether the item
constitutes an entering skill, an acceptable or minimum standard, or a
superior standard, as well as weighting for importance. The entering skill
measures the extent to which ability to perform (pass the item, master the
content) is required for entrance to the grade or instructional level for which
the test is intended. The acceptable or minimum standard indicates mastery
of the content such that passing the item is a measure of acceptable or successful achievement at the end of that grade or instructional unit. The
superior standard represents a judgment that to do well on the item is to
demonstrate superior achievement for the age or instructional unit.
Weighting for importance involves the judgment of how many items or how
much weight to assign to the particular categories in the test specifications.

Item writing and review. This is the second stage in which judgments
may affect fairness. Here the test specifications translate into directions for
item writers and item reviewers. This stage is critical in terms of meeting the
needs to avoid stereotyping and to include positive representation of
minorities and women. One of the most common problems found in reviewing items and tests is the lack of representation of minorities and women in
nonstereotypical settings. The most obvious instances of discriminatory
presentation of these groups may be eliminated, only to find that the elimination occurs to an extreme, resulting, for example, in few instances of reading
passages that include content about black or Hispanic Americans. (Green,
1973, recommends that members of each of the groups concerned participate
in constructing the examination, so that a more heterogeneous set of biases
are built into tests. See also Tidwell, 1979, for a similar recommendation on
representing racial, sexual, religious, cultural, and SES groups in the item
writing and item review stage.) Directions to item writers must include
references to resources about minorities and women which provide the source
material for passages in reading, history, social studies, science, and other

areas of study. Omissions are difficult, and in some cases impossible, to rectify once items have been tried out.

Item tryout. This stage also involves a judgment that will later be evaluated by test users in assessing the fairness of the test. The judgment involves determining the major subgroups taking the test for whom it is important to obtain sufficient representation in item studies for group analysis. Estimates of the characteristics of potential test users, or identification of the groups for whom the test developer will claim that the test is fair, will dictate the selection of students for item tryouts. Statistical procedures for examining item bias will be used on the responses for these groups of students. Another set of judgments enters into the choice of the statistical procedure and the definition of biased and unbiased items using that particular statistical procedure(s). The definition is not strictly a statistical one; sample size and magnitude of differences will affect the acceptance or rejection of items regardless of the statistical test. The rationale and decisions made by the test developer at this stage also need to be documented and made public for others to examine. This suggests that external judges may also be useful here, until procedures become more codified.

Selection of the final items. This stage provides a final item pool or test that can again be reviewed for fairness with respect to stereotyping, representation of women and minorities, estimates or descriptions of the balance of material judged to be equally familiar to subgroups, and estimates of opportunity to learn. Here the overall balance in representation of society in terms of diverse social groups can be described and judged as acceptable or deficient. The match of the test with the specifications, with the identification of categories of content, skills, and presentation format, is detailed. Judges may again provide a final review for the major areas included in judgmental reviews of item bias or fairness, as well as the general directness and simplicity of directions and the grouping of similar item types.

Development of norms and scales. The development of norms, scales, standards, or final domain classifications provides another instance in which judgments enter the test development process. As with item tryouts, special groups may be identified for norms, such as urban pupils, high and low SES schools, students requiring special administration procedures (e.g., the handicapped), and other categories. The development of standards, as with minimum competency tests, directly involves the use of judges, and studies have utilized teachers as well as parents in an examination of standards (Jaeger et al., 1980). Perceptions of the fairness of the test and the use of test results should be affected by representation in the process and knowledge of the outcomes.

This framework shows that judgments are involved at every stage of test development, as well as in the use of test results. I turn now to an examination of the procedures that have been used to judge item bias—first, for stereotyping, positive representation, and familiarity, and second, for judgments of opportunity to learn and overlap with curriculum and instruction.

Judgments of Stereotyping, Representation, and Familiarity

Experts develop their expertise by a variety of relevant experiences, according to Coffman (1977), and the function of judgmental methods in item bias is to represent as many experiences as may be relevant to perceptions of the fairness of the test items and to student motivation, and perhaps performance. The accommodation is reached in the current development of tests through two approaches: providing instructional materials and guidelines, as well as training, to judges, and increasing in the judging process the representation of other "experts" who are particularly aware of stereotyping, demeaning material, and the need for representation of specific groups in our culture.

The inclusion of guidelines and training is necessary for several reasons. Guidelines insure that the variety of types of stereotypical behavior are brought to the attention of reviewers, writers, and editors. Training to identify instances of such behavior helps to ensure the consistent application of guidelines. Not all members of particular groups will have had the same experiences or awareness of the implications of specific experiences. Judges are likely to differ on their sensitivity to the guidelines and to the subtle and not so subtle forms that bias can take. "Expert" judges will, in some sense, be more keenly attuned to these forms. For example, an item may describe government personnel interacting with consumer or civil rights groups. Is there subtle discrimination in the following references to the characters in the situation?

William Lawrence, Executive Director of the Federal Commission; George Donner, Executive Director of the Federal agency; Esther Misen, an official of the consumer group; Al Juarez, an official of the labor group; and Richard Sherman, former Commissioner of the (federal agency).

In this example, the males have their titles given whereas the female and the Hispanic person do not. Will all judges identify this distinction? Another example can be cited in the illustrations for a grade 2 reading test:

There are illustrations of a boy and a woman watching TV. The TV screen shows the boy watching a cowboy and a football player, showing the full figures in action, and the woman sees the face (only) of another woman on TV. The TV woman's face is smiling; there is no identification of the female adult as active or engaged in an occupation or sport. Another "pretty face"?*

*The general principles that underlie much of expert judgment have been formally stated by Harms (1978), drawing on the ideas of John Rawls. Harms specified two major principles (stated in language appropriate for twelfth-grade reviewers used in his study): (1) Within a defined us-

The few instances in which judges have been checked for agreement show individual differences in their ratings, as might well be expected.

Guidelines and tally forms. To gauge the level of analysis of behavior that can be conducted for item text and illustrations, consider the categories in Table 2.1 used by Jacklin to examine sex bias in early readers (which could be applied to minority group representation also). These categories were used to classify adult and juvenile characters, female and male, in each of the four main areas: main or secondary character, type of environment, behavior exhibited, and types of consequence of behavior. These are the types of behavior to which judges need to be sensitive, as well as the language usage and stereotyping phrases given in more detail in the guidelines of publishers. Macmillan (1975) has made available a comprehensive and detailed publication, *Guidelines for creating positive sexual and racial images in educational materials.* The section of guidelines for treatment of races and minorities concerns general content and avoiding racial and minority stereotypes in art. The guidelines are especially helpful in moving from identifying negative examples, e.g., racial paternalism, to positive representation: "Include minority figures who created their own opportunities, solutions, and achievements and helped others. Treat minority heroes in depth, not in passing mention. Use minority persons as central, three dimensional characters in stories and examples" (p. 35).

The Macmillan guidelines for minorities focus on specific groups—black Americans, American Indians, Hispanic Americans, Asian Americans, and Jewish Americans. Also included are subject area guidelines that provide a thoughtful discussion of the problems and issues in increasing representation of minorities and women in areas such as social studies. The guidelines recommend that reading materials include an overall 50-50 representation of the sexes, and that approximately one-fourth or more of the female characters be in activities that are central, outside the home, active, physically demanding, exciting, highly valued in our culture, instructive, fun, and that require initiative and leadership. Similarly, about one-fourth or more of the characters should be males in activities that are secondary, inside the

---

age, test items should not "turn off" students so that they are unable to do as well as their abilities would indicate; and (2) All students should have equality of opportunity to respond. The principles were translated into nine criteria or guidelines. These guidelines are: (1) an item must not contain any information that could be offensive to a student's religion or culture; (2) an item must be nonsexual in the sense that it must not be designed to offend either sex group; (3) an item must not include depictions of any group that are degrading or stereotypic; (4) an item must not portray groups as unequal in ability; (5) an item must not, by content or form, cause students to be "turned-off" so that they may not do as well as they are able; (6) the content of the test item must not reflect information and/or skills that may not be expected to be within the educational background of all students or groups taking the test; (7) the content of the item must not contain any clues or information that could be seen to work to the benefit of any group or either sex; (8) the content of the item must be familiar to all and not specific to any one group or sex; and (9) group specific language, vocabulary, or reference pronouns (*he, she*, etc.) must not be included in items.

TABLE 2.1. Categories Used by Jacklin to Examine Sex Bias in Beginning Readers

CATEGORIES
1. Main and secondary characters
2. Type of environment:
     Home
     Outdoors
     Place of business
     School
3. Behavior exhibited:
     Nurturant (helping, praising, serving)
     Aggressive (hitting, kicking, verbal put-downs)
     Self-care (dressing, washing)
     Routine-repetitive (eating, going to school)
     Constructive-productive (building, writing story, planning party)
     Physically exertive (sports, lifting heavy objects)
     Social-recreational (visiting someone, card games)
     Fantasy activity (doll play, cowboys and Indians)
     Directive (initiating, directing, demonstrating)
     Avoidance (stop trying, run away, shut eyes)
     Statement about self—positive, negative, neutral ("I have blue eyes." "I'm too stupid.")
     Problem-solving (producing idea, unusual combinations)
     Statements of information ("I know . . ."; non-evaluative observations about other people)
     Expression of emotion (crying, laughing)
     Conformity (express concern for rules, social norms, others' expectations, do as told)
     General motor (trivial motor behavior such as dropping something, looking for something,
        listening)
4. Types of consequences:
     Positive consequences—
     From others—directed toward subject (praise, recognition, support, signs of affection)
     From self—self-praise, satisfaction
     From situation—reaching goal, unintended positive results
     Chance
     Author's statement, text
     Negative consequences—
     From others—directed toward subject (criticism, correction, rejection of ideas)
     From self
     From situation—inability to reach goal, unintended negative results
     Chance
     Author's statement, text
     *Neutral consequences—*not clearly positive or negative

Source: Saario, T. N., Jacklin, C. N., & Tittle, C. K. Sex role stereotyping in the public schools.
Harvard Educational Review, 1973, *43*, 392–393. © 1973 by President and Fellows of Harvard
College.

home, observing, and that express emotion, show social concern, show concern for appearance, minister to the needs of others, and scold.

     Other examples of guidelines available include McGraw-Hill's *Guidelines
for equal treatment of the sexes* (1974) and *Multiethnic publishing guidelines*
(1968), and the *Guidelines for the representation of exceptional persons in
educational material* (National Center of Educational Media and Materials
for the Handicapped, 1979). The Council on Interracial Books for Children
(1980) also publishes guidelines and sources. Major test publishers have also
prepared guidelines for reviewers and/or writers, as well as publications

describing the procedures for developing tests that are fair to minorities, women, and exceptional persons.* A number of professional organizations also have developed guidelines, e.g., *Guidelines for nonsexist use of language in NCTE publications* (National Council of Teachers of English, n.d.), and the *Guidelines for nonsexist language in APA journals* (American Psychological Association, 1977). *The handbook of nonsexist writing* (Miller & Swift, 1980) provides a useful perspective on linguistic change by tracing the origins of some of our current usage, and suggesting alternatives.

Specific examples of the types of analysis being done in current test development are shown in Tables 2.2. and 2.3. Table 2.2 shows the categories in the coding system used as one part of the fairness analysis of the *Metropolitan Achievement Tests.* The analysis of illustrations in the Metropolitan categorized children and adults separately, according to three categories: male taller than female, female taller than male, and female same height as male. The classification of illustrations was in response to a criticism that boys are often shown as taller than girls, when in fact children of the same age are very similar in height regardless of sex. The Metropolitan analysis also included a variant of the tally of male nouns and pronouns and female nouns and pronouns used by Tittle, McCarthy, and Steckler (1974) to show the ratio of references of males to females (The Psychological Corporation, 1978a). Donlon et al. (1977) also describe in detail a variant on count-

TABLE 2.2. Categories for Analysis of Gender-Balance

1. OCCUPATIONS
   Female Traditional: Nurse, Teacher, Librarian, Secretary, etc.
   Male Traditional: Laborer, Professional, Principal, Boss, etc.
   Female Non-traditional: Professional, Laborer, Boss, Principal, etc.
   Male Non-traditional: Nurse, Teacher, Secretary, etc.

2. ACTIVITIES
   Female Traditional: School, Playing with Dolls, Onlookers, Domestic Chores
   Male Traditional: School Sports, games, other physical activities, adventurer, etc.
   Female Non-traditional: Sports, games, physical activity
   Male Non-traditional: Domestic Chores, Child rearing, etc.

3. ROLES
   Active: Main character, problem solver, giving help/gift
   Passive: Secondary character, needing help, recipient of help/gift

4. EMOTIONS
   Female Traditional: Fear, nurturance/tenderness, dependency, etc.
   Male Traditional: Aggression, courage, emotional strength, "strong silent type"
   Female, Male Non-traditional: Cross-sex stereotypes

Source: Jensen and Beck (1979). © 1979, American Personnel and Guidance Association. Reprinted with permission.

*Appreciation is expressed to the following publishers for their generosity in supplying descriptions of their procedures and samples of forms and publications: American College Testing Program, CTB/McGraw-Hill, Educational Testing Service, Instructional Objectives Exchange, Science Research Associates, and The Psychological Corporation.

TABLE 2.3. Character Tally Form—Science Research Associates

Identification of Level and Form	Form _____ Copy Art	Form _____ Copy Art
Age		
Child/Adolescent		
Adult		
Elderly		
Group		
Asian American		
Black		
Native American		
Spanish American		
White		
Ethnic (other)		
Not Identified		
Handicapped		
Activity		
Active		
Passive		
Neutral		
Role		
Traditional		
Nontraditional		
Neutral		
Adult Role Model		
Worker		
Parent		
Character Development		
Major		
Minor		
Incidental		
Setting		
City		
Suburban		
Rural		
Neutral		

Source: Developed 1977 by Science Research Associates, Inc. Reprinted by special permission.

ing nouns and pronouns as a rough indicator of sex balance. For these counts, as well as the classifications into categories (see below), good agreement among judges can be obtained (e.g., Donlon et al., 1977) and can be expressed as percentage overlap using Scott's (1955) index, π, or chi-square.

Table 2.3 shows the categories used by Science Research Associates (SRA) to tally male or female characters in items. One tally sheet is completed for males and one for females. This table also provides a form that integrates representation for major groups of concern in fairness. In chapter 9, Raju presents an SRA summary form for either artwork or copy for subtests, levels, forms, or other major groupings of items (see Table 9.7). These tally forms and summary forms could be used to describe item pools or item domain specifications as well as the standardized tests with which they are currently used. The judgments used to make the easily understandable description provided by the tallies will do much to increase the perceptions that tests are fair in the area of representing minorities.

Expert judges. As noted earlier, expert "judges" or representatives of special groups can be used at all stages of test development. In a few instances, this is apparently done. However, the more common procedure appears to be to involve these representatives at the item writing stage, item review stage or, alternatively, at the stage when items are put into final test forms. Ideally, all racial and sex groups would be represented in the pool of item writers (as is done in the *ACT Assessment* Program, Schmeiser, personal communication, 1980). Several publishers also maintain files or national panels of minority reviewers, in addition to the test specialists who carry out their own internal reviews. Often, external judges who indicate that an item is biased are asked to identify the source of bias. As noted by one publisher, "Comments of the reviewers provide valuable insights into the subtleties of racism, stereotyping, and other inappropriate attitudes" (Lyster, personal communication, 1980). A sample form used by CTB/McGraw-Hill for this purpose is shown in Table 2.4. A similar form is used to review the artwork for tests for content bias.

Judges typically are sent the publisher's guidelines, along with general comments to identify items that have stereotyped or demeaning content or is likely to be unfamiliar to a particular group. For the new edition of the *Stanford Achievement Test,* the broad categories suggested to reviewers were: status; stereotype; familiarity; offensive use of language; and other to be specified by reviewer (unpublished material, The Psychological Corporation,

TABLE 2.4. Item Bias Review Form—CTB/McGraw-Hill

TRYOUT EDITION

Level_____ Content Area_____

Directions: For each item, check either the "Not Biased" or the "Biased" column. For each item checked in the "Biased" column, give the reason for your evaluation.

Page nr	Item nr	Item Evaluation		Explanation
		Not Biased	Biased	

Note: Reprinted by permission of the publisher, CTB/McGraw-Hill, Del Monte Research Park, Monterey, Calif. 93940.

1980). Hambleton (1980a) has provided an example of an item bias review form that includes some of these categories. This form is presented in Table 2.5.

In an adaptation of a review form for criterion-referenced item pools, Dunning and Maruhnich (1980) included a section on item bias review. Five questions were specified:

Does the item contain any references which could be construed as biased in terms of race, ethnic origin, or cultural background?
. . . in terms of sex or sexual orientation?
. . . in terms of socioeconomic status?
. . . in terms of age?
. . . in terms of religious affiliation or belief?

Each item was then checked as satisfactory, questionable, unsatisfactory, or not applicable. The form was used in the process of developing a 2000-item pool for the state of Delaware. Part of the training of item reviewers included a discussion of item bias and the presentation of sample items illustrating bias. Differences among item writers, item editors, and measurement specialists in the categorization of items on the five questions on item bias led the authors to conclude that

particular training in the recognition and avoidance of bias in items be conducted. This training also should prepare item writers to differentiate between those items in which bias is a relevant concern and those in which it is not a pertinent consideration. This training should focus item writers' attention on the subtlety of bias and particular wording which can signal the presence of bias in items. (p. 26)

Harms (1978) used an instructional module for twelfth-grade student raters and still had 22% of the raters who did not reach the standard level of identifying four of five biased items. Thus, individual differences among judges are likely to remain even with training.

Educational Testing Service (ETS), as part of its test sensitivity review process (Hunter & Slaughter, 1980), will train test development staff to be test sensitivity reviewers. The description of the review process includes test evaluation criteria as well as guidelines for the recognition of unacceptable stereotypes and a helpful list of caution words and phrases, e.g., *backward, barbarian, birthrate, class, colonialism, crime, culturally disadvantaged, developing nation, gangs, ignorant, illegitimate,* and *inferior.*

Before examining the judgmental methods applied to the match between test, curriculum, and instruction, several issues have been raised by the discussion thus far. No systematic studies of the number of judges required in any particular review procedure and their distribution by type of group exist, and only a few studies of the agreement among judges expected to represent the same set of relevant experiences. Earlier reports by Spencer (1973),

TABLE 2.5. Item Bias Review Form

Reviewer: _____ Date: _____

Objective: _____

Place the numbers of the test items to be reviewed in the appropriate boxes below. Next, read each test item and answer the eight questions. Use "✔" for *YES* answers and "X" for *NO* answers.

	Test Item Ratings							

1. Is the item free of offensive sexual, cultural, racial, and/or ethnic content?
2. Is the item free of sexual, cultural, racial, and/or ethnic stereotyping?
3. Is the item free of language which would be offensive to a segment of the examinee population?
4. Is the item free from descriptions which would be offensive to a segment of the examinee population?
5. Will the activities or situations described in the item be familiar to all examinees?
6. Will the words in the item have a common meaning to all examinees?
7. Is the item free of difficult vocabulary and/or sentence structure?
8. Will the item format be familiar to all examinees?

Source: Hambleton (1980a). Reprinted by permission of the author.

Armstrong (1972), and Ozenne, Van Gelder, and Cohen (1974) as well as the informal summaries of minority reviewers given here indicate that some proportion of items *are* identified as biased. Also, the items identified as biased or unfair vary by minority group and for women.

Typically, items are reviewed by the publisher's staff before being sent to reviewers. Not all items judged as unfair by a group will be identified by internal staff. Another issue is that of evaluating the "accuracy" of external judges, and if some of the dimensions they apparently use for judgment can be described for internal staff.

The Ozenne et al. (1974) report includes the reasons given by members of an 11-person review panel for identifying items as biased. In that particular instance, the reasons can be grouped into two language areas—(1) different use of words in a youth culture and differences between Spanish and English, and (2) the familiarity category—differences due to urban-rural, socioeconomic, and geographic statuses.

Boldt et al. (1977) identified four sociolinguistic principles relevant to examining fairness or bias in tests: pragmatics, processing, formality, and redundancy. The sociolinguistic view argues that age, sex, social class, ethnic group, and geographic location all condition the language of a particular individual. These variables are part of *pragmatics*—the frame of reference or values of the item writer and the test taker. *Processing* involves the clarity with which sets of items require the same combination of information processing skills. *Formality* means that the greater the distance between the variety of English familiar to an individual and that used in a test, the greater the potential for linguistic difficulty. The *redundancy*-reducing rules characteristic of written English may also cause difficulty for individuals whose familiarity with formal written English is limited.

The principles were applied to two subtests of the armed services selection battery. For one subtest the three judges agreed closely; on a second subtest there was less agreement. It appeared, however, that "the four principles can, with further experimental refinement, be used to identify potential sociolinguistic problems in test items" (Boldt et al., 1977, p. 27). Polin and Baker (1979) appear to have included a variable related to the sociolinguistic ones above, that of linguistic complexity. Linguistic complexity has several parts: vocabulary used in the item is consistent with specifications for item difficulty; words do not have different or unfamiliar meanings for different groups of students; and the item language structure (compound and complex sentences) is consistent with the test specifications for item difficulty.

There are a number of questions here that can be researched. Despite criticisms of testing, there are more, not fewer, tests being given, and the development of tests is not limited to a few test publishers. Those concerned with the development of state and district testing programs will have opportunities to examine their own use of expert judges more systematically. There is a body of rich psychological literature on the nature of expert judgment (see, for example, Doherty, 1980). As the dimensions on which it appears experts judge stereotyping and differential familiarity are refined, we may be able to identify those judges who use the dimensions most consistently. Similar issues will apply to another area in which tests have been called biased—that of the opportunity to learn the skills and content of the items in the evaluation test.

Judgments of Items, Curricula, and Opportunity to Learn

The admonition to examine or to select a test for its congruence with the curriculum is a basic tenet of educational evaluation, whether for assessment of individual pupils or programs. This tenet, however, is not well met in practice. Charges of test bias also include the criticism that tests do not measure what is taught in the classroom. Inner-city teachers have argued that tests are biased because inferences are made that programs are not effective and/or that their children fail to learn. As Hanson, Schutz, and Bailey (1980) noted, "Testing children on what they have not been taught and then stigmatizing their 'failure to achieve' is a fundamental form of discrimination" (p. 21). Thus, it is appropriate to examine here the judgmental methods that have been developed to meet this facet of test and item bias, one directly concerned with the construct validity of inferences made from test scores. In the evaluation context, the inferences made on the basis of tests include no changes due to treatment and no differences in the effects of different treatments. In the individual score context, the inference is that the student did not, sometimes translated to *cannot*, learn "reading comprehension," "mathematical problem solving," or whatever the label on the particular test. The validity of any of these inferences depends on the match between curriculum and instruction (i.e., opportunity to learn) and test items. In the terminology used by Cook and Campbell (1979), we are concerned here with the construct validity of the "treatment" as well as the construct validity of the test.

The issue of whether broad, generalized goals or specific objectives of education should be measured has been debated widely. The debate became more defined with the evaluation of government-sponsored curriculum development projects in the 1960s and sharpened with the evaluation of government-sponsored program evaluation of compensatory education programs. Glaser's (1963) seminal article on criterion-referenced testing focused the debate on the contrast between the norm-referenced and criterion-(objectives-) referenced instruments, and encouraged the development of objective- and domain-referenced measures as well as the specification of the technical characteristics of these instruments. Judgmental methods have been applied in ratings of the relevance of objectives to domain statements and in ratings of the match between items and objectives. These judgments typically have been either yes/no or degree of certainty ratings of congruence.

Rovinelli and Hambleton (1977) and Hambleton (1980b) considered the various judgments, rating procedures, and statistics applicable for content specialists in their assessment of criterion referenced test item validity. The authors also presented several rating forms and the results of small-scale studies on the consistency among judges. Hambleton (1980a) provided a set of review methods for criterion-referenced test items, and Dunning and Maruhnich (1980) also supplied an example of an item pool review form used for the state of Delaware. Some recent test standardizations have incorporated teacher ratings. For example, the 1978 edition of the Metropolitan collected teacher questionnaires. The percentage of teachers who reported teaching each objective during a specified school year have been compiled (The Psychological Corporation, in press). Ratings of the overlap of objectives specified for the basic skills improvement policy in Massachusetts and standardized test items have been carried out (Madaus et al., 1979). Teachers and others were asked, How many of the fourteen reading skills (or thirty-eight mathematics skills) of the Massachusetts Basic Skills are measured by at least one item on the test? ____No. of skills; ____% of Skills.

More recently, these judgments have taken two directions. The first direction is the attempt to classify at a greater level of specificity the characteristics of the item, and the curriculum format, substance, and skill/process required. The second is the use of teacher, student, or external ratings of the opportunity to learn the item in the instructional process as an index of the match of instruction, curriculum, and test items.

A historical review of the use of taxonomic, or descriptive, categories in scientific classification was recently completed by Travers (1980). Many inventories of specific objectives in education have been published, with little impact. The exception has been the widespread use of the taxonomy of educational objectives edited by Bloom (1956). According to Travers, however, the taxonomy has no theoretical underpinning such as that characterizing earlier classifications in other areas of science. While Travers argues for Piaget's work as being useful since it may yield a taxonomy for the cognitive domain based on the formal properties of knowledge, this approach does not appear in recent writings on classifications suggested for tests (e.g., Bormuth, 1970; Gagné & Merrill, 1976; Kirsch & Guthrie, 1980; Kretschmer, 1972; Lucas & McConkie, 1980). Nor does it appear in the classification schemes that have been developed for early readers (Hanson, Schutz, & Bailey, 1977), for elementary school tests of mathematics (Kuhs, et al., 1979) or other examples (see below).

The taxonomies in use in test development programs vary according to subject matter areas, but they have reflected the approach of the taxonomy edited by Bloom (e.g., the classification of mathematics skills used by the Educational Testing Service: recall factual knowledge, perform mathematical manipulations, solve routine problems, demonstrate comprehension of mathematical ideas and concepts, solve nonroutine problems requiring insight or ingenuity, and apply higher mental processes to mathematics). Alternatively, the classification schemes have been highly specific.

Several studies have demonstrated the importance of the classification schemes and analysis of the curriculum and test congruence for evaluation and program improvement. Anderson (1975) analyzed the effects of schools in a small-scale study in the South. Both his study and Bianchini's report (1977) were based on examining the vocabulary in use in instruction. Anderson showed that the opportunity to learn vocabulary words varied with the school setting. Bianchini described the situation in the California Miller-Unruh Statewide Testing Program for grade 1: in the first five years (1966–1970), the *Stanford Reading Test* was used, and some 65% of first-graders had reading scores in the 1st quartile of the national norms, while the statewide median was at the 38th percentile rank. When the test was changed to the *Cooperative Primary Reading Test* in 1971, the statewide median remained the same as the national norm sample. Bianchini attributes the shift not to "easier" norms on the Cooperative test, but to an increase in overlap between vocabulary in the first-grade readers and the test. The overlap for the Stanford test and the readers was 19%; overlap for the Cooperative test and the readers was 55%. Lewy (1972) showed differences in opportunity to learn and test performance in mathematics, geography, and literature in a study in Israel. Teachers identified the items that students of their class did not have an opportunity to study. Cooley and Leinhardt (1978), in a preliminary report of findings in a large-scale study of reading and math instruction and student gain in grades 1 and 3, concluded that "the most useful construct in explaining achievement gain is the opportunity that the children had to learn the skills assessed in the achievement test, especially as represented by the measures of overlap between the curriculum and the post-test" (p. 5). They argue also that program evaluators run the risk of attributing instructional effectiveness to specific programs or ways of teaching when it is really a matter of differences in opportunity to learn.

The *opportunity to learn* construct is important regardless of the approach taken to test construction, the items selected for scoring as "program sensitive," or other suggested approaches to "program fair" evaluation, e.g., Angoff, 1975; Cahill et al., 1977; Hanson et al., 1977, 1980; Lewy, 1972; Rakow, Airasian, & Madaus, 1975; Thompson, 1971. The category systems used in several major studies of the congruence of tests and curriculum are examined next, then the approaches to judging opportunity to learn. All of these judgmental methods bear on the question raised by Cronbach: Why should *that* be measured? Although the studies have used norm-referenced tests, they are just as applicable to objective- and domain-referenced measures.

Content classification schemes. Several studies have examined the relationship between classifications of curricula and test content in early reading. Jenkins and Pany (1976, 1978) reported analyses of seven reading series and five reading achievement tests for grades 1 and 2. "Bias" was estimated by comparing the overlap. Overlap was reported in terms of achievement test grade-equivalent scores expected if the words were mastered in the curriculum and included as achievement test items. The authors surveyed first- and second-grade books from seven basal reading series and used teachers' manuals to compile alphabetized word lists for each series. They also prepared alphabetized word lists of all words in the tests and subtests of word recognition. Overlap was assessed by comparing word lists to determine the total number of word matches per grade level. Total number of word matches yielded a raw score that was then converted to a grade-equivalent score. The procedures involved two people independently matching the reading test and curriculum word lists; another person compared the lists and reconciled disagreements. Two persons computed the scores independently. The results showed that there were discrepancies between grade equivalents both between tests for a single curriculum and on a single test for different reading curricula. The "bias" was not uniform for these achievement tests. The authors examined the implications of selecting different tests for student evaluation, curriculum evaluation, teacher evaluation, reading placement, and educational research.

Armbruster, Stevens, and Rosenshine (1977) compared three curricula and two tests at the third-grade level, examining the match on reading comprehension categories. Frequencies of exercises and items were obtained for 16 categories: detail; paraphrase level 1; paraphrase level 2; cloze sentences; classifying; following directions; sequence; drawing conclusions; main idea; supporting information; cause and effect; words in context; figurative language; fantasy-reality; mood-setting; and character's emotions and traits. Only the curriculum written exercises designed to be completed by all students were coded; an interrater reliability (percentage agreement) of .81 was obtained using 3 blocks of 40 randomly selected items from the 3 curricula.

The reading series differed in its relative emphasis on reading comprehension, and the two standardized tests were similar in relative emphasis of reading comprehension. Only 6 of the 16 categories were common to all texts and tests, however, and "skills in the tests tend to be factual items entailing locating information in the presented text, whereas two of the three curricula give heavier emphasis to comprehension skills that appear to require inference, interpretation, indentification of relationships, and synthesis" (Armbruster et al., 1977, p. 10). The authors indicate that the extent to which such mismatches have any practical significance is not known for reading comprehension. The 16 categories did not examine such variables as amount of information and order of information, which are predictive of reading task difficulty (e.g., Kirsch & Guthrie, 1980).

A series of reports and presentations from the Institute for Research on Teaching and the College of Education at Michigan State University have been based on analyses of fourth-grade mathematics textbooks and tests. Porter et al. (1977, 1978) have argued that "practical significance" in program evaluation is not dependent on the "size of effect" as estimated by statistical indices that do not describe what was measured. They have called for, and designed materials to obtain, a description of the substantive characteristics of both curriculum and test. In the initial study of fourth-grade tests, three factors were used to describe items: Mode of Presentation, Nature of Material, and Operations. Mode of presentation had three categories: (1) graphs, figures, tables, etc.; (2) operation(s) specified; and (3) operation(s) not specified. Nature of the Material had 14 categories, e.g., single digits, single and multiple digits, multiple digits, etc. Operations had 12 categories, e.g., add, subtract without borrowing, subtract with borrowing, and so on.

The categories were independently classified by three researchers, and 98% of the items in the four standardized tests were found to be classifiable, using a criterion of agreement by two out of three of the raters. Interrater reliabilities were represented by the percentage of possible pairs of raters agreeing. The results of the analyses showed similarities and differences between tests on the factors; it was inferred that a total score would be likely to vary in sensitivity to any given instructional program. The tests were reasonably consistent in treatment of whole number computational skills, but differed in areas such as applications involving graphs, tables, and number sentences.

The factors and categories were slightly revised when the analysis was extended to look at classroom instructional materials. Table 2.6 lists the categories in each of the three factors as revised (Kuhs et al., 1979). Factor I, General Intent, has a focus on both the general intent and the format of presentation. The three categories of intent are conceptual understanding, skill acquisition, and application of skills or concepts. Factor II, Nature of the Material, examines whether the problem deals with whole numbers, fractions, decimals, geometry, or measurement. Factor III, Operations, examines the type of operation that must be applied to the material, e.g., ordinary arithmetic operations, order, estimating. The usual order of teaching has influenced the ordering of the categories in the factors. Kuhs et al. (1979) described and gave examples of classifying items and provided sample items to check understanding of the classification categories. Items were classified at the most complex level appropriate.

Porter et al. (n.d.) and Freeman et al. (1980) reported on the analysis of student study exercises in three widely used textbooks of fourth-grade mathematics. Each item in each exercise was classified on all three factors; the sum across exercises gave totals for each cell for each textbook. Three indices were derived: (1) percentage of items, providing a measure of emphasis on a given topic throughout a book; (2) percentage of lessons, giving an index of dispersion—whether items on a topic were concentrated in a few lessons or

TABLE 2.6. Taxonomy for Classifying Elementary School Mathematics Content

Factor I General Intent	Factor II Nature of the Material	Factor III Operations
Level	*Level*	*Level*
1 Conceptual understanding with pictorial models	1 Single digit/basic number facts	1 Identify equivalents
2 Conceptual understanding without pictorial models	2 Single & multiple digit	2 Order
3 Mathematical skills, reading graphs, etc.	3 Multiple digit numerals	3 Add without carrying
4 Computation/numeration skills	4 Number sentences/phrases	4 Add with carrying
5 Applications involving graphs, tables, etc.	5 Algebraic sentences/phrases	5 Add columns
6 Applications without graphs, etc.	6 Single or like fractions	6 Subtract without borrowing
	7 Unlike fractions	7 Subtract with borrowing
	8 Mixed numerals	8 Multiply
	9 Decimals	9 Divide without remainder
	10 Percentages	10 Divide with remainder
	11 Measurement	11 Combine
	12 Essential units of measurement	12 Apply concepts (terms)
	13 Geometry	13 Apply properties
	14 Other	14 Identify place value
		15 Estimate

Source: Adopted from Kuhs et al. (1979). Reprinted by permission.

distributed (estimated by dividing the number of lessons having at least one item corresponding to a given cell by the total number of lessons for that text); and (3) proportion of items within each lesson, dealing with a given topic.

The overlap in tests and texts was examined using the item percentages and an adjusted lesson percentaged measure (dividing the sum of the proportion of items in each lesson that dealt with a topic by the total number of lessons in the book). Criteria for core curricula common to texts (common to the three texts and representing at least .5% of adjusted lesson percents for each) and tests (at least one item common to four of the five tests) were used. The authors identified 27 core topics, and 21 topics showed at least some overlap between tests and texts (Kuhs et al., 1980). There were six core topics in both texts and tests. In a further analysis comparing the percentage of topics in a text matched by at least one item on a test, the results ranged from 22% to about 46%.

Porter and his associates have employed standardized tests and texts in their work. Similar judgments of other texts, using the same level of specificity, could either replace or anchor ratings of objectives- and domain-referenced tests. Roudabush (1977), for example, described a panel of teachers and a panel of mathematics experts who rated the *Prescriptive Mathematics Inventory* objectives as: appropriate for all sixth-grade students, appropriate for many sixth-grade students, or appropriate for some sixth-grade students. Objectives rated appropriate for all sixth-grade students were considered basic objectives in mathematics; content analysis of texts, or the methods described below, could supplement such judgments.

Direct judgments of opportunity to learn. As Leinhardt and Seewald (1980) have remarked, the content analysis procedures described above have two drawbacks for program evaluation. The first is that the approach considers only material in the formal curriculum, not actual instruction by the teacher, and second, that it does not yield a metric readily incorporated into analysis (as a predictor of student gain, for example): "Just as it is inappropriate to examine posttest differences without pretest information, it is also inappropriate to ignore variation in the opportunity to learn the material that is being tested" (p. 7).

The Instructional Dimensions Study (IDS) included about 400 first- and third-grade classrooms, examining reading and mathematics instruction. In an interview at the end of the year, teachers were asked to estimate the percentage of students who had been taught the minimum material necessary to pass the item (similar to earlier work in the International Educational Achievement Study and Lewy's work). Also, a curriculum analysis of material covered by students was completed. Other studies, however, have used both teacher estimates for individual students and computer analyses. Teachers have been asked to identify for each student for each item whether or not the student (1) has been taught the information required to answer the item, and (2) is familiar with the type of item format. (An estimate of 30 minutes is given for a teacher to complete the task of marking each item for each of 10 children.) Directions to teachers were,

We are trying to determine how closely this test measures what your students have been *taught*. To do this, we would like you to estimate which items on the CTBS you have taught to each student. . . . This is the same test that "Joey" (name of student on the booklet) took. . . . Start with number 1 and circle the item number if "Joey" was *taught* the information required to get this item correct. . . please take into account the way the item is presented as well as the content of the item. (Seewald, 1979, pp. 1–2)

The teacher's estimate includes both curriculum and teacher presentation but may also have a component of teacher expectation of performance.

The computer analysis constructs a dictionary of test-relevant information for each student (e.g., vocabulary words given in text) and information needed to "pass" an item. The dictionaries are matched to determine what percentage of the test has been covered through curriculum presentation. (This procedure requires large amounts of information on each curriculum, to be entered, sorted, and merged with student files.)

A basic regression analysis is used for data analysis, with the posttest score as the dependent variable, and the pretest, overlap, and perhaps other variables entered as covariates. In the IDS and other studies a measure of overlap has been an important variable in predicting end-of-year performance. The estimates using curriculum analysis are lower than teacher estimates, but the regression analysis remains essentially the same, regardless of which estimate is used. The teacher estimate has apparent advantages in relevance and perhaps cost.

Tenenbaum and Miller (1977) used a different method to examine congruence between items in a norm-referenced test and curriculum content in a program evaluation. In a field test of Project Information Packages (PIPs), data were sought through daily lesson plans that teachers were requested to turn in. The procedures were: to formulate rules to describe the knowledge and skills in each item in each subtest; to examine project curricula for the presence of the rules and appropriate content keyed to each item; to have the curricula entered on a daily record for each pupil listed; and to declare a match when the curricula taught to each pupil overlapped with the curricula keyed to a test item. An application of the rules developed for math story problems is given below.

Item: Which of these figures has the least number of line segments?

△ ○ ⬡ ▭

Rule: In order to respond correctly to this item a pupil must have been
    taught
        (a) recognition of planar shapes: triangle, rectangle, circle, and
            hexagon
        (a1) same scale
        (b) concepts: counting, least number, line segments
        (c) vocabulary (sight recognition and understanding): figures,
            least, number, line, segments. (Tenenbaum & Miller, 1977, p. 3)

The percentage of items congruent in the fourth-grade PIP-specified
materials and Metropolitan items ranged from 17% to 100%; for grade 8 the
overlap ranged from 7% to 70% on four subtests (3 items to 28 items).

As part of a study of Basic Skills Learning Centers, Hanson et al. (1980)
reported the use of three alternative types of instruments: (1) standardized
achievement tests (SAT), (2) program attainment tests (PAT), and (3) instructional accomplishment inventories (IAI). Although the method of judging items and curriculum content was not reported, the three types vary in
the degree of match to the subject matter instruction. The PAT is referenced
to a segment of instruction, typically 30 to 50 hours in length, and is scored
as percentage of items correct. The IAI is constructed to reflect the common
content within a grade, i.e., what *all* texts at the grade emphasize and what
all teachers view as important for instruction at that grade.

The issues that have arisen in judgments of opportunity to learn center on
the development of classification systems for content analysis and further
development and testing of teacher judgments that incorporate both curriculum and classroom instruction. Further work on classification schemes
may hasten the integration of cognitive psychology and measurement. While
we are far from meeting Travers's criteria for taxonomies, the extension of
the reading and mathematics analyses to higher grade levels and to other
subject areas will contribute to this long-term goal. One researchable issue in
the use of teacher judgments of overlap is the information the teacher is
weighting or combining in making the judgment that an individual student
has been taught a specific test item. Other topics for study include individual
teacher reliability of judgment and consistency across teachers.

RECOMMENDATIONS FOR
TEST DEVELOPERS AND TEST USERS

The review of the judgmental procedures in use, in ongoing test development and program evaluation, recognizes the importance of increasing the
test user's perception of the fairness of items, tests, and evaluations. Perceptions of fairness can be increased by using judgments at several stages of the
test development process and by involving both representatives of groups
concerned with fairness and test users in the judgmental process.

It has been suggested here that the formulation of a set of procedures is underway to meet the concerns of test users as well as focus on both content and construct validity. This formulation or paradigm may become established so that both users and test developers will agree that the procedures involved, judgmental and statistical, result in a test that is judged to be fair to individuals and groups, provided that the paradigm is followed. Parts of the paradigm or a set of procedures are identifiable in the judgmental methods, and it is possible now to make recommendations for their implementation. It is also anticipated that these recommendations may be changed, as further study and experience provide the basis for other procedures.

A crucial part of increasing perceptions of fairness is that the results of the judgmental methods used at different times must be summarized *and reported* so that users can incorporate that information in their own judgments. Therefore, the recommendations that follow identify not only specific procedures for use, but also emphasize the preparation of reports to inform users and policy makers of the results of such procedures.

Increasing Representation and Equal Familiarity

Test items should not have demeaning or stereotyped views of minorities, women, or other groups of concern. Therefore, define several stages, ideally at the test planning, item writing, item review, and final test assembly stages, for representatives of particular groups to provide judgments. The following guidelines are suggested:

1. Use at least two representatives from each group as expert judges.
2. Ask these expert judges to state the reason for identifying particular items as unfair.
3. Provide judges with a rating form (e.g., Table 2.4 or 2.5) and general categories, such as status, stereotype, familiarity, and offensive use of language.
4. Provide all reviewers with guidelines, such as the Macmillan (1975) *Guidelines for creating positive sexual and racial images in educational materials,* or those developed by other publishers (see chapter 9).
5. Summarize the results of the judgments and examine agreement among judges. Evaluate judges and retain those who are most sensitive to a wide variety of subtle forms of discrimination and who suggest ways to improve content.
6. Publish a report on the review procedures and their results. Report the number of items recommended for deletion or modification by reviewers and show the action taken by giving percentage of items in each category actually deleted or modified.

Unless there is an assessment of the overlap of tests and instruction, it is difficult, perhaps impossible, to draw policy implications from program evaluation. Therefore, the following guidelines are suggested:

1. Review carefully the reasons for administering any test. Clarify the level of specificity needed for use by administrators, curriculum supervisors, and teachers.
2. Consider whether the test is to be "program fair," either to a single program or to several programs. (*Program* here can mean either a specific text/curriculum, an instructional procedure, or a combination of both.)
3. Survey the existing classification schemes, e.g., Kuhs et al. (1979). Select one if available. If none is available, consider the development of such a scheme, particularly if program improvement is a goal and if it is important to be able to describe the test and the curriculum in similar terms.
4. Use the classification scheme with at least two judges.
    a. Obtain estimates of agreement between judges in classifications.
    b. Report the results of classifications of tests and curricula and the agreement between judges.
5. If effectiveness of schools or program comparisons is of interest, obtain also teacher ratings of opportunity to learn individual items for each student. These ratings may also be useful for program improvement (e.g., teacher conferences, identification of pupils with special needs).
6. Use the variables of item-curriculum match and/or opportunity to learn in examining program outcomes and interpreting the scores of individual pupils.

Monitoring the Fairness Procedures

A gap often develops between the procedures set as ideals and their implementation. These guidelines should lead to improvement:

1. Establish an external "blue ribbon" committee to represent the interests of test users (minorities, women, teachers, students).
2. Use this committee to review the recommendations of the entire set of procedures for fairness. Obtain their judgments of the likely fairness of any test built using these procedures.
3. After the first set of tests (or an item pool) is developed, and periodically thereafter, ask these judges to take the examination (or a random set of items) to review items for each of the major areas covered by these recommendations.

Further Research

The use of expert judges, the idea of procedures to increase perceptions of test fairness, the increasing concern with the overlap of curricula and tests, and the estimates of opportunity to learn all suggest areas for research. As mentioned earlier, there is an existing psychological literature of studies on the use of judges and expert judgment, as well as the work of Porter and his associates on teacher judgments as influenced by tests and curricula. It will be particularly of interest to establish the main categories that "expert" judges use in identifying biased or unfair items. Also, can the "best" set of expert judges be identified? And what are the criteria for such a set? Such studies will assist in training new judges and test development staff. Can the accuracy of staff be increased by practice and standard examples?

The problem of determining the level of specificity in classification schemes is a recurring one, as is the meaningfulness of the classification schemes to users—students, teachers, curriculum specialists, administrators and policy makers, such as school board members and funding agency staff. There is a concern for the scientific criteria that such classifications must meet, but pragmatic criteria also play an important role. Some of the research in this area will be done in collaboration with the psychologists who are examining the cognitive components of tasks. Estimates of the opportunity to learn given by different methods can be compared, as well as examined for their relationships to outcome and other program measures (e.g., resources and teacher's aides). Do teacher estimates correlate highly with estimates obtained by examining documents such as class lesson plans? Are some teachers "better" at providing estimates than others? What are our criteria for "better"? Can methods of estimating opportunity to learn vary by grade level and subject matter?

Fundamentally, however, the goal of much of the research is to increase perceptions of the fairness of tests and the accuracy of inferences, thereby increasing the use of test results. Do these procedures provide further evidence for construct validity and increase the use of test results? Are we identifying procedures that increase perceptions of test fairness? These questions also need answering and provide a challenge to the use of judgmental methods in studies of items and test bias and test fairness.

REFERENCES

American Psychological Association. *Guidelines for nonsexist language in APA journals.* Washington, D.C.: Author, 1977.

Anderson, L. W. *Opportunity to learn test bias and school effects.* Paper presented at the annual meeting of the National Council of Measurement in Education, Washington, D.C., April 1975.

Angoff, W. H. *The investigation of test bias in the absence of an outside criterion.* Paper presented at the National Institute of Education Conference on Test Bias, Annapolis, Md., December 1975.

Armbruster, B. B., Stevens, R. O., & Rosenshine, B. *Analyzing content coverage and emphasis: A study of three curricula and two tests* (Technical Report No. 26). Urbana-Champaign: Center for the Study of Reading, University of Illinois, 1977. (ERIC Document Reproduction Service No. ED 136 238)

Armstrong, R. A. *Test bias from the non-Anglo viewpoint: A critical evaluation of intelligence test items by the members of three cultural minorities.* Unpublished doctoral dissertation, University of Arizona, 1972.

Bianchini, J. C. Achievement tests and differential norms. In M. J. Wargo & D. R. Green (Eds.), *Achievement testing of disadvantaged and minority students for educational program evaluation.* Monterey, Calif.: CTB/McGraw-Hill, 1977. Pp. 157–181.

Bloom, B. S. (Ed.). *Taxonomy of educational objectives: The classification of educational goals. Handbook I: Cognitive domain.* New York: McKay, 1956.

Boldt, R. F., Levin, M. K., Powers, D. E., Griffin, M., Troike, R. C., Wolfram, W., & Ratliff, F. R. *Sociolinguistic and measurement considerations for construction of Armed Services Selection Batteries* (Final Report), October 1975–June 1977. Princeton, N.J.: Educational Testing Service, 1977. (ERIC Document Reproduction Service No. ED 151 405)

Bormuth, J. R. *On the theory of achievement test items.* Chicago: University of Chicago Press, 1970.

Boruch, R. F., & Gomez, H. Sensitivity, bias, and theory in impact evaluations. *Professional Psychology,* 1977, *8,* 411–434.

Breland, H. M., & Ironson, G. H. *Defunis* reconsidered: A comparative analysis of alternative admissions strategies. *Journal of Educational Measurement,* 1976, *13,* 89–99.

Cahill, V. M., Airasian, P. W., Madaus, G. F., & Pedulla, J. J. *Insensitivity of the total test score for identifying achievement differences between groups.* Paper presented at the annual meeting of the American Educational Research Association, New York, April 1977.

Cervantes, R. A. *Problems and alternatives in testing Mexican American students.* Paper presented at the annual meeting of the American Educational Research Association, Chicago, April 1974. (ERIC Document Reproduction Service No. ED 093 951)

Coffman, W. E. Sex differences in responses to items in an aptitude test. In *Eighteenth yearbook of the National Council on Measurement in Education,* 1961, 117–124.

Coffman, W. E. Classical test development solutions. In M. J. Wargo & D. R. Green (Eds.), *Achievement testing of disadvantaged and minority students for educational program evaluation.* Monterey, Calif.: CTB/McGraw-Hill, 1977. Pp. 103–119.

Cole, N. S., & Nitko, A. J. Measuring program effects. In R. A. Berk (Ed.), *Educational evaluation methodology: The state of the art.* Baltimore: Johns Hopkins University Press, 1981. Pp. 32–63.

Cook, T. D., & Campbell, D. T. *Quasi-experimentation: Design and analysis issues for field settings.* Chicago: Rand McNally, 1979.

Cooley, W. W., & Leinhardt, G. *Design and educational findings of the Instructional Dimensions Study.* Paper presented at the annual meeting of the American Educational Research Association, Toronto, March 1978.

Council on Interracial Books for Children. *Guidelines for selecting bias-free textbooks and storybooks.* New York: Author, 1980.

Cronbach, L. J. Validity on parole: How can we go straight? In W. B. Schraeder (Ed.), *New directions for testing and measurement* (No. 5)—*Measuring achievement: Progress over a decade.* San Francisco: Jossey-Bass, 1980. Pp. 99–108.

Doherty, M. E. *Brunswick and the nature of expert judgment.* Paper presented at the annual meeting of the American Psychological Association, Montreal, September 1980.

Donlon, T. F. *Content factors in sex differences on test questions.* Paper presented at the meeting of the New England Educational Research Organization, Boston, June 1971.

Donlon, T. F., Ekstrom, R. B., & Lockheed, M. E. The consequences of sex bias in the content of major achievement test batteries. *Measurement and Evaluation in Guidance,* 1979, *11,* 202–216.

Donlon, T. F., Ekstrom, R. B., Lockheed, M., & Harris, A. *Performance consequences of sex bias in the content of major achievement test batteries* (Final Report). Princeton, N.J.: Educational Testing Service, 1977.

Dunning, T. L., & Maruhnich, N. *Test item development: An empirical study of practical problems.* Paper presented at the annual meeting of the American Educational Research Association, Boston, April 1980.

Dwyer, C. A. The role of tests and their construction in producing apparent sex-related differences. In M. A. Wittig & A. C. Peterson (Eds.), *Sex-related differences in cognitive functioning.* New York: Academic Press, 1979. Pp. 335–353.

Freeman, D. J., Kuhs, T. M., Porter, A. C., Knappen, L. B., Floden, R. E., Schmidt, W. H., & Schwille, J. R. *The fourth grade mathematics curriculum as inferred from textbooks and tests.* Paper presented at the annual meeting of the American Educational Research Association, Boston, April 1980.

Gagné, R. M., & Merrill, M. D. The content analysis of subject matter: The computer as an aid in the design of criterion-referenced tests. *Instructional Science,* 1976, *5,* 1–28.

Glaser, R. Instructional technology and the measurement of learning outcomes. *American Psychologist,* 1963, *18,* 519–521.

Green, D. R. *Racial and ethnic bias in achievement tests and what to do about it.* Del Monte, Calif.: CTB/McGraw-Hill, 1973.

Hambleton, R. K. *Review methods for criterion-referenced test items.* Paper presented at the annual meeting of the American Educational Research Association, Boston, April 1980. (a)

Hambleton, R. K. Test score validity and standard-setting methods. In R. A. Berk (Ed.), *Criterion-referenced measurement: The state of the art.* Baltimore: Johns Hopkins University Press, 1980. Pp. 80–123. (b)

Hanson, R. A., Schutz, R. E., & Bailey, J. D. *Program-fair evaluation of instructional programs: Initial results of the Kindergarten Reading Readiness Inquiry* (Technical Report 57). Los Alamitos, Calif.: Southwest Regional Laboratory for Educational Research and Development, 1977.

Hanson, R. A., Schutz, R. E., & Bailey, J. D. *What makes achievement tests tick: Investigation of alternative instrumentation for instructional program evaluation.* Los Alamitos, Calif.: Southwest Regional Laboratory for Educational Research and Development, 1980. (mimeo)

Harmes, R. A. *The development, validation and application of an external criterion measure of achievement test item bias.* Paper presented at the annual meeting of the National Council on Measurement in Education, Toronto, March 1978. (ERIC Document Reproduction Service No. ED 157 902)

Hunter, R. V., & Slaughter, C. D. *ETS test sensitivity review process.* Princeton, N.J.: Educational Testing Service, 1980.

Jaeger, R. M., Cole, J., Irwin, D. M., & Pratto, D. J. *An iterative structured judg-*

ment process for setting passing scores on competency tests, applied to the North Carolina high school competency tests in reading and mathematics. Greensboro: Center for Educational Research and Evaluation, University of North Carolina, 1980.

Jenkins, J. R., & Pany, D. *Curriculum biases in reading achievement tests* (Technical Report No. 16). Urbana-Champaign: Center for the Study of Reading, University of Illinois, November 1976. (ERIC Document Reproduction Service No. ED 134 938)

Jenkins, J. R., & Pany, D. Curriculum biases in reading achievement tests. *Journal of Reading Behavior,* 1978, *10,* 345-357.

Jensen, M., & Beck, M. D. Gender balance analysis of the Metropolitan Achievement Tests, 1978 edition. *Measurement and Evaluation in Guidance,* 1979, *12,* 25-34.

Jones, L. V. Three major movements: Contributions and limitations. In W. B. Schraeder (Ed.), *New directions for testing and measurement* (No. 5)—*Measuring achievement: Progress over a decade.* San Francisco: Jossey-Bass, 1980. Pp. 65-67.

Kirsch, I. S., & Guthrie, J. T. Construct validity of functional reading tests. *Journal of Educational Measurement,* 1980, *17,* 81-93.

Kretschmer, J. C. Subject matter as a factor in testing comprehension. *Reading World,* 1972, *11,* 275-285.

Kuhn, T. S. Objectivity, value judgments, and theory choice. In T. S. Kuhn (Ed.), *The essential tension.* Chicago: University of Chicago Press, 1977.

Kuhs, T. M., Schmidt, W. H., Porter, A. C., Floden, R. E., Freeman, D. J., & Schwille, J. R. *A taxonomy for classifying elementary school mathematics content* (Research Series No. 4). East Lansing, Mich.: Institute for Research on Teaching, Michigan State University, April 1979.

Leinhardt, G., & Seewald, A. M. *Overlap: What's tested, what's taught?* Paper presented at the annual meeting of the American Educational Research Association, Boston, April 1980.

Lewy, A. Opportunity to learn and achievement in three subject matter areas. *Journal of Experimental Education,* 1972, *41,* 68-73.

Linn, R. L. Test design and analysis for measurement of educational achievement. In W. B. Schraeder (Ed.), *New directions for testing and measurement* (No. 5)—*Measuring achievement: Progress over a decade.* San Francisco: Jossey-Bass, 1980. Pp. 81-92.

Lucas, P. A., & McConkie, G. W. The definition of test items: A descriptive approach. *American Educational Research Journal,* 1980, *17,* 133-140.

Macmillan. *Guidelines for creating positive sexual and racial images in educational materials.* New York: Author, 1975. (Available from the publisher, 866 Third Avenue, N.Y., N.Y., 10022.)

Madaus, G. F., Airasian, P. W., Hambleton, R. K., Consalvo, R. A., & Orlando, L. R. *Development and application of criteria for screening commercial standardized tests for the Massachusetts basic skills improvement policy.* Boston: Massachusetts State Department of Education, April 1979. (ERIC Document Reproduction Service No. ED 174 652)

McCarthy, K. *Sex bias in tests of mathematical aptitude.* Unpublished doctoral dissertation, City University of New York, 1975.

McGraw-Hill. *Recommended guidelines for multiethnic publishing in McGraw-Hill Book Company publications.* New York: Author, 1968.

McGraw-Hill. *Guidelines for equal treatment of the sexes in the McGraw-Hill Book Company publications.* New York: Author, 1974.

McKenna, B. What's wrong with standardized testing? In National Education Association, *Standardized testing issues: Teachers' perspectives* (Reference and Resource Series). Washington, D.C.: National Education Association, 1977. (ERIC Document Reproduction Service No. ED 146 233)

Medley, D. M., & Quirk, T. J. The application of a factorial design to the study of cultural bias in general culture items on the National Teacher Examination. *Journal of Educational Measurement,* 1974, *11,* 235-245.

Miller, C., & Swift, K. *The handbook of nonsexist writing.* New York: Lippincott & Crowell, 1980.

Milton, G. A. *Five studies of the relation between sex-role identification and achievement in problem solving* (Technical Report 3). New Haven: Yale University, 1958.

National Center of Educational Media and Materials for the Handicapped. *Guidelines for the representation of exceptional persons in educational materials.* Columbus: Ohio State University, 1979.

National Council of Teachers of English. *Guidelines for non-sexist use of language in NCTE publications.* Urbana, Ill.: Author, n.d.

Nitko, A. J. Problems in the development of criterion-referenced tests: The IPI Pittsburgh experience. In C. W. Harris, M. C. Alkin, & W. J. Popham (Eds.), *Problems in criterion-referenced measurement* (CSE Monograph Series in Evaluation, No. 3). Los Angeles: Center for the Study of Evaluation, University of California, 1974. Pp. 59-82.

Ozenne, D. G., Van Gelder, N. C., & Cohen, A. J. *Achievement test restandardization: Emergency School Aid Act National Evaluation.* Santa Monica, Calif.: System Development Corporation, 1974. (ERIC Document Reproduction Service No. ED 101 017)

Perloff, R. M., Padgett, V. R., & Brock, T. C. Sociocognitive biases in the evaluation process. In R. M. Perloff & E. Perloff (Eds.), *New directions for program evaluation* (No. 7)—*Values, ethics and standards in evaluation.* San Francisco: Jossey-Bass, 1980. Pp. 11-26.

Polin, L., & Baker, E. L. *Qualitative analysis of test-item attributes for domain-referenced content validity judgments.* Paper presented at the annual meeting of the American Educational Research Association, San Francisco, April 1979.

Porter, A. C., Kuhs, T. M., Freeman, D. J., Floden, R. E., Knappen, L. B., Schmidt, W. H., & Schwille, J. R. *Is there a core curriculum in elementary school mathematics? A textbook perspective.* East Lansing: Institute for Research on Teaching, Michigan State University, n.d.

Porter, A. C., Schmidt, W. H., Floden, R. E., & Freeman, D. J. *Impact on what? The importance of content covered.* Paper presented at the first annual meeting of the Evaluation Research Society, Washington, D.C., October 1977.

Porter, A. C., Schmidt, W. H., Floden, R. E., & Freeman, D. J. Practical significance in program evaluation. *American Educational Research Journal,* 1978, *15,* 529-539.

Rakow, E. A., Airasian, P. W., & Madaus, G. F. *A comparison of the sensitivity of two item selection techniques for program evaluation.* Paper presented at the annual meeting of the National Council on Measurement in Education, Washington, D.C., April 1975.

Rawls, J. *A theory of justice.* Cambridge: Harvard University Press/Belknap, 1971.

Roid, G. H., & Haladyna, T. M. The emergence of an item-writing technology. *Review of Educational Research,* 1980, *50,* 293–314.

Roudabush, G. E. Program evaluation using criterion-referenced tests. In M. J. Wargo & D. R. Green (Eds.), *Achievement testing of disadvantaged and minority students for program evaluation.* Monterey, Calif.: CTB/McGraw-Hill, 1977. Pp. 249–268.

Rovinelli, R. J., & Hambleton, R. K. On the use of content specialists in the assessment of criterion-referenced test item validity. *Dutch Journal of Educational Research,* 1977, *2,* 49–60.

Saario, T. N., Jacklin, C. N., & Tittle, C. K. Sex role stereotyping in the public schools. *Harvard Educational Review,* 1973, *40,* 386–416.

Samuda, R. J. *Psychological testing of American minorities: Issues and consequences.* New York: Harper & Row, 1975.

Schmeiser, C. B. *The effect of cognitive skill level on the performance of black and white examinees on black and white social studies test content.* Paper presented at the annual meeting of the American Educational Research Association, San Francisco, 1979.

Schmeiser, C. B. *Analysis of the impact of skill category on the performance of black and white examinees on black and white English test content.* Paper presented at the annual meeting of the American Educational Research Association, Boston, April 1980.

Science Research Associates. *Fairness in educational materials: Exploring the issues.* Chicago: Author, 1976.

Scott, W. A. Reliability of content analysis: The case of nominal scale coding. *Public Opinion Quarterly,* 1955, *19,* 321–325.

Seewald, A. M. *Directions for obtaining overlap estimates from teachers in LD/NRS study.* Pittsburgh: Learning Research and Development Center, University of Pittsburgh, 1979. (mimeo)

Sherman, S. W. *Multiple choice test bias uncovered by use of an "I don't know" alternative.* Paper presented at the annual meeting of the American Educational Research Association, San Francisco, April 1976.

Spencer, T. L. An investigation of the National Teacher Examination for bias with respect to black candidates. *Dissertation Abstracts International,* 1973, *33* (8).

Tennenbaum, A. B., & Miller, C. A. *The use of congruence between the items in a norm-referenced test and the content in compensatory education curricula in the evaluation of achievement gains.* Paper presented at the annual meeting of the American Educational Research Association, New York, April 1977. (ERIC Document Reproduction Service No. ED 141 395)

The Psychological Corporation. *Metropolitan Achievement Tests* (Special Report Number 15). New York: Author, 1978. (a)

The Psychological Corporation. *Metropolitan Achievement Tests* (Special Report Number 16). New York: Author, 1978. (b)

The Psychological Corporation. *Content validity of the Mathematics Instructional Tests and Mathematics Tests of the survey batteries* (1978 Edition). New York: Author, in press.

Thompson, R. E. *Investigations of the appropriateness of the College Board Science Tests for students of different high school courses* (TDR-71-2). Princeton, N.J.:

Educational Testing Service, September 1971. (ERIC Document Reproduction Service No. ED 057 086)

Tidwell, R. *Guidelines for reducing bias in testing.* Los Angeles: Instructional Objectives Exchange, 1979.

Tittle, C. K. Fairness in educational achievement testing. *Education and Urban Society,* 1975, *8,* 86–103.

Tittle, C. K., McCarthy, K., & Steckler, J. F. *Women and educational testing: A selective review of the research literature and testing practices.* Princeton, N.J.: Educational Testing Service, 1974.

Travers, R. M. W. Taxonomies of educational objectives and theories of classification. *Educational Evaluation and Policy Analysis,* 1980, *2,* 5–23.

Tyler, R. W. Comments. In M. J. Wargo & D. R. Green (Eds.), *Achievement testing of disadvantaged and minority students for educational program evaluation.* Monterey, Calif.: CTB/McGraw-Hill, 1977. Pp. 324–329.

Tyler, R. W. Three major movements: As viewed from three perspectives. In W. B. Schraeder (Ed.), *New directions for testing and measurement* (No. 5)—*Measuring achievement: Progress over a decade.* San Francisco: Jossey-Bass, 1980. Pp. 69–72.

Williams, R. L., Mosby, D., & Hinson, V. Critical issues in achievement testing of children from diverse ethnic backgrounds. In M. J. Wargo & D. R. Green (Eds.), *Achievement testing of disadvantaged and minority students for educational program evaluation.* Monterey, Calif.: CTB/McGraw-Hill, 1977. Pp. 41–72.

3 USE OF EXPERIMENTAL DESIGN IN STATISTICAL ITEM BIAS STUDIES

CYNTHIA BOARD SCHMEISER

INTRODUCTION

BECAUSE OF THE complexities inherent in the test development process, test constructors are continually striving to identify and implement the most efficient and effective set of procedures that will ensure that the examinations so produced are reliable and valid indicators of examinee behavior. Concomitant with these efforts is a concern for ensuring that the examinations are free of bias for the intended examinee population and intended test use. In the past decade, these efforts and concerns have led to a proliferation of research studies examining various aspects of the issue of test item bias. Although these studies have differed in their theoretical perspective, statistical basis, and results, there seems to be a common premise upon which the research of item bias in achievement testing has been and should continue to be based: *to assist test constructors in developing an efficient and effective set of procedures which can be used to develop items and, ultimately, to assemble tests that are free of bias for the intended examinee population and test use.* Based upon this premise, it seems reasonable to propose the following three goals of item bias research:

1. To establish a set of guidelines, or procedures, that can be used by test constructors to eliminate apparent biases in the language, subgroup references and characterizations, and content sampling of items and tests as a whole;
2. To identify one or more statistical methods that can be appropriately used by test constructors under specified conditions to identify which, if any, items in a test are biased for one or more subgroups; and
3. To identify the potential variables or factors that may be responsible for bias in a particular test for a particular subgroup in an effort to determine what, if any, changes should be made in the test development process to minimize or prevent the possible inclusion of biased items in future tests.

To date, two major approaches have been used to study the issue of item bias, each of which has focused upon one of the first two goals of item bias research. The first approach, as described by Tittle in chapter 2, comprises the judgmental methods. These methods are intended to detect item bias through subjective, judgmental means before the test is administered and data are gathered. Efforts have been made and are currently under way to establish procedures and guidelines that provide systematic, standardized approaches to eliminating and preventing apparent bias in items and tests during the early stages of the test development process (i.e., in the editorial and test assembly stages). These methods, therefore, have focused on the first goal of item bias research. The second approach, as described by Angoff and Ironson in chapters 4 and 5, respectively, comprises the statistical item bias methods. These methods deal with item bias through objective, statistical means at the later stages of the test development process (i.e., once the items have been administered). The statistical methods have focused on the second goal of item bias research and have been doing so in two ways: (1) by applying a particular statistical method to a particular test to identify whether the test contains items that are biased for particular subgroups, and (2) by comparing several different statistical methods to determine how each method functions under a particular set of conditions (see chapter 6 for a detailed review of these studies).

In a sense, both of the judgmental and statistical approaches to the study of item bias are serving a *quality control* function in the test development process by providing either subjective (i.e., through the judgmental approach) or objective (i.e., through the statistical approach) information that can be used to eliminate biased items or bias within the items in a test, whether such modification occurs at an early stage of the test development process or at a later stage of the process (i.e., after the test or the items have been administered). Doubtless both of these approaches attend to different characteristics of items and tests, and because of this, the results of each approach should be used jointly. What seems to be lacking in these approaches to item bias research, however, is a systematic investigation of the *procedures* and *assumptions* that are used by test constructors to develop items and assemble tests, procedures that traditionally have been based, by and large, upon common sense and judgment. Such research, as contrasted to quality control research, would be *experimental* in nature, aimed at questioning the procedures and assumptions upon which tests are developed in an effort to determine what, if any, changes should be made in the test development *process* to minimize or prevent the possible inclusion of biased items in future tests.

Based upon this characterization of the two major existing approaches to the study of item bias, it seems reasonable to suggest that there may be a third approach to the study of item bias which may contribute unique insights into the problem of item bias, one that is applicable at the intermediate stages of the test development process and is based upon the principles of experimental design. This research would have as its focus the third goal of item bias research.

The purpose of this chapter is to describe this third approach to the study of item bias and how it might be applied in various settings. Because this approach is based upon the principles of experimental design, many concerns that are pertinent to this approach are equally as pertinent to other statistically based item bias methodologies. Thus, a secondary purpose of this chapter is to review the principles of experimental design that are crucial to planning any item bias study, regardless of the approach taken.

Rationale for the Experimental Design Approach

Basically, there are three reasons why an experimental design approach to the study of item bias would be beneficial to test constructors.

First, the experimental design approach to the study of item bias can provide an objective, systematic means by which test developers can evaluate the stated and unstated assumptions and procedures that are used to develop tests to find out whether the procedures do, in fact, cause bias or can be used to eliminate potential sources of bias in the tests for particular subgroups. All test developers begin with some idea of what a test should measure, often resulting in a table of specifications (or test blueprint) that defines the content and skills to be measured in the test. In standardized tests, this table is generally based upon curriculum surveys, content expert judgment, as well as psychometric expertise; in classroom tests, this table is usually based upon expert judgments regarding correspondence of test content to the amount of time spent teaching, significance of the topic, and relationship to the curriculum. Ultimately, tables of specifications arise out of a set of assumptions, based partly upon objective data and partly upon expert judgment, which can be systematically used and replicated to develop a test. Often these tables do not specify:

1. the general types of items to be used (e.g., objective or essay);
2. the specific item formats to be used (e.g., multiple-choice, matching, true-false);
3. the specific item response formats to be used (e.g., single correct answer, best answer, combinational format);
4. the specific contexts within which the content and skills are to be tested (e.g., the context of information within which certain skills are to be tested);
5. the various approaches to measure the content and skills (e.g., passage or stimulus-related items as opposed to discrete items);
6. the language to be used in the items (e.g., representation of subgroups, roles of subgroups); and
7. the characteristics of the examinee population (e.g., race, ethnicity, sex) for which the test is intended.

Although these characteristics must be considered in designing tables of specifications, the decisions that are made with respect to these test characteristics frequently depend upon judgments—judgments about efficiency of approach, effectiveness of approach, and validity of approach. One advantage of the experimental design approach to the study of item bias is that both of these stated (i.e., tables of specifications) and unstated (i.e., other test characteristics) assumptions and procedures used to develop the items and ultimately to assemble the tests can be examined empirically to study the effect that the procedures have on the performance of various subgroups.

Second, the experimental design approach can provide additional information that can supplement both the judgmental and statistical approaches. The process of testing the assumptions and procedures of the test development process can contribute evidence that can support or question the judgmental procedures. The procedures used in the test development process, beginning with the assumptions underlying the table of specifications and continuing through the procedures used in the editorial and test assembly stages, can be examined in an objective way, and the results can be used to supplement the results of the judgmental procedures.

The results obtained through the experimental design approach can also be used in conjunction with the results obtained through the statistical procedures. As previously described, the statistical methods provide one type of objective data to test developers through analyses of tests (or items) once the tests (or items) have been administered. In one sense, this "ex post facto" approach is not particularly effective in determining why particular items are biased and what can be done to avoid the recurrence of such biased items in future tests. In fact, when a statistical method identifies items as biased, the test constructor has a limited number of actions that can be taken. For instance, if the statistical method is conducted after pretesting the items, the test constructor can either eliminate the items from consideration during final test assembly or revise the items in hopes of eliminating the bias and repretesting the modified items before use, a luxury not always available to test constructors. If the method is conducted after administration of the final test, the test constructor can rescore the test not using the biased items (hence, possibly decreasing test reliability and jeopardizing content validity) or retain the items in the test if the detected bias is "balanced" for the subgroups being examined. (The notion of balancing bias within a test will be discussed in a subsequent section of this chapter.) These limitations stem partially from the fact that in the ex post facto type of bias study, items are considered to be fixed, that is, all items about which inferences are to be drawn are included in the experiment, resulting in conclusions that are specific to a single item as an entity and are not generalizable to other seemingly similar items.

What appears to be one advantage of the experimental approach to the study of item bias is its provision for a systematic way of evaluating the developmental processes used by test constructors in an effort to determine whether such processes result in the development of items that are biased for one or more subgroups before the test is assembled. In this way, items are considered to be random, that is, the items studied are considered to be a random sample from a population of items about which inferences are to be drawn. This permits the researcher to draw conclusions about the *processes* being investigated rather than about specific items. Through this objective source of information, test constructors can modify their procedures and assumptions to eliminate the development and inclusion of such items in future examinations in a replicable and systematic fashion. In addition, if the experimental design approach identifies a developmental procedure as being responsible for the development of biased items, the effectiveness of the statistical approaches in identifying such biased items can be evaluated and compared. Such evidence can be obtained to supplement further the investigation and comparison of the existing statistical methods.

This information about test development processes is particularly important in view of current and possible future testing legislation (i.e., truth-in-testing), whereby items and tests may be required to be released to the examinees after administration. Under these circumstances, the usefulness of identifying particular items that are biased after a test has been administered becomes secondary to the usefulness of detection procedures, processes, or assumptions that lead to the development of items that are free of bias. In such a testing climate, items may be reused only rarely, and because of this, it may not be of great interest to identify in an ex post facto fashion those items that are biased. Through the experimental approach, however, the goal of identifying procedures and processes that produce unbiased items becomes of paramount importance to test constructors, as such processes can be applied and replicated in a systematic fashion to produce one or more forms of an examination.

Collectively, the information provided by all three approaches to the study of item bias should be used to investigate the issue of item bias. The unique perspectives provided by each approach at various stages of the test development process should be carefully considered by the test developer to ensure that the tests being developed are as free of bias as possible.

Third, the experimental design approach to the study of item bias has the advantages inherent in good experimental design. As described by Lindquist (1953), a good experimental design will:

1. insure that the observed treatment effects are *unbiased** estimates of the true effects;

Unbiased, as used by Lindquist in this instance, refers to the equivalence of a parameter and the expected value of some estimate of the parameter. This connotation of the word *unbiased* should not be confused with the various definitions of the lack of item or test bias.

2. permit a quantitative description of the precision of the observed treatment effects regarded as estimates of the "true" effects;
3. insure that the observed treatment effects will have whatever degree of precision is required by the broader purposes of the experiment;
4. make possible an objective test of a specific hypothesis concerning the true effects; that is, it will permit the computation of the relative frequency with which the observed discrepancy between the observation and hypothesis would be exceeded if the hypothesis were true; and
5. be *efficient*; that is, it will satisfy these requirements at the minimum "cost," broadly conceived. (p. 6)

Through well-planned experimental design studies, the researcher's questions can be identified before the "experiment" is conducted, randomization can be employed, and methods of control can be instituted over sources of variability both directly and indirectly related to the purposes of the study. The principles associated with randomization and control in experimental design are more fully described in the next section.

REVIEW OF THE EXPERIMENTAL DESIGN APPROACH

In this section, an overview of basic experimental design principles will be provided and will be followed by a description and discussion of two studies illustrating the application of the experimental design approach to the study of item bias.

Definition of Experimental Design

Experimental design, broadly defined, is a process of investigation of scientific or research hypotheses by obtaining observations under controlled conditions whereby one or more variables are manipulated and their effects observed while other conditions are held constant. According to Kirk (1968), this process consists of five stages:

1. Formulate statistical hypotheses and make plans for the collection and analysis of data to test the hypotheses ...
2. State decision rules to be followed in testing the statistical hypotheses.
3. Collect the data according to plan.
4. Analyze the data according to plan.
5. Make decisions concerning the statistical hypotheses based on decision rules and inductive inferences concerning the probable truth or falsity of the research hypotheses. (p. 1)

Independent and dependent variables. Basic experimental designs of item bias studies usually involve one or more variables that are manipulated by the researcher (independent variables), one or more variables that are used by the researcher to classify or group subjects (independent variables), and one or more variables that are expected to change as a result of the manipulation of the independent variables (dependent variables). (For the purpose of simplicity, only a single dependent variable will be assumed in this review.)

The use of one or more independent variables to group subjects is a distinguishing feature of the experimental design approach, for in item bias studies the researcher is interested in the effects that the manipulation of certain independent variables has on the dependent variable *for specific groups.* Such groups might be based upon such unmanipulable characteristics (i.e., attribute variables) as sex, race, or ethnicity. For example, in an item bias study, one might manipulate item format (independent variable), group subjects on the basis of race and sex (grouping independent variables), and examine the impact of item format on subject performance (dependent variable).

Randomization.   Randomization is one of the primary advantages of experimental design. As defined by Kerlinger (1973), randomization "is the assignment of objects (subjects, treatments, groups) of a universe to subsets of the universe in such a way that, for any given assignment to a subset, each member of the universe has an equal probability of being chosen for that assignment" (p. 123). As applied to sampling of subjects in an experimental design, randomization is accomplished by the random selection of subjects, random assignment of subjects to groups, and/or random assignment of experimental treatments to subjects (or groups). Practically speaking, in most item bias studies, subjects cannot be randomly assigned to groups since most group membership is based upon such unassignable characteristics as sex, race, and ethnicity. In these instances, however, the researcher should try to randomly select subjects within the intact groups and randomly assign experimental treatments to subjects within groups.

The principle of randomization can also be applied to the independent variable(s) being manipulated in a study. Suppose a researcher wanted to examine whether either of two innovative item formats differentially affected the performance of two particular subgroups in a particular content area. In this case, it is important for the researcher to select a random sample of items from the universe of all possible items that could be written in each item format in the particular content area so that the items used in the study represent the theoretical universe of all such items. Regardless of the procedure or assumption being tested through the experimental design approach, the researcher should try to obtain as large a sample of items as possible (and reasonable) from the universe in order to be able to make "strong" inferences from the observed data about the *procedure* or *assumption* being investigated. Because the researcher wishes to make inferences about test development procedures rather than about specific items, items can be considered to be random, and to make such inferences as strong as possible, the sample of items should be as large as possible. With larger samples of items comes less measurement error, and systematic error variance can be more effectively isolated from random error variance.

If randomization is successfully completed, then the experimental groups can be considered statistically equivalent, in a probabilistic sense. From a pragmatic perspective, randomization can be effectively applied to studies of item bias through the random selection of subjects within intact groups, random assignment of treatments to subjects within groups, and random sampling of items from the universe of all possible such items identified with the procedure or assumption being tested. In this way, the maximum use of randomization, given the fixed constraints of group membership, can be made.

Experimental control is of critical importance to experimental design. Through randomization with the manipulation of one or more independent variables, while using other independent variables to group subjects, the researcher can have more confidence that the relations discovered are the relations the researcher thinks they are, since such relations are observed under carefully controlled conditions. A well-conducted experimental research study may well yield information that variable A is related to variable B.

Ex Post Facto Research

With the preceding definition of experimental design, perhaps it would be useful to distinguish between experimental design and ex post facto research. Ex post facto studies have been defined by Kerlinger (1973) as "a systematic empirical inquiry in which the scientist does not have direct control of independent variables because their manifestations have already occurred or because they are inherently not manipulable. Inferences about relations among variables are made, without direct intervention, from concomitant variation of independent and dependent variables" (p. 379).

In experimental design, the researcher manipulates an independent variable, or variables, and observes a dependent variable to see if the variation expected or predicted from the independent variable occurs. The researcher predicts from one or more independent variables to a dependent variable. To achieve control, the researcher uses randomization with the active manipulation of the independent variable(s) while grouping subjects on the basis of other independent variables of interest. The researcher can then cautiously assume, other things being equal, that the dependent variable is varying as a result of the manipulation of the independent variable(s).

In contrast, in ex post facto research, a dependent variable is observed as the independent variable is observed, before, after, or simultaneously with the observation of the dependent variable. The basic difference between the two types of research is in the direct control of the independent variable. In experimental research, the independent variable is manipulated, which is rather direct control. In ex post facto research, direct control is not possible, as neither experimental manipulation nor random sampling or assignment of treatments can be used by the researcher. The researcher usually must a take a situation as it is and untangle it as well as possible.

Most previous studies of statistical item bias methods which have focused upon the application of a particular statistical method or comparisons among methods can be characterized as ex post facto research studies. In most of these studies, no experimental manipulation of an independent variable or randomization occurred. By and large, two subgroups took one particular examination, and the results were analyzed by one or more statistical procedures. Doubtless the ex post facto type of research is valuable, especially with regard to the second goal of item bias research; however, because of the lack of randomization and experimental manipulation of an independent variable, these studies cannot be considered true experimental design studies and are thereby limited in their applicability and generalizability to the test development process.

Quasi-experimental designs.   According to Campbell and Stanley (1966), quasi-experimental designs can be considered a special case of ex post facto research where an attempt to gain control of independent variables is made through statistical and other means. As is the case with ex post facto research in general, a quasi-experimental design approach to the study of item bias would have limited applicability to the third goal of item bias research and would perhaps be more useful in studies pertaining to the second research goal. In such cases where the experimental design approach is not practical or feasible, the researcher is advised to consult Cook and Campbell (1979) for more information about quasi-experimental designs and analyses.

Purposes of Control in Experimental Designs

Three purposes of control can be exerted in experimental designs: (1) estimate the magnitudes of the sources of variability in the dependent variable; (2) add precision to the experiment by accounting for independent variables that the researcher feels may affect the investigation; and (3) minimize random error variance. Each of these purposes is discussed briefly in this section.

To estimate the magnitudes of the sources of variability in the dependent variable.   First, through experimental control the researcher tries to identify the sources of variability in the dependent variable. By "decomposing," or separating, the total observed variability of the dependent variable, the researcher is able to estimate the variability due to the independent variables in the study, the interaction between the independent variables in the study, and error. Through randomization of the manipulated independent variables and random sampling of test materials and intact groups, the researcher can have considerable assurance that over replications of the study no systematic effects will distort the results.

To add precision to the experiment.   Second, in certain instances the researcher may have reason to believe that the results of the study may be affected by independent variables other than those being actively manipulated or used as the primary grouping variables in the study. For instance, the researcher might believe that these variables could affect the outcomes of the study and might therefore decide to include the variables in the study not only to obtain further information but to add precision to the experiment by further minimizing random error variance. Such variables might include socioeconomic class, motivation level, cognitive style, testwiseness, or achievement level.

To add precision to the experiment by accounting for such variables, the researcher may decide: (1) to hold the variable constant, (2) to build the variable into the experimental design, (3) to match subjects on the variable, and/or (4) to statistically control for the variable. Each of these methods is described below.

First, the researcher, can add precision to the experiment by *holding the variable constant* for all subjects; that is, subjects can be chosen so that they are as homogeneous as possible on the variable of interest (such as using one geographic region, socioeconomic class, or grade). In general, however, this is probably not a practical solution in item bias studies, as it severely limits the generalizability and the practical usefulness of the results.

The second way to add precision to the experiment is to *build the variable into the design* as an additional independent variable. In this method, levels or intervals are defined along the scale of values of the variable, and subjects within any level are assigned to treatments at random. As is true with the variable used as the primary grouping variable of interest in a study, these variables are also usually classificatory in nature (e.g., social class, geographical location, ability level, socioeconomic level), rather than manipulable independent variables. To the extent of the relationship between the variable and the dependent variable in the population, such a procedure can result in control of an important source of error variance and hence can improve the precision of the experiment (Feldt, 1958). Various methods for building the variable into a design as an independent variable have been described in most textbooks on experimental design as *blocking, stratifying,* and *leveling*.

For example, suppose an item bias researcher suspects that achievement level might be a source of variability in an item bias study of the effect of a potential source of bias on the performance of two subgroups. In this case, the researcher may wish to categorize each subgroup into high, middle, and low achievement levels to improve the precision of the experiment by controlling for the variability of that factor. In addition, such leveling or blocking upon the achievement level of examinees in each subgroup may be particularly useful if, for instance, a researcher believes that there may be either a floor or a ceiling effect on the test for a particular subgroup or if the researcher believes that certain test development procedures, practices, or assumptions may be biased for one ability group but not for others.

This method of adding precision to the experiment should be used whenever the researcher believes that a variable may have a differential effect upon the outcome measure of the study (i.e., significant interaction between the two variables), given that the researcher has data on the variable before the experiment is begun. If this method is used, however, the researcher should select an appropriate design and statistical method to analyze the outcomes of the study.

The third way to add precision to the experiment is to *match subjects on one or more variables* and randomly assign the subjects to treatments, if possible. In a sense, matching is a special case (two-group) of the second way of adding precision to the experiment by building the variable into the design.

Jensen (1980) has suggested the use of matched groups and pseudogroups when a significant item-by-group interaction is obtained in an analysis of variance procedure to determine whether the interaction is attributable solely to differences in ability level or to some other factor (i.e., cultural differences). The *matched groups* approach, as suggested by Jensen, involves matching subjects on the total test score distribution by pairing individuals from the two subgroups on total test score. The analysis is then rerun using the matched groups, and if the result is nonsignificant, he concludes that the significance of the result from the unmatched groups was due to the groups' difference in ability level.

Unfortunately, matching has several limitations that must be considered. First, the variable being used to match the subjects should be substantially related to the dependent variable. If it is not, matching will be a waste of time and may be misleading. Second, if the researcher wants to match on more than one variable, the attrition rate of the subjects will be high because of the difficulty of finding matched subjects on more than one or two variables. Third, matching on one variable (e.g., social class) does not guarantee that the groups are equivalent in other respects (e.g., achievement level). Fourth, if the means of the groups to be matched are substantially different, then matching may produce unwanted regression effects that are independent of any effects of the experimental treatment. Campbell and Stanley (1966) describe these regression effects in detail. Ideally, one would want to match on "true" characteristics rather than on observed characteristics. However, the estimation of true characteristics is problematic as well and must be cautiously considered.

Jensen also suggests the use of *pseudogroups*, whereby a subgroup of persons from one subgroup is formed to conform to the distribution of total test scores in another subgroup, or vice versa. Again, the interaction of item-by-pseudogroup is tested, and, if significant, then he concludes that the effect is probably due to a difference in ability rather than to a cultural difference.

Even in spite of the limitations of matching, *the researcher should seriously consider matching subjects or using pseudogroups in any statistical study of item bias*. With the exception of the latent trait approaches, all other statistical item bias studies will, in all likelihood, benefit from this type of control. The increase in precision gained by accounting for the effect of other independent variables used as the basis for matching will probably outweigh the limitations involved (see, for example, the matched groups studies by Angoff & Ford, 1973, and Cotter & Berk, 1981). If, on the other hand, the limitations associated with matching subjects are judged by the researcher to outweigh the advantages, then randomization or building the variable into the design may be more suitable alternatives. If matching is used, however, it should be used cautiously, and an appropriate statistical analysis should be conducted.

Finally, *statistical control* can be used to add precision to the experiment by isolating and quantifying the variability of the variable of interest. When the researcher suspects that uncontrolled variables may be present in an experiment, he/she can use statistical controls to make adjustments on the final observations to account for any measured lack of initial equivalence. This may be particularly effective in those instances where building the variable into the design or matching is not possible before the experiment is conducted, although statistical control can be used jointly with any of the other methods of control. Analysis of covariance (ANCOVA) is one such method of statistical control, and it can be a useful technique if the assumptions regarding the nature of the relationship between the variable (or covariate) and the dependent variable and the homogeneity of this relationship from treatment to treatment are fulfilled. In deciding whether to use leveling or statistical controls such as ANCOVA, Feldt (1958) suggests that leveling or stratification be used when the correlation between the particular variable and dependent variable is less than .40 and recommends that covariance might be more effective when the correlation is .60 or more. Obviously, it is important for the researcher to analyze the particular variables involved in the study when data are available and consider the sample size, statistical assumptions, and advantages of each technique before selecting a method to improve the precision of the experiment.

To minimize random variance. The third purpose of control in experimental designs is to minimize the error, or random variance. Error variance is the variability of a measure due to random fluctuations and, therefore, is unpredictable. It is associated with errors of measurement and the reliability of measures. Obviously, as more control is exerted on the experimental situation and conditions, less error due to errors of measurement and to random variance occurs. Although the previous discussion has focused on the importance of control in designing an item bias study to minimize error variance, it is also an important consideration while the study is actually being executed. That is, in order to minimize error variance, the researcher should strive to administer the experimental instrument under standardized conditions that are as similar to the actual test administration conditions as possible (e.g., time, testing conditions).

Furthermore, the larger the sample of items used to represent the procedures being investigated, the smaller the error variance will be with respect to the test development procedure. With a small sample of items, it would not be possible to identify and extract systematic error variance from random error variance. This will affect the resulting inferences about the procedures being investigated. One way to minimize random error variance is to increase the number of items. Such a technique is reasonable in the experimental design approach since the researcher is interested in examining the potential bias of a test development procedure rather than the potential bias of individual test items. As contrasted to the test constructor's concern for efficient testing by maximizing reliability and validity with the smallest number of items within specified time constraints, the researcher using the experimental design approach should use as many items illustrating the procedures being investigated as is reasonable and possible. Or, if time is limited and a large sample of subjects is available, the researcher can administer smaller, but different, samples of items to different subjects. This would involve a matrix sampling design.

Although this brief description of the effects of experimental control is not meant to be exhaustive, it has been presented to acquaint the researcher with some of the considerations involved in planning and conducting an experimental study. With these general considerations in mind, two illustrations of the application of the experimental design approach to the study of item bias follow.

Illustrative Studies Using the Experimental Design Approach

The purpose of this section is to describe two studies conducted by the author using the experimental design approach. Because of the limited number of studies that have been conducted via this approach, these two studies are provided as practical examples of types of research and are not intended to be "ideal" illustrations.

Test development procedures studied. Both studies were intended to examine a potential source of bias for two selected subgroups: test content—the vehicle or passage that is used to elicit the skills being examined on an examination. Many achievement tests have included content that could be labeled "traditional" in nature: content that is emphasized in the curriculum which may predominantly reflect the white culture. This test development practice was examined in the following two studies by developing test materials based upon content identified with the white culture and content identified with the black culture. All the test materials used in the studies that pertained to a particular *ACT* subtest were developed according to the same table of specifications; that is, the materials differed only in the cultural context within which these skills were tested. Although the skills themselves might be considered as one source of bias, they are representative of the skills taught in high schools and colleges nationwide. The basic assumption underlying the studies was that test content reflecting the majority culture may favor members of that culture, and conversely, test content reflecting the minority culture may favor minority subgroup members. Thus, consistent with the experimental approach, test content was the test development practice being questioned and the independent variable being manipulated.

General description of the instruments.   The test materials used in these studies were developed for inclusion in two subtests of the *ACT Assessment* examination—the English Usage Test and the Social Studies Reading Test. The *ACT* tests are oriented toward major areas of secondary and postsecondary instructional programs rather than toward a factorial definition of various aspects of intelligence. Whether the tests should be classified as measures of achievement, aptitude, or developed ability is mainly an academic issue. In terms of construction, the tests might best be regarded simply as measures of academic development which rely partly on the examinees' reasoning abilities and partly on their knowledge of subject-matter fields but which emphasize their abilities to use both.

The tasks presented in the *ACT* tests are intended to be intricate in structure, comprehensive in scope, and educationally significant rather than narrow, artificial tasks that are included in tests solely on the basis of their statistical correlation with a criterion. Consequently, the *ACT* tests are multifaceted examinations that include several multiple-choice item formats (i.e., passage-related items and discrete items) that are intended to measure the problem solving abilities of examinees.

The format of the *ACT* English Usage Test consists of several prose passages with certain portions underlined and numbered. For each underlined portion, four alternative responses are presented. The examinee must decide which alternative is most appropriate in the context of the passage. The Social Studies Reading Test contains two item formats: one type is based on reading passages, and the second is based on general background or information obtained primarily in high school social studies courses. All items are multiple-choice with four alternatives.

Method of data analysis.   The examples presented next use analysis of variance procedures to analyze the data with an experimentwise significance level of .01. This resulted in an alpha level of .001 for the individual tests in the analyses. Although the analysis of variance procedure is convenient and easy to use, other methods of data analysis are available and may be considered more appropriate by the researcher. In fact, any analysis based upon the linear model could be used in the experimental design approach to the study of item bias (e.g., regression, generalizability).

In this type of analysis, bias is defined as a statistically significant procedure-by-group interaction. This is indicative of the presence of a test development procedure that is relatively more difficult for members of one group than for another. As contrasted to studies using statistical methods to identify particular items that are biased, studies using the experimental approach concentrate on detecting biases in *procedures*. The researcher, however, should be cognizant of the different definitions of bias associated with various statistical analyses. The method of data analysis selected should be based upon the definition of bias consistent with the researcher's intent.

Study #1

Purpose. The purpose of the first study was to examine whether test materials reflecting black or white culture in two subject areas (English usage and social studies) differentially affected the test performances of black and white examinees. To do this, test materials were developed, reflecting both black and white cultures, in each of the subject areas. Data resulting from the study were used to address the following questions:

1. Were the performances of black and white examinees differentially affected by black and white English content? By black and white social studies content?
2. Did the performance of black and white examinees differ within a subject area? That is, did one subgroup significantly outscore another?
3. Did the average difficulty level of the black and white tests differ within a subject area? That is, was one test significantly harder for the two subgroups than the other?
4. Did the mean item discrimination indices, item omission indices, and reliability coefficients for the test materials differ for black and white examinees?

Collectively, these questions were intended to examine the impact of test content on black and white examinee performance and on test characteristics.

Instruments. As previously described, the test materials used in this study were developed for inclusion in the *ACT* English Usage Test and the *ACT* Social Studies Reading Test. Two English usage tests were randomly selected from among the test materials available, one pertaining to black culture (18 items) and one to white culture (17 items). The test based on content identified with the white culture was based upon the topic of fast food restaurants. The second test was written from a black viewpoint and was based on a black woman's reflections on her Civil War experiences.

Three social studies tests were also randomly selected from the available test materials, two of which were written from a black viewpoint and pertained to black culture. Each test contained a passage based on the history of blacks in America, including the struggle for legal and civil rights in the nineteenth and twentieth centuries. The first black test (B_1) had 20 items; the second (B_2) had 21. The third social studies test (W_1) was based on white content; it contained 20 items dealing with seventeenth-century English history.

The black and white English tests were combined and administered as a single test to the same group of examinees; the three social studies tests were administered as individual tests to three different groups. A summary of the tests used is given in Table 3.1.

TABLE 3.1. Description of Tests: Study #1

Culture Reflected in Test	Subject Matter of Test	
	English Usage[a]	Social Studies
White	17 items	20 items (W_1)
Black	18 items	20 items (B_1)
		21 items (B_2)

[a]The English Usage tests were combined for administration.

Sample. The four tests were administered to examinees at randomly selected test centers in various testing locations across the nation. Approximately half of the examinees in each location were black and about half were white. Each examinee took only one of the four experimental tests; the tests were randomly distributed to the examinees and arranged so that each was completed by some examinees in every testing site. The tests were administered under standardized, but unspeeded, conditions, with 20 minutes allotted for completion. A total of 266 examinees took the English test. For the social studies tests, 272 examinees took B_1, 280 took B_2, and 252 took W_1. On all four tests, exactly half the examinees were black and half were white.

Analysis. The effect of black and white English content on black and white examinee test performance was determined using a Type I analysis of variance (Lindquist, 1953), or a two-factor experiment with repeated measures on one factor. The analysis for social studies content was a two-factor analysis of variance. In both analyses the two factors were test content and race. Test performance was computed as the proportion of items answered correctly to avoid the complexities of an unbalanced analysis of variance design. Point-biserial discrimination indices were computed for the items using the total scores of the examinees on the corresponding *ACT* national tests (English Usage Test and Social Studies Reading Test). The number of omissions for each group was calculated as the average number of omits on the last five items of the test. Internal consistency (KR_{20}) reliability coefficients also were calculated for the black and white examinees on each test, separately.

Results. The results of analyses of the effect of black and white test content on performance by race are shown in Tables 3.2 and 3.3. The mean test performances and standard deviations for both black and white examinees are shown in Table 3.2 for the two parts of the English test and for the three social studies tests. In Table 3.3, analysis of variance tables are presented for all three analyses.

The lack of a significant interaction between test content and performance by race on the English test suggests that black and white examinees were not shown to respond differentially to black and white content. The significant content main effect ($p \leq .001$) indicates that the black content was easier than the white content for both black and white examinees. In addition, the

TABLE 3.2. Black and White Examinee Test Performance: Study #1

	Black Examinees		White Examinees		Combined Races
Test Content	M	SD[a]	M	SD[a]	M
I. *English Tests*					
black content	44.11	17.67	57.56	17.09	50.84
white content	31.76	15.01	41.84	16.09	36.80
combined tests	37.94		49.70		43.82
II. *Social Studies Tests B_1 and W_1*					
black content	40.66	18.68	50.52	20.96	45.59
white content	42.94	17.47	52.14	18.60	47.54
combined tests	41.80		51.33		46.56
III. *Social Studies Tests B_2 and W_1*					
black content	35.71	16.82	42.55	18.63	39.13
white content	42.94	17.47	52.14	18.60	47.54
combined tests	39.32		47.35		43.33

[a]Standard deviations for combined races and tests are not provided.

TABLE 3.3. Analysis of Variance Summary Tables: Study #1

Source	df	MS	F
I. *English Usage Test*			
Between Subjects			
Race	1	18416.049	46.607[a]
Subjects within race	264	395.131	
Within Subjects			
Content	1	26208.188	175.780[a]
Race × content	1	376.778	2.528
Content × subjects within race	264	149.097	
II. *Social Studies Tests B_1 and W_1*			
Content	1	498.149	1.379
Race	1	11927.480	33.030[a]
Content × race	1	13.670	.038
Within cells	520	361.111	
III. *Social Studies Tests B_2 and W_1*			
Content	1	9376.410	29.306[a]
Race	1	8426.277	26.336[a]
Content × race	1	186.073	.582
Within cells	528	319.954	

[a]$p \leq .001$

white examinees scored higher than the black examinees on both parts; consequently, the main effect for race was significant ($p \leq .001$). The scores on the black content were slightly more variable for the black examinees than for white examinees, and the scores on the white content were slightly more variable for the white examinees than for black examinees.

In the analysis of variance for social studies tests B_1 and W_1, the interaction of content and race also was nonsignificant. The test of the main effect of content was not significant, indicating that the two tests were not significantly different in difficulty for the combined races. The test of the effect for race was significant ($p \leq .001$), with the scores for the white examinees being higher and slightly more variable on both tests than the black examinees' scores.

In the analysis for the effect of social studies tests B_2 and W_1 on performance by race, the interaction again was nonsignificant. Both tests of the main effects were significant ($p \leq .001$), indicating that although whites outscored blacks on both tests, both blacks and whites scored higher on the white test. Again, the scores for the white examinees on both tests were slightly more variable than the black examinees' scores.

The mean *item discrimination* values were higher for the white examinees on all tests. In addition, the indices computed for the white examinees tended to be higher for the black content than for the white content. There were no consistent effects for the discrimination values computed for items taken by the black examinees. These results suggest that: (1) higher and lower ability white examinees appeared to be consistently differentiated more effectively than were higher and lower ability black examinees regardless of test content, and (2) the black content appeared to differentiate higher and lower ability white examinees better than did the white content.

The mean number of *omissions* can be used as a gross indicator of the speededness of a test: the greater the mean number of omissions, the more speeded the test. One might expect that since white examinees typically outscore black examinees, they might tend also to omit fewer items, regardless of test content. That was not the case in this study. The mean number of omissions computed for both races on the English test indicates that white examinees tended to omit more items on the black content than did black examinees, and that black examinees tended to omit more items on the white content than did white examinees.

For all three social studies tests, the mean number of omissions for the black examinees was greater than for the whites, and both blacks and whites omitted more items on the black tests than on the white test.

The internal consistency (KR_{20}) *reliability* coefficients computed for both black and white tests on the basis of the black and white examinees were tested for population equality using a procedure described by Feldt (1969). In none of the comparisons did the reliability coefficients based on black and white examinees on the same test differ significantly.

Discussion.   Although white examinees scored higher than black examinees regardless of test content, the lack of significant interactions between test content and test performance by race in either English or social studies suggests that black and white content did not appear to differentially affect black and white test performance. These results are in contrast to those found by Medley and Quirk (1974). Their study examined the performances of black and white examinees on black, modern, and traditional test items contained on the general culture section of the *National Teacher Examination*. The results indicated that blacks outscored whites on black content. In the current study, however, no consistent effects were found for black and white test forms in either English or social studies. That is, the black content (or white content) did not appear to be systematically easier or harder for either group in English or social studies. It is possible that this result is specific to a given test rather than directly related to the test's content.

Examination of the mean item discrimination values indicated that higher and lower ability white examinees appeared to be differentiated more effectively than black examinees regardless of test content, and that white examinees appeared to be differentiated better with tests of black content than with those of white content. No systematic differences in discrimination indices were found for black examinees on either test. Collectively, these results suggest that no systematic, reliable effect of test content on examinee performance was reflected through this characteristic.

The results for the mean number of item omissions for the English and social studies tests tended to differ, as expected. In English, whites and blacks tended to omit items more frequently in the tests containing content related to the other race. In social studies, black examinees omitted more items in both the black and white tests than did white examinees, with the most omissions occurring on the black test. The effect of omissions and speededness, to an extent, is unclear from these results, but it is possible that the effect may be related to the particular subject area (English or social studies) or to the particular test. Further research should be aimed at clarifying this effect.

The difference between the KR_{20} coefficients for the black and white examinees was within the range attributable to sampling errors at $p = .001$. Thus, the tests were not shown to have significantly different internal consistency reliabilities for the two samples. (See Reynolds, chapter 8, for the test of significance between two reliability coefficients.)

Implications.   The results obtained in this study for two major subject matter areas do not indicate a differential effect of test content on examinee performance by race. They do, however, support trends found by Dreger and Miller (1960, 1968) and Shuey (1966), indicating that white examinees tend to outscore black examinees.

The results of this study should be tempered by the fact that only limited samples of behavior in each subject matter domain were obtained from the examinees. It seems logical, therefore, that future research into the effect of test content on test performance should be aimed at obtaining a larger sample of materials to afford a greater number of comparisons within each subject area, so that general trends across subject areas can be identified. If test content does indeed tend to affect black and white examinee performance differentially, resulting in one race receiving an advantage over another, then developers of such tests should try to eliminate biased content in their tests by modifying their test development procedures. If test content does not seem to differentially affect black or white examinee performance, then the use of diverse cultural content in such tests probably can be recommended for its own sake. Given the great cultural diversity of individuals who now are seeking access to higher education, there is much to commend the inclusion of content materials reflecting that diversity, so long as the content does not have an adverse effect on the particular cultural group.

Study #2

Purpose. The second study was conducted after Study #1 in an effort to examine the effect of test content on black and white examinee performance using a larger sampling of content. A secondary purpose of the study was to examine the effect of a second potential source of bias, namely skill level, on black and white examinee performance.

Most tables of specifications used by test constructors include several levels of skills, and the purpose of this study was to examine the effect of this test development practice on the performance of black and white examinees using test materials developed in English.

Specifically, this study attempted to answer the following questions:

1. Are the overall performances of black and white examinees differentially affected by black and white English test content?
2. Does skill category differentially affect black and white examinee performance on black and white English test content?
3. Do the reliability coefficients for the black and white English tests differ for black and white examinees?

Instruments. The test materials used in this study were developed for inclusion in the *ACT* English Usage Test. Four tests, two reflecting black culture and two reflecting white culture, were randomly selected from among the available test materials and were administered in the 1979 fall pretesting administration of the *ACT Assessment*. All tests contained a 225-word passage and 30 multiple-choice test items. The tests reflecting content identified with the white culture were based on the topics of the development of chewing gum (White Test #1) and word puzzles (White Test #2); the tests reflecting content identified with the black culture were based on the topics of biracial adoption (Black Test #1) and a biographical sketch of Booker T. Washington (Black Test #2).

Skill, as used in this study, will refer to the type of basic element of effective expository writing measured by a test question. The five skill categories used in this study were: punctuation, grammar, sentence structure, diction and style, and logic and organization. These categories are defined below.

1. punctuation: punctuation and graphic conventions, such as the use and placement of commas, colons, semicolons, dashes, hyphens, parentheses, apostrophes, and quotation, question, and exclamation marks
2. grammar: agreement between subject and verb and between pronouns and their antecedents, adjectives and adverbs, and conjunctions
3. sentence structure: relationships between/among clauses, placement of modifiers, parallelisms, and shifts in construction
4. diction and style: precision in word choice, appropriateness in figurative language, and economy in writing
5. logic and organization: logical organization of ideas, paragraphing, transition, unity, and coherence

Sample. The tests were administered to examinees under standardized testing conditions, as described in Study #1. A random sample comprised of 146 black and 146 white examinees took each test.

Analysis. The effect of test content and skill category on the performance of black and white examinees was analyzed using a four-factor analysis of variance. The four factors were: (1) race (black, white); (2) test content (black, white); (3) test within test content (Test #1, Test #2); and (4) skill category (punctuation, grammar, sentence structure, diction and style, logic and organization).

The factors of race, test content, and skill category were considered fixed, and the factor of test within test content was considered random. Test performance and internal consistency reliability coefficients were computed exactly as they were in Study #1.

Results. The results of the analysis of the effect of skill category on black and white examinee performance on the black and white test content are presented below and relate to each of the objectives of this study.

1. Are the performances of black and white examinees differentially affected by black and white English test contents?

The results of the analysis of variance are reported in Table 3.4. The interactions between race and test content and between race and test within test content were all nonsignificant, indicating that black and white examinees were not shown to respond differentially to the black and white English test content. The main effect for test content was not significant, indicating that the black and white content were not significantly different in difficulty for the combined races. The main effect for race, however, was significant ($p \leq .001$), with white examinees scoring higher than black examinees, regardless of test content. In addition, the effect of test within test content was significant ($p \leq .001$), indicating that the tests, two of which were based upon each of the two types of content (black and white), were different in dif-

TABLE 3.4. Analysis of Variance Summary Table: Study #2

Source	df	MS	F
Race	1	30.0169	656.5632[a]
Test content	1	1.9070	.4307
Skill category	4	3.8773	3.0706
Test within test content	2	4.4276	35.3360[a]
Race × test content	1	0.4432	9.8271
Race × skill category	4	0.2410	10.4329
Test content × skill category	4	0.1281	.1015
Race × test within test content	2	0.0451	.3599
Skill category × test within test	8	1.2627	38.3698[a]
Race × test content × skill category	4	0.1442	6.2424
Persons within race × test within test content	1160	0.1253	[b]
Race × skill category × test within test content	8	0.0231	.6471
Persons × skill category within race × test within test content	4640	0.0357	[b]

[a]$p \leq .001$
[b]No F tests for these effects

ficulty for the combined races. This effect is shown in Figure 3.1. The mean proportions of items answered correctly by the combined races are reported in parentheses in the figure.

The mean proportions of items answered correctly for the two races combined suggest that Black Test #1 (biracial adoption) and the White Test #2 (word puzzles) may have been more difficult for both black and white examinees than were the other black and white tests, respectively.

2. Does skill category differentially affect black and white examinee performance on black and white English test content?

Again, referring to Table 3.4, the main effect for skill category was nonsignificant, indicating that the five skill categories were not significantly

FIGURE 3.1. Test within test content, Study #2

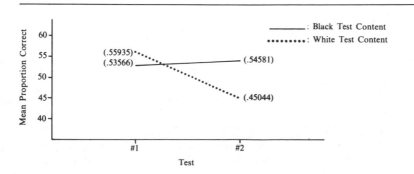

different in difficulty across test content, test within test content, and race. The interactions between race and skill category; test content and skill category; race, test content, and skill category; and race, skill category, and test within test content were all nonsignificant. The interaction between skill category and test within test content was significant ($p \leq .001$), indicating that the five skill categories were significantly different in difficulty for *all* examinees for the two tests based upon each of the black and white content. This interaction is shown in Figure 3.2. In addition, the mean proportions of items answered correctly by the combined races and the number of items comprising each skill category are shown in Table 3.5.

These results suggest that the diction and style items may have been more difficult for all examinees in Black Test #1 than they were in the other three

FIGURE 3.2. Skill category x test content, Study #2

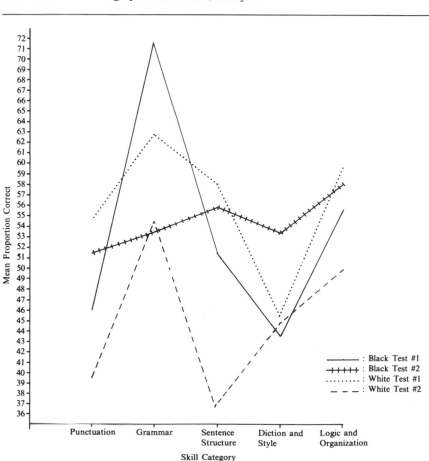

TABLE 3.5. Mean Proportion of Items Correct for the Interaction between Skill Category and Test within Test Content: Study #2

Test Content	Skill Category				
	Punctuation	Grammar	Sentence structure	Diction & style	Logic & organization
Black Test #1	.46095	.71301	.51252	.43691	.55525
number of items	5	5	6	7	7
Black Test #2	.51597	.53766	.55865	.53732	.57962
number of items	3	5	8	10	4
White Test #1	.54246	.62602	.57577	.45354	.59930
number of items	5	5	7	7	6
White Test #2	.39589	.54109	.36651	.45146	.49753
number of items	5	5	7	6	7

tests, but easier for all examinees in Black Test #2 than they were in the other three tests. Similarly, the grammar items may have been more difficult for all examinees in Black Test #2, but easier for all examinees in Black Test #1 than they were in the other three tests. Except for Black Test #2, the grammar items seemed to be the easiest type overall for all examinees. The same trend occurred in the two white tests. Punctuation, sentence structure, and logic and organization seemed to be more difficult for all examinees in White Test #2 than they were in the other three tests, and easier for all examinees in White Test #1 than they were in the other tests.

3. Do the reliability coefficients for the black and white English test differ for black and white examinees?

To assess the homogeneity of the items contained in the four tests, KR_{20} coefficents and the corresponding standard errors of measurement were computed for black and white examinees separately. The results are shown in Table 3.6. The resulting internal consistency values were tested for population equality using a procedure described by Feldt (1969). In none of the

TABLE 3.6. Reliability Coefficients and Standard Errors of Measurement: Study #2

Test	Number of Items	Race	KR_{20}	SE_{meas}
Black Test #1	30	black	.76	2.40
		white	.76	2.35
Black Test #2	30	black	.69	2.62
		white	.77	2.44
White Test #1	30	black	.70	2.46
		white	.66	2.27
White Test #2	30	black	.75	2.30
		white	.79	2.38

comparisons did the reliability coefficients based on black and white examinees on the same test differ significantly ($p = .001$).

Discussion. Although white examinees scored higher than black examinees regardless of test content, skill category, or test within test content, the lack of significant interactions between race and test content in this study suggests that the performance of black and white examinees did not appear to be differentially affected by either black or white English test content.

Second, the lack of any significant interactions between skill category and race or test content suggests that the skill categories did not appear to differentially affect black and white examinee performance on black and white English test content.

Third, the differences between the reliability coefficients for black and white examinees on the black and white content were within the range attributable to sampling errors. Thus, the four tests used in this study were not shown to have significantly different internal consistency reliabilities for the two races.

The effect of test within test content found to be statistically significant in this study may be attributable to the differences in difficulty between the two tests based upon black content and between the two tests based on white content. Specifically, Black Test #1 and White Test #2 appeared to be more difficult for all examinees than were the other two tests. These results suggest that the two tests within each of the two test content areas, and, consequently, the skills measured by the items in these tests, were not parallel in difficulty, as intended.

These results, however, must be tempered by the fact that only limited samples of black and white test content and skills were used in the study. As a result, the design may not have had sufficient power or "sensitivity" to detect the significance of some of the effects as would have been the case if a larger sample of content and skills had been used. Thus, future efforts should be aimed at obtaining a larger sample of items measuring each skill category in each of the black and white test content areas.

Implications. Given the limitations of this study, however, the results do support trends found in Study #1, indicating that white examinees tend to score higher than black examinees. Moreover, the results of this study also support the results of Study #1 and the findings of Schmeiser (1978), indicating that test content does not appear to be a source of bias in black and white examinee test performance.

Although the results of this study did not suggest that skill category is a source of bias in black and white examinee test performance, the significant results suggest that the effect of skill category on examinee performance, regardless of race, may well be particular to the specific test. That is, there seemed to be a differential effect of the skill categories between tests of the same content, implying that the two tests based on the black content and the two tests based on the white content were not similar in difficulty nor in the difficulty of the skills being measured by each for all examinees, regardless of race. However, there did not seem to be a consistent differential effect of the skill categories on the performance of black and white examinees on black and white test content, perhaps due to the limited sampling of test materials used in the study. Further investigation of this variable should therefore be conducted.

Discussion of the Two Illustrative Studies

Although the two studies were not meant to serve as ideal item bias studies, they have been presented to illustrate the advantages of the experimental design approach to the study of item bias. Specifically, these studies have:

1. illustrated the testing of procedures and/or assumptions used in the test development process to discern whether these particular variables could be sources of bias for two subgroups studied (Item Bias Research Goals #1 and #3);
2. presented suggestions related to the adoption (or continuation) of a test development practice in the test development process (Item Bias Research Goal #3);
3. provided an objective way of studying item bias through experimental design by using randomization, manipulating independent variables, and grouping subjects on the basis of another independent variable of interest;
4. identified the effects on the dependent variable due to such independent variables as race, test content, test within test content, and skill category;
5. illustrated the use of randomization by using more than one instrument selected as representative of the domain of all such test materials (i.e. several passages based on the content of each culture);
6. illustrated the use of randomization by randomly selecting the examinees within intact groups and randomly assigning test materials to examinees within groups; and
7. reduced error variance by administering all tests under standardized conditions and by administering as many items illustrating the procedures as was reasonable, given the time constraints and sample size.

One final advantage of the use of the experimental design approach to the study of item bias demonstrated by these two examples is the sequencing of research studies. In Study #1, only one test reflecting white culture and one test reflecting black culture were developed in English. The results of this study deserved qualification for this reason. In Study #2, an attempt to overcome this limitation was made by developing two tests reflecting each culture. Although the sample of test materials was still limited, an effort was made in the second study to improve upon the limitations cited in the first study.

Although these examples have limitations, they are intended to illustrate the traditional experimental process: define a problem and plan for the collection and analyses of data, exert experimental control, perform the experiment, analyze the results, and interpret the results. Such sequencing of research studies over time permits the researcher to conduct an initial study, examine the results, and design a second study to explore further the results obtained in the first study. After examining the results obtained in the first study, the researcher may decide to reexamine the test development procedure under different conditions (e.g., different subject area, different groups), overcome or improve upon any limitations encountered in the first study (e.g., limited samples of examinees or content), or examine additional variables suggested by the results of the first study (e.g., a new test development procedure or variation thereof). The sequencing of studies also allows the researcher to obtain more information about the procedures being investigated and to have more confidence in the obtained results.

Obviously no one study can answer all questions. However, there is no limit to the number of studies that could be conducted, and each new study should capitalize upon the results of all previous studies. This process can clearly strengthen the conclusions and generalizations that can be drawn by the researcher about the effect that certain test development procedures have on examinee subgroup performance and their implications for the test development process.

Clearly, all tests, whether teacher-made or standardized, are evolving rather than static instruments. With changes in culture and changes in instruments (i.e., test specifications) over time, the conclusions about bias with respect to a particular procedure will also change. It seems reasonable to suspect, then, that a procedure that was found to be free of bias 20 years ago may not necessarily be free of bias today. Thus, the continuous study of procedures should be undertaken by test developers.

RECOMMENDATIONS FOR
TEST DEVELOPERS AND TEST USERS

This section presents several suggestions pertaining to practical application of the experimental design approach in item bias studies, alternatives available to test developers when a biased test development procedure is detected, and topics for future item bias studies.

Practical Application of the Experimental Design Approach

In the preceding sections of this chapter, several suggestions have been presented for the researcher to consider while planning a statistical item bias study, with particular emphasis upon the use of the experimental design approach. At the risk of oversimplification, these suggestions are summarized in Table 3.7 for use in planning such a study. This list is intended to serve as a practical checklist and is not intended to exhaust all the concerns involved in conducting a study.

TABLE 3.7. Checklist for Use in Planning a Statistical Item Bias Study

_____ 1. Formulate the problem and state the hypothesis
_____ 2. Specify the decision rules to be followed in testing the hypothesis
_____ 3. Identify operationally the independent variable to be manipulated (i.e., test development procedure or assumption to be tested)
_____ 4. Identify the independent variables to be used to classify the subjects
_____ 5. Identify the dependent variable to be measured
_____ 6. Determine whether additional independent variables should be considered in the
design and, if so, select an appropriate method of accounting for such variables
_____ 7. Select an appropriate statistical design and corresponding analysis procedure
_____ 8. Identify the subgroup population to be studied
_____ 9. Identify the universe of test materials employing the procedure to be studied
_____10. Randomly sample the universe of test materials (or develop the test materials) using
as large a sample as possible
_____11. Randomly sample the subgroup populations
_____12. Randomly assign test materials to subjects
_____13. Plan for and collect the data under standardized conditions
_____14. Analyze the data using an analysis that is appropriate for the design
_____15. Interpret the results of the data within any possible limitations of the study
_____16. Formulate new hypotheses for a subsequent study based upon the results
_____17. Plan a subsequent study

From a practical standpoint, it seems reasonable at this point to examine
the alternatives that test constructors must consider when the results of
studies indicate that a particular test development procedure or assumption
may produce biased items.

Alternatives Available to Test Developers When a Biased Procedure is Detected

If, in an experimental series of studies of item bias, consistent significant
results are obtained in a series of studies, indicating that a particular procedure, assumption, or practice may be a source of bias for a particular
subgroup, the test developer is faced with a decision as to how to apply such a
result in a practical way. Before such a decision is made, however, the
generalizability of the research must be considered, to assure that the conclusions reached are directly related to the questions studied and to the popula-
tion(s) of examinees who take (or will take) the instrument(s) in question.

For instance, suppose a particular practice was tested in the context of a
mathematics test, although the practice itself is used to develop examinations
in other content areas (e.g. English, natural or social science). To conclude
that such a practice should be adopted as part of or eliminated from the test
development process in all content areas might be an overgeneralization, as
the results pertained to only one particular test. Thus, test developers should
be wary of such generalizations, especially when recommending changes in
general test development practices.

Moreover, they should be sensitive to another type of overgeneralization
related to subgroups. Any person can be classified into a number of

subgroups related to race, sex, ethnicity, geographic location, achievement level, social class, or some other criterion. Because of the multiplicity of classifications, it is important for test developers to be sensitive to the particular groups being examined in a study, so that unwarranted generalizations are not made. For example, suppose a particular testing practice for a particular test is found to be biased for black and white examinees. To conclude "the test is biased" is misleading, as such a statement implies that the test is biased for *all* examinees, regardless of race. This misstatement is similar to stating that "a test is not valid" without qualifying the context of test score use. The biased nature of a test development practice is directly related to the particular subgroup(s) studied, and not necessarily to all subgroups. Further, if a practice is found to produce items that are biased against a certain subgroup, one cannot directly conclude that it is biased against each individual member of that subgroup. Bias with respect to a subgroup does not necessarily imply bias with respect to each member of that subgroup.

If the results of a series of item bias studies consistently indicate that a particular test construction practice produces biased items for a particular subgroup or subgroups, several alternatives are available to the test developer.

Balance the bias in the test. In recent years, the method of balancing bias within a test has been suggested when significant item biases favor either one or another subgroup or cancel each other altogether. At this point, the decision as to whether to balance the bias in the test may be dependent upon which one of three conceptualizations of test item bias is adopted: (1) bias in total test scores; (2) bias in a certain number or proportion of the items in the test; and (3) bias in the procedures used to develop the test.

If one accepts the first conceptualization of bias, then a test is viewed as an instrument leading to a total score almost in a criterion validity sense. (See the discussion of this issue by Shepard, chapter 1.) In this conceptualization of bias, the notion of balancing bias within a test may be a reasonable alternative in that total test scores will be "equalized" with respect to biasedness.

If one accepts the second conceptualization of bias, then a test is viewed as a collection of individual test items. In this case, the notion of balancing bias will probably not be an acceptable alternative, as conveyed by Jensen (1980): "A test in which large item biases balance each other so as not to favor either group in the total score is no more desirable or defensible than a test in which the item bias preponderantly favors one group. There is only one satisfactory solution for significantly biased items: elimination" (p. 441). Clearly, Jensen feels that a test does not become less biased by merely balancing significantly biased items. (See Berk, Introduction, for further comments on this point.)

If one accepts the third conceptualization of bias, then a test is considered to be unbiased to the extent that the procedures used to develop the test are unbiased. Again, in this case the notion of balancing bias within a test may not be an acceptable solution. To balance biased items in a test has little impact upon the test development process in the future. In other words, by including items in a test that result from a biased test development procedure and by exerting no effort to prevent the further development of such items by modifying the procedures used to develop them, test developers have not learned much of anything.

Consequently, depending upon the conceptualization of bias one adopts, different conclusions about the usefulness of balancing bias within a test will result.

Change the test development procedures to prevent such items from being developed in the future. The second alternative available to test developers when a test construction practice is found to produce biased items is to change the procedure to prevent such items from being developed in the future. This action is a more reasonable approach, especially if the procedure does not have a direct impact upon the test specifications. For instance, suppose the variable or procedure found to be biased for a particular subgroup is one that is outside the specifications of the test. Such variables might include item format, item wording, contextual material, and so on. In this case, changing or eliminating the test development procedure would probably not affect the content validity of the test as a whole. Moreover, introducing a change in the test development process to eliminate the production of such items in the future can probably be relatively easily implemented. Thus, when a procedure is found to produce biased items, the test developer may decide to change the procedure if such a change will not have a substantial impact upon the test specifications.

Retain current test development procedures. There may be instances, however, when the test developer may decide to continue using the test development procedure, even though the procedure is found to produce biased items. This may occur when the procedure has a substantial impact upon the test specifications. For instance, suppose that in an English test all punctuation items were found to be biased against black examinees who comprise 35% of the examinee population. Further suppose that these skills have been documented as essential skills by content experts and national survey data, thus leading to their inclusion in the table of specifications. In cases where the variables or procedures are critical to the content validity of a test and are reflected in the table of specifications, the test developer has two alternatives: to change the test specifications to exclude such content from future examinations or to retain the current test specifications. The first option in this situation has serious implications for the content validity of the test; that is, the test will no longer include the English skills considered essential. The second option limits the predictive validity of the test in that its predictive validity for the black subgroup is suspect. Obviously, neither option is inherently more acceptable than the other.

Whatever decision is reached by the test developer, it must be based upon careful consideration of all the aspects of the situation, including the results and implications of the results of the research, the importance of the biasing variable and its relationship to the test development process, the nature of the change to be implemented, and the potential impact of such a change on the content and predictive validity of the test for all subgroups.

Suggestions for Future Experimental Studies of Item Bias

Several suggestions for future experimental studies of item bias are listed below. Although these suggestions are not meant to be comprehensive or exhaustive, they have been provided to illustrate the types of test development procedures and practices that could be tested through the experimental design approach to the study of item bias.

Portrayal of various subgroups with respect to occupations, hobbies, sports, etc.

Active vs. passive roles of various subgroups

Appropriateness of test content for particular ages and grades

Use of language

Item types (objective vs. subjective types, types of objective items—matching, true-false, multiple-choice)

Item formats (correct response, best response, combinational formats)

Item formats oriented toward the exception (use of NOT, EXCEPT formats)

Item context (passage vs. discrete items, word problems vs. formula problems)

Context of content (content relating to the culture of a particular subgroup as opposed to another)

Cognitive skill levels (Bloom's taxonomy or other such taxonomies)

Speeded vs. power tests

Use of symbols vs. verbal explanations

Use of Guttman's facet design to develop items vs. other item development techniques

Specific editorial techniques (neutral references vs. balance of references)

Visual materials vs. verbal descriptions of data (graphs and charts vs. verbal descriptions of data)

Item flaws (incomplete stems, length of alternatives, specific determiners, window dressing, clues in stem corresponding to correct answer, etc.)

Types of various response alternatives (use of none of the above vs. all of the above)

Reading level of various item types

It is important to recognize that regardless of the variable, procedure, or assumption being studied, the future of item bias research does not rest solely with the researcher or test developer. Rather, future item bias research should be a cooperative venture by test developers (and/or researchers) and content experts to plan the study, interpret the results, and consider future studies. Moreover, all three approaches to the study of item bias should be pursued by the test developer and content expert, as each approach offers unique, yet complementary, information that should be used in any item bias study. To proceed without the perspectives of each of these three approaches will probably lead to limited results and fallacious interpretations. Item bias research needs and deserves the contributions of all three approaches.

REFERENCES

Angoff, W. H., & Ford, S. F. Item-race interaction on a test of scholastic aptitude. *Journal of Educational Measurement,* 1973, *10,* 95–105.

Campbell, D. T., & Stanley, J. C. *Experimental and quasi-experimental design for research.* Chicago: Rand McNally, 1966.

Cook, T. D., & Campbell, D. T. *Quasi-experimention: Design and analysis issues for field settings.* Chicago: Rand McNally, 1979.

Cotter, D. E. & Berk, R. A. *Item bias in the WISC-R using black, white, and Hispanic learning disabled children.* Paper presented at the annual meeting of the American Educational Research Association, Los Angeles, April 1981.

Dreger, R. M., & Miller, K. S. Comparative psychological studies of negroes and whites in the United States: 1959–1965. *Psychological Bulletin,* 1960, *57,* 361–402.

Dreger, R. M., & Miller, K. S. Comparative psychological studies of negroes and whites in the United States: 1959–1965. *Psychological Bulletin,* 1968 (Monograph Supplement, *70* (3), Part 2).

Feldt, L. S. A comparison of the precision of three experimental designs employing a concomitant variable. *Psychometrika,* 1958, *23,* 335–353.

Feldt, L. S. A test of the hypotheses that Cronbach's alpha or Kuder-Richardson coefficient twenty is the same for two tests. *Psychometrika,* 1969, *34,* 363–373.

Jensen, A. R. *Bias in mental testing.* New York: Free Press, 1980.

Kerlinger, F. N. *Foundations of behavioral research* (2nd ed.). New York: Holt, Rinehart & Winston, 1973.

Kirk, R. E. *Experimental design: Procedures for the behavioral sciences.* Belmont, Calif.; Brooks/Cole, 1968.

Lindquist, E. F. *Design and analysis of experiments.* Boston: Houghton Mifflin, 1953.

Medley, D. M., & Quirk, T. J. The application of a factorial design to the study of cultural bias in general culture items on the National Teacher Examination. *Journal of Educational Measurement,* 1974, *11,* 235–245.

Schmeiser, C. B. *The impact of black and white English test content on black and white student performance and selected test characteristics.* Paper presented at the annual meeting of the American Educational Research Association, Toronto, March 1978.

Shuey, A. *The testing of Negro intelligence* (2nd ed.). New York: Social Science Press, 1966.

4 USE OF DIFFICULTY AND DISCRIMINATION INDICES FOR DETECTING ITEM BIAS
WILLIAM H. ANGOFF

INTRODUCTION

THERE IS general agreement among test specialists that simple differences between groups—differences in means, standard deviations, and skewness, for example—are not by themselves evidence of test bias. What *may* be evidence of bias are differences between groups in relationships between tests and criteria, between items and tests, and between individual items and other items measuring the same ability and administered in the same context. More generally, the evaluation of bias must come either from an examination of the internal components in the test in relation to one another or from an examination of the test data in the context of other empirical data and theory independently developed. It is in this sense that the item-by-group interaction is of particular interest here, rather than the simple variance of the main effects.

It should be understood, in the discussion of item-bias methodology that follows, that proper methods of test development require extensive and careful judgmental review of all items from the point of view of ethnic and sex bias, among others, before they are accepted for inclusion in the test. The role of the methods to be discussed here is to serve only as a further check, in the event that one or more biased items have escaped the attention of the reviewers. As is suggested in the closing paragraphs of this chapter, and as has been urged by many other writers in the past, statistical methods are only supplemental to human judgment, certainly no substitute for it.

REVIEW OF METHODS

Delta-plot Method
The delta-plot method described by Angoff (1972; also Angoff & Ford, 1973) goes back to early days in psychometrics when L. L. Thurstone de-

scribed its use in connection with his Method of Absolute Scaling (1925). The method calls for the calculation of item-difficulty values, i.e., p values, for two different groups on a number of items that sample a single content or skill domain, in which it may reasonably be assumed that the item difficulties will order themselves in the same way for different groups of individuals. Each p value is converted to a normal deviate with an arbitrarily chosen mean and standard deviation. (The values 13 and 4, respectively, are typical; normal deviates so transformed are called *deltas*.)

The pairs of deltas (one pair for each item) are plotted on a bivariate graph, each pair represented by a point on the graph, where the delta values of one group are read on the abscissa and the delta values of the other group are read on the ordinate. As in the usual correlation diagram, the plot of these points will appear in the form of an ellipse, this one extending from lower left to upper right. If the two groups are drawn from the same or very similar populations, the scatterplot of these points will fall on a long, narrow ellipse, often representing a correlation of .98 or even higher, indicating that the rank order of difficulty of these items is essentially the same for the two groups. It also indicates that the spacing between indices is not changing more rapidly in one group than in the other; for if it were, the plot would not be linear, but curvilinear.

When the samples differ somewhat in level of ability, the points will still fall in a long, narrow ellipse but will be displaced vertically or horizontally, depending on which group is the abler one. Even when the groups differ in dispersion, the points will still fall in the same type of ellipse, but the ellipse will be tilted at an angle more or less steeply than 45°, depending on which group's deltas are the more dispersed. However, when the two groups differ in *type*, or when the items do not all have the same meaning for the two groups, the deltas will not fall in precisely the same rank order for the two groups, and the correlation represented by these points will be lower than .98, sometimes substantially lower. The items falling at some distance from the plot may be regarded as contributing to the item-by-group interaction. These are the items that are especially more difficult for one group than for the other, *relative to* the other items; and they are the items that appear to represent a different "psychological meaning" to the members of each group. A clinical review of the items that fall at some distance from the plot may reveal that the group for which they are inordinately difficult may not have had the same amount of exposure to the concepts measured by these items as did the other group. It is in this sense that the items are referred to as "biased" items.

As described in an earlier paper (Angoff & Ford, 1973), the formal procedure for measuring the departure of each item from the plot is to calculate its distance from the major axis of the ellipse. The equation of the major axis may be given in the form, $y = ax + b$, where

$$a = \frac{(s_y^2 - s_x^2) \pm \sqrt{(s_y^2 - s_x^2) + 4r_{xy}^2 s_x^2 s_y^2}}{2r_{xy} s_x s_y} \tag{1}$$

and

$$b = M_y - aM_x. \tag{2}$$

(It is recalled that the variables x and y are, respectively, the delta-values for the two groups under consideration. Thus M_x and s_x, for example, denote the mean and standard deviation of deltas for the group whose deltas are referred to the x axis, and r_{xy} denotes the correlation between the deltas for the two groups.) The formula for the distance d_i of each point i in the plot to the line (the major axis of the ellipse) is given as

$$d_i = \frac{ax_i - y_i + b}{\sqrt{a^2 + 1}} \tag{3}$$

Since the correlation coefficient represented by the plot of the deltas for the two groups expresses the degree to which the items have the same rank order of difficulty in the two groups, it also expresses (inversely) the item-by-group interaction. Another index of item-by-group interaction is the standard deviation of the d_i values. In order to make these standard deviations comparable from one plot to another, it is convenient to set the standard deviation of the deltas themselves at unity, in which case the standard deviation of the d_i values, $s_d = \sqrt{1 - r_{xy}}$, becomes a function of the correlation itself. Although the point is perhaps an obvious one, it should be mentioned that as the correlation between the delta values departs from unity by what may appear to be small amounts, the standard deviation of the distances from the points to the major axis increases by large amounts. Thus, a plot representing a correlation of .92 shows a standard deviation of these distances twice as large (and a variance four times as large) as would be found in a plot for a correlation of .98.

The nature of the bias under study is well illustrated in the delta-plot method. If, for example, we were to plot a set of deltas for blacks drawn from the general population against the deltas for the same items for whites, similarly drawn from the general population, we would find an elliptical swarm of items whose major axis falls to one side of the 45° line through the origin, indicating that as a group the items are more difficult for blacks than for whites. In recognition of this fact, the procedure for evaluating bias in the individual items is to measure their distance from the major axis of the ellipse defined by the items themselves, rather than from the 45° line (i.e., the equal-difficulty, equal-dispersion line). The justification for this choice is that virtually all data yielded by random selection methods reveal this disparity; and although the disparity is, to be sure, the result of social and educational bias, the bias we are seeking to investigate here is a bias of another sort, one that goes beyond the basic social bias. Here, we are willing to assume that the content of the test is a reasonable representation of the more general educational goals, and the items sought in the item bias study are those that are deviant, granted the acceptability of those goals. Focusing our attention on the departure of the items from the line defined by the items themselves illustrates our interest in the item-by-group interaction *by itself*, quite apart from the main effects, i.e., the variation between or among groups and the variation among items.

Figures 4.1, 4.2, and 4.3 illustrate the application of the delta-plot procedure. Figure 4.1 shows a plot of paired deltas for two random samples of black students (Samples 1 and 2) who took a form of the 70-item *Preliminary Scholastic Aptitude Test* (*PSAT*)-Verbal. In order to produce this plot, each of the two samples was subjected to an item analysis, which yielded a *p* value

FIGURE 4.1. Delta plot for random (unselected) samples of blacks (*PSAT*-Verbal). Reprinted, with permission, from W. H. Angoff and S. F. Ford. Item-race interaction on a test of scholastic aptitude. *Journal of Educational Measurement*, 1973, *10* (2), p. 98.

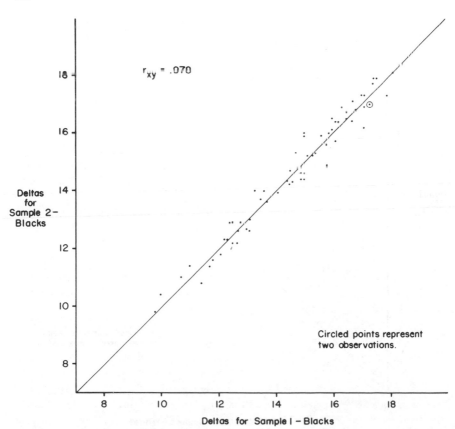

$r_{xy} = .070$

Deltas for Sample 2 – Blacks

Circled points represent two observations.

Deltas for Sample 1 – Blacks

for each of the 70 items. The p values were each converted to deltas, as described above, and the pairs of delta values (one for each sample) were plotted, one pair for each of the 70 items in the test. As may be seen from the plot, the paired deltas, as expected, describe a 45° line out of the origin, with little dispersion ($r = .978$) about that line.

Figure 4.2 shows a similar plot for two random samples of white students (Samples 5 and 6). As with the plot for the black students, this plot also describes a 45° line out of the origin, similarly with little dispersion ($r = .987$) about the line.

Figure 4.3 also shows a plot of deltas, but this time based on the deltas for Sample 1 (black students), plotted on the abscissa, paired with the deltas for Sample 5 (white students), plotted on the ordinate. This time, the plot, while differing very little in slope from the 45° line, is clearly displaced to the right,

FIGURE 4.2. Delta plot for random (unselected) samples of whites (*PSAT*-Verbal). Reprinted, with permission, from W. H. Angoff and S. F. Ford. Item-race interaction on a test of scholastic aptitude. *Journal of Educational Measurement*, 1973, *10* (2), p. 99.

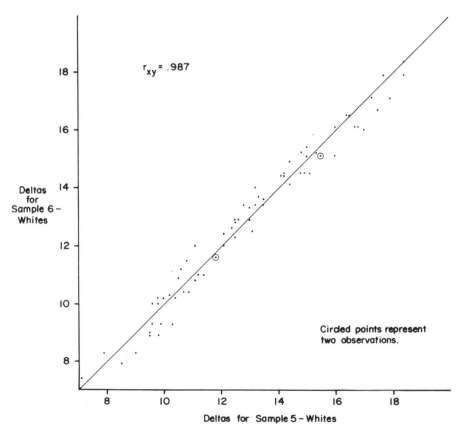

FIGURE 4.3. Delta plot for unselected sample of blacks vs. unselected sample of whites (*PSAT*-Verbal). Reprinted, with permission, from W. H. Angoff and S. F. Ford. Item-race interaction on a test of scholastic aptitude. *Journal of Educational Measurement*, 1973, *10* (2), p. 100.

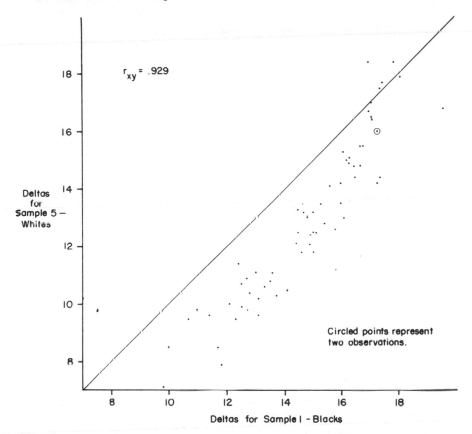

indicating that the items are generally harder for the black students, as a group, than for the white students. Moreover, this biracial plot is clearly more dispersed ($r = .929$) than is the case for two random samples drawn from the same population, as illustrated in Figures 4.1 and 4.2. In Figure 4.3, any item points found to be substantially divergent from the swarm of points (i.e., whose distances from the major axis of the ellipse are inordinately greater than the others) are identified as *outliers* and examined for possible bias.

The delta-plot method and its derivative statistics have had several uses in addition to the identification of biased items. Their use in score equating (absolute scaling) has already been mentioned. They have also been used successfully in operational work in standardizing and equating item difficulties (Thurstone, 1947), in the study of cultural and sex differences (Angoff &

Ford, 1973; Angoff & Herring, 1976; Breland et al., 1974; Coffman, 1961, 1963), in equating scores across tests for groups presumed to be culturally different (Angoff & Modu, 1973; Angoff & Stern, 1971), and in studies of English-language ability for different cultural and lingual groups (Alderman & Holland, 1981; Angoff & Sharon, 1971, 1974). The delta-plot method has been useful in detecting errors in scoring keys and, in the sense that it identifies items having different "psychological meaning" for different groups, it has also had successful application in identifying obsolete or obsolescent items, and items whose difficulty is affected by changes in speededness, context, or even item and test format. Finally, the method, in addition to being useful in these several applications, seems to be a valuable tool to use in assessing the extent to which the members of two cultures, for whom the items of a test are reasonably appropriate, view the items in the same way; specifically, the correlation represented by the plot may be used as an index of the similarity, in a particular dimension, between two cultural groups. (See the studies of culturally different groups cited above.)

Modifications and Variations of the Delta-plot Method

Sinnott (1980) proposes a way of determining the precise nature of the major axis line in the event that biased (i.e., discrepant) items are found. In order to decrease the likelihood that such biased items would contribute to the determination of that line, the following steps are taken:

1. Calculate a preliminary line based on all items.
2. Remove the items that are identified, on the basis of their distance from the line, as biased.
3. Calculate a new line based on the remaining items.
4. Readmit the items removed in Step 2 to the set of points.
5. Repeat Step 2.

If the items to be removed on the basis of the new line are the same as those removed the previous time, the process is discontinued, and the line calculated in Step 3 is defined as the line of best fit. If the items are not the same, the process is continued.

It is clear that the delta-plot procedure, which is described for the case of two groups, may be generalized to several groups considered simultaneously (Angoff, 1975). As in the case of the two-group comparison, a line can be determined running through the major axis of the multidimensional ellipsoid, and a perpendicular distance can be found between the item point in the hyperspace and that major axis line. Sinnott (1980) provides formulas for determining the equation of the line and for determining the distance of each point to the line. This development will prove to be useful in situations where there may be some question of the applicability of a single set of test items to several groups, a problem confronted in the study by Alderman and Holland (1981) and in the study by Angoff and Sharon (1974). In such studies, items found at inordinately great distances from the major axis of the ellipsoid would have to be investigated further by considering the plots of the groups two at a time to determine which group(s) is contributing most heavily to the magnitude of that distance. The method should also be of value in considering the degree to which several disparate (e.g., national) groups may be considered members of a common general culture, and is particularly applicable in countries such as our own whose population is composed of many diverse subgroups. It would also be of interest to compare the degree of diversity among the subgroups across the geographical regions of the country and perhaps also to track changes in the diversity over the course of time.

One of the methods chosen by Rudner, Getson, and Knight (1980) in their comparative study of item bias studies is a variation of the delta-plot method. In conducting their analyses, they form a distribution of within-group p values and calculate the mean and standard deviation of p values for each group. They then determine within-group z values for each item, where $z_i = (p_i - M_p)/s_p$, and where M_p and s_p are, respectively, the mean and standard deviation of the p values. The plot of the paired z values, which yields a major axis line with a 45° slope and zero intercept, is used as the reference line against which item-point discrepancies are measured.

Echternacht (1974) also describes a variation of the delta-plot method. He suggests converting the raw p values to deltas, as is done in the first method described above. Instead of examining the plot of one group's deltas against another's, however, Echternacht computes the differences between the corresponding delta values for the two groups and tests the distribution of those differences for normality. He also requires that, within sampling limits, the differences between paired delta values be constant across all items, which is to say that he assumes equal dispersions of the deltas in the two groups.

Coffman (1961, 1963) has described yet another variation of the method of plotting item difficulties for the two groups under study. His procedure calls for plotting the paired values of 2 arcsin $\sqrt{p}$, where p, as before, is the proportion of the group answering the item correctly. The advantage here is that all item-difficulty values, so transformed, have the same variance error ($1/N$, where N = number of cases in the sample), a characteristic not shared by the p value (Plake & Hoover, 1979–1980). The disadvantage is that, like p values, they are bounded, and therefore yield a curvilinear plot when the groups under study have widely different means, as is the case when black and white performances are studied. By way of contrast, the advantage of the transformation to deltas is that it tends to rectify such plots and permits the conduct of far simpler analyses than would be possible with curvilinear plots of items. Indeed, this was the principal reason for the use of the normal deviate in Thurstone's work in absolute scaling.

Limitations of Delta-plot Methodology

The delta-plot type of method has its limitations, to be sure. Elizabeth Stewart (personal communication) has pointed out that a highly discrepant item in a plot between two groups that perform at widely different levels is also very likely to be a highly discriminating item for the same reason (i.e., that it discriminates sharply between a high-scoring and low-scoring group). This being the case, the method may well identify as biased, or discrepant, items that are simply highly discriminating.

The same observation—that the delta-plot method tends to confound item discrimination with item difficulty—has been made by other investigators. Cole (1978), Hunter (1975), and Lord (1977), for example, have pointed out that unless all the items in the plot have the same discriminating power, the delta-plot may yield misleading results when the groups under consideration score at widely different ability levels. The delta, as described above, is derived from the proportion of individuals in the specific groups answering the item correctly, a value that may be found on the item response curve corresponding to the mean ability score of the group. As may be seen in Figure 4.4, the difference in proportion-pass for the two groups on the more discriminating item is considerably greater than is the difference in proportion-pass on the less discriminating item, even when the items are of the same difficulty (i.e., when the points of inflection of the two item response curves correspond to the same value on the scale of ability). This being the case, it is probable that the items identified as biased by the delta-plot method may in fact not be biased, but only give that appearance because the item is highly discriminating. It would be unfortunate, then, if action were to be taken to remove such an item on the basis of that appearance alone, since it would lead to the ultimate removal of the most useful items in the pool.

One solution to this difficulty, apart from going to more complex and

FIGURE 4.4. Item response curves for two items of the same general difficulty, but of different discriminating power

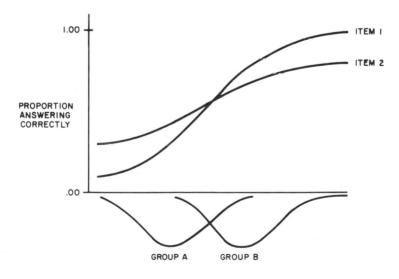

GROUP A   GROUP B

costly methods involving the formal use of item response curves, is to construct plots based on groups that have been matched beforehand on ability, as was done in the Angoff and Ford (1973) study. There, the groups that were used to study bias in the verbal items were first matched on their math scores; the groups used to study bias in the math items were first matched on their verbal scores. Although the circumstances in the conduct of that study did not permit matching on more relevant variables (for example, matching on external verbal scores for studying verbal items and matching on external math scores for studying math items), such matching should greatly reduce the artifactual character of the findings. Even more, it would separate considerations of ability from the more pertinent considerations of ethnicity, and permit the examination of ethnic bias in a purer form. Such studies, coupled with studies of pseudogroups as described by Jensen (1980, pp. 450, 451)—studies of groups matched on ethnicity, but differing by specified amounts on relevant, but external, test scores—should also be illuminating (also see Schmeiser, chapter 3).

Another possibility for improving the delta-plot procedure is to use the available data in an effort to provide an estimate of item difficulty, independent of the ability of the particular group of individuals taking the item (Lorr, 1944). This would suggest dividing the normal deviate, z, corresponding to the p value for the item, by the correlation between the item and the ability in question, or, as an approximation to this correlation, the item-test correlation. These newly derived z values (z', to distinguish them from unadjusted z's) represent estimates of the ability at which the probability of passing the item is .50. A plot of these z' values, or a plot of recomputed Δ values (Δ', where $\Delta' = 4z' + 13$), might avoid some of the pitfalls, discussed here, of the unadjusted Δ values.

The foregoing adjustment in the deltas is one that may have some promise. It is important, however, at the same time to draw attention to the relative unreliability of item biserials. It is therefore possible that they may introduce more instability into the statistics than correction. Nevertheless, the adjustment is something to be considered.

The criticisms of the delta-plot procedure are quite valid. With appropriate controls for differences in the abilities of the major and minor groups and with an adjustment for item-test correlation, however, it is likely that the method will yield results more closely approximating those given by the more sensitive item characteristic curve (ICC) methods. In addition, the delta-plot procedure is clearly far simpler and much less expensive than ICC methods, and it has applications in some types of cross-cultural studies not shared by the other methods.

Table 4.1 attempts to summarize the advantages and disadvantages of the delta-plot procedure. It also provides some replies to the stated disadvantages and offers suggestions for adjustments in the procedure that may help to overcome those disadvantages.

TABLE 4.1. Summary of Advantages and Disadvantages of the Delta Method

Advantages	Disadvantages	Responses to Stated Disadvantages
1. Simple in its execution 2. Inexpensive 3. Easily explained; lends itself to graphical description 4. Does not require much data to achieve stability 5. Provides useful information for the study of cultural differences	1. Delta values are not equally reliable; arcsin transformation would make them so	1. When groups are of equal ability, plot of arcsin transformations is not noticeably different from delta plot. When groups are not of equal ability, the arcsin transformation yields a curvilinear plot
	2. Positions of bivariate points are confounded with item discrimination. This confounding may cause misclassification of items as to "bias," if conditions are such that the groups are widely different in ability *and* if the item discriminations vary widely	2. It is possible that a confounding problem can be overcome if deltas are unregressed by dividing each delta by its item discrimination index. In any case, it can be dealt with by matching the groups on a highly correlated external variable

Analytical Methods

The principal emphasis in the description of the delta-plot method is that it is essentially a graphical procedure for studying item-by-group interaction. Analytical methods for carrying out such studies are also available (e.g., Angoff & Sharon, 1974; Cardall & Coffman, 1964; Cleary & Hilton, 1968). The design suggested by Cardall and Coffman is a two-factor design with repeated measures on one factor. Several random samples are drawn from each of the basic groups (ethnic or sex groups, for example) under comparison, and a difficulty index is calculated for each item for each sample within each group. The variance of item difficulties across samples within groups provides the estimate of error. As indicated earlier, Coffman (1961, 1963) and, in this context, Cardall and Coffman (1964) suggest transforming the item p values to arcsin values, and $\emptyset = 2 \arcsin \sqrt{p}$, in order to control the sampling variances of the item difficulties. When so transformed, the sampling variance for any item, regardless of its difficulty, is $1/N$ (Plake & Hoover, 1979–1980). As pointed out above, such a transformation may not be advantageous in studying delta plots. However, it would seem to be highly advantageous in the conduct of analysis of variance (ANOVA).

The foregoing procedure is an important and useful one for examining the test as a whole in what might be regarded as a preliminary step. Once it is determined that the item-by-group interaction is significant, it would then be in order to identify the items that are the principal contributors to the interaction.

The use of an error term involving differences among samples within groups suggests that items should be regarded as discrepant only when the item-by-group interaction is clearly greater than the interaction of items with samples within groups. It is not entirely clear, however, that such samples should necessarily be drawn at random from the group. It can be argued that the yardstick for evaluating bias should be the variance that would be observed among widely different samples for whom a test is considered appropriate, within the large basic (e.g., ethnic or sex) group. Thus, for example, if a test is considered, or found to be, appropriate for urban whites in the Northeast as well as for, say, rural whites in the South, then the variation observed for these groups should be used as a baseline for evaluating the interaction of item-by-ethnic group.

Using the delta-plot method for illustration, one would choose two widely different types of groups of the same ethnic (or sex) background, for whom all the items in the test are considered appropriate and acceptable, and use a band as large as $\pm 3s_d$ on either side of the main diagonal of that ellipse to identify biased items in a cross-ethnic ellipse. Any item that falls outside that band in a plot where item bias is under investigation would be regarded as a significantly discrepant item, quite possibly biased in the educational or social sense.

There is another lesson to be learned from the ANOVA studies of item-by-group interaction: The use of the interaction of items with individuals within groups as an error term is not especially useful, because we know beforehand that it will almost inevitably yield significant results. Even with tests of moderate length and relatively small sample sizes, the number of degrees of freedom will be so large as to render any effect significant, even though its contribution to the total may be very small; and this is precisely what occurred in the Cleary and Hilton (1968) study and in the Angoff and Sharon (1974) study. It also appeared in the ANOVA of the *Wechsler Intelligence Scale for Children (WISC)* Vocabulary subtest, reported by Jensen (1980, p. 556). Much to be preferred is the procedure followed by Cardall and Coffman (1964), in which the interaction of items with random samples within groups were used to represent the error term. Better yet, in this writer's opinion, is the use of clearly nonrandom samples within groups, as suggested above.

One possible drawback to the ANOVA procedure is that it is sensitive to differences in dispersions of item difficulties between, or among, the groups, and may yield significant results, even when there is no item-by-group interaction in the sense defined by the delta plot. In that procedure, it is recalled, an item's contribution to the item-by-group interaction is measured from the major axis of the elliptical swarm, just as one finds it. That is, the slope of the line is not assumed to be 45°, as is the case with the ANOVA procedure or with the Echternacht procedure, but is defined only by the data themselves. With a 45° line imposed on a plot whose slope is not 45° (i.e., whose groups do not yield equal dispersions of item difficulties), it can be predicted that the most difficult and least difficult items are the ones that will necessarily contribute heavily to the item-by-group interaction and will therefore be identified as biased for artifactual reasons, due to the choice of methodology, and not because such items are inherently discrepant.

Delta-decrement Analyses

The nature of the item-by-group interaction variance has been subjected to further scrutiny by Jensen (1980, pp. 434–435, 441–442), who separates the variance into two components: (1) the ordinal interaction variance, in which the items in the minor group, while not necessarily of equal difficulty as those in the major group, nevertheless display themselves in the same rank order as do those in the major group; and (2) the disordinal interaction variance, in which the items in the minor group have a different rank order from those in the major group. Especially of interest are those situations where most of the items are harder for the minor group than for the major group, but where some items are easier for the minor than for the major group. Jensen suggests that in those situations, disordinal effects would be indicated by the difference between the rank-order correlation (rho) and the product-moment correlation (Pearson r) between the two sets of item difficulties (see Reynolds, chapter 8), and would be a more compelling sign of biased items than would the simple ordinal effects.

An editorial note might be inserted here to the effect that items that are *easier* for the minor group than for the major group may be a matter of some interest, perhaps. The identification of such items, however, is not usually fundamental to the social and educational purpose of the investigation, which more often is designed to identify items that are biased *against* members of the minor group, that is, items that are inordinately *harder* for them.

The inference—perhaps one he does not intend—may be drawn in Jensen's treatment of the ordinal-disordinal distinction that only a disordinal arrangement of item difficulties will cause the Pearson r to depart from 1.00. This is not so, of course. Item difficulties may arrange themselves in the same rank order for the two groups, but because of different intervals, or spacing, between them, may yield a Pearson r lower than 1.00. Possibly in recognition of this, Jensen later proposes in his treatment of this method of analysis to correlate the delta decrements rather than the deltas themselves.

The delta-decrement analysis is conducted as follows: The items are first arranged in rank order in terms of their deltas as observed in the major group. Delta differences (decrements) are calculated between the most difficult item and the next most difficult item ($\Delta_1 - \Delta_2$), between that item and the next ($\Delta_2 - \Delta_3$), and so on through the list of items. Deltas for the minor group are arranged in the order determined for the major group, and delta decrements are calculated again, this time based on the minor group's performance. Finally, the two sets of delta decrements are correlated to yield rho (ρ) and also to yield the Pearson r. The value, $1 - \rho^2$, is the disordinal component of the interaction; $\rho^2(1 - r^2)$ is the ordinal component, and $\rho^2 r^2$ is the residual variance.

Unfortunately, Jensen does not make clear just what the relationship is between correlations based on delta decrements and those based on the deltas themselves, and why a delta-decrement analysis is to be preferred to one based on the deltas themselves. An elucidation of this issue would contribute greatly to an understanding of the bias question.

Item Discrimination Procedure

Green and Draper (1972) have developed a procedure for evaluating bias by means of an item selection procedure. A summary of their procedure and their study appears in Green (1971). Seven groups of subjects were chosen—three high-SES white, one low-SES white, two low-SES black, and one low-SES Chicano—and in each group the items of an existing test in the *California Achievement Test (CAT)*-70 battery were separated into the "best" half and "worst" half on the basis of their item-test (point-biserial) correlations. Each of the seven groups was paired with each of the remaining six, and biased items were defined as those selected as "best" in one group, but not in the other. The *proportion* of biased items was defined as the number of items identified as biased, divided by the number of items in the half-test (half the number of items in the test). (In Figure 4.5 the number of "biased" items equals the number of those in quadrant P plus the number of those in quadrant Q. The proportion of biased items equals the number in quadrants P + Q, divided by the number in the half-test.) As would be expected, the proportions of biased items found in this analysis were smaller for like groups (same SES level or same ethnic group) than for unlike groups.

FIGURE 4.5. Plot of point-biseral correlations for two groups

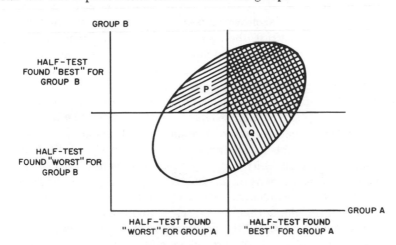

Green and Draper also correlated the scores composed of items biased against one group in a pair with scores composed of items biased against the other group in the pair and found that in many instances, even when corrected for unreliability, the correlations were low, suggesting that the tests composed of items identified as biased in this study were measuring different abilities.

The reliabilities of the full-length tests were uniformly high for all seven groups, ranging from .90 to .93. Analyses by subtests in the battery and by half-tests showed nonsignificant differences in reliability for major and minor groups.

Studies of the mean differences between the major and minor groups on the tests composed of "biased" items showed that items chosen as "best" for a group (in terms of the item point-biserials) tended to favor that group in its mean performance. That is, items chosen as "best" for a major group increased the disparity in means between the major and minor groups; items chosen as "best" for a minor group reduced the disparity in means between major and minor groups.

Studies of the foregoing kind can be highly informative and should go hand in hand with studies of item difficulty. If one considers again the model of the bivariate plot, one can imagine the point-biserial correlations for one group plotted against the point-biserial correlations for another group, as shown in Figure 4.5. As with the delta plot, the location of the bivariate plot and the correlation represented by it would reflect the degree to which the items generally discriminate to the same degree or in the same rank order for the two groups. Then too, as with the delta plot, outlier items can be identified and examined for the reasons underlying their differing biserials.

In any future study conducted along the lines followed by Green and Draper, however, it would be useful, as with studies making use of the delta-plot method, to match the groups that are being studied for ethnic differences on a relevant cognitive variable. As has been shown by several writers, (e.g., Hunter, 1975), the traditional measures of item difficulty and item discrimination are confounded and group-dependent. Unless the more sophisticated (and more demanding) ICC methods are used, it would be important to employ special control methods.

In his 1975 paper, Hunter reviewed not only the delta-plot method presented by Angoff (1975), but also the work of Green and Draper (1972) in their study of bias in item discrimination. In connection with the latter review, Hunter constructs a hypothetical test of six unbiased items of equal quality but different difficulty and shows that the point-biserial correlations would necessarily be different for the different items in such a test, simply as a result of their difficulty characteristics. Therefore, assuming that each item is more difficult for blacks than for whites, it would have to follow that different items would be selected to constitute the "best" half-tests for the two groups, *even though* the items are all of equal quality. Specifically, the overlap between the two best half-tests in his hypothetical example would be only 50 percent, and the percentage of all items defined as biased by Green and Draper also as 50%, in spite of the fact that all six items were actually unbiased. Hunter shows that these results are a necessary consequence of the items in his example not all being "centered" in difficulty for the same group. As indicated earlier, the results are unrelated to differences in quality in the items, since all items are initially equal in quality.

Hunter goes on to show that, contrary to the conclusions drawn by Green and Draper, the half-test chosen as "best" for the blacks is not different in function from the half-test chosen as "best" for the whites, since the nonlinear correlation between the tests would be 1.00 if they were long enough to be perfectly reliable.

Further, the fact that the mean black-white score difference on the half-test chosen as "best" for whites is greater than that for blacks is also a difficulty-determined result and therefore probably artifactual.

Finally, Hunter maintains that the product-moment correlations between the items "biased" against blacks and the items "biased" against whites are less than unity is probably also an artifact of the mean difference between the groups on each of the items, since their nonlinear correlations are probably close to 1.00.

On an entirely different level of discourse, it is significant that Green and Draper found items "biased," in terms of their own definition, against one group or the other, even when they compared two similar groups, e.g., two white suburban, high-SES groups. Inasmuch as it is difficult to understand what meaning "bias" can have in such a context, it can only be concluded that the method they choose for defining bias, or their definition of bias, may be in need of reconsideration. By their definition, some items would be found to be biased against one group or the other, even if the two groups were only randomly different. This would have to be so since the point-biserial index is relatively unreliable and yields considerably less than perfect correlations even between two highly similar groups. Even with Hunter's concerns aside, an alternative method of defining bias might be one that was suggested earlier in this paper: to define the maximum number of allowable disagreements by comparing the point biserials in two socially or culturally disparate groups for whom all the items are considered appropriate and acceptable. Then, any items in a black-white comparison found to be in excess of that number would be taken to be symptomatic of possible bias. Thus, for example, in comparing two groups of *different* types (white suburban, high SES vs. black urban, low SES), 38% of the items in the Green and Draper study are found to be in disagreement. In comparing two groups of the *same* type (white suburban, high SES), however, one finds that as many as 28% of the items are in disagreement. Instead, then, of reporting all 38% as "biased" items, one might use the 28% as an acceptable baseline number and report 38% − 28%, or 10%, as biased.

Item-group (Partial) Correlation

Stricker (1981) is investigating the usefulness of yet another index of item bias, suggested by F. M. Lord. The index, $r_{ig.t_\infty}$, is the correlation between success on the item and group membership, with true scores on the test (with the item omitted) partialed out. This index is highly attractive, at least in theory, since it incorporates the sense of what has already been regarded by several investigators as the criterion method. This is the method of examining the difference between the three-parameter item response curves for the two groups under consideration, a method that by its nature automatically controls, or matches, on ability. The advantage of the $r_{ig.t_\infty}$ index over the criterion method is that, like the delta-plot procedure and its variations, it is likely to be far less costly in computer software, in running time, and especially in the amount of data required to achieve desired levels of reliability. Whether it actually proves to be effective as an index of item bias remains to be seen in empirical comparisons that may be carried out in the future.

RECOMMENDATIONS FOR
TEST DEVELOPERS AND TEST USERS

Out of a review of theoretical and empirical considerations in the comparison of the several item-difficulty and item discrimination (biserial) methods come the following suggestions for evaluating the usefulness of any index of item bias:

1. Any index or procedure for evaluating bias should incorporate in it some control on the level of ability of the groups under study. The ICC method, Scheuneman's (1979; see Ironson, chapter 5) chi-square method, and the $r_{ig.t_\infty}$ index, for example, already contain this control. The delta-plot procedure has already been applied with such controls, although more relevant controls are needed than those used in the Angoff and Ford (1973) study. Any future application of the delta-plot method or the point-biserial approach used by Green and Draper should make use of such controls.
2. Supplementary to the use of controls is the use of pseudogroups, as suggested by Jensen (1980, pp. 450–451), in which two groups of the *same* ethnic background, but differing in means by an amount equal to that typically observed in cross-ethnic comparisons, are analyzed. If studies reveal that the same discrepancies are found in pseudogroup comparisons as are found in the cross-ethnic comparisons, then the conclusion might be drawn that the discrepancies are not associated with ethnic differences, but simply with ability differences. (See Schmeiser, chapter 3, for a further discussion of possible designs.)
3. The control variable should be highly correlated with, and external to, the

test; ideally, it should be a variable that has already been examined and declared free of bias. If this step is not followed, then issues of circularity in the logic of the investigation will be raised, and however trivial the circularity may be, the credibility of the investigation will be adversely affected if the circularity is not eliminated, or, at least, dealt with in some other way.

4. A baseline study should first be undertaken comparing two groups of the same ethnic background, as diverse as possible, yet remaining within the previously agreed-upon, or determined, bounds of proper administration and use of the test. One (extreme) example might be the comparison of Northeastern urban, high-SES whites vs. Southern rural, low-SES whites (but, as suggested above, after controlling on ability). Assuming that all the items are appropriate for both groups, the outer limit of the index of bias for the groups might be used as the outer limit of acceptability for the study of two ethnically different groups (again controlling on ability).

5. Related to the foregoing is that significance tests conducted in connection with item bias studies are probably less informative than they may appear to be: first, because any level of item-by-group interaction can attain statistical significance with enough cases, and second, because the choice of the error term is not a closed matter, but depends on the nature and purpose of the study.

   Also related to this area of interest is that the use of significance levels in identifying biased items is similarly not as helpful or necessary as it may appear, principally because the level of significance chosen for this purpose is purely arbitrary and often reflects only the predilections of the investigator. What is needed is simply a well-rationalized index that expresses the degree, or amount, of item-by-group interaction reflected by the item in question and a sufficiently large sample size to insure a reasonable level of stability.

6. Studies of the reliability of each proposed index should be undertaken in any comparison of the usefulness and effectiveness of the indices. Such studies can be carried out very simply by a replication of, say, a black-white comparison, and a correlation of the indices for the items in question across the two comparisons. In the delta-plot method, for example, this would involve correlating the d_i values for two replications of the study. Reliability studies of this sort can be made as complex as one wishes, but if properly executed, can lead to important and useful insights into the subtler differentiating characteristics of the various methods and their cost-benefit features.

7. In undertaking a study of the sensitivity of one or more indices of bias, it would be useful as a step in the validation process to analyze a test in which several items known or expected to be biased have been "planted," with the expectation that an appropriate statistical analysis would identify them as different in some significant way from the other items in the test.

If, in the analysis, one or another of the indices fails to identify the planted items, then clearly, that index is in need of critical examination.

At some point in this discussion of item-bias methodology some mention ought to be made of the fact that bias in its more general sense goes far beyond the statistics alone. There should be an educational or psychological rationale for deciding that a statistically biased item is indeed biased. Consider that in some of our analyses it has been found that items concerning percentages appear to be especially more difficult for blacks than for whites, relative to the other items in the tests. Guided by the statistics alone one might conclude that since such items are "biased," they should be removed from the test. On the other hand, if these items are tapping knowledges and skills that are needed for survival in our society, then, biased in the statistical sense or not, they should remain. It is plain that the problem revealed by the statistics in the analyses cited here lies, not in the items, but in the quality of the training that students receive in dealing with the knowledges and skills under consideration.

Often, too, an item found to be biased statistically may be biased in the general sense when used in one context or for one purpose, but not necessarily biased when used in other contexts and for other purposes. Consider, for example, the item, "Name three parks in Manhattan." Obviously, if this item is to be used in a general information test, one could quite reasonably argue that the item is biased and unfair; people who live at some distance from Manhattan do not have the same opportunities to learn about its parks as those who live close to it. Suppose now we introduce the fact that this item, along with others like it, is to be used to select Manhattan taxicab drivers. Under these circumstances, then, we may take the opposite position, that the item is, after all, quite fair, even if it is "biased" against non–New Yorkers, since Manhattan taxicab drivers should be expected to know their territory. We have here an illustration of the familiar principle that item fairness and test fairness are concepts and characteristics that must be evaluated in terms of the purpose of the instrument and its intended use, not solely on the basis of the bare statistics.

It may therefore be useful to work toward defusing the bias issue by acknowledging that what we are considering here are not necessarily *item-bias* methodologies but only *item-discrepancy* methodologies. It should be understood that the presence or absence of bias is unavoidably a matter for human judgment, for which the statistical analysis is only a useful tool. It would probably clear the air considerably if we reserved the use of "bias" for its important social role and referred to the methods under present consideration in appropriately parsimonious terms. These methods are, after all, only item-discrepancy methods; they should not be credited with a higher function than they are capable of serving.

REFERENCES

Alderman, D. L., & Holland, P. W. *Item performance across native language groups on the Test of English as a Foreign Language* (TOEFL Research Reports, Report 9; ETS Research Report 81-16). Princeton, N.J.: Educational Testing Service, 1981.

Angoff, W. H. *A technique for the investigation of cultural differences.* Paper presented at the annual meeting of the American Psychological Association, Honolulu, September 1972. (ERIC Document Reproduction Service No. ED 069686)

Angoff, W. H. *The investigation of test bias in the absence of an outside criterion.* Paper presented at the National Institute of Education Conference on Test Bias, Annapolis, Md., December 1975.

Angoff, W. H., & Ford, S. F. Item-race interaction on a test of scholastic aptitude. *Journal of Educational Measurement*, 1973, *10*, 95-105.

Angoff, W. H., & Herring, C. L. Study of the appropriateness of the Law School Admission Test for Canadian and American students (Report No. LSAC-71-1). In Law School Admission Council, *Reports of LSAC sponsored research: Volume II, 1970-1974.* Princeton, N.J.: Law School Admission Council, 1976.

Angoff, W. H., & Modu, C. C. *Equating the scales of the Prueba de Aptitud Academica and the Scholastic Aptitude Test* (Research Report No. 3). New York: College Entrance Examination Board, 1973.

Angoff, W. H., & Sharon, A. T. A comparison of scores earned on the Test of English as a Foreign Language by native American college students and foreign applicants to U.S. colleges. *TESOL Quarterly*, 1971, *5*, 129-136.

Angoff, W. H., & Sharon, A. T. The evaluation of differences in test performance of two or more groups. *Educational and Psychological Measurement*, 1974, *34*, 807-816.

Angoff, W. H., & Stern, J. *The equating of the scales for the Canadian and American Scholastic Aptitude Tests* (Project Report 71-24; CEEB RDR 71-72, No. 4). Princeton, N.J.: Educational Testing Service, 1971.

Breland, H. M., Stocking, M., Pinchak, B. M., & Abrams, N. *The cross-cultural stability of mental test items: An investigation of response patterns for ten sociocultural groups* (Project Report 74-2). Princeton, N.J.: Educational Testing Service, 1974.

Cardall, C., & Coffman, W. E. *A method for comparing the performance of different groups on the items in a test* (College Entrance Examination Board Research and Development Report 64-5, No. 9; ETS Research Bulletin 64-61). Princeton, N.J.: Educational Testing Service, November 1964.

Cleary, T. A., & Hilton, T. L. An investigation of item bias. *Educational and Psychological Measurement*, 1968, *28*, 61-75.

Coffman, W. E. Sex differences in responses to items in an aptitude test. In *Eighteenth yearbook of the National Council on Measurement in Education*, 1961, 117-124.

Coffman, W. E. *Evidence of cultural factors in responses of African students to items in an American test of scholastic aptitude* (Research and Development Reports). New York: College Entrance Examination Board, 1963.

Cole, N. S. *Approaches to examining bias in achievement test items.* Paper presented at the annual meeting of the American Personnel and Guidance Association, Washington, D.C., March 1978.

Echternacht, G. A quick method for determining test bias. *Educational and Psychological Measurement,* 1974, *34,* 271–280.

Green, D. R. *Racial and ethnic bias in test construction.* Monterey, Calif.: CTB/McGraw-Hill, 1971.

Green, D. R., & Draper, J. F. *Exploratory studies of bias in achievement tests.* Paper presented at the annual meeting of the American Psychological Association, Honolulu, September 1972. (ERIC Document Reproduction Service No. ED 070 794)

Hunter, J. E. *A critical analysis of the use of item means and item-test correlations to determine the presence or absence of content bias in achievement test items.* Paper presented at the National Institute of Education Conference on Test Bias, Annapolis, Md., December 1975.

Jensen, A. R. *Bias in mental testing.* New York: Free Press, 1980.

Lord, F. M. A study of item bias, using item characteristic curve theory. In Y. H. Poortinga (Ed.), *Basic problems in cross-cultural psychology.* Amsterdam: Swets and Zeitlinger, 1977. Pp. 19–29.

Lorr, M. Interrelationships of number-correct and linear scores for an amount-limit test. *Psychometrika,* 1944, *9,* 17–30.

Plake, B. S., & Hoover, H. D. An analytical method of identifying biased test items. *Journal of Experimental Education,* 1979–80, *48,* 153–154.

Rudner, L. M., Getson, P. R., & Knight, D. L. A Monte Carlo comparison of seven biased item detection techniques. *Journal of Educational Measurement,* 1980, *17,* 1–10.

Scheuneman, J. D. A new method of assessing bias in test items. *Journal of Educational Measurement,* 1979, *16,* 143–152.

Sinnott, L. W. *Differences in item performance across groups* (ETS Research Report 80-19). Princeton, N.J.: Educational Testing Service, 1980.

Stricker, L. J. *A new index of differential subgroup performance: Application to the GRE Aptitude Test* (GRE Board Professional Report GREB No. 78-7P; ETS Research Report 81-13). Princeton, N.J.: Educational Testing Service, 1981.

Thurstone, L. L. A method of scaling educational and psychological tests. *Journal of Educational Psychology,* 1925, *16,* 263–278.

Thurstone, L. L. The calibration of test items. *American Psychologist,* 1947, *2,* 103–104.

5

USE OF CHI-SQUARE AND LATENT TRAIT APPROACHES FOR DETECTING ITEM BIAS

GAIL H. IRONSON

INTRODUCTION

IN RECENT YEARS there has been a proliferation of statistical techniques for measuring item bias. These techniques differ in their conceptualization of bias, theoretical soundness, statistical complexity, sample size requirement, and cost. The two major approaches to measuring bias reviewed in this chapter share a common conceptualization of bias. This conceptualization pertains to how they address the problem of how much of the observed difference between majority and minority groups is due to ability and how much is due to bias. In any bias study, the researcher seeks to assess the bias in a measuring instrument by a criterion that is presumably less biased. Here, one can start by assuming that the test as a whole is less biased than the individual items, or that we can find some collection of relatively unbiased items. Ability is measured by the best unbiased estimate, using information from the whole test or a subset of items that are relatively unbiased. It is important to note that these approaches will not detect pervasive bias, which affects all items equally.

Thus, the chi-square and latent trait approaches deal with the problem posed by possible differences in ability of the samples by estimating ability from information provided by the test as a whole and then comparing performance of different ethnic groups for subjects matched on ability. Items are examined for bias based on the distribution of correct responses across ability levels. *An item is considered unbiased if individuals with equal ability, but from different groups, have the same probability of answering the item*

The author would like to thank Robert L. Brennan, Gregory Camilli, Michael V. Levine, Robert L. Linn, Robin I. Lissak, Frederic M. Lord, Leonard A. Marascuilo, Ronald J. Mead, and Janice D. Scheuneman for facilitating work on this chapter and offering many helpful suggestions. Of course, the responsibility for the accuracy of all statements made in the chapter rests with the author.

117

correctly. As Shepard, Camilli, and Averill (1980) have noted, "It is presumed that it is worthwhile to use internal criteria to eliminate relatively biased items, and that, when an external criterion is ultimately applied, the total test will be less biased as a result" (p. 6).

These procedures are designed to be insensitive to the different shapes of the distribution of the group abilities in question. Scheuneman (1980b) pointed out that "because they attempt to circumvent the problems posed by differences in ability, these procedures are intuitively pleasing and very promising for the study of bias" (p. 141).

Latent trait theory, or item response theory, makes use of an *item characteristic curve* (ICC). Several sources are available for introductory reading on this topic (Hambleton & Cook, 1977; Hambleton, Swaminathan, Cook, Eignor, & Gifford, 1978; Warm, 1978). ICCs depict the relationship between ability and the probability of answering the item correctly. In general, as the former increases, so does the probability of the latter. The curves are usually described by a cumulative logistic or normal ogive function. Three parameters may be used to describe such a curve:

1. the difficulty parameter, given by the ability level corresponding to the inflection point of the curve (e.g., if guessing is zero, the difficulty is the ability level at which the probability of a correct response is .50);
2. the discrimination value, proportional to the slope of the curve at the inflection point; and
3. the probability of examinees of infinitely low ability getting the item right (sometimes called the *guessing parameter*).

An item that is *unbiased* should have the *same* ICC in both groups. *Biased* items, such as those pictured in Figure 5.1, will have *different* ICCs. One can see in Item A that, for equal ability whites and blacks, whites have a greater chance of getting the item right. Thus, the item is biased against blacks. Item B illustrates nonuniform bias. At low abilities, the item is biased against whites; at high abilities, it is biased against blacks.

The most statistically complex latent trait model makes use of all three parameters in describing an item in each group. The measures most often used to index bias for the three-parameter model are: (1) the area between the curves (Rudner, 1977a) and (2) the hypothesis test of the equality of the three parameters across ethnic groups (Lord, 1977, 1980).

Another latent trait model, the *Rasch model*, uses only one parameter, the difficulty parameter, to describe an item. The discrimination of the items is set to a constant. The two most common procedures used for measuring bias with this model (Draba, 1977; Durovic, 1975a, 1975b; Wright, Mead, & Draba, 1976) are to examine the differences in difficulty levels of an item across ethnic groups and to examine the fit of the item in each ethnic group. Items C and D (Figure 5.1) illustrate these types of bias.

The *chi-square techniques* (Scheuneman, 1979b; Shepard et al., 1980)

FIGURE 5.1. Illustration of items biased by various techniques

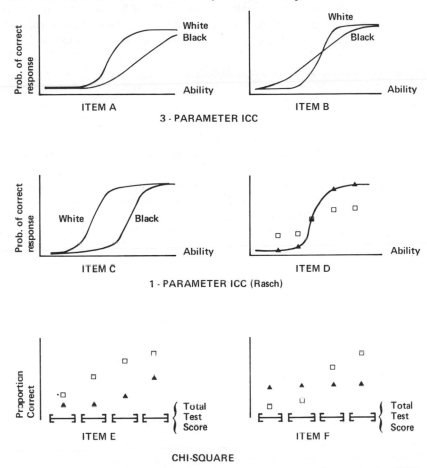

may be viewed as rough practical variations of the ICC procedure. The ability scale is divided into discrete units; the continuous curve is replaced by estimation of a few points. Therefore, an assumption of a theoretical model for the curve is not necessary. Performance of the ethnic groups is compared within each ability category. Items E and F illustrate this approach.

The *three-parameter ICC* procedure is the most theoretically sound and statistically complex procedure for measuring bias (Bejar, 1980; Hunter, 1975; Lord, 1980; Petersen, 1977). The sample invariant nature of the parameter estimates makes it less likely to artifactually label an item as biased when true differences in group means are present. Furthermore, difficulty and discrimination indices are less confounded. Thus, it offers several important advantages over the delta-plot procedure, which is greatly influenced by the distribution of ability (for groups differing in ability, a large p

difference is expected for discriminating items), confounds proportion correct with guessing and discrimination, and is limited to identifying bias only where an item favors the group as a whole (i.e., it misses nonuniform bias) (see Angoff, chapter 4, for a detailed description of the delta-plot method).

Several investigators (Craig & Ironson, 1981; Ironson & Subkoviak, 1979; Rudner & Convey, 1978; Rudner, Getson, & Knight, 1980; Shepard et al., 1980; Subkoviak, Mack, & Ironson, 1981) have found empirical support for the three-parameter ICC procedure. This procedure, however, requires a high degree of statistical sophistication, a program (LOGIST) that is costly to run (though available at no charge), and a large sample size.

In contrast, the Rasch model is less complex and the program (BICAL) is less costly to run (though must be purchased), and the model requires comparatively smaller samples. The chi-square type procedures are the easiest to understand, are the least costly, and require the smallest sample size. In fact, computations can be done by hand. Although they are less elegant statistically, they offer a very practical and attractive alternative to the latent trait models.

A general review of the comparative theoretical and empirical validity of classical and latent trait approaches to measuring item bias may be found in Ironson (1981).

The purpose of this chapter is to describe the computational and conceptual aspects of the procedures. The chapter does not focus on empirical studies except insofar as it helps in comparing or evaluating an index. The procedures are reviewed in ascending order of complexity: from chi-square techniques, to the Rasch model, to the three-parameter model.

REVIEW OF CHI-SQUARE TYPE TECHNIQUES

In this section, two chi-square techniques are described in detail. The first, $\chi^2_{correct}$ (Scheuneman, 1975, 1979b), focuses on correct responses to a given item. The second, χ^2_{full} (Camilli, 1979; Nungester, 1977), includes both correct and incorrect responses in the analysis. The following topics are covered: (1) definition, (2) assumptions, (3) choice of ability intervals, (4) calculations for chi-square indices, (5) some procedures for further interpretation, (6) hypotheses being tested, (7) other procedures for analyzing contingency tables, and (8) comparison of $\chi^2_{correct}$ and χ^2_{full}.

Definition

According to Scheuneman (1975), "an item is unbiased if, for all individuals having the same score on a homogeneous subtest containing the item, the proportion of individuals getting the item correct is the same for each population group being considered" (p. 2).

Several investigators (Baker, 1981; Camilli, 1979) have noted that

Scheuneman's (1979b) procedure is based only on correct responses to an item. This prompted Camilli (Shepard et al., 1980) to adopt a χ^2_{full} procedure, which incorporates both correct and incorrect responses in the calculation of the chi-square index. It is interesting to note, though, that Nungester (1977) had used this procedure previously. Both procedures, $\chi^2_{correct}$ and χ^2_{full}, involve only two steps: (1) three to five ability intervals are established, and (2) the chi-square value is then calculated and tested for statistical significance.

Assumptions

The chi-square techniques assume that a test is (1) valid, so that the total test score may be used as an estimate of ability, (2) reliable within usual standards, and (3) homogeneous. One of the advantages of the techniques is the absence of an assumption about the shape of the distribution of observed scores. These scores do not have to be normally distributed or representative of the distribution of ability in the population of interest. Sample size, however, is constrained by the required expected cell frequencies.

Choice of Ability Intervals

The first step in performing any chi-square procedure is to divide the total score scale into ability intervals or score levels. To do this, one needs several distributions (use Table 5.1). In columns 2 and 3, standard frequency distributions of total test scores are given separately for each group. In columns 5 and 6, distributions of the number of correct responses to the given item for each ethnic group are given. If χ^2_{full} is to be calculated, the distributions of the number of incorrect responses given in columns 7 and 8 should also be obtained. Scheuneman (1979b, p. 145) suggested the following three criteria for determining the intervals:

1. A minimum of 10 to 20 observed correct responses per cell should be used. Expected frequencies should be at least 5 per cell, a usual recommendation for the chi-square procedure (calculation of expected frequencies is described in the next section).
2. Some minimum number of incorrect responses in each score interval (not necessarily in each ethnic group) should be expected. If the χ^2_{full} is used, an expected frequency of 5 per cell is also needed for the incorrect responses. Observed incorrect responses of 10 to 20 per cell will usually give the required expected number. This should be checked, however.
3. Within the limits of satisfying the above constraints, one must decide whether ability intervals are to cover approximately the same width in terms of total score scale, or approximately the same number of people (ethnic groups combined); or, as Scheuneman suggests, "so that the smallest cell frequency is about the same at each ability level (except where slightly larger cell frequencies are required to include a sufficient

TABLE 5.1. Distributions for Selecting Interval Cutoffs: Item 8

Total Score Scale	Number with Each Score		Cum. Total	Correct		Incorrect	
	White	Black		White	Black	White	Black
1	0	6	6	0	0	0	6
2	1	4	11	0	0	1	4
3	1	15	27	0	0	1	15
4	2	41	60	0	3	2	38
5	3	56	129	0	2	3	54
6	13	71	213	4	5	9	66
7	17	98	328	2	12	15	86
8	24	128	480	1	18	23	110
9	36	148	664	4	23	32	125
10	28	142	834	6	17	22	125
11	58	129	1021	16	24	42	105
12	57	112	1180	9	18	48	94
13	69	96	1355	9	19	60	77
14	80	92	1527	15	16	65	76
15	74	85	1686	15	13	59	72
16	107	81	1874	25	19	82	62
17	78	59	2011	19	12	59	47
18	78	60	2149	23	17	55	43
19	93	60	2302	25	14	68	46
20	95	47	2444	35	12	60	35
21	110	33	2587	45	8	65	25
22	109	32	2728	52	12	57	20
23	93	21	2842	51	9	42	12
24	96	20	2958	43	9	53	11
25	86	11	3055	48	4	38	7
26	80	7	3142	47	2	33	5
27	65	7	3214	41	2	24	5
28	54	8	3276	32	5	22	3
29	47	7	3330	35	5	12	2
30	54	7	3391	39	4	15	3
31	29	0	3420	25	0	4	0
32	28	4	3452	28	4	0	0
33	14	2	3468	14	2	0	0
34	12	1	3481	12	1	0	0
35	2	0	3483	2	0	0	0
TOTAL:	1793	1630					

number of incorrect responses)" (p. 145). Usually, 3 to 5 intervals are chosen. With larger samples, the number of intervals may be increased.

At first, it may appear simple to divide the combined populations into quintiles, or five equally spaced score intervals. Practical problems generally prevent this from working smoothly. Table 5.1 shows data for a difficult item ($p = .30$) given to roughly equal-sized samples of blacks and whites. Equal score width intervals would yield intervals of 1–7, 8–14, 15–21, 22–28, and 29–35. To satisfy a minimum of 10 observed correct responses per cell for whites, however, the cutoff in the lowest interval must be raised to 9. In addition, the top interval of 29–35 must be changed if one wants to perform the χ^2_{full}. With a lower limit of 29, the expected black incorrect frequency is below 5 (3.65). Changing the top category to 28–35 will bring the expected frequency to 6.58.* Note that had the division been made on the basis of quintiles, $3483/5 = 697$, the starting levels would have been 1–9, 10–13, 14–18, 19–23, and 24–35, allowing wider intervals for the end categories. These work well for this example, but for many applications where the sample sizes are smaller, the category score levels may need to be adjusted.

In general, most of the difficulty in setting intervals stems from the necessity of having an adequate number of observations from each group in the upper and lower ability intervals. This is complicated by several factors, including the overlap of the groups on the total score scale, the relative sizes of the groups, the difficulty of the item, and whether $\chi^2_{correct}$ or χ^2_{full} are to be performed. These factors are discussed below.

1. In cases with roughly equal-sized groups but with a sizable difference in total score means, the lower limit of the top category is usually set by securing enough high-ability blacks who get the item wrong; the upper limit of the bottom category is set by securing enough low-ability whites who get the item right. In addition, expected frequencies may be low in the following categories:
   a. low-ability whites getting it right;
   b. high-ability blacks getting it right;
   c. high-ability whites getting it wrong;
   d. low-ability whites getting it wrong.
2. If the black group is smaller, as is typically the case, intervals will need to be changed to bring their expected frequency to the accepted level.
3. For an easy item, the top ability interval usually needs to be expanded so that enough people get the item wrong; for a difficult item, the bottom ability interval needs to be expanded so that enough people get the item right (as is the case in Table 5.1).
4. Since $\chi^2_{correct}$ does not specifically consider incorrect responses, it does not constrain the expected frequency of incorrect responses. Often, as in the example, the top category can be narrower with $\chi^2_{correct}$. This is particularly acute with an easy item, since it is hard to find high-ability whites and blacks who get it wrong. For this reason, Scheuneman's $\chi^2_{correct}$ procedure handles easy items more readily than Camilli's χ^2_{full} procedure.

As mentioned previously, at the current time the computation of chi-square is a two-step procedure. First, the distributions listed in Table 5.1 are used to set the interval score limits. Next, these score limits are set (usually

---

*This change of interval due to one score point can have a marked effect on the calculated chi-square. With the score of 28 in the second ability interval, $\chi^2_{correct}$ is 8.564 (4 df, $n.s.$), χ^2_{full} is 14.11 (5 df, $p < .05$); with 28 in the top interval, $\chi^2_{correct}$ drops to 7.03 (4 df, $n.s.$), and χ^2_{full} drops to 10.63 (5 df, $p < .05$).

individually for each item) and the second set of output is obtained (Table 5.2). Expected frequencies should be checked, and if they are adequate, interpretation of the results should follow. This procedure can be done by hand.

Several computer programs are available to facilitate computation. One advantage of the χ^2_{full} procedure is that, once the ability-score interval limits are set, the chi-square can be calculated by use of the usual chi-square program included in most standard statistical packages. In addition, an algorithm has been suggested by Camilli (personal communication, 1980) to enable the whole process to be performed in one computer program. Finally, Rudner (1977d) has developed a program to calculate the $\chi^2_{correct}$.

Calculations for Chi-square Indices

Intermediate steps for computation of Scheuneman's $\chi^2_{correct}$ are shown in Table 5.2, and of Camilli's χ^2_{full} in Tables 5.2 and 5.3. The example used here is adopted from Scheuneman (1979b) because the sample sizes are realistic for most practical uses.

Scheuneman's $\chi^2_{correct}$. Once the ability-score intervals are established, three pieces of information are obtained in Table 5.2:

1. the *number* of each ethnic group at each total score interval,
2. the *observed frequency* getting the item correct in each ability-score level within each ethnic group, and

TABLE 5.2. Computation of Scheuneman's $\chi^2_{correct}$

Score Level	Number with Scores in Each Level			Obtained Frequency (Item Correct)		
	Black N_{1j}	White N_{2j}	Total $N_{.j}$	Black O_{1j}	White O_{2j}	Total $O_{.j}$
($j = 1$)13-14	25	315	340	22	300	322
($j = 2$)12	24	110	134	18	99	117
($j = 3$)10-11	48	118	166	23	93	116
($j = 4$)1-9	65	92	157	14	33	47
TOTAL	$N_{B.} = 162$	$N_{W.} = 635$	$N_{..} = 797$	$O_{B.} = 77$	$O_{W.} = 525$	$O_{..} = 602$

Score Level	Proportion Correct $= O/N$			Expected Frequency	
	Black $P_{1j} = O_{1j}/N_{ij}$	White $P_{2j} = O_{2j}/N_{2j}$	$P_{.j} = O_{.j}/N_{.j}$	Black $E_{1j} = P_{.j}N_{1j}$	White $E_{2j} = P_{.j}N_{2j}$
($j = 1$)	.88	.9524	.9471	23.68	298.32
($j = 2$)	.75	.9	.8731	20.96	96.04
($j = 3$)	.4792	.7881	.6988	33.54	82.46
($j = 4$)	.2154	.3587	.2994	19.46	27.54
TOTAL	$P_{BT} = .4753$	$P_{WT} = .8267$	$P_{(B+W)T} = .7553$	97.64	504.36

Note: Based on data from Scheuneman (1979).

3. the *expected frequency* getting the item correct within each ethnic group if the item had a common p value within the interval.

In order to clarify how each of these quantities is calculated, the following notation is introduced. Let i and j be subscripts denoting ethnic group and score level, respectively. Thus, in this example, i and j can take on these values:

$$i = \begin{cases} 1 \text{ black} \\ \\ 2 \text{ white} \end{cases} \qquad j = \begin{cases} 1 \text{ highest-score (13–14) group} \\ 2 \\ 3 \\ 4 \text{ lowest-score (1–9) group} \end{cases}$$

N_{ij} = number of people in the ith ethnic group and jth score group
O_{ij} = observed frequency of correct (O'_{ij} = incorrect) response in the ith ethnic group and jth score group
E_{ij} = expected frequency of correct (or E'_{ij} incorrect) response in the ith ethnic group and jth score group
P_{ij} = proportion of subjects getting the item correct in the ith ethnic group and jth score group

The Ns are obtained from the frequency distribution for the entire test; Os are obtained from the frequency distribution of the number correct (or incorrect for O's in Table 5.3) on a particular item.

In Table 5.2, N_{13} = 48 blacks received a score of 10 or 11 on the test. Of these, O_{13} = 23 got the item right and O'_{13} = 25 (Table 5.3) got it wrong. The E values are calculated by

$$E_{ij} = P_{.j} N_{ij}, \tag{1}$$

where $P_{.j} = (O_{1j} + O_{2j})/(N_{1j} + N_{2j})$. For example, E_{13} is the expected frequency for blacks in ability level 3.

$$E_{13} = P_{.3} N_{13} = \left(\frac{O_{13} + O_{23}}{N_{13} + N_{23}} \right) N_{13}$$

$$E_{13} = \left(\frac{23 + 93}{48 + 118} \right) 48 = (.6988)\ 48 = 33.54.$$

$P_{.j}$ is the best unbiased estimate of the difficulty of a given item for the combined group in a given ability level. In other words, if an item were unbiased it should be equally difficult for both blacks and whites. The best estimate of what this "common" difficulty would be is $P_{.j}$, which is just the total number of blacks and whites getting the item correct in a given interval divided by the total number of blacks and whites scoring in that interval. In Table 5.3, $Q_{.j}$ is the unbiased estimate of proportion incorrect within an ability interval; $Q_{.j} = 1 - P_{.j}$ or $Q_{.j} = (O'_{1j} + O'_{2j})/(N_{1j} + N_{2j})$. Values for obtained, expected, and proportion correct and incorrect are reported in Tables 5.2 and 5.3.

TABLE 5.3. Computation of $\chi^2_{incorrect}$

Score Level	Obtained Frequency (Item Incorrect)		Proportion Incorrect	Expected Frequency	
	Black O'_{1j}	White O'_{2j}	$Q_{\cdot j} = 1 - P_{\cdot j}$	Black $E'_{1j} = (1 - P_{\cdot j})N_{1j}$	White $E'_{2j} = (1 - P_{\cdot j})N_{2j}$
13–14	3	15	.0529	1.3225	16.6635
12	6	11	.1269	3.0456	13.959
10–11	25	25	.3012	14.4576	35.5416
1–9	51	59	.7006	45.539	64.4552

Note: Based on same data as Table 5.2.

To calculate Scheuneman's $\chi^2_{correct}$, only the correct answers (see Table 5.2) are used. The equation is:

$$\chi^2_{correct} + \sum_{j=1}^{J} \frac{(E_{1j} - O_{1j})^2}{E_{1j}} + \sum_{j=1}^{J} \frac{(E_{2j} - O_{2j})^2}{E_{2j}}. \tag{2}$$
$$\text{(blacks)} \qquad\qquad \text{(whites)}$$

For this example, there will be eight contributions, one for each ability level in each ethnic group.

$$= \frac{(23.68 - 22)^2}{23.68} + \frac{(20.96 - 18)^2}{20.96} + \cdots + \frac{(82.46 - 93)^2}{82.46}$$
$$+ \frac{(27.54 - 33)^2}{27.54}$$

These quantities sum to 7.912. Scheuneman suggests using $(I - 1)(J - 1)$ degrees of freedom where I is the number of ethnic groups and J is the number of score groups. In this example, a value of $\chi^2_3(.95) = 7.81$ would be necessary as a cutoff for labeling an item as biased. Since the obtained value of 7.912 is greater, the item is labeled as biased. A word of caution is appropriate here. Scheuneman (1979b) stressed that "because the modified procedure does not include incorrect responses, the obtained distribution of chi-square values may not always approximate the appropriate chi-square distribution, particularly if the sample sizes for the groups being compared are quite different, or the cell frequencies are all very large" (p. 147).

Other indices of the amount of bias in a given item include the size of chi-square value, which is only appropriate if the number of intervals is the same for each item, and the p value associated with the chi-square, which is only an approximation since the distribution of the statistic is not chi-square.

Several investigators besides Scheuneman have noted that the $\chi^2_{correct}$ index is not distributed as a chi-square statistic (Baker, 1981; Camilli, 1979; Marascuilo & Slaughter, 1981). Obviously, it does not include the incorrect responses. In addition, Marascuilo and Slaughter (1981) point out that the expected values in the columns do not sum to the observed values in the columns (for example, black expected values sum to 97.64, but the observed values sum to 77). The resulting statistic cannot have a chi-square distribution.

Signed $\chi^2_{correct}$. Using a large chi-square value as an index of bias gives no indication of the direction of bias. Ironson and Subkoviak (1979) and Shepard et al. (1980) have used signed indices to specify the direction of bias. Within each ability level and for each ethnic group is a contribution of $(O - E)^2/E$ to the chi-square index of bias. If the observed number of correct responses for an ethnic group is less than expected, an item may be considered biased against that group at that ability level. Assigning one sign to bias against blacks (say, positive) and another sign to bias against whites (say, negative), one may attach a sign to the $(O - E)^2/E$ contribution, summing these over ability levels and ethnic groups to arrive at a signed chi-square. For the item in Table 5.2, for equal ability whites and blacks, whites have a greater chance of getting the item right. Thus, the item is biased against blacks, and the $\chi^2_{correct}$ would have a positive sign.

Signed χ^2_{full}. For Camilli's χ^2_{full} procedure, one sign may be attached to each 2×2 table before summing over ability levels. If the direction of bias is consistent across ability levels, the signed and unsigned indices result in the same conclusions about item bias. However, when discrepancies are large, but compensating across ability groups (such as when the item characteristic curves cross), the signed index will be smaller.

Camilli's χ^2_{full}. There are several different equations available for calculating Camilli's χ^2_{full}. The first, adapted from Camilli (personal communication, 1980), involves computing a second table (see Table 5.3) for the incorrect responses. The χ^2_{full} will be the sum of the chi-squares from the correct and incorrect tables:

$$\chi^2_{full} = \chi^2_{correct} + \chi^2_{incorrect}$$

The equation may be written as follows:

$$\chi^2_{full} \begin{cases} \chi^2_{correct} = \sum_{j=1}^{J} \frac{(E_{1j} - O_{1j})^2}{E_{1j}} + \sum_{j=1}^{J} \frac{(E_{2j} - O_{2j})^2}{E_{2j}} \\ + \\ \chi^2_{incorrect} = \sum_{j=1}^{J} \frac{(E'_{1j} - O'_{1j})^2}{E'_{ij}} + \sum_{j=1}^{J} \frac{(E'_{2j} - O'_{2j})^2}{E'_{2j}} \end{cases} \qquad (3)$$

where:

$E'_{ij} = (1 - P_{.j})N_{ij} = Q_{.j}N_{ij}$, for example,
$E'_{13} = (1 - P_{.3})N_{13} = Q_{.3}N_{13} = (.3012)\,48 = 14.4576$, and
O'_{ij} = observed number of people in ethnic group i and score level j who get the item wrong.

Calculations for the χ^2_{full} illustrating the contribution from each individual cell (ethnic group, score level, and correct/incorrect response) are given in Table 5.4 using Equation 3:

$$\chi^2_{full} = \chi^2_{correct} + \chi^2_{incorrect} = 7.91 + 17.72 = 25.63$$

$$= \frac{(23.68 - 22)^2}{23.68} + \frac{(20.96 - 18)^2}{20.96} + \cdots + \frac{(35.5416 - 25)^2}{35.5416}$$

$$+ \frac{(64.4552 - 59)^2}{64.4552}$$

The degrees of freedom for testing this statistic have been defined by Holland (Scheuneman, 1981, p. 63, n.1), Mellenbergh (1980), and Scheuneman as $(i - 1)j$ [i = ethnic groups, j = ability levels] = $(2 - 1) 4 = 4$, in this example.

A second method for calculating χ^2_{full} has been offered by Holland (Scheuneman, 1981, p. 63, n.1). The advantage of this method is that it can be calculated from the correct response information found in Table 5.2. The equation is:

$$\chi^2_{J(I-1)} = \sum_{j=1}^{J} \frac{(E_{1j} - O_{1j})^2}{E_{1j}(1 - P_j)} + \sum_{j=1}^{J} \frac{(E_{2j} - O_{2j})^2}{E_{2j}(1 - P_j)} \qquad (4)$$
$$\quad\quad\quad\quad \text{(black)} \quad\quad\quad\quad\quad \text{(white)}$$

$$\chi^2_{4(2-1)} = \frac{(23.68 - 22)^2}{23.68(1 - .9471)} + \frac{(20.96 - 18)^2}{20.96(1 - .8731)}$$

$$+ \frac{(33.54 - 23)^2}{33.54(1 - .6988)} + \frac{(19.46 - 14)^2}{19.46(1 - .2994)}$$

$$+ \frac{(298.32 - 300)^2}{298.32(1 - .9471)} + \frac{(96.04 - 99)^2}{96.04(1 - .8731)}$$

$$+ \frac{(82.46 - 93)^2}{82.46(1 - .6988)} + \frac{(27.54 - 33)^2}{27.54(1 - .2994)}$$

$$= 18.730(\text{black}) + 6.916(\text{white}) = 25.647.$$

Finally, the easiest way to calculate χ^2_{full} is by constructing a 2 × I table (right/wrong by ethnic group) for each level of ability. Thus:

	$j = 1$		$j = 2$		$j = 3$		$j = 4$	
Black	22	3	18	6	23	25	14	51
White	300	15	99	11	93	25	33	59

where the four levels will each contribute to the overall chi-square by using the following equation:

$$\begin{array}{|c|c|} \hline a & b \\ \hline c & d \\ \hline \end{array} \qquad \frac{N(ad - bc)^2}{(a + c)\,(b + d)\,(a + b)\,(c + d)} \qquad (5)$$

$$\chi^2_{full} = \chi^2_1 + \chi^2_2 + \chi^2_3 + \chi^2_4 = 2.42 + 4.00 + 15.47 + 3.73 = 25.62$$

Some Procedures for Further Interpretation

Having determined that the chi-square is significant, and the item is therefore biased, one might wish to investigate the level at which the differences are most marked. Looking at the difference in p values between blacks and whites, we see that at each level whites have a higher proportion of correct answers. This seems to be most pronounced at score level 3, where the white $p = .7881$ and the black $p = .4792$.

The equality of p values at each score level can be formally tested by use of a chi-square with 1 degree of freedom. Familywise error rate can be controlled by dividing an overall $\alpha = .05$ by the number of score levels. Since $.05/4 = .0125$, the value of chi-square necessary for rejection of the hypothesis of equality of p's is $\chi^2_{1,(.9875)} = 6.25$. The only value exceeding this is 15.47 at level 3.

If there are a priori reasons for believing an item will be biased against one specific group, the statistical power of the test may be improved by performing a directional test using normal curve statistics. The hypothesis of equality of p's is rejected if Z critical <

$$Z_{obtained} = \frac{p_{1j} - p_{2j}}{\sqrt{p._j(1 - p._j)\left(\dfrac{1}{N_{1j}} + \dfrac{1}{N_{2j}}\right)}} \qquad (6)$$

TABLE 5.4. Illustrations and Contributions for Three Methods of Calculating χ^2_{full}

Score Level	Correct Black	Correct White	Incorrect Black	Incorrect White	Holland Black	Holland White	2 × 2 Tables
(j = 1) 13–14	.1192	.0095	2.1278	.1661	2.253	.1788	2.42
(j = 2) 12	.4180	.0912	2.8659	.6272	3.294	.7189	4.001
(j = 3) 10–11	3.3122	1.3472	7.6840	3.1257	10.997	4.473	15.475
(j = 4) 1–9	1.5319	1.0825	.6549	.4617	2.187	1.545	3.729
TOTAL	5.4435	2.5304	13.3326	4.3807	18.730	6.916	
	$\chi^2_{cor} = 7.912$		$\chi^2_{inc} = 17.713$		$\chi^2 = 25.65$		$\chi^2_{2 \times 2} = 25.62$
		$\chi^2_{full} = \chi^2_{cor} + \chi^2_{inc} = 25.63$					

Note: Based on same data as Table 5.2.

For the data in Table 5.2,

$$Z_1 = -1.56 \qquad Z_2 = -2.00 \qquad Z_3 = -3.93 \qquad Z_4 = -1.94$$

Since $Z_{\text{critical } (.0125 = .05/4)} = -2.24$, the bias is concentrated in the third score group.

Hypotheses Being Tested

Marascuilo and Slaughter (1981) point out that the alternative hypotheses being tested by χ^2_{full} and χ^2_{correct} are different. Let $\Delta_j = p_{1j} - p_{2j}$ so that Δ_j represents the p value difference between whites and blacks at ability level j. Then the hypothesis being tested by use of the χ^2_{full} is given by a set of j pairwise hypotheses:

$$H_o: \Delta_j = 0.$$
$$H_a: \Delta_j \neq 0.$$

Note that the alternative makes no statement about the equality or inequality of the Δ_j values.

The hypothesis being tested by the use of χ^2_{correct} is:

$$H_o: \Delta_1 = \Delta_2 = \cdots = \Delta_j = 0$$
$$H_a: \psi \neq 0,$$

where $\psi = \sum\limits_{j=1}^{J} d_j \Delta_j$ and $\sum\limits_{j=1}^{J} d_j = 0.$

The alternative states that at least one contrast involving the Δ_j's is different from zero. Which contrast must be determined by a complex post hoc analysis. The alternative here is difficult to interpret, but the method will have its greatest utility when not all of the Δ_j's $= 0$. However, since the Scheuneman χ^2_{correct} alternative is an omnibus form of χ^2_{full} (because Scheuneman tests all possible contrasts in the Δ_j values), it has less power than χ^2_{full}, provided comparisons are restricted to investigations of the Δ_j values alone (Marascuilo & Slaughter, 1981).

Other Procedures for Analyzing Contingency Tables

Marascuilo and Slaughter (1981) suggest four other nonparametric techniques for analyzing bias. Among these, the two most practical techniques will be described here.

A procedure referred to as method 3 can be used to test the null hypothesis:

$$H_o: \Delta_1 = \Delta_2 = \cdots = \Delta_j = 0 \text{ against the alternative}$$
$$H_a: \Delta_1 = \Delta_2 = \cdots = \Delta_j = \Delta_o.$$

Thus, the alternative states that all the Δ_j (or p value differences between ethnic groups at level j) are equal to a common value. Note that the alternative for Camilli's χ^2_{full} makes no statement about the equality or inequality of the Δ_j's. In terms of latent trait theory, method 3 represents a test of identity of ICCs versus an alternative of parallelism. Method 3 is based on the assumption that, if a difference exists, it is constant for all levels of j. The simplest way to test this is given by Maxwell (1961). The statistic

$$Z = \frac{1}{\sqrt{J}} \sum_{j=1}^{J} Z_j \qquad (7)$$

is calculated. In this example,

$$= \frac{1}{\sqrt{4}}(-1.56 - 2.00 - 3.93 - 1.96) = -4.71.$$

Using the normal probability or distribution table, Z obtained is less than $Z_{\text{critical}} = -1.645$ ($\alpha = .05$); H_o is rejected. A second procedure, formulated by Cochran (1954), enables one to calculate confidence intervals for Δ_o.

Method 4 in the Marascuilo and Slaughter (1981) paper tests the hypothesis:

$$H_o: \Delta_1 = \Delta_2 = \cdots - \Delta_j = \Delta_o \text{ against the alternative}$$
$$H_a: H_o \text{ is false.}$$

In this procedure, the null hypothesis is that the differences in p values at each level are equal to a constant. The other null hypotheses all set the difference to zero. Method 4 is sensitive to a score group by ethnic-group interaction. It provides a test of parallelism against nonparallelism, i.e., it is a test of equal item discrimination. If the null hypothesis is rejected, the item has differential levels of bias across the range of the test. From Marascuilo and McSweeney (1977, chap. 9), one calculates:

$$U_o' = \sum_{j=1}^{J} \hat{W}_j(\hat{\Delta}_j - \hat{\Delta}_o)^2 \qquad (8)$$

where $\hat{\Delta}_o = \sum_{j=1}^{J} \dfrac{\hat{W}_j \hat{\Delta}_j}{\sum\limits_{j=1}^{J} \hat{W}_j}$ with $\hat{W}_j = \dfrac{1}{SE_{\hat{\Delta}_j}^2}$.

For the example,

$$SE_{\hat{\Delta}_1}^2 = .004368 \qquad SE_{\hat{\Delta}_2}^2 = .008631 \qquad SE_{\hat{\Delta}_3}^2 = .006614$$

$$SE_{\hat{\Delta}_4}^2 = .005100. \text{ Therefore,}$$

$$\hat{\Delta}_o = \frac{\dfrac{-.0724}{.004368} + \cdots + \dfrac{-.1433}{.005100}}{\dfrac{1}{.004368} + \cdots + \dfrac{1}{.005100}} = -.1571$$

U_o' is compared to χ_{J-1}^2. Here, H_o is not rejected.

Marascuilo and Slaughter (1981) suggest using methods 3, 4, and χ^2_{full} in combination. This allows one to study guessing, difficulty, and discrimination. Further procedures, and details of those discussed here, may be found in that paper.

Several investigators (Camilli, 1979; Marascuilo & Slaughter, 1981; Mellenbergh, 1980) have suggested the use of *log-linear models* as an efficient way to analyze contingency tables for bias. The responses to each item can be conceptualized in a three-way table: score level × ethnic group × response (correct or incorrect). To use the model, one must carefully specify the null and alternative hypotheses. The models may be used to test whether there is a main effect of score group, ethnic group, or an interaction of score group and ethnic group. If a model including only a constant and score group can adequately fit the data, there is no bias. If a term including ethnic group is necessary in addition, then there is uniform bias.. (For all score categories, the difference between response ratios of blacks and whites is constant.) If that model does not fit the data, a parameter for the interaction between score group and ethnic group is needed, and the item is nonuniformly biased.

Good general explanations of log-linear models have been presented by Bishop, Fienberg, and Holland (1975), Fienberg (1977), and Knoke and Burke (1980). In addition, computer programs such as ECTA (Goodman & Fay, 1974) and BMDP3F (Dixon & Brown, 1977) are available. Finally, the most detailed paper applying these models to bias is Mellenbergh's (1980).

Comparison of $\chi^2_{correct}$ and χ^2_{full}

In this section, the differences and similarities between the two indices are discussed.

Differences.   The major differences between $\chi^2_{correct}$ and χ^2_{full} are examined first.

1. *Statistical distribution.* Camilli's χ^2_{full} is distributed as a chi-square statistic. As has been noted by Scheuneman and several other investigators, Scheuneman's $\chi^2_{correct}$ is not. Scheuneman includes only correct responses, whereas Camilli's χ^2_{full} includes both correct and incorrect responses. There is no known sampling distribution for the $\chi^2_{correct}$ statistic.

2. *Hypotheses tested.* Each method has power against some very specific alternatives. Method 1 may be seen as a test based on partitioning of a total chi-square into four orthogonal pairwise comparisons. Scheuneman tests whether or not there is some contrast involving comparisons that is different from zero.

3. *Degrees of freedom and power.* $\chi^2_{correct}$ uses $(I - 1)(J - 1)$, where I is the number of ethnic groups and J is the number of score groups. χ^2_{full} uses $(I - 1)J$. As the degrees of freedom increase, the critical value of chi-square necessary to reject the null hypothesis increases, making it more difficult to reject the null hypothesis. However, the obtained value of χ^2_{full}

will be greater than χ^2_{correct} because χ^2_{full} includes more cells (the incorrect responses) in the computation. In determining which procedure is more powerful, one must ascertain whether the increase in one degree of freedom is offset by the larger chi-square obtained from the addition of J cells from the incorrect responses. χ^2_{full} may be broken down into the sum of $\chi^2_{\text{correct}} + \chi^2_{\text{incorrect}}$. A discussion of the relative contribution of items to the two components will be undertaken later in the chapter.

4. *Cutoffs for ability intervals.* With some items, different cutoffs for the score intervals may be necessary for the two procedures. In general, the inclusion of the incorrect responses in χ^2_{full} will decrease the lower limit of the uppermost ability interval. This accommodates the requirement that an adequate expected frequency of *incorrect* responses be present. The hardest place on the ability continuum to find an adequate number of incorrect responses is among very able people. This is especially true if the item is easy. Thus, Camilli's χ^2_{full} is likely to have a wider top ability interval with a lower cutoff.

5. *Sensitivity to contributions of different cells.* Scheuneman's χ^2_{correct} is relatively insensitive to certain contributions from the top ability group. Consider, for example, an easy item. For high-ability people, answering it incorrectly may be largely random. Since the expected frequency of incorrect responses is low, and this expected frequency appears in the denominator of the contribution to the chi-square, the contribution is likely to be large. Therefore, random variation would be receiving a lot of weight if the incorrect responses were included. Added to this is the concern that the top ability groups are not really matched on total test score. The whites in that category typically have a wider variance in total test score, whereas blacks tend to be concentrated toward the lower cutoff. One could argue that the reverse problem is present for using correct responses in the bottom ability category, particularly for difficult items. However, the situation is not symmetrical because the expected frequencies are not as low, due to guessing, and the difference in total test score (mean) in the low-ability group is generally much smaller, particularly since the sample size tends to be smaller for the low-ability group.

6. *Sample size.* The sample size required is less for χ^2_{correct}. This is because it is not necessary to have expected frequencies of 5 for the incorrect responses. Scheuneman (1981) reports that in several large-scale studies the smallest group size was between 90 and 150. Including the incorrect responses would have meant that many items could not be tested. In a certification exam for social workers, fewer than half could be tested with χ^2_{full} (Scheuneman, 1979a). Another example of the occurrence of this problem was evident in a study of an examination used for selecting police recruits. With fewer than 150 blacks, Ironson, Craig, and Canger (1981) found that fewer items could be evaluated with the χ^2_{full} procedure as compared with the χ^2_{correct} procedure.

7. *Evaluating easy and difficult items.* Following the same reasoning, very easy items will be easier to evaluate with $\chi^2_{correct}$ since only correct responses are considered. Difficult items will be hard to evaluate with either Scheuneman's $\chi^2_{correct}$ or Camilli's χ^2_{full} because the frequency of correct responses will be low, thus making it harder to satisfy the requirement of expected (correct) frequencies.

8. *Agreement and disagreement of the two methods.* The methods should agree most for items that are difficult, and least for items that are easy. The easier the item, the more likely the χ^2_{full} will identify it as biased and the more likely $\chi^2_{correct}$ will not. To demonstrate this point, χ^2_{full} may be broken down into two components: $\chi^2_{correct}$ and $\chi^2_{incorrect}$. Scheuneman's chi-square corresponds to $\chi^2_{correct}$, whereas Camilli's χ^2_{full} contains both. For an easy item, $\chi^2_{incorrect}$ will be large and $\chi^2_{correct}$ will be small. Therefore, Scheuneman's $\chi^2_{correct}$ would be small and Camilli's χ^2_{full} would be large. For a difficult item, $\chi^2_{incorrect}$ will be small and $\chi^2_{correct}$ will be large. Therefore, both Scheuneman's and Camilli's chi-squares will be large. This is illustrated by the two examples in this chapter. The item in Tables 5.2 and 5.3, which is easy ($p = .755$), has a $\chi^2_{correct}$ of 7.912, and a $\chi^2_{incorrect}$ of 17.713. The item in 5.1, which is difficult ($p = .297$), has a $\chi^2_{correct}$ of 7.029 (8.564) and a $\chi^2_{incorrect}$ of 3.6137 (5.5419), depending on the cutoffs for the intervals chosen.

9. *Validity.* Evidence for the validity of Scheuneman's $\chi^2_{correct}$ comes from convergent validity studies using real data (Ironson, 1978; Ironson & Subkoviak, 1979; Nungester, 1977; Rudner & Convey, 1978; Shepard et al., 1980), from simulated data or computer-generated bias (Merz & Grossen, 1979; Rudner et al., 1980), and from a comparison of the performance of the index in a white/white versus a black/white comparison (Ironson & Subkoviak, 1979). (For the case where bias is known to be absent [white/white comparison], about 5% should be identified as biased, assuming a significance level of 5%.) Furthermore, moderate reliability (.627) has been found for the procedure (Scheuneman, 1980a).

   The evidence for Camilli's χ^2_{full} comes from several studies, one by Nungester (1977), another by Shepard et al. (1980). Burrill (see chapter 6) provides a comprehensive review of these studies as well as those cited previously.

   Two newer studies (Craig & Ironson, 1981; Subkoviak et al., 1981) provide additional evidence for the validity of the procedures where tests have been constructed with biased items "planted" in them.

Similarities. Both methods share several advantages and disadvantages. Three advantages are listed below:

1. *Intuitively understandable to the practitioner.* This is the most important advantage, since the basic question is whether different ethnic groups of the same ability have the same probability of getting the item right.

2. *Smaller sample sizes.* The sample sizes required for the chi-square procedures (a minimum of 100–200 have been recommended for each group) need not be as large as those required for the latent trait techniques. It is important to note, however, that although the question of sample size has been addressed from the point of view of the minimum number necessary to satisfy the requirements of the chi-square test, the question of a minimum sample size necessary for obtaining a reliable and accurate estimate of bias has not been addressed. It may be that a much larger sample size is necessary for the latter.
3. *Significance tests.* Both procedures are associated with significance tests that permit dichotomous biased/unbiased classifications.

The disadvantages that the two procedures have in common are delineated next.

1. *Arbitrariness in setting cutoffs for the intervals.* Within the constraints set for the procedures by the required expected frequencies, there are a variety of possible cutoffs. The magnitude of the chi-square could easily change as the cutoffs change, as was illustrated earlier.
2. *Problems in using the total test score as a measure of ability.* Both methods assume the total test score is a valid measure of ability. Given the nature of the information, total test score is a reasonable choice. However, it does have several weaknesses. First, the total test score is *not perfectly reliable;* true score matching might be an alternative. Second, the total test contains biased items. Suppose, for example, that there is more bias against blacks than against whites. The total test score would then underestimate black ability. Whites and blacks matched on total test score would then represent higher ability blacks compared with lower ability whites. If these two groups have the same probability of answering the item correctly, the item is really biased against blacks because higher ability blacks should do better if the item were not biased. However, it will appear to be unbiased. Similarly, an item that is flagged as biased may be more biased than it looks. The conclusion is that constant bias may be absorbed into the scale; thus, by using total test score as a measure of ability, *constant bias will be overlooked.* Third, sometimes ethnic groups in the same total test score interval may not have the same mean test score. This will occur if the distributions of total test score within an interval are different, especially at the highest level of ability. Therefore, *groups may not really be matched on ability.* Due to differences in group means within "matched" intervals, regression artifacts may still cause the appearance of bias.
3. *Sensitivity to the distribution of total test scores.* Nungester (1977) points out how the chi-square approach is sensitive to total score distributions. An example in which two groups perform identically within an interval but have dissimilar total score distributions is shown in Table 5.5. Even

TABLE 5.5. Sensitivity of Chi-square to Total Score Distributions

Total Score	N		Observed Correct	
	Group 1	Group 2	Group 1	Group 2
1	200	10	40 (20%)	2 (20%)
2	160	30	48 (30%)	9 (30%)
3	120	50	48 (40%)	20 (40%)
TOTAL	480	90	136	31

though the two groups perform identically at each total score, the interval 1–3 would have a nonzero chi-square since $O_1 = 136 \neq E_1 = (136 + 31)/(480 + 90) \times 480 = 140.6$ and $O_2 = 31 \neq E_2 = (136 + 31)/(480 + 90) \times 90 = 26.4$. Thus, by changing the distribution, different expected values would emerge, inflating the χ^2. Rudner (1977c) also demonstrated that the χ^2 can become quite inflated when the total observed score distributions differ.

4. *Sensitivity to differential sample sizes of ethnic groups.* Baker (1981) noted that the Scheuneman chi-square procedure is confounded by unequal sample sizes for the two groups. He demonstrated that "two sets of identical pseudo item characteristic curves could lead to different χ^2 values and possibly different conclusions concerning item bias if they were based upon different group size ratios" (p. 60). Comparing equal sample sizes ($N = 800$), he obtained a Scheuneman χ^2 of 11.814 (3 *df*, $p < .05$); with a 10 to 1 ratio of sample sizes ($N = 440$), it dropped to 1.80 (3 *df*, *n.s.*).

In responding to Baker's criticism, Scheuneman (1981) indicated that using χ^2_{full} gives similar results (with $N = 400$ whites, 400 blacks, $\chi^2_4 = 30.437, p < .001$; with $N = 400$ whites, 40 blacks, $\chi^2_4 = 6.6411, p > .15$) and his example with a 10 to 1 ratio has less power (440) than that with equal size samples. It has been demonstrated that the relative contributions of the two groups to the resultant index are the same for both procedures. This relative contribution is greater for the smaller sized minority group (see Table 5.4). Two factors help explain this: (1) Baker (1981) points out that the combined p within a given ability level will be closer to the p for the majority group; (2) for each of the four contributions (black correct/black incorrect/white correct/white incorrect) of $(O - E)^2/E$ within a given ability level, the largest contribution will be determined by the smallest E in the denominator.

5. *Failure to utilize all available information.* Neither procedure focuses on the continuous, quantitative nature of the underlying variable (Marascuilo & Slaughter, 1981). Instead, the underlying variable (ability) is treated essentially in categorical fashion.

REVIEW OF LATENT TRAIT TECHNIQUES

One-parameter, or Rasch, Model

The one-parameter model, based on the work of Georg Rasch (1960, 1966, 1980), has been developed and applied to testing problems by Wright and his associates (Wright, 1977; Wright & Panchapakensan, 1969; Wright & Stone, 1979). A simplified description of the mathematical and theoretical principles of this model has been presented by Ryan and Hamm (1978). In this model, the probability of a correct response is a function of an examinee's ability and only one item parameter, *difficulty*.

The one-parameter model may be viewed from one of two positions. The first is as a special case of the three-parameter logistic model where only the difficulty parameter is permitted to vary. If the data fit the simpler one-parameter model, it makes sense to use this model for the sake of parsimony and economy.

The other viewpoint, a philosophical one, holds that the Rasch model is the very definition of measurement (Mead, 1980). That is, in order to measure a variable with "specific objectivity," certain conditions must be present (these are listed as 1 and 2 under "Assumptions"). The family of models proposed by Rasch is the only one that meets these conditions (Mead, 1980).

Assumptions. The Rasch model is based on several measurement conditions:

1. A more able person always has a better chance of success on an item than does a less able person;
2. Any person has a better chance of success on an easy item than on a difficult one;
3. These conditions can only be the consequence of the person's and the item's position on the trait, and so they must hold regardless of the race, sex, etc., of the person measured. (Wright et al., 1976, p. 7)

These conditions lead to the following simplifying assumptions of the one-parameter model: (1) there is no guessing on the test, and (2) all items are equally discriminating. In addition, the conditions imply that (3) only tests that are homogeneous can be considered. For example, a math test requiring verbal skill, where students who score low on verbal ability would not understand the statement of the problem, would not be homogeneous.

A major consequence of these considerations is that it is possible to derive an estimator for each parameter that is independent of all other parameters.

All the information contained about a person's ability is contained in the simple, unweighted count of the number of items he [or she] answered correctly. Raw score is a sufficient statistic for ability. For item difficulty, the sufficient statistic is the number of persons who responded correctly to the item. (Wright et al., 1976, p. 8)

Measurement of bias. There are two primary methods for measuring bias with the Rasch model. As in the three-parameter ICC approach, if the item is unbiased, examinees with the same ability, but from different ethnic groups, have the same probability of answering the item correctly. The first method, illustrated by biased item C in Figure 5.1, analyzes the difficulty shift. The second method, illustrated by biased item D in Figure 5.1, analyzes the fit of each item to the model in each group.

The first step in *analyzing the difficulty shift* is to obtain the difficulty parameters for the items within each group separately. BICAL (Wright & Mead, 1978) is a convenient program for this step. Then, the *most direct method of measuring bias is by calculating the difference in difficulty value for each item estimated separately for the two groups, but equated onto the same scale* (Draba, 1978; Wright et al., 1976). A t statistic is used for this purpose (note that this particular t ratio does not account for differences in size):

$$t = \frac{d_1 - d_2}{\sqrt{SE_1^2 + SE_2^2}} \, , \tag{9}$$

where d_1 and d_2 are respective difficulties for the given item in groups 1 and 2, and SE_1 and SE_2 are the respective standard errors in the two groups. If t is large, an item is relatively more difficult for one group and is thus biased. Draba (1977) suggests a cutoff value of 2.4 for identifying biased items.

Since the parameters of the items are determined separately within each group, even if the items as a whole are more difficult for one group than for the other group, their difficulties will be centered at zero within *each group*. Therefore, the t measure is a measure of *relative* item difficulty difference. Wright et al. (1976) question, Do the items maintain their relative difficulties for the new sample, regardless of its distribution of ability? As Shepard et al. (1980) indicate, one problem with this approach is that it assumes the data satisfy the assumptions of the model, i.e., that guessing is zero and discrimination is constant.

A second approach used by Durovic (1975a, 1975b) and Wright et al. (1976) involves *analyzing the fit* of each item in each group. An unbiased item should either fit or fail to fit the model in a similar manner for both groups; thus, it relates to the dimension being measured in the same way for each group. If an item is biased, it may be measuring different abilities in the different groups. Consistent with this notion, Durovic (1975b) operationally defined bias as follows: "An item is biased for members of a group if on that item, for members of the group, a mean square fit of the item to the Rasch model is obtained which differs, by greater than one, from the mean square fit obtained for members of the other group" (p. 4).

The *mean square total item fit statistic* is calculated via the BICAL program. Each group would be run separately. First, for each item in each group a chi-square statistic with one degree of freedom is computed as:

$$\chi_1^2 = Z_{vi}^2 = \frac{[x_{vi} - E(x_{vi})]^2}{V(x_{vi})} \, , \tag{10}$$

where:

x_{vi} = person (v)'s score on item i;
$E(x_{vi})$ = expected response predicted by the model; and
$V(x_{vi})$ = variance of the expected value.

The mean square for the total (overall) fit of an item, i, is given by:

$$V_i = \sum_v^n Z_{vi}^2 \left(\frac{L}{(n - 1)(L - 1)} \right) \, , \tag{11}$$

where L is test length and n is the number of persons in the calibration sample. This mean square has an expected value of one and a standard error of $2L/(n - 1)(L - 1)$.

Thus, first, a residual—the person's obtained response minus the expected response based on the model—is calculated. Next, the residuals are standardized. Then the mean squared residual is calculated within each group. An index of bias used by Shepard et al. (1980) was the difference in mean square fit, that is, the absolute value of the differences in mean squared residuals for the two groups. This fit index will be large if the item in question is relatively more discriminating in one group than in another, or if there is a difference in guessing between the two groups.

There are other fit statistics in the BICAL program that are useful in determining reasons for misfit (Lang, 1978). The *between-group fit statistic* estimates how well an item fits the model for each score-level group and may be used to help determine whether item difficulty estimates are actually free from the ability distribution of the sample. The *item residual discrimination index* is an index of the slope of the ICC as estimated by the data. It helps determine whether the assumption of equivalent item discrimination is being met.

Other indices that have been used to measure bias via the Rasch model, aside from the t statistic, or difference in mean square fit, are the difference in item difficulty (weighted) and the signed and unsigned area indices. A discussion of the calculation of the area between curves is deferred until the section on the three-parameter model.

Since it is not the purpose of this chapter to review empirical studies, a few pertinent studies will be highlighted only briefly, but enough to report mixed results (see Burrill, chapter 6, for a further discussion of these studies). Durovic (1975b) analyzed a 14-item test for black/white differences using the fit statistic. His analysis identified two items, both of which received empirical verification from two reviewers. Draba (1978) carried out a difficulty shift analysis and then a fit analysis. In two simulation studies, the one-parameter model correlated only moderately with generated bias. Merz and Grossen

(1979) found that a Rasch area index correlated from .20 to .96 with generated bias. They did not compute difficulty differences; had they, the Rasch procedure would have performed better since guessing and discrimination parameters were held constant.

Rudner et al. (1980) found the Rasch model difference in difficulty was better than the fit statistic, but it was not as good as Scheuneman's $\chi^2_{correct}$, and it was about the same as the transformed item difficulty procedure. When discrimination was held constant, the Rasch difficulty index performed about the same as the three-parameter bias index. It should be noted that, in their study, bias was generated using the three-parameter model.

In a study using empirical data, Shepard et al. (1980) found that both the Rasch difficulty differences and signed areas had a near perfect correlation ($r \geq .99$) with the Angoff transformed item difficulty. The researchers explained this relationship as follows:

In the Rasch model, an efficient estimate of item difficulty depends on the quantity $ln\ p/q\ (=\ -ln\ q/p)$ (Wright, 1977, p. 100). In the TID-Angoff method, item difficulties are transformed by the inverse normal transformation, $\phi^{-1}\ (p)$. Birnbaum (1968) has shown that $(ln\ p/q)/1.7$ is a very close approximation of $\phi^{-1}\ (p)$. Obviously, two functions that differ mainly by a constant multiplier will be very highly correlated. (p. 40)

They concluded:

Although the Rasch model may not have good substitutes in other measurement applications, for all practical purposes the TID-Angoff method can be considered equivalent to the ICC-1 for detecting item bias. Since the TID-Angoff method is much easier to use, it is obviously preferred. (p. 40)

It should be noted, however, that the instruments used in the study did not satisfy the Rasch assumptions (p. 18). Finally, inconsistent relationships among the three-parameter and one-parameter indices were also found. A recent study by Douglass (1981) reported poor performance of the Rasch model used for measuring bias. It should be noted, however, that the investigation involved a speeded test.

There is some disagreement regarding the minimum sample size required for this procedure. Tinsley and Dawis (1975a) recommend 500 in each group; Durovic (1975a) used 367 blacks and 575 whites; Wright (1977) says 100 is sufficient, although more should be used if diverse groups are to be compared. Lord (1979) suggests that a small number (200) can justify use of the Rasch model. Finally, studies have shown that difficulty parameters can be estimated fairly well with small samples of, say, 250 (Ree & Jensen, 1980).

Implementation. Many researchers implementing the Rasch model for measuring bias have focused on either a fit analysis or a difficulty shift analysis. These will often tap different kinds of bias, however, and the inclusion of misfitting items (and of misfitting people) may adversely affect the calibration of the difficulty estimates.

In order for a test to be unbiased, the variable measured by the test should be well defined in each group such that the items fit the model in each group and the difficulty of an item does not shift significantly. An all-inclusive procedure should address three questions (Wright et al. 1976):

Which items are biased and for whom?
Which items define the trait to be measured?
Which persons are properly measured by items that define the trait? (p. 1)

The following procedure, suggested by Mead (personal communication, 1981), would be comprehensive:

1. Calibrate the items separately for each group. Perform a fit analysis, removing the items that do not fit (and those that are biased according to the fit criterion).
2. Perform a difficulty shift analysis, removing items whose equated difficulty parameter is significantly different between groups.
3. Examine the fit of each person to the pattern of responses expected by the model. This enables the researcher to detect a possibly biased (or inappropriate) measurement for an individual.

Advantages and disadvantages. The major advantages accrue from the theoretical model and the focus on the difficulty parameter that researchers have been able to estimate fairly well. The major disadvantages stem from the fact that many items do not fit the model, and, in some cases, a simpler procedure may measure as well in the bias context. In addition, Rentz and Bashaw (1975, pp. 41–43) noted that the fit index is highly affected by sample size, and the user is likely to reject items that ought not to be rejected.

Three-parameter Model

According to the three-parameter model, an unbiased item should have the same item characteristic curves in both groups. Figure 5.1 illustrates two items that are biased. One advantage of the three-parameter technique is that it is not limited to a uniform bias favoring one group (illustrated in item A). It also identifies nonuniform bias, such as item B, where members of one group are favored at low-ability levels, and members of another group are favored at high-ability levels.

The three-parameter model is sometimes regarded as the standard by which all other methods are to be compared because of its theoretical soundness. This theoretical underpinning is the *invariance property* of the estimated parameters. *Invariance* means that the shape of the ICC is not dependent on the particular distribution of ability in the sample. The probability of success of examinees at a given level (Θ) is independent of how many examinees are at any other given level of Θ. This is discussed further in Guion and Ironson (in press), Hambleton and Cook (1977), and Hambleton et al. (1978). Invariance does not mean that the same numerical value will always be obtained for an item's parameters, regardless of the parameterization group. Scaling with different groups of examinees is likely to produce a different set of scale values for the parameters. The invariance notion, however, specifies that this relationship will be linear. In the traditional item analysis, changes in the sample yield unpredictable differences in the item statistic. Rudner (1977b) offers a good illustration of the invariance notion. The important point here is that the parameter estimates on different scales can be placed easily on the same scale via a linear transformation, if they are estimated accurately and the model holds. (It should not be assumed that parameters can be estimated equally accurately regardless of the sample. For example, there may be too little data in the ability region which is most critical for estimating the item parameters.)

Assumptions. The three-parameter model assumes that (1) the normal ogive or logistic model adequately represents the data, and (2) the test is unidimensional.

Unidimensionality is usually tested by performing a factor analysis. Reckase (1979) investigated the strength of the one- and three-parameter procedures when the unidimensionality requirement was violated. He suggested that the first factor should account for 20% of the variance in order to assure stable item parameters. He also found that the three-parameter model fits the data significantly better than the one-parameter model.

LOGIST. The LOGIST program (Wood & Lord, 1976; Wood, Wingersky, & Lord, 1976) may be used to estimate the parameters for each item and an ability for each person.* The three-parameter model used to describe an ICC in that program (Hambleton & Cook, 1977, p. 82) is:

$$P_g(O) = c_g + (1 - c_g) \frac{e^{Da_g(\Theta - b_g)}}{1 + e^{Da_g(\Theta - b_g)}} . \tag{12}$$

This equation is a logistic model introduced by Birnbaum (1968) in Lord and Novick (1968). It calculates the probability of success ($P_g[\Theta]$) for a person of ability Θ on item g that has parameters a_g (discrimination), b_g (difficulty), and

---

*Several other programs, such as ANCILLES (Urry, 1976), are available for parameter estimation. A discussion of the accuracy of the methods may be found in Ree (1979) and Swaminathan and Gifford (1980). Although ANCILLES requires less computer time and is less expensive to run, in general the LOGIST maximum likelihood estimates for item parameters and ability are superior to ANCILLES, especially for short tests (Swaminathan & Gifford, 1980). Another program, named CARIF (Lissak & Wytmar, 1981), can be used in conjunction with LOGIST to calculate the ICC and item information functions from the parameter estimates. It incorporates these analyses into one computer run and uses direct output from LOGIST.

c_g (guessing). D is set to 1.7, a value chosen so that the logistic model would closely approximate a normal one.

Input to LOGIST requires that one specify if, for each person, the item was right, wrong, omitted, or not reached.

Sample size. In order to obtain stable, accurate estimates of the parameters, large sample sizes are recommended. The specific sample size depends on which parameter one wishes to estimate accurately. Lord (1968) and Swaminathan and Gifford (1980) examine the recovery of item parameters. For example, for estimating the a parameter (which is less stable than estimates of the b parameter, but more stable than estimates of the c parameter), as many as 50 items and 1,000 subjects have been recommended. In practice, getting convergent estimates for the c parameters presents the most problems. Shepard et al. (1980), using a sample of 1,593, found that almost 40% of the c parameters did not converge.

Hulin, Lissak, and Drasgow (1981) have investigated the recovery of an ICC (by Monte Carlo methods) instead of focusing on individual item parameters. They found acceptably low error for samples of 30 items and 1,000 subjects *or* 60 items and 500 subjects for the three-parameter data, and 30 items and 500 subjects for two-parameter data.

Measurement of bias. Green and Draper (1972) introduced the notion of examining observed ICCs to indicate bias. Subsequently, several researchers (Linn & Harnish, 1981; Linn et al., 1980; Lord, 1977, 1980; Pine, 1975; Rudner, 1977a) adapted the three-parameter item characteristic curve model for use in investigating item bias. Parameters are usually, but not always, estimated separately for each group. Procedures used to compare the ICCs of the two groups include the following:

1. Difference between ICCs as measured by the *area* between the curves (signed or unsigned) or summed squared differences;
2. A *test of parameter equality* as measured by a composite test of simultaneous differences in a, b, and c parameters (or an investigation of differences in the b parameter alone or the a parameter alone);
3. A measure of *lack of fit* derived from an examination of differences between observed data and what would be expected from an estimated model;
4. An estimation of confidence intervals around ICCs; and
5. A test measuring differences in empirical response functions.

Several of the above procedures are described in this section. The first procedure, one adapted by Ironson and Subkoviak (1979), makes use of Rudner's (1977a) area measure. The second procedure involves the application of weighted mean square item bias statistics. The third procedure described is a two-stage procedure proposed by Lord (1980), culminating in a simultaneous test of the equality of item parameters between groups. Some procedures described by Linn et al. (1981) are then presented, followed by some tests of dif-

ferences in empirical response functions. A discussion of equating procedures is incorporated into the parts describing the Ironson and Subkoviak
procedure and Lord's procedure. Other procedures are noted where appropriate.

The *Ironson and Subkoviak (1979) procedure* using *Rudner's (1977a) area
measure* involved three steps:

1. LOGIST runs were completed separately for blacks and for whites. To
   avoid problems in estimating convergent c parameters, these were set to
   $.75(1/r)$, where r is the number of options in a multiple-choice question.
2. Since the LOGIST runs were group-referenced (the mean ability, $\hat{\Theta}$, is zero
   and the variance of $\hat{\Theta}$ is 1), the item parameters had to be put on the same
   scale. The b values, or difficulty values, estimated on whites and blacks
   should be linearly related. The objective at this point is to obtain the
   equation of the line relating the black and white b values.

   In pursuing an approximate procedure, a cross plot of b values should
   be obtained, as shown in Figure 5.2. One group is arbitrarily picked as
   the "base" group, the other as the "comparison" group. In this example,
   whites have been arbitrarily picked as the base group, blacks as the comparison group. For illustrative purposes particular features of Figure 5.2
   are exaggerated. The scatter of the points about the line is very much
   larger than what is normally found. Similarly, the slope and the intercept
   of the line are not meant to represent statistics computed from a real data
   set.

   "Interocular analysis," or eyeballing of the plot, should reveal which
   items are aberrant (lie far off the line). Although one could remove the

FIGURE 5.2. Crossplot of difficulty values for two groups to be used in determining
equating line

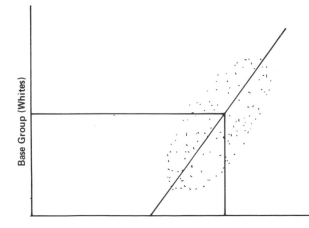

Comparison Group
(Blacks)

aberrant items before calculating the equating line, a better procedure would be to weight the outliers less heavily. There is no one "best" line currently in use. The regression line should *not* be used, because it is not symmetrical. The major axis may be used (see Angoff & Ford, 1973, for the formulas for its calculation), but that is imperfect because it fails to take into account the differential accuracy in estimating the b's and the outlier problem. Furthermore, Lord (personal communication, 1981) points out another reason why the major axis is incorrect. Suppose the b's define a principal axis with a slope of 1, where $\sigma_{\hat\theta} = 1$ for whites. If it is decided to arbitrarily set $\sigma_{\hat\theta} = 2$ instead, the new plot of b's will not have a principal axis with a slope of 2, as is logically required by the arbitrary choice of the unit.

A refinement that takes errors of estimation into account was proposed by Mosteller and Tukey (1976). Linn et al. (1980) selected equating constants so that the weighted mean and variance of the b_i's in the comparison group were equal to the weighted mean and variance of the original b_i's in the base group (b_i is the difficulty value for item i in a given group). The weight for each item was determined by taking the inverse of the larger sampling variance for b_i from either the base or comparison group. This results in less weight (for determining the equating constants) being given to items whose difficulty parameter was poorly estimated (large sampling variance). Detailed formulas for this procedure are given in Linn et al. (1980). Further work on the equating line is the progress at Educational Testing Service (ETS).*

Suppose the equating line for b is given by:

$$b_i^{\text{base}} = M b_i^{\text{comp}} + D, \tag{13}$$

where M and D are the equating constants, then the line used to equate a parameters would be

$$a_i^{\text{base}} = a_i^{\text{comp}}/M. \tag{14}$$

The parameters for the base group are left unchanged. The equated parameters for the comparison group would be arrived at by entering the old, unequated value on the right side, yielding equated values on the left side. C values are already on the same scale.

3. With the parameters now on the same scale, several indices (as indicated before) may be calculated. One such index (the one we used) was suggested by Rudner (1977a). It involves calculating the area between the black and white ICCs. The *unsigned area bias index* was calculated by adding successive rectangles whose width was .005 and whose height was the abso-

---

*Frederic Lord, Marilyn Wingersky, or Martha Stocking should be contacted for the most current information (Educational Testing Service, Princeton, N.J. 08540).

lute value of the difference between the probability of getting the item right at each particular ability level.

A *signed index* may be calculated by attaching a sign to the height of each rectangle. One may arbitrarily choose a positive sign to represent bias against blacks. Thus, at a particular Θ, if the white Pg (Θ) is above the black Pg (Θ), a positive sign would be attached.

Unfortunately, the foregoing procedures have several inherent problems: (1) the c's are fixed rather than estimated; (2) an equating line that is not entirely satisfactory must be used; and (3) biased items may have been used to estimate ability.

Linn et al. (1980, 1981) used several area measures as well as a measure that involved computing the sums of squared differences between ICCs. Their indices were: (1) base high area: the area between the group curves in which the base group ICC is above the comparison group ICC; (2) base low area: the area between the group curves in which the base group is below the comparison group ICC; (3) absolute difference: the sum of (1) and (2); and (4) square root of the sum of squares: the square root of the sum of squared differences between ICCs in the region $\Theta = -3$ to $\Theta = +3$. These indices were computed in both a weighted and an unweighted manner. The former were weighted according to the stability of the estimates of the ICCs at various levels of Θ. Details of the procedures may be found in Linn et al. (1980).

Weighted mean square item bias statistics. Weighting is currently being used to address several problems in item bias research. First, as was noted earlier, one should not assume that parameters can be estimated equally well regardless of the sample. Large observable differences in curves may be found simply because there are too little data in the ability region where data are critical for estimating the item parameters. In addition, the distribution of ability in one group may be such that only a poor estimate of item performance can be obtained over the range containing most of the examinees in another group. Second, items with different parameters may make virtually the same predictions about persons over the range of their application. Third, the anticipated use of the test scores renders the same amount of bias much less acceptable over one range than over another.

The first two problems may be addressed by considering the weighted mean square difference between item response functions, where the weights are obtained from the number of examinees available for item calibration at each ability level. Earlier weighted mean square item bias statistics gave equal weights to all abilities in an interval and zero weight outside the interval (Linn et al., 1980, 1981). Current research by the Illinois Item Bias group (Levine, Wardrop, & Linn, 1982) suggests that a conservative set of weights can be obtained first by smoothing the empirical distribution of estimated ability and then by assigning each ability the weight equal to the minimum of the two smoothed histograms. The third problem mentioned above could be addressed by choosing arbitrary weights that reflect the specific requirements of a given application.

The distribution of the general weighted item bias statistic has been derived. It has been shown that under most conditions the statistic is the sum of the squares of three normal variables with different variances and zero means. The variances are eigenvalues of a matrix computed using the weights, the estimated three-parameter logistic parameters, and the covariance matrix of estimated parameters (Levine, 1981). The statistic is being evaluated with reading test data classified by race, SES, and grade level (see Levine, Wardrop, & Linn, 1982).

Lord's (1980) two-stage procedure begins as follows:

1. Estimate approximately the item parameters for all groups combined, standardizing on the b's* and not on Θ. (Standardizing on the b's means choosing a LOGIST option for the b scale to have its mean set at 0 and standard deviation at 1; all parameters for all groups are then on the same scale. If the usual method of standardizing on Θ were used, the item parameters for each group would be on a different scale, and would have to be equated by the procedure noted previously.)

2. Fix the c's at the values obtained in step 1. Reestimate the a's and b's separately for each group, standardizing on the b's.

3. For each item, compare the item characteristic curves or parameters obtained in step 2. A significance test (described shortly) may be used for this purpose. Notice that for the procedure just outlined, the same c is used for a given item in both groups. Therefore, we would functionally be testing only for a difference in a and b parameters. (p. 217)'

A second stage, also described by Lord (1980, p. 220), was suggested by Marco (1977). Lord notes that if many of the items are biased the test is not unidimensional, and the black Θ and white Θ scales will not be comparable. Therefore, this second stage proceeds as follows:

1. Remove items found biased by the first stage. The remaining items may be considered to be unidimensional.
2. Combine all groups and estimate Θ for each individual. These Θ's are all comparable.
3. For each group separately, while holding Θ fixed for all individuals at the values obtained in step 3, estimate the a and b for each item. Do this for all items including those previously removed.
4. Compare estimated item characteristic (response) functions or parameters using the hypothesis testing procedure described next. The Θ scale from this procedure is applicable to all groups and thus legitimizes the resulting comparisons.

*Lord recommends removing very easy and very hard items and items with low a before standardizing on the b's, because the b for these items has high sampling errors. These items should be omitted only from standardization.

Lord (1980, pp. 218–223) suggested using a *statistical significance test for comparing the parameters of an item across ethnic groups*. The null hypothesis of equality of b's, $b_{i1} = b_{i2}$, can be performed by comparing the difference between the black and white b for a given item, $b_{i1} - b_{i2}$, to an estimate of the standard error of this difference. These sampling variances are estimated by asymptotic formulas. An analogous separate significance test can be used with the a parameters. A preferable procedure, however, would be to test both the equality of the a and b parameters for an item in two groups simultaneously. This technique weights the a and b differences by various entries in the variance-covariance matrix combined for the two groups. The test uses a chi-square statistic with two degrees of freedom (Morrison, 1967, p. 129). More specifically, for an item i, given groups 1 and 2, the chi-square is given by

$$\chi_i^2 = (V_{i1} - V_{i2})' \left(\frac{1}{\Sigma_{i1} + \Sigma_{i2}} \right) (V_{i1} - V_{i2}), \tag{15}$$

where V_{i1} and V_{i2} are the vectors of a and b parameters for the subgroups 1 and 2, and Σ_{i1} and Σ_{i2} are the covariance matrices for the vectors of a and b parameters. This significance test is carried out separately for each item by computing the χ_i^2 for each item and comparing it to the critical value in a chi-square table.*

For testing the equality of three parameters, ETS researchers use the same chi-square test employed for testing two parameters, but with three degrees of freedom. It is somewhat analogous to Hotelling's T^2 test except that the T^2 test estimates the variances used to test the significance of the means. In this application, the variances of $\hat{a}$, $\hat{b}$, and $\hat{c}$ are known (approximately).

As Lord (1980) points out, there are several problems with the above test:

1. If the test contains biased items, unidimensionality and local independence are violated. Thus, purifying the test by the two-stage process outlined above is recommended.
2. The significance test is asymptotic.
3. The test assumes the Θ's are known rather than estimated.
4. The test only applies to maximum likelihood estimates.

Bougon and Lissak (1981) also point out that the test may be unreliable because we do not know the preasymptotic distribution of a, b, and c. It is not known how close the convergence of the maximum likelihood estimates $\hat{a}$, $\hat{b}$, and $\hat{c}$ are to a, b, and c for middle sample theory, and the distribution of $\hat{\Theta}/\Theta$ is sample-dependent (because the form of the likelihood function is assumed to be known), which may lead to detecting bias that is artifactual. An exact

---

*More information about this test and an appropriate computer program may be obtained by contacting Marilyn Wingersky, ETS, Princeton, N.J. 08540 (*Note*: Wingersky, 1977).

preasymptotic solution for the difference between two ICCs derived from maximum likelihood estimates is not available.

Other procedures have been used that focus on a particular parameter. Pine (1977; Martin, Pine, & Weiss, 1978) used an elliptic D value to measure bias, defined as the perpendicular distance of each item's difficulty (b) from the major axis of the ellipse relating the b values of the two racial groups. In his procedure, the a and b parameters were estimated separately for each group; c was fixed at .25 since the multiple-choice items studied had four alternatives. Shepard et al. (1980) looked at the difference in discrimination (a) parameters, and the difference in difficulty (b) parameters in addition to the area and simultaneous parameter testing procedure. Pine and Weiss (1976) focus on the latent trait difficulty parameter only.

Significance test for equality of parameters versus area measure. We have very little information on how these two measures relate, but it should be noted that they might not necessarily agree in detecting items as biased. The only study where both the simultaneous parameter testing procedure and the area measure were calculated found low correlations between them (Shepard et al., 1980).

Linn et al. (1980) noted that item parameters may be different when in fact no practical difference in the ICCs exists. The illustration they give is:

Group 1 $a = 1.8, b = 3.5, c = .2$
Group 2 $a = 0.5, b = 5.0, c = .2$

They suggest that bias based on differences in estimated difficulty or discrimination parameters may be misleading, and that studying differences in ICCs is the approach that focuses on the information of practical concern (the difference in the probability of answering the item correctly for persons of equal ability from different groups).

It should also be kept in mind, however, that an asymptotic significance test is available for testing the equality of parameters, whereas no significance test for the area measure has yet been completed (work on one is in progress).

Lack of fit. One of the problems in using the latent trait approach is the requirement of large samples for the different ethnic groups. In practice, a minority group size of between 100 and 300 and a majority group size of 1,000 or more for a given study is not unusual.

Linn and Harnisch (1981) adopted an interesting lack of fit procedure to deal with this problem. All cases in the sample were combined, and estimates of a, b, and c were made for each item, Θ for each person. Then, for each person, the probability of a correct answer was calculated from the three-parameter logistic model. The estimates based on the model could be averaged over members of a subgroup and compared to the observed proportion correct for that subgroup. The researchers used two indices to measure bias: (1) $D_i = O_i - P_i.$, where O_i is the proportion of persons in a given group answering item i correctly, and $P_i.$ is the expected proportion of persons (according to the model) answering the item correctly; (2) a standardized difference score for each item for each subgroup,

$$Z_i = \frac{1}{N_g} \sum_{j \in g} \frac{U_{ij} - P_{ij}}{\sqrt{P_{ij}(1 - P_{ij})}} , \qquad (16)$$

where:

$U_{ij} = 1$ if person j answers item i correctly, and 0 otherwise;
N_g = number of persons in group g; and
P_{ij} = estimated probability that person j would answer item i correctly, based on the fitted model from combined groups.

These indicate the degree to which members of a particular subgroup perform better or worse than expected on that item, and help to identify items that are unusually easy or difficult for members of a subgroup.

Lack of person fit. As in the one-parameter model, one may determine if a test score is appropriate for a person by examining whether his or her responses deviate from what is expected according to the model (Levine & Drasgow, 1980; Levine & Rubin, 1979).

Visual method using standard errors of ICCs. Linn et al. (1980, 1981) used a visual procedure to compare ICCs for two groups plotted on a common scale. Groups were matched on two out of three characteristics (grade, income, or race), and standard errors of the ICCs were plotted to better evaluate if observed differences in ICCs might be due to error. Detailed formulas for approximating the standard error of a point on an estimated ICC can be found in Linn et al. (1980).

Comparing empirical item response functions. Work is in progress at the University of Illinois on other latent trait procedures that test the equivalence of two empirical item response functions (EIRF). These procedures may be viewed as somewhere between the ICC and chi-square (Scheuneman's χ^2_{correct} and Camilli's χ^2_{full}) in approach. They differ from the chi-square procedures discussed earlier in this chapter in that those use total score for the purposes of matching on ability, whereas the EIRF procedures estimate ability from use of Θ obtained from the latent trait model. They also differ from the ICC approaches just discussed inasmuch as they compare observed empirical characteristic curves instead of comparing theoretical ICCs derived by solving for a, b, and c from empirical data.

One procedure for testing the equivalence of two EIRF was used by Hulin, Komocar, and Drasgow (1980), and is appropriate for two-parameter data only. It involves linearizing the empirical characteristic curves by use of a logit transformation on the proportion correct and subsequently using an F test to examine the equivalence of two regression lines.

A method developed by Bougon and Lissak (1981) involves testing for differences between empirical response functions at various levels of ability: a series of t ratios is combined into a single B statistic. Calculation of a C statistic from summing squared t ratios can also be obtained. The C statistic would be particularly useful when the empirical curves cross. Both statistics have an associated sampling distribution. An empirical study comparing the B, F, and chi-square methods for examining bias has been conducted by Goldberg (1981).

Although these two procedures are promising, they are as yet unpublished and unevaluated. It is therefore suggested that any potential user of the techniques follow the most recent literature on them.

Advantages and disadvantages. Latent trait theory, or item response theory, is the most theoretically sound approach to the study of item bias, due to its property of parameter invariance. Parameters from different samples should be linearly related; items whose parameters are not linearly related violate the unidimensionality assumption and, therefore, may be biased because they are measuring something different for a particular ethnic group. The invariance property implies that differences in ability should not create artifactual instances of bias (as would be a criticism of classical measures). In addition, item difficulty parameters from this procedure are less confounded with differences in item quality and guessing than classical p values.

The three-parameter model is more realistic than the one-parameter model since having an a and a c parameter seems to fit the data better (particularly where guessing is involved). In practice, however, the a and c parameters do not exhibit the strong invariance of the b (Ree & Jensen, 1980). Correlations for b are about .90, for a, about .70, and for c, much less.

The analysis is complex, expensive, and requires a larger sample size than the simpler Rasch model. In fact, Lord (1979) justifies use of the Rasch model with small numbers (e.g., 200), but suggests estimating c and setting them all equal, rather than setting c to zero. A major problem with using LOGIST is getting convergent estimates of the c parameters. It is also sometimes difficult to get stable estimates of the other parameters. For example, if a is low, the b value may not converge.

Latent trait curves are also not entirely independent of the distribution of ability, as smaller sizes in the ends of the distributions will result in poorer estimation at the ends of the curves and different displacements of the curves because of unreliability.

The validity of the three-parameter area model, the three-parameter index that has been most widely used to date, has been explored in simulation studies (Merz & Grossen 1979; Rudner et al., 1980), with real data (Ironson &

Subkoviak, 1979; Linn et al., 1980, 1981; Rudner & Convey, 1978; Shepard et al., 1980), and with real data having biased items "planted" (Craig & Ironson, 1981; Subkoviak et al., 1981). The findings of these have been generally supportive of the superiority of the method (Ironson, 1981), but its validity and the validity of the other three-parameter indices have not been thoroughly investigated. Also, it is not fully understood just what kinds of items are biased (Lord, 1977).

RECOMMENDATIONS FOR
TEST DEVELOPERS AND TEST USERS

The chi-square and latent trait procedures examined in this chapter represent the extremes of a spectrum, from the most statistically elegant (the three-parameter model) to the most practical (Scheuneman's $\chi^2_{correct}$ or Camilli's χ^2_{full}). Studies have shown that, while there is enough agreement among the methods to offer evidence that they are measuring the same construct (bias), they are not interchangeable. The agreement between the chi-square and three-parameter ICC procedures is generally highest, and the chi-square procedure may be viewed as a rough approximation to the more complicated three-parameter latent trait procedure.

Since these techniques use only an internal criterion, they are apt to be most useful during test development. Summaries of the advantages and disadvantages of the chi-square and latent trait approaches (one-parameter and three-parameter procedures) are presented in Tables 5.6 and 5.7, respectively. Practically speaking, however, the choice will be governed primarily by the sample size and cost.

If a large enough sample is available, the three-parameter method is recommended. If both samples are large, the area or simultaneous hypothesis test for the equality of the parameters is appropriate. For the case where one sample is small and one is large, Linn's lack of fit procedure may be used. In the case where one is particularly interested in a visual approach, estimation and plotting of the standard errors of ICCs is helpful. If a smaller sample (for both groups) is available, a chi-square procedure should be used. Where possible, the χ^2_{full} should be utilized because it has a known sampling distribution. The one-parameter model is not specifically endorsed at this time because of its mixed support. It should be noted, however, that new evidence on these procedures is constantly evolving, so it behooves the user to continually evaluate new findings in the field.

There are still many issues that need to be addressed in the domain of item bias methodology. First, we need to explore further the theoretical differences in the methods. It is hoped that this chapter constitutes one step in that direction. Second, we need more information on the reliability of the methods. Scheuneman's (1980a) study began this examination. Third, we need to

TABLE 5.6. Summary of Advantages and Disadvantages of Two Chi-square Type Procedures

Advantages	Disadvantages
Scheuneman's $\chi^2_{correct}$	
1. Small sample size required, about 100 per group minimum	1. Not distributed as chi-square, sampling distribution of index is unknown
2. Very easy items can be evaluated	2. No standard computer programs are available
3. Random variation in top ability group gets less weight	
4. Demonstrated usefulness in a variety of studies	
Camilli's χ^2_{full}	
1. Distributed as a chi-square	1. Larger sample size needed, about 200 per group
2. Computer programs available	2. Difficult to evaluate very easy items
3. Generally more powerful	
Both procedures	
1. Significance test available so items may be dichotomized as biased/unbiased	1. Further analysis needed to determine direction and source of bias
2. Intuitively easy to understand	2. Do not handle difficult items well (need adequate number of correct responses)
3. Good for rapid screening	3. Arbitrariness in cutoffs may cause problems
4. Procedure can be extended to more than two groups	4. Total test score is an imperfect measure of ability
5. Sample size is smaller than for latent trait theory	5. Procedures are sensitive to the distribution of total test scores
6. Procedures are less sensitive to shape of distributions than "classical" procedures	6. Procedures are sensitive to differential sample size of ethnic groups
7. Cost is minimal	

know more about how validly the procedures perform in correctly identifying "truly" biased items as biased, and "truly" unbiased items as unbiased. Validity studies have been conducted using simulated data or real data with unknown "true" amounts of bias. We are beginning to explore how well the methods work in detecting "planted" biased items. We need to know more, however, about what makes an item biased. The fourth and fifth issues, then, refer to its usefulness and impact. Does use of the methods help us understand the nature of bias? What effect does removing the bias items have? (For example, does removing biased items reduce adverse impact without impairing predictive validity?) The sixth area would address statistical issues. For example, what is the sampling distribution of the area measure? (As noted, work is progressing on this by researchers at the University of Illinois.) To what extent are the various indices robust to violations of their assumptions?

Other more specific questions warrant attention. First, all of the methods assume the test is homogeneous. Should unidimensionality be tested within each ethnic group separately, or for the total group combined? Since one of the methods proposed for measuring bias is comparing the factor structures

TABLE 5.7. Summary of Advantages and Disadvantages of Two Latent Trait Approaches

Advantages	Disadvantages
One-parameter or Rasch Approach	
1. Theoretical ability and parameter estimation are independent. Total test score is a sufficient statistic for ability; parameter invariance	1. Assumptions of no guessing and equal discrimination are not practical
2. Smaller sample size required as compared to three parameter	2. Larger sample required when compared to the chi-square or transformed difficulty technique
3. Item fit statistics are available	3. Difficulty difference and signed area correlate highly (.99) with Angoff transformed difficulty, an easier procedure requiring a smaller sample size
4. Person fit can be calculated	4. Empirical support is mixed
5. Focuses on one parameter, the one that can be measured with the greatest confidence	
6. Computer program, BICAL, is available	
Three-parameter approach	
1. Latent trait parameter invariance implies that differences in ability will not create artifactual instances of bias	1. Complex computer analysis; difficulty encountered in estimation of parameters, especially c
2. Difficulty parameter less confounded with discrimination and guessing than p value	2. Large sample size required
3. Superiority in several studies	3. Expensive to run LOGIST
4. Including a and c parameters is more realistic and fits data better	4. Precision of estimation of a and c is weak
5. Computer programs such as LOGIST and ANCILLES are available for estimating parameters.	5. Ability distributions influence accuracy of estimation at ends of curves
6. Asymptotic significance test associated with testing for equality of parameters is available	6. Problems encountered in determining equating line
	7. Fit statistics are not generally available yet

(see Reynolds, chapter 8), it does not entirely make sense to require unidimensionality for the combined group prior to a bias analysis. It may make more sense to check for unidimensionality in the majority group *only* a priori.

One of the primary advantages of the latent trait and chi-square techniques is that they attempt to be uninfluenced by the distribution of ability in the sample. Controlling for ability is laudable, and these procedures do improve over earlier procedures (such as Angoff's delta plot), but they control imperfectly for ability. The distribution of ability does have some effect on estimation. Even more importantly, since ability is estimated from internal information, the presence of biased items will affect that estimation. In particular, if the bias is constant, the ability scales will be systematically distorted. For this reason, these procedures all measure *relative,* rather than absolute, bias, i.e., they are all fundamentally item-by-group interaction measures.

For the reasons mentioned previously, a two-stage procedure (analogous to the one used by Lord) is recommended where possible. In the first stage, the most biased items should be detected and removed. In the second stage, ability should be estimated from the remaining items, and bias should be calculated using this refined measure of ability.

Where possible, the bias of the test as a whole should be checked via an "unbiased" external criterion. Although the item bias methods are useful in their own right, and valid to the extent that the test as a whole is less biased than the individual items, they only measure one kind of bias.

Finally, these statistics should be viewed as tools in decision making and not as ends in themselves. As I noted in an earlier article (Ironson & Subkoviak, 1979), in addition to the statistical index of bias, a judgment should be made about the fairness of an item. The example cited was asking for the temperature at which one bakes a cake. This item may be statistically biased against males, but it may be appropriate if the purpose of the test is to select a cook.

REFERENCES

Angoff, W. H., & Ford, S. F. Item-race interaction on a test of scholastic aptitude. *Journal of Educational Measurement*, 1973, *10*, 95–105.

Baker, F. B. A criticism of Scheuneman's item bias technique. *Journal of Educational Measurement*, 1981, *18*, 59–62.

Bejar, I. I. Biased assessment of program impact due to psychometric artifacts. *Psychological Bulletin*, 1980, *87*, 513–524.

Birnbaum, A. Some latent trait models and their use in inferring an examinee's ability. In F. M. Lord & M. R. Novick, *Statistical theories of mental test scores*. Reading, Mass.: Addison-Wesley, 1968. Pp. 397–422.

Bishop, Y. M., Fienberg, S. E., & Holland, P. W. *Discrete multivariate analysis: Theory and practice*. Cambridge, Mass.: MIT Press, 1975.

Bougon, M. G., & Lissak, R. I. *Detecting item bias using the three-parameter logistic model and the B and C statistics*. Paper presented at the annual meeting of the American Psychological Association, Los Angeles, August 1981.

Camilli, G. A critique of the chi-square method for assessing item bias. Unpublished paper, Laboratory of Educational Research, University of Colorado, Boulder, 1979.

Cochran, W. G. Some methods for strengthening the common χ^2 tests. *Biometrics*, 1954, *10*, 417–451.

Craig, R., & Ironson, G. H. *The validity and power of selected item bias techniques using an a priori classification of items*. Paper presented at the annual meeting of the American Educational Research Association, Los Angeles, April 1981.

Dixon, W. J., & Brown, M. D. (Eds.). *BMDP-77 manual*. Berkeley and Los Angeles: University of California Press, 1977.

Douglass, J. B. *Item bias, test speededness, and Rasch tests of fit*. Paper presented at the annual meeting of the American Educational Research Association, Los Angeles, April 1981.

Draba, R. E. *The identification and interpretation of item bias* (Research Memorandum No. 26). Chicago: Statistical Laboratory, Department of Education, University of Chicago, 1977.

Draba, R. E. The Rasch model and legal criteria of a "reasonable" classification. Unpublished doctoral dissertation, University of Chicago, 1978.

Durovic, J. J. *Application of the Rasch model to civil service testing.* Paper presented at the annual meeting of the Northeastern Educational Research Association, Grossinger's N.Y., October 1970. (ERIC Document Reproduction Service No. ED 049-305)

Durovic, J. J. Definitions of test bias: A taxonomy and illustration of an alternative model. Unpublished doctoral dissertation, State University of New York at Albany, 1975. (a)

Durovic, J. J. *Test bias: An objective definition for test items.* Paper presented at the annual meeting of the Northeastern Educational Research Association, Ellenville, N.Y., October 1975. (ERIC Document Reproduction Service No. ED 128 381) (b)

Fienberg, S. E. *The analysis of cross-classified categorical data.* Cambridge, Mass.: MIT Press, 1977.

Goldberg, J. The application of item bias procedures to the cross-cultural assessment of attitudes. Unpublished master's thesis, University of Illinois, 1981.

Goodman, L. A., & Fay, R. *ECTA program: Description for users.* Chicago: Department of Statistics, University of Chicago, 1974.

Green, D. R., & Draper, J. F. *Exploratory studies of bias in achievement tests.* Paper presented at the annual meeting of the American Psychological Association, Honolulu, September 1972. (ERIC Document Reproduction Service No. ED 070 794)

Guion, R. M., & Ironson, G. H. Latent trait theory for organizational research. *Organizational Behavior and Human Performance,* in press.

Hambleton, R. K., & Cook, L. L. Latent trait models and their use in the analysis of educational test data. *Journal of Educational Measurement,* 1977, *14,* 75-96.

Hambleton, R. K., Swaminathan, H., Cook, L. L., Eignor, D. R., & Gifford, J. A. Developments in latent trait theory: Models, technical issues, and applications. *Review of Educational Research,* 1978, *48,* 467-510.

Hulin, C. L., Lissak, R. I., & Drasgow, F. *Effect of sample size and test length on IRT parameter estimation.* Paper presented at the annual meeting of the American Psychological Association, Los Angeles, August 1981.

Hulin, C. L., Komocar, J., & Drasgow, F. *Applications of item response theory to analysis of attitude scale translations* (Technical Report 80-5). Urbana-Champaign: University of Illinois, July 1980.

Hunter, J. E. *A critical analysis of the use of item means and item-test correlations to determine the presence or absence of content bias in achievement test items.* Paper presented at the National Institute of Education Conference on Test Bias, Annapolis, Md., December 1975.

Ironson, G. H. *The comparative validity of classical and latent trait approaches to the measurement of item bias.* Paper presented at the annual meeting of the National Council on Measurement in Education, Los Angeles, April 1981.

Ironson, G. H., Craig, R., & Canger, J. *The adaptation of item bias techniques for selection tests.* Paper presented at the annual meeting of the American Psychological Association, Los Angeles, August 1981.

Ironson, G. H., & Subkoviak, M. A comparison of several methods of assessing item bias. *Journal of Educational Measurement,* 1979, *16,* 209-225.

Knoke, D., & Burke, P. J. *Log-linear models* (University Papers Series, No. 20). Beverly Hills, Calif.: Sage, 1980.

Lang, D. An investigation of test item bias using the Rasch logistic response model. Unpublished master's thesis, Bowling Green State University, 1978.

Levine, M. V. *Weighted item bias statistics* (Report 81-5). Urbana-Champaign: Department of Educational Psychology, University of Illinois, 1981.

Levine, M. V., & Drasgow, F. Appropriateness measurement: Basic principles and validating studies. In D. J. Weiss (Ed.), *Proceedings of the 1979 Computerized Adaptive Testing Conference.* Minneapolis; Computerized Adaptive Testing Laboratory, University of Minnesota, 1980. Pp. 322–344.

Levine, M. V., & Rubin, D. B. Measuring the appropriateness of multiple-choice test scores. *Journal of Educational Statistics,* 1979, *4,* 269–290.

Levine, M. V., Wardrop, J. L., & Linn, R. L. *Weighted mean square item bias statistics.* Paper presented at the annual meeting of the American Educational Research Association, New York, March 1982.

Linn, R. L., & Harnish, D. Interactions between item content and group membership on achievement test items. *Journal of Educational Measurement,* 1981, *18,* 109–118.

Linn, R. L., Levine, M. V., Hastings, C. N., & Wardrop, J. L. *An investigation of item bias in a test of reading comprehension* (Technical Report No. 163). Urbana Champaign: Center for the Study of Reading, University of Illinois, March 1980.

Linn, R. L., Levine, M. V., Hastings, C. N., & Wardrop, J. L. Item bias in a test of reading comprehension. *Applied Psychological Measurement,* 1981, *5,* 159–173.

Lissak, R. I., & Wytmar, III, R. CARIF: A computational program for item information functions and item characteristic curves. *Behavior Research Methods & Instrumentation,* 1981, *13,* 360.

Lord, F. M. An analysis of the Verbal Scholastic Aptitude Test using Birnbaum's three-parameter logistic model. *Educational and Psychological Measurement,* 1968, *28,* 989–1020.

Lord, F. M. A study of item bias, using item characteristic curve theory. In Y. H. Poortinga (Ed.), *Basic problems in cross-cultural psychology.* Amsterdam: Swets and Zeitlinger, 1977. Pp. 19–29.

Lord, F. M. *Small N justified Rasch methods.* Paper presented at the Computerized Adaptive Testing Conference, Minneapolis, June 1979.

Lord, F. M. *Applications of item response theory to practical testing problems.* Hillsdale, N.J.: Lawrence Erlbaum Associates, 1980.

Lord, F. M., & Novick, M. R. *Statistical theories of mental test scores.* Reading, Mass.: Addison-Wesley, 1968.

Marascuilo, L. A., & McSweeney, M. *Nonparametric and distribution free methods for the social sciences.* Monterey, Calif.: Brooks/Cole, 1977.

Marascuilo, L. A., & Slaughter, R. E. Statistical procedures for identifying possible sources of item bias based on chi-square statistics. *Journal of Educational Measurement,* 1981, *18,* 229–248.

Marco, G. L. Item characteristic curve solutions to three intractable testing problems. *Journal of Educational Measurement,* 1977, *14,* 139–160.

Martin, J., Pine, S., & Weiss, D. J. *An item bias investigation of a standardized aptitude test* (Research Report No. 78-5). Minneapolis: Psychometric Methods Program, University of Minnesota, 1978.

Maxwell, A. E. *Analyzing qualitative data.* London: Methuen, 1961.

Mead, R. J. Using the Rasch model to identify person-based measurement disturbances. In D. J. Weiss (Ed.), *Proceedings of the 1979 Computerized Adaptive Testing Conference.* Minneapolis: Computerized Adaptive Testing Laboratory, University of Minnesota, 1980. Pp. 285–300.

Mellenbergh, G. Contingency table models for assessing item bias. Unpublished manuscript, March 1980. Psychologisch Laboratorium Universiteit van Amsterdam, Weesperplein 8, 1018 XA Amsterdam, Netherlands.

Merz, W. R., & Grossen, N. F. *An empirical investigation of six methods for examining test item bias.* Paper presented at the annual meeting of the National Council on Measurement in Education, San Francisco, April 1979. (Final report submitted to the National Institute of Education, Grant NIE 6-78-0067, California State University, Sacramento, 1979) (ERIC Document Reproduction Service No. ED 178 566)

Morrison, D. F. *Multivariate statistical methods.* New York: McGraw-Hill, 1967.

Mosteller, F., & Tukey, J. W. *Data analysis and regression.* Reading, Mass.: Addison-Wesley, 1976.

Nungester, R. J. An empirical examination of three models of item bias. (Doctoral dissertation, Florida State University, 1977). *Dissertation Abstracts International,* 1977, *38,* 2726A. (University Microfilms No. 77-24, 289)

Petersen, N. S. *Bias in the selection rule: Bias in the test.* Paper presented at the Third International Symposium on Educational Testing, University of Leyden, Netherlands, June 1977.

Pine, S. M. *Application of the latent trait test model for reducing ethnic bias in testing.* Paper presented at the annual meeting of the Psychometric Society, Princeton, N.J., 1975.

Pine, S. M. Applications of item characteristic curve theory to the problem of test bias. In D. J. Weiss (Ed.), *Applications of computerized adaptive testing* (Research Report 77-1). Minneapolis: Department of Psychology, Psychometric Methods Program, University of Minnesota, March 1977. Pp. 37–43.

Pine, S. M., & Weiss, D. J. *Effects of item characteristics on test fairness.* (Research Report No. 76-5). Minneapolis: Department of Psychology, Psychometric Methods Program, University of Minnesota, December 1976.

Rasch, G. *Probabilistic models for some intelligence and attainment tests.* Copenhagen: Denmarks Paedagogiske Institut, 1960.

Rasch, G. An individualistic approach to item analysis. In P. F. Lazarsfeld & N. W. Henry (Eds.), *Readings in mathematical social science.* Chicago: Science Research Associates, 1966. Pp. 89–108.

Rasch, G. *Probabilistic models for some intelligence and attainment tests.* Chicago: University of Chicago Press, 1980.

Reckase, M. D. Unifactor latent trait models applied to multifactor tests: Results and implications. *Journal of Educational Statistics,* 1979, *4,* 207–230.

Ree, M. J. Estimating item characteristic curves. *Applied Psychological Measurement,* 1979, *3,* 371–385.

Ree, M. J., & Jensen, H. E. The effects of sample size on linear equating of item characteristic curves. In D. J. Weiss (Ed.), *Proceedings of the 1979 Computerized Adaptive Testing Conference.* Minneapolis: Computerized Adaptive Testing Laboratory, University of Minnesota, 1980. Pp. 218–228.

Rentz, R. R., & Bashaw, W. L. *Equating reading tests with the Rasch model.* Athens, Ga.: Educational Resource Laboratory, 1975.

Rudner, L. M. *An approach to biased item identification using latent trait measurement theory.* Paper presented at the annual meeting of the American Educational Research Association, New York, April 1977. (a)

Rudner, L. M. *A closer look at latent trait parameter invariance.* Paper presented at the annual meeting of the New England Educational Research Organization, Manchester, N.H., 1977. (b)

Rudner, L. M. *Efforts toward the development of unbiased selection and assessment instruments.* Paper presented at the Third International Symposium on Educational Testing, University of Leyden, Netherlands, June 1977. (c)

Rudner, L. M. An evaluation of select approaches for biased item identification. Unpublished doctoral dissertation, Catholic University of America, 1977. (d)

Rudner, L. M., & Convey, J. J. *An evaluation of select approaches for biased item identification.* Paper presented at the annual meeting of the American Educational Research Association, Toronto, March 1978. (ERIC Document Reproduction Service No. ED 157 942)

Rudner, L. M., Getson, P. R., & Knight, D. L. A Monte Carlo comparison of seven biased item detection techniques. *Journal of Educational Measurement,* 1980, *17,* 1-10.

Ryan, J. P., & Hamm, D. M. *An introduction to the Rasch latent trait psychometric model.* Columbia: College of Education, University of South Carolina, 1978.

Scheuneman, J. D. *A new method of assessing bias in test items.* Paper presented at the annual meeting of the American Educational Research Association, Washington, D.C., April 1975. (ERIC Document Reproduction Service No. ED 106 359)

Scheuneman, J. D. *Academy of Certified Social Workers: Report on minority performance.* Princeton, N.J.: Educational Testing Service, June 1979. (a)

Scheuneman, J. D. A new method for assessing bias in test items. *Journal of Educational Measurement,* 1979, *16,* 143-152. (b)

Scheuneman, J. D. *Consistency across administrations of certain indices of bias in test items.* Paper presented at the annual meeting of the American Educational Research Association, Boston, April 1980. (a)

Scheuneman, J. D. Latent trait theory and item bias. In L. J. T. van der Kamp, W. F. Langerak, & D. N. M. de Gruijter (Eds.), *Psychometrics for educational debates.* Chicago: Wiley, 1980. Pp. 139-151. (b)

Scheuneman, J. D. A response to Baker's criticism. *Journal of Educational Measurement,* 1981, *18,* 63-66.

Shepard, L. A., Camilli, G., & Averill, M. *Comparison of six procedures for detecting test item bias using both internal and external ability criteria.* Paper presented at the annual meeting of the National Council on Measurement in Education, Boston, April 1980.

Subkoviak, M. J., Mack, J. S., & Ironson, G. H. *Item bias detection procedures: Empirical validation.* Paper presented at the annual meeting of the American Educational Research Association, Los Angeles, April 1981.

Swaminathan, H., & Gifford, J. Estimation of parameters in the latent trait model. In D. J. Weiss (Ed.), *Proceedings of the 1979 Computerized Adaptive Testing Conference.* Minneapolis: Computerized Adaptive Testing Laboratory, University of Minnesota, 1980. Pp. 372-385.

Tinsley, H. E., & Dawis, R. V. An investigation of the Rasch simple logistic model:

Sample free item and test calibration. *Educational and Psychological Measurement*, 1975, *35*, 325–339.

Urry, V. W. Ancillary estimators for the item parameters of mental tests. In W. A. Gorham (Chair), *Computerized testing: Steps toward the inevitable conquest* (PS-76-1). Washington, D.C.: Personnel Research and Development Center, U.S. Civil Service Commission, 1976. (NTIS No. PB 261 294).

Warm, T. A. *A primer of item response theory* (Technical Report No. 941078). Oklahoma City: U.S. Coast Guard Institute, Department of Transportation, 1978. (NTIS No. ADA063072).

Wingersky, M. S. Test whether the item parameters estimated by LOGIST for two separate groups differ significantly. Unpublished manuscript, Educational Testing Service, 1977. (Draft)

Wood, RL, & Lord, F. M. *A user's guide to LOGIST* (ETS Research Memorandum 76-4). Princeton, N.J.: Educational Testing Service, 1976.

Wood, RL, Wingersky, M. S., & Lord, F. M. *LOGIST: A computer program for estimating examinee ability and item characteristic curve parameters* (ETS Research Memorandum 76-6). Princeton, N.J.: Educational Testing Service, 1976.

Wright, B. D. Solving measurement problems with the Rasch model. *Journal of Educational Measurement*, 1977, *14*, 97–116.

Wright, B. D., & Mead, R. J. *BICAL: Calibrating items and scales with the Rasch model* (Research Memorandum No. 23A). Chicago: Statistical Laboratory, Department of Education, University of Chicago, 1978.

Wright, B. D., Mead, R. J., & Draba, R. *Detecting and correcting test item bias with a logistic response model* (Research Memorandum No. 22). Chicago: Statistical Laboratory, Department of Education, University of Chicago, 1976.

Wright, B. D., & Panchapakesan, N. A procedure for sample-free item analysis. *Educational and Psychological Measurement*, 1969, *29*, 23–48.

Wright, B. D., & Stone, M. H. *Best test design*. Chicago: MESA Press, 1979.

6 COMPARATIVE STUDIES OF ITEM BIAS METHODS
LOIS E. BURRILL

INTRODUCTION

ATTEMPTS TO identify bias at the level of the individual item, rather than at the test level, are relatively recent. Most frequently, item bias has been defined operationally as whatever a particular statistical procedure is picking up.

The two preceding chapters have described a number of specific methods of identifying item bias. The various procedures differ in their conceptualization as well as in their computation and interpretation. They also differ in their susceptibility to confounding by other artifacts of item construction or examinee ability. Some important questions are thereby raised: Are these procedures all tapping the same theoretical construct? Is there such a thing as statistical item bias? If they are all in some respects similar, in what ways are they different? Which approach is more accurate or, at least, most promising in informing decisions about item development and test construction? What follows is a brief review of the handful of studies that have addressed these comparative questions.

REVIEW OF STUDIES COMPARING ITEM BIAS METHODS

In order to determine which of the proposed methods of detecting item bias is most successful in accomplishing that end, a number of researchers have conducted comparative studies, applying several procedures to the same item pool or pools administered to carefully defined samples. Perhaps more importantly, several recent studies have also sought to evaluate their statistical findings in terms of size of item pools or samples required, time- and cost-effectiveness, and other criteria in order to recommend to other researchers which procedures might be most useful in particular situations.

Comparative Studies Using Simulated Data

Several researchers have attempted to compare proposed procedures for detecting item bias by applying the methods to simulated data. Such data may be generated using a Monte Carlo procedure in such a way as to establish a priori both the amount and the nature of the bias in each test. Thus, methods may be evaluated not only for their relative similarity, but also for the extent of "spurious" bias they may detect.

Rudner, Getson, and Knight (1979) study. Rudner and his colleagues investigated five bias identification procedures (transformed item difficulties, three-parameter item characteristic curves (ICCs), one-parameter ICCs, chi-squares with five intervals, and chi-squares with multiple intervals). The simulated data were generated using Birnbaum's (1968) three-parameter cumulative logistic model to relate item and examinee characteristics to item responses. Item bias was introduced in the difficulty and discrimination parameters by manipulating the standard deviations of these parameters. Four amounts of bias in discrimination, four amounts in difficulty, and four test lengths (20, 40, 60, and 80 items) were used to produce a total of 64 sets of test conditions. Two groups of 1,200 examinees were also drawn with one standard deviation difference between them in mean level of performance. The amount of bias generated for each item in this simulation was then correlated with the amount of bias detected by each of the five selected procedures.

For the transformed item difficulty method, two sets of p values were computed for the two groups and transformed to normal deviates. The values were plotted, and their distance from the 45° line through the origin was computed as a measure of relative item bias. Note that this procedure constitutes a modification of the original Angoff (1972) procedure (see chapter 4).

Two sets of ICC parameters were estimated for each item by applying Urry's (1975) iterative minimum chi-square procedure separately to the item responses of the two groups. The parameter values were equated, and the area between the estimated equated ICCs was used as the measure of item bias.

For the Rasch (one-parameter) procedure, difficulty estimates for each of the items for the two groups were computed separately, and a test of mean square fit of the items to the Rasch model was computed for each item. The difference in residuals was used as the bias measure (see Durovic, 1975).

Each item was tested individually for bias using Scheuneman's (1975) modified chi-square technique with two groups and five total score intervals. The measure of bias for each item was the value of the chi-square divided by its associated degrees of freedom. Each item was also tested with a modification of this technique which increased the number of score intervals to the highest possible number of cells, with the restriction that each cell have an expected value of 5.

COMPARATIVE STUDIES OF METHODS   163

Rudner and his colleagues found that all techniques, except the multiple-interval chi-square, showed slight increases in correlations between detected bias and generated bias with increases in test length. The sharpest increase was between 20 and 40 items for ICC-3.

Since the three-parameter model was used to generate the data base, one might expect a bias detection method based on that model to recover effectively the simulated bias. Although the correlation between generated and detected bias across all item lengths and types of generated bias was highest for ICC-3 ($r = .79$), the chi-square method with five score intervals was similarly effective ($r = .72$), as was the transformed item difficulty method ($r = .67$). Least effective overall was the Rasch model ($r = .55$). It should be noted that increasing the number of intervals in the chi-square procedure decreased, rather than increased, accuracy measured in terms of correlation with generated bias ($r = .61$).

When no bias was introduced in the difficulty parameter and all generated bias was attributable to group differences in item discriminations, the chi-square method with five intervals was most effective in recovering bias ($r = .81$), followed by the Rasch model procedure ($r = .71$). Least sensitive to differences in discrimination was the transformed item difficulty procedure ($r = .47$). It is interesting to note that, although the Rasch model does not parameterize discrimination, the goodness-of-fit approach of Durovic (1975) was found to be sensitive to discrimination differences. As larger amounts of bias were introduced in the difficulty parameter, correlations between generated and detected bias increased for the ICC-3 and transformed item difficulty procedures and declined for ICC-1.

When simulated bias was introduced solely in the difficulty parameter, the transformed item difficulty and chi-square (with five intervals) were most effective with correlations of .87 and .84, respectively. Correlations for the Rasch ICC-1 increased with greater amounts of bias in discrimination from .50 to .58; for the ICC-3, they remained relatively stable. The correlations for both chi-square procedures and transformed item difficulties steadily decreased as increases in bias were introduced into the discrimination parameter.

Intercorrelations among the five bias detection procedures revealed highest agreement between the chi-square method (with five intervals) and the transformed item difficulty procedure, and between the two chi-square methods (both $r = .85$). Correlations of the Rasch procedure with the others were consistently low (all $r < .40$).

Rudner and his colleagues concluded that three of the investigated procedures produced fairly accurate estimates of the generated item bias: ICC-3, chi-squares with five intervals, and transformed item difficulties. The ICC-3 procedure depends on accurate parameter estimates. The chi-square's effectiveness depends on interval estimates of ability. The transformed item difficulty method is insensitive to bias in item discrimination.

In a later publication (Rudner, Getson, & Knight, 1980) the authors added two additional procedures to their previous research: transformed item difficulties using the major axis of the scatterplot and delta values (cf. Angoff & Ford, 1973) and Rasch model using absolute values of the differences in difficulty values, rather than fit statistics. The two transformed item difficulty procedures performed similarly (intercorrelation .78). The Rasch procedure using the difficulty values correlated more highly with the other procedures than did the fit statistic method ($r = .57$ to .74), but was still not as sensitive to generated bias across all levels of bias and test length as ICC-3 or chi-square with five intervals.

Merz and Grossen (1979) study. Merz and Grossen used four sets of simulated data to compare transformed item difficulty (TID), point-biserial correlation, chi-square, factor analysis, one-parameter, and three-parameter item characteristic curve procedures. Although a three-parameter model was used to generate data, Merz and Grossen manipulated only the difficulty parameter. (Difficulties were restricted to a range from .15 to .92.) All tests were 60 items in length. The authors used two difficulty levels: 60% of the items correct (on the average) and 80% correct. Within each difficulty level two degrees of bias were introduced: 10% and 20% biased. Although data sets with zero bias were generated, Merz and Grossen reported no data for these sets.

For data generation, bias was defined as a difference of .70 or more in the area between the ICCs of the two groups, using Rudner's (1977) formula. Methods were equated by converting all bias estimates to z scores. Distributions of all item parameters and of examinee ability were normal. The same average percentage correct for total score for the two groups of hypothetical examinees in each data set was maintained by biasing 50% of the items in favor of each group, in order that test characteristic curves be similar for the two groups. Data were generated for 1,000 examinees in each group for each data set.

Merz and Grossen parameterized data for the three-parameter method using Urry's (1970) approach. Areas were computed using Rudner's (1977) procedure. The z scores for the area for each item were computed. For the one-parameter method, data were calibrated separately for each group using the BICAL program (Wright, Mead, & Draba, 1976). Areas and z scores were computed as for the three-parameter method. Item-total point-biserial correlations were computed for each group, and the difference between the two correlations expressed as a z score was used as a measure of bias. For the transformed item difficulty procedure, item difficulties were computed for each group and transformed to z scores. The distance from a 45° hypothetical regression line through the origin was used as the measure of bias. (Note that this is a modification of the Angoff, 1972, procedure.) The total score distribution was divided into eight intervals (60% correct data sets) or six intervals (80% correct) to obtain data for the chi-square procedure. The signed chi-square expressed as a z score was used as a bias measure. For the factor analysis method, group membership was used as a dummy variable along with item responses in computing an intercorrelation matrix that was then reduced with principal components analysis. The factor structure was rotated using varimax rotation. Bias was identified by factor loadings of items on the largest factor loading for that group membership. Again z scores were computed.

Correlations between the amount of generated bias and the amount of identified bias ranged from .07 to .98. The point-biserial method detected biased items poorly in comparison with other methods. Transformed item difficulty correlated .95 to .97 with generated bias across all conditions. Correlations for one- and three-parameter procedures were very high and chi-square only somewhat lower. The data for factor analysis were high for three of the four data sets.

In addition to correlations, Merz and Grossen also presented data on the accuracy of bias identification. One- and three-parameter procedures, transformed item difficulty, and factor analysis consistently identified more biased items than had been generated. Transformed item difficulty method exceeded 80% correct identification under all four conditions; the point-biserial method consistently underidentified the biased items.

Merz and Grossen concluded that the procedure that appeared to function best was transformed item difficulty. The only method they determined to be functioning poorly, however, was point biserial. Decisions among the other procedures should probably be based on other considerations, such as size of examinee group and computational resources.

It should be noted that the balancing of bias in both directions in this study was deliberately chosen as a way to avoid confounding of bias with ability. Such an assumption of equal ability is usually unwarranted in the real world. As Merz pointed out in the handout for the National Council on Measurement in Education session in which this study was presented, "Devising a method to deal with the confounding of bias and ability is crucial if the goal of debiasing is to be reached" (p.3).

Groome and Groome (1979) study. In another study, the Groomes compared transformed item difficulties (a modification of the Angoff, 1972, procedure developed by Merz and Rudner, 1978) and the three-parameter ICC method, based on simulated data generated using that ICC methodology. Four 60-item tests were developed, and each group contained 1,000 examinees. Test 1 had a normal distribution of parameters with no biased items; Test 2 had a uniform distribution of parameters with no biased items; and Tests 3 and 4 had distributions parallel to Tests 1 and 2, but with generated item bias. Correlations computed between known-to-be-biased and identified-as-biased items by the transformed item difficulty procedure were .95 for the normal distribution and .90 for the uniform distribution of item parameters.

Summary. The results of these data simulation studies are of value, even though unusually large item pools and examinee groups were used to obtain stable estimates for the ICC methods. Prepublication item tryouts, even for many large publishing ventures, rarely test this many examinees. More importantly, the nature of a simulation is that decision rules and operational definitions must be created arbitrarily. Since the rules used are those of the three-parameter model, it seems unlikely that any other procedure would "recover" the inserted bias as well as that model and even less likely that any other procedure would "recover" more of the inserted bias. It would be an example of circular thinking, however, to assume from this that the problem of determining (or deducing) a "best method" is thereby solved. Simulations are useful only in experimenting with the theoretical structure of the bias definition of interest. Before final decisions are made, responses made by real people taking real test questions must be studied carefully across the most promising methods of bias detection.

Comparative Studies Using Empirical Data

Very few studies comparing various identification methods have been made using "real" data; that is, comparing the performance of actual persons on actual test items. The few studies that have been reported, however, have tended to yield similar information.

Nungester (1977) study. Using data from the *Florida Statewide Ninth-Grade Test,* Nungester (1977) examined sex bias items and then compared empirically Angoff's (1972) delta-plot procedure, Scheuneman's (1975) method of chi-square analysis, and Fishbein's (1975) p value difference technique. He found rank order correlations from .65 to .77 for English items and from .87 to .98 for mathematics items. These findings led to the conclusion that, at least for sex bias, similar results could be expected from all three methods. His efforts to analyze the nature of the content of biased items were inconclusive. When items that were found to be biased by each procedure were removed, very slight decreases in reliability were found for the remaining items. Since Nungester did have a twelfth-grade test to use as a criterion, he was able to establish that removal of the items did tend to improve predictive validity, though only slightly.

Nungester also subjected items from these "finished" tests to what he described as a "standard item analysis." Thus, he also removed items with unacceptable discrimination indices or difficulty values (for this sample) and found that the removal of these items improved the test's reliability and validity for the sample to a greater extent than did the removal of "biased" items. He concluded that the effect of bias is not large on well-constructed tests and that the best justification for using these techniques is that they call attention to the problems of item and test bias.

Rudner and Convey (1978) study. Rudner and Convey compared four approaches, including transformed item difficulties, chi-square analysis,

ICCs, and factor scores, using data from *Stanford Achievement Test, Primary II Reading Comprehension*. They studied the various methods both in two samples from different populations (hearing and hearing-impaired) and in two subsamples from the same (hearing) population.

For the transformed item difficulty procedure, Rudner and Convey obtained a normal deviate score for each item and then plotted the pairs on a bivariate graph. They then measured the distance of each plotted item from the 45° line, not from the major axis of the actual ellipse formed by the items. This produced the distance estimate they used in generating an index of bias for each item. This procedure, though referenced to Angoff (1972), is in fact a modification of that original method.

For the ICC model, they applied Urry's (1975) iterative minimum chi-square procedure to the item responses of each group. The areas between estimated equated ICCs served as indices of bias.

For the factor-score method, Rudner and Convey computed the interitem product-moment correlations of the responses made by the two groups, and the matrix was reduced using ·principal components factor analysis. The resultant matrix was rotated to simple structure and factor scores were computed. Separate *t*-tests were computed. Those factors that showed significant differences ($p < .001$) between mean culture groups were identified as biased. Each item's factor loading on those factors serves as the bias index.

Finally, Scheuneman's (1975) chi-square technique was used, employing two culture groups and five score intervals. Two indices were developed: the magnitude of the chi-square, and one minus the probability associated with that chi-square. (No mention is made of the degrees of freedom used.)

When indices of bias were obtained for all items and methods, the methods were compared using Pearson product-moment correlations. Two items could not be parameterized because of their near-zero item-test correlations. Rudner and Convey also had difficulties with the chi square method due to disproportionate score distributions. Consequently, they ended up using four intervals rather than five.

The highest correlation obtained was between ICC and chi-square ($r = .67$). The correlation between chi-square and transformed difficulties was .59. The factor-score and chi-square ($1 - p$) approaches showed the least degree of similarity with the other approaches.

Rudner and Convey had set their same-culture groups to have significantly different abilities, so that these groups could serve as a check on whether the methods were picking up something other than bias. The transformed difficulty method did not appear to do so. In the ICC approach, two items showed aberrance between these two groups greater than that observed in the diverse-culture comparison. The factor-score method picked up about as much difference between these groups as in the diverse-culture comparison. The chi-square method did not identify items as biased for these groups.

Rudner and Convey concluded that ICC theory and transformed item difficulty approaches appeared to be the most attractive among the methods studied. They questioned using chi-square with groups as large as those they tested. They also cautioned against possible systematic inflation of the chi-squares when groups are too disproportionate in size. (This is a factor that can be controlled easily, however.)

Laksana (1979) study. Laksana applied the three-parameter ICC and ANOVA methods to data collected on the *Iowa Tests of Basic Skills* vocabulary and mathematics subtests at several levels in order to investigate both racial and sex bias (also see Coffman, chapter 9). He examined the degree of agreement between the two methods. The ANOVA procedure used in this study involved the arcsin transformation of p values. The index of bias was the arcsin difference obtained for each item. Under the ICC procedure, possibly biased items were identified by the size of the area between the two curves; Laksana established both absolute and signed aberrances, but used only signed aberrance as the index of bias for each item. Rank correlations between the two bias indices were obtained. The median correlation obtained was .40, leading Laksana to conclude that the procedures were identifying rather different sets of possibly biased items. The ANOVA method, he concluded, was practical, but not comprehensive; the ICC method was more comprehensive, but was impractical since large numbers of examinees and items are required for reliable parameter estimates.

Intasuwan (1979) study. Three approaches were compared by Intasuwan (1979) using data from the International Association for the Evaluation of Educational Achievement (IEA) *Reading Comprehension Test* (groups being English, American, and New Zealand teenagers). The approaches compared were the three-parameter ICC, Rasch model, and chi-square methods. Correlations between these methods ranged from .51 to .98, the latter being between the Rasch and chi-square methods.

Ironson and Subkoviak (1979) study. Ironson and Subkoviak compared delta plots, point-biserial discrimination indices, chi-squares, and the three-parameter ICC technique using samples of blacks and whites tested as part of the National Longitudinal Study (NLS) of 1972. (For a description of the NLS, see Hilton & Rhett, 1973.) The delta plots were made using Angoff and Ford's (1973) procedure. An unsigned index of bias was computed using absolute differences between white and black point-biserial item-total score correlations. The procedure was analogous to the one employed by Green and Draper (1972). Ironson and Subkoviak used Scheuneman's (1975) chi-square procedure, computing both signed and unsigned indices. For the ICC method, the LOGIST computer program of Wood and Lord (ETS) was employed (see Ironson, chapter 5); the unsigned measure of bias was based on the size of the area between the curves.

Ironson and Subkoviak did not find the discrimination-differences approach to correlate significantly with any other method. The unsigned indices correlated weakly among the other methods; the strongest relationship was found between the ICC and chi-square methods ($r = .485$). Signed indices increased the magnitude of the correlations substantially. Using the 24 most biased items identified by each method, a percentage agreement index was computed for each pair. The only pairs with greater-than-chance agreement were chi-square and ICC (54.2%), transformed difficulty and ICC (33.3%), and transformed difficulty and chi-square (37.5%).

A number of other facets to this research are worthy of mention here. As Ironson and Subkoviak stated the problem, there are a number of methods proposed for identifying bias and "no clear guidelines for choosing among them" (p. 209). Since the size of the sample required and the costs associated with various methods vary considerably, the choice of a method has practical ramifications. If all methods identify the same pool of biased items, one could simply choose the simplest and least expensive approach. If the methods yield different results, however, how should one determine which ones are most valid?

The authors also discussed the question of true differences in ability between groups. Throughout the research literature on item bias, it has been assumed that differences do indeed exist at the present time, for whatever reasons, among the performance levels of groups identified by ethnic membership. It remains then for bias to be identified as separate and distinct from true difference, just as "noise" is differentiated from the "signal," to borrow an analogy from engineering technology. Some methods proposed for identification of item bias attempt to control for differences in ability; others attempt to use statistical tools that are not sensitive to difficulty, with more or less success. Ironson (1978) was the first researcher since Angoff and Ford (1973) to attempt to match samples of different ethnicity for ability prior to the analysis of bias. Unlike the Angoff and Ford (1973) and Burrill (1981) studies, however, where external matching variables were used, Ironson used the total subtest score as the matching variable.

Ironson and Subkoviak suggested three approaches that appear to have great potential for detection of *relative* item bias. First, the latent trait procedures, restricted by their requirements for large samples and long subtests as well as their computational costs, may be feasible for developers of large-scale testing programs. For smaller-scale research studies, the chi-square procedure and Angoff's transformed difficulty procedure would be more practical. Discrimination procedures appear to be inadequate.

Shepard, Camilli, and Averill (1980) study.   Shepard et al. defined bias as a contextual property—an "anomaly in a context of other items" (p. 4)—and point out that this is different from the notion of unfairness. Their study used data from the Lorge-Thorndike test, a group-administered mental ability test having separate verbal and noverbal sections, given to black, white, and Chicano pupils in grades 4, 5, and 6. The same white sample was used in comparisons with blacks and with Chicanos, with about 500 pupils in each sample. The samples contained roughly the same proportion of each grade group.

The procedures that were compared included chi-square (both Scheuneman's procedure and a modification suggested by Camilli, 1979), Angoff's delta-plot or transformed item difficulty procedure, point-biserial difference, and various indices derived from both three-parameter latent trait methodology and one-parameter (Rasch) techniques, for a total of 15 different indices, both signed and unsigned. Separate analyses were made using an external criterion as an ability estimate, as well as the usual total test score (internal criterion) estimate. The external criterion variable was the score on *Raven's Coloured Progressive Matrices,* a "culture-fair" test of Spearman's g-factor, presumed to be less biased than the test containing the items being examined. It should be noted that Angoff's delta-plot procedure does not lend itself to use of an external criterion in this way, so such analyses were not attempted.

Shepard and her colleagues felt that the three-parameter latent trait methodology offered the most theoretically defensible possibility for identifying biased items and planned their study to investigate how closely other procedures could approximate its findings. They ran into trouble, however, since their samples were not large enough for analysis using these procedures. They also found problems with the Raven's test as an external criterion because their samples experienced ceiling effects with this measure.

Since there is a "method effect" in any significance tests applied across methods, the more important findings are embedded in the correlations among methods and in the percentage of agreement among methods in the identification of extreme items. Correlations between chi-square procedures and the ICC-3 area, the Angoff procedure and the ICC-3 area, and the Angoff and chi-square procedures were all moderate and (though somewhat lower) approximate those found by Ironson and Subkoviak (1979). The Angoff procedure also correlated very highly with one-parameter difference in b's and signed areas ($r \geq .99$).

Correlations represent relationships across the whole range of items in a test and the index values assigned to those in the middle are of less concern in this context than the consistency of identification in the tail (unsigned) or tails (signed) of the distribution. Shepard et al. used inspection of histograms displaying the distribution of item bias values for each data set to identify "outliers." Thus, the number of items identified as anomalous was different for various procedures, ranging from 3 (out of 90) for signed Scheuneman chi-squares to 16 and 19 for the Wingersky (1977) indices for three-parameter and one-parameter methods, respectively. The closest agreements were among the Camilli chi-square and Scheuneman's signed chi-square. A looser cluster was formed by the Angoff procedure, Rasch b differences, and Rasch signed and unsigned areas. It is interesting to note that 46 out of the 90 items were not identified as biased by any procedure in the black-white comparison with an internal criterion. One item was identified by 10 of the 15 procedures; 1 by 9; 2 by 7; 2 by 6; 3 by 5; 7 by 4; 4 by 3; 7 by 2; and 17 by only one procedure. (Most of those 17 were identified by point-biserial or Wingersky procedures.)

Despite the limitations of the external criterion, it is instructive to examine how well each procedure correlated with itself using internal and external criteria of ability. Correlations were all moderate to high for the various chi-square and ICC-3 indices, and .99+ for all ICC-1 indices except fit statistics. Despite the magnitude of these correlations, it seemed clear that changing the criterion did make a difference. Since the external criterion was a nonverbal test, it is not surprising that most correlations improved in those data sets for the nonverbal portion of the Lorge-Thorndike test. (This was not true for unsigned chi-square procedures for Chicanos.)

Shepard et al. concluded that the relationships among the various methods are strong enough to be taken as evidence of convergent validity, which is "sufficient to hearten a measurement theorist." However, "the practitioner is more likely to be struck by the serious method effects observable in the results" (p. 74). They suggest that the three-parameter methods are the most theoretically sound. But when samples or pools are not of sufficient size, Shepard et al. recommend that the Camilli chi-square procedure be used, adding that bias indices should always be considered indicative data and should not be used as the sole basis for accepting or rejecting an item. They also suggest that the Angoff procedure may be used instead of the Rasch model for bias detection.

Burrill (1981) study. Burrill compared seven procedures: four difficulty procedures, including Angoff delta-plot or transformed item difficulty, two item-test correlation procedures (biserial and point-biserial correlations) and Scheuneman's chi-square technique. Fourteen item pools in three tryout forms, administered in the item analysis phase of the development of the *Metropolitan Readiness Test* (*MRT,* 1976 edition) were used, and data for beginning first-graders were analyzed. Randomly selected samples of blacks and whites and samples matched pairwise on an external correlated variable (1965 *MRT* total score) were compared, as were two random samples of white children. Latent trait methodologies were eliminated from this study because of their requirements for large samples and long item pools. (Although Burrill investigated a total of 204 items, they were in three forms and could not be considered unidimensional pools.)

Data obtained for each procedures across the three pairs of samples were analyzed at two levels. Rank order correlations were computed between pairs of procedures, for each pair of samples, and for each item pool. Second, editorial or observational analyses were conducted, looking only at items identified as extreme both in terms of relative position within the distribution of indices and in terms of absolute rank order. All four difficulty procedures ("raw" p values, arcsin transforms, difference between delta transforms, and the Angoff delta-plot procedure) were very highly correlated with each other; though as expected, the Angoff distance values correlated less well with the other three than those others correlated with each other. For every comparison between procedures, the correlations were lowest for the random samples of blacks and whites. The procedure of first reducing mean differences between the groups by "matching" on a correlated external variable improved the correlations in all cases, but differentially across procedures.

Correlations between the two "discrimination" indices were extremely high across all item pools and for all three pairs of samples. (Medians of 14 correlations = .922, .975, and .974.) Almost no correlations of one discrimination procedure with one difficulty procedure reached significance. Among the few that were significant, many were negative.

The chi-square procedure correlated moderately well with all the difficulty procedures—in the .60s for random samples of blacks and whites and in the high .70s for matched samples and for the two random white samples. Thus, although related to the difficulty procedures, chi-square seemed to be picking up something not identified by the difficulty procedures, especially when the children differed in ability level.

Correlations of the Scheuneman chi-square with the discrimination procedures were stronger than those between the discrimination and difficulty procedures, but, in general, were extremely modest. Again several of the significant correlations were negative. Except for these somewhat isolated cases, chi-square did not appear to be closely related to the discrimination procedures.

One measure of an item's extreme position (anomaly) within an item pool was determined by using an arbitrary cutoff of one and one-half standard deviations from the mean of the distribution of signed item indices for the pool. If the distributions for the 14 item pools investigated were normal, a total of 29 items would be expected to be identified as extreme. Although the various procedures identified groups of from 22 to 32 items in the three pairs of samples, none of the procedures was really consistent in identifying the same items in both matched and random samples of the two ethnic groups without also identifying "bias" within the two random white samples as well. A total of 24 items were identified consistently by at least one procedure—ranging from a low of 4 for the chi-square procedure to a high of 9 for arcsins, point biserials, and Angoff's delta-plot. Of these 24 items, 6 were identified by all 4 difficulty procedures and 5 others by both discriminations. Of the 4 identified by chi-squares, one was also identified by all difficulty procedures and one by both discrimination indices.

A similar analysis was also conducted using ranks of first, second, last, or next-to-last within the item pool, for a possible total of 56 "extreme" items to be identified. The same criterion of consistency was applied, requiring identification in both matched and random samples of two ethnic groups, but not in the two random white samples. The Angoff procedure identified the highest number with 22, followed by the other difficulty procedures, the discrimination procedures and, finally, chi-squares (identifying only 12). A total of 49 items were identified by all the procedures combined—of which 21 had been identified previously by the one-and-one-half standard deviation definition of extreme. (Note that three items previously identified as extreme were not so identified by the rank definition.)

The performance of the chi-square method in this study was disappointing. It should be noted, however, that sample sizes were very small and many items exhibited differential validity, even when the number of intervals was reduced from five to three. Furthermore, "signing" is artificial in chi-squares, and the real value of the chi-square may be lost by this procedure. The results of the study suggest the Angoff procedure is worthy of recommendation, not only on the grounds of consistency of item bias identification, but also in terms of efficiency, cost-effectiveness, and interpretability to the lay public, who constitute the primary audience for the findings of bias studies.

Tentative Generalizations from Recent Studies

There is still much needed research to be done, but we are now at a point when some tentative generalizations may be drawn from the studies that have been conducted to date. The following comments summarize some general themes.

Statistical item bias is not *the same as judgmental item bias.* The items identified as biased by various statistical procedures are not the same ones that are identified by panels of minority judges or item editors as offensive, denigrating, or insulting to individuals of some population subgroup. Nor are they the items that experts tend to identify as requiring a cultural background outside the experience of disadvantaged or culturally different persons. The two approaches will yield different (though sometimes overlapping) information and cannot be considered as alternatives to each other. Rather, test developers should build both procedures into their test construction methods.

All statistical procedures devised to date are "relative" methods. The present conceptualizations of bias in an item involve its "not fitting in" with some other group of items with which it had been thought to belong. This is true whether one uses matched or random samples and whether one uses internal or external criteria of ability. Thus, bias is not necessarily some inherently "bad" characteristic of an item; it is dependent on the pool of items with which the particular item is being compared.

In this respect, then, bias in the sense of unfairness to some group cannot be eliminated during test construction by rejecting items that do not meet a particular standard of comparability with other items. What the process can do is to improve the homogeneity of the test being constructed so that each item is yielding information parallel to that yielded by each other item. The final test must then be evaluated for fairness or bias in terms of the use to which test scores are put in decision making.

Having said that item bias or lack of bias is relative does not, of course, reduce the importance of the process or the necessity for its appropriate application during test development. Although most researchers have conceived of item bias procedures as improving validity, it may be more realistic to visualize them as concerned more with internal consistency or reliability—a necessary, but not sufficient, prerequisite of validity.

Differences in ability between examined groups are very hard to eliminate as a confounding factor.   It must be taken as a given, at least for the present, that true differences in ability exist between most groups—whether ethnic-, cultural-, or sex-identified divisions within the population. This being so, procedures have to be evaluated on the basis of their ability to overcome these differences. The latent trait models are by their nature most successful in this regard. The chi-square procedure proposed by Scheuneman is also appealing in this respect, since it uses several levels of ability, rather than a mean performance. The Angoff procedure, because of its measurement of outliers, also seems to be quite satisfactory in this context. Yet studies using matched samples show that even chi-square and Angoff procedures can be improved by first reducing the differences in ability of the groups being compared.

Correlations among procedures are necessary evidence of convergent validity, but not sufficient for deciding which procedure to use.   Studies that have been done to date all seem to confirm that latent trait indices, chi-square analyses, and Angoff's delta-plot procedures are moderately highly correlated. However, correlations are based on the full range of items in the pool, whereas bias decisions are affected by the correlations only at the tail or tails of the distribution. Here the relationships are not as high, and further research efforts need to focus on this issue.

The notion of "signing" bias indices, though attractive, may be very misleading.   When an average ability level for each group is used as the zero point and aberrance is defined as distance from that point, direction of bias is deceptively easy to assign. In procedures like chi-square or the latent trait methods, where several levels of ability are compared across samples, differences in opposite directions at different levels may be observed. This important characteristic of aberrance may be lost when a sign must be given to some summing of these differences. This is especially true when the aberrances tend to "average out."

No useful conclusions about why certain items are biased can yet be drawn from studies conducted to date.   Once items are identified as outliers, traditional item editorial procedures can frequently confirm that some distractor was operating differently for the samples. Usually, however, one cannot deduce any logical reason why this should be true. Indeed, some of

Scheuneman's most recent work suggests that placement on the page, order of distractors, and other artifacts of format may have more to do with the bias identification than the content of the item itself (Scheuneman, 1978; see also chapter 7). And in Nungester's earlier work, editorial procedures using ethnic item data, but without any formal bias identification procedures, worked very well in eliminating "bad items." For the moment, then, we do not know how to avoid writing biased items but must decide simply whether or not to reject the items once they have been identified. Much additional research is needed in this area.

Bias researchers are restricted in their choice of procedures by several practical considerations. Few persons contemplating bias studies have access to samples of 1,000 persons or to the extensive computer time required for the three-parameter analysis—even if they have item pools of 60 items. Rasch procedures, though somewhat less restrictive, are yet fairly expensive and require large samples. Both the chi-square and Angoff procedures may be used with smaller samples and shorter tests, and both may be computed by hand, if necessary. Therefore, in most instances, researchers will be restricted to a choice between one or the other of these more classical test construction procedures. The weight of preference between these two seems to be on the side of the chi-square procedure for most studies, but with Angoff's delta-plot procedure running a very respectable second place. The other procedures appear to have been eliminated from further consideration by the weight of the research reported previously.

For those who have appropriate item pools and samples, as well as access to computer time—especially those using latent trait methodology for their test construction for other reasons—the ICC procedures offer psychometrically compelling approaches to the identification of biased items. Which of a number of indices derived from latent trait methods may be best for this purpose has not been determined, however. (See Ironson, chapter 5, for a further discussion of this issue.)

RECOMMENDATIONS FOR
TEST DEVELOPERS AND TEST USERS

Those who plan to incorporate bias detection into their test-development activities should base their decision making about what procedure to use on three basic criteria. First, it is important to use a procedure that has been shown to have "psychometric respectability"—a method that can be defended as appropriate. To date, four procedures appear to qualify under this criterion: latent trait methods, both one- and three-parameter models, chi-square analysis, and Angoff's transformed item difficulty or delta-plot procedure.

Second, it is realistic for any test developer to add a second level of decision-making rules for selecting a procedure—the time-effectiveness and cost-effectiveness of the method. There are substantial differences among the procedures in these regards, as well as constraints in the number of items and number of examinees necessary to obtain estimates.

It is often vital, however, to add a third level of decision making: the criterion of interpretability or ability to explain the procedure to a lay public. Item bias is not, at its heart, a statistical concept, but rather a philosophical and emotional one. The tools we have designed to identify what should, perhaps, be more accurately labeled "item discrepancy," or differential performance, are statistical tools. They are useful to us and we understand them as test developers. Whether they can be explained convincingly to the lay public or to the court judges—in litigation involving discrimination in testing—is another issue that cannot be disregarded in planning any item bias research for a current or future test.

Having surveyed briefly what has been learned and, in passing, mentioned several issues yet to be resolved, it remains to offer some practical guidelines for test developers. The following list is suggestive, but not exhaustive.

1. *Do not rely on statistical item bias detection alone.* Plan to have a panel of reviewers edit the items for bias (see Tittle, chapter 2). They will need some training, especially if they are not test construction experts. Laypersons may tend to confuse nonparallel difficulty of an item with bias. Increase your own editors' sensitivity to bias, as well. Plan some way of identifying the degree of test bias that may yet be present in the finished test, even after judgmental and statistical bias analyses have been conducted, In other words, plan a three-pronged program to reduce bias in your final product.
2. *If you are developing your test using latent trait methodology, by all means use indices from that process as indicators of item bias.* Be aware, however, in making that decision that samples of less than 1,000 (in the case of three-parameter) or 500 (in the case of Rasch) may yield unstable results. Be sure your item pool is reasonably large and that your budget for computer time is realistic.
3. *If you are using more traditional test development procedures, choose between chi-square analysis and Angoff's delta-plot procedure—or better yet, consider both.* If you are most concerned about bias only against the minority group, you may prefer delta plot; if you are concerned more with differential validity, you may prefer chi-square. Neither procedure is likely to yield an enormous number of aberrant items. Both are fairly easy to compute, although determining the appropriate cells for the chi-square method is not a mechanistic process. Both are easily explainable to the lay public.
4. *Regardless of which procedure you select, consider trying to reduce somewhat any extreme differences in true ability you anticipate may exist between your samples.* You might consider dropping cases beyond, for ex-

ample, one and one half or two standard deviations from the mean of their own sample. Alternatively, you may wish to pull samples matched on an external correlated variable such as another (preferably well-accepted) measure of the same trait or aptitude. As an internal criterion, total score on the item pool being examined may also be used as a matching variable. (See Schmeiser, chapter 3, for further discussion of matching.)

5. *Do not set in advance any particular cutoff as an absolute, arbitrary definition of "biased."* Rather, rank the items from worst to best in terms of the bias index you have selected. Then drop items using the rank as one (but not the only) criterion until you have an item pool of the required size. If you wish to then judge the degree to which you have eliminated bias by noting whether there are any items left beyond some preplanned goal or cutoff, fine, but remember that present definitions of item bias are relative; there is no inherently "right" cutoff. The longer the test, the more "wobble" there will be in the way any two groups respond to the same questions. Some wobble will always remain.

6. *Do not abandon other, more traditional, methods for rejecting or including items in the final test.* Many items identified by bias procedures are poor items anyway—ones that traditional editing would also reject. Look carefully at others. If there is reason to believe that the position of various distractors or the item's placement on the page was the real reason for aberrant performance, consider carefully whether the item should be discarded. If you are building an achievement test, do not forget the content outline or set of objectives that guided original test development. For example, if all or most of the items testing a certain skill are among the outliers, can you really just dump them without violating the content validity of your final product? Check to see if perhaps the directions for that particular task may have been unclear in some way that is causing one group to misperceive the intent of the items.

7. *Do not be surprised that you can find no logical reason for an item to have behaved peculiarly.* Do not automatically throw the item back into the pool if you cannot explain why it was identified as an outlier. In sum, selecting items for a final form has never been a clerical task or one easily defined by a set of rules. Although bias indices should inform decisions, judgment is still paramount. To date, about the only kind of decision you can make is to include or to reject the item.

8. *Be prepared to explain to several different publics what you have done and why.* The primary consumers of your explanation will be students, parents, school personnel, and the general public, rather than other test developers. Technical jargon will not help; graphics will, as will a clear description of what the procedure you have used to identify item bias can and cannot accomplish. In many respects, the process is at least as important as the outcome.

REFERENCES

Angoff, W. H. *A technique for the investigation of cultural differences.* Paper presented at the annual meeting of the American Psychological Association, Honolulu, September 1972. (ERIC Document Reproduction Service No. ED 069 686)

Angoff, W. H., & Ford, S. F. Item-race interaction on a test of scholastic aptitude. *Journal of Educational Measurement,* 1973, *10,* 95–105.

Birnbaum, A. Some latent trait models and their use in inferring an examinee's ability. In F. M. Lord & M. R. Novick, *Statistical theories of mental test scores.* Reading, Mass.: Addison-Wesley, 1968. Pp. 397–422.

Burrill, L. E. A comparative investigation into the identification of ethnic bias in items assessing current educational status. Unpublished doctoral dissertation, Fordham University, 1981. (Available from author, The Psychological Corporation, 757 Third Avenue, New York, N.Y. 10017.)

Camilli, G. A critique of the chi-square method for assessing item bias. Unpublished paper, Laboratory of Educational Research, University of Colorado, Boulder, 1979.

Durovic, J. J. *Test bias: An objective definition for test items.* Paper presented at the annual meeting of the Northeastern Educational Research Association, Ellenville, N.Y., October 1975. (ERIC Document Reproduction Service No. ED 128 381)

Fishbein, R. L. *An investigation of the fairness of the items in a test battery.* Paper presented at the annual meeting of the National Council on Measurement in Education, Washington, D.C., April 1975. (ERIC Document Reproduction Service No. ED 111 837)

Green, D. R., & Draper, J. F. *Exploratory studies of bias in achievement tests.* Paper presented at the annual meeting of the American Psychological Association, Honolulu, September 1972. (ERIC Document Reproduction Service No. ED 070 794)

Groome, M. L., & Groome, W. R. *Item bias identification: A comparison of two approaches.* Paper presented at the annual meeting of the National Council on Measurement in Education, San Francisco, April, 1979. (ERIC Document Reproduction Service No. ED 174 685)

Hilton, T. L., & Rhett, H. *The base-year survey of the national longitudinal study of the high school class of 1972* (Final Report, Contract No. OEC-0-72-0903, Office of Education, National Center for Education Statistics, U.S. Department of Health, Education, and Welfare). Princeton, N.J.: Educational Testing Service, June 1973.

Intasuwan, P. A comparison of three approaches for determining item bias in cross-national testing (Doctoral dissertation, University of Pittsburgh, 1979). *Dissertation Abstracts International,* 1979, *40,* 2613A. (University Microfilms No. 79-24, 720)

Ironson, G. H. A comparative study of several methods of assessing item bias (Doctoral dissertation, University of Wisconsin, Madison, 1977). *Dissertation Abstracts International,* 1978, *38,* 7285A. (University Microfilms No. 78-04, 425)

Ironson, G. H., & Subkoviak, M. J. A comparison of several methods of assessing item bias. *Journal of Educational Measurement,* 1979, *16,* 209–225.

Laksana, S. Application of analysis of variance approach and item characteristic approach for assessing item bias in the ITBS Form 7 (Doctoral dissertation, University of Iowa, 1979). *Dissertation Abstracts International*, 1979, *40*, 2615A. (University Microfilms No. 79-24, 495)

Merz, W. R., & Grossen, N. *An empirical investigation of six methods for examining test item bias.* Paper presented at the annual meeting of the National Council on Measurement in Education, San Francisco, April 1979. (Final report submitted to the National Institute of Education, Grant NIE 6-78-0067, California State University, Sacramento, 1979) (ERIC Document Reproduction Service No. ED 178 566)

Merz, W. R., & Rudner, L. M. *Bias in testing: A presentation of selected methods.* Paper presented at the annual meeting of the American Educational Research Association, Toronto, March 1978. (ERIC Document Reproduction Service No. ED 164 610)

Nungester, R. J. An empirical examination of three models of item bias (Doctoral dissertation, Florida State University, 1977). *Dissertation Abstracts International*, 1977, *38*, 2726A. (University Microfilms No. 77-24, 789)

Rudner, L. M. An evaluation of select approaches for biased item identification. Unpublished doctoral dissertation, Catholic University of America, 1977.

Rudner, L. M., & Convey, J. J. *An evaluation of select approaches for biased item identification.* Paper presented at the annual meeting of the American Educational Research Association, Toronto, March 1978. (ERIC Document Reproduction Service No. ED 157 942)

Rudner, L. M., Getson, P. R., & Knight, D. L. *The effect of various test and item properties on five approaches to biased item detection.* Paper presented at the annual meeting of the National Council on Measurement in Education, San Francisco, April 1979.

Rudner, L. M., Getson, P. R., & Knight, D. L. A Monte Carlo comparison of seven biased item detection techniques. *Journal of Educational Measurement*, 1980, *17*, 1-10.

Scheuneman, J. D. *A new method of assessing bias in test items.* Paper presented at the annual meeting of the American Educational Research Association, Washington, D.C., April 1975. (ERIC Document Reproduction Service No. ED 106 359)

Scheuneman, J. D. *Further considerations in the assessment of bias in test items.* Paper presented at the annual meeting of the American Psychological Association, Toronto, August 1978.

Shepard, L. A., Camilli, G., & Averill, M. *Comparison of six procedures for detecting test item bias using both internal and external ability criteria.* Paper presented at the annual meeting of the National Council on Measurement in Education, Boston, April 1980.

Urry, V. W. A Monte Carlo investigation of logistic mental test models. Unpublished doctoral dissertation, Purdue University, 1970.

Urry, V. W. *Ancillary estimators for the parameters of mental test models.* Paper presented at the annual meeting of the American Psychological Association, Chicago, August 1975.

Wingersky, M. S. Test whether the item parameters estimated by LOGIST for two separate groups differ significantly. Unpublished manuscript, Educational Testing Service, 1977. (Draft)

Wright, B. D., Mead, R. J., & Draba, R. *Detecting and correcting test item bias with a logistic response model* (Research Memorandum No. 22). Chicago: Statistical Laboratory, Department of Education, University of Chicago, 1976.

7 A POSTERIORI ANALYSES OF BIASED ITEMS

JANICE DOWD SCHEUNEMAN

INTRODUCTION

OVER THE PAST decade a number of statistical procedures for the detection of item bias have been introduced and their validity investigated, as in the studies reported in the preceding chapters. Relatively little work, however, has been done concerning how the statistical results are to be used once they have been obtained. One reason for this may be that only recently, as results have begun to accumulate from numerous studies with little increase in the understanding of the bias process, has it become apparent that this is a problem area.

When many of us first began working on the topic of bias, the isolation of items that seemed to be biased for or against a particular group appeared to be the bulk of the task. We naively assumed, as many investigators are assuming today, that a review of such items would readily reveal the source of the apparent bias, that the problem could then be easily corrected with suitable modifications or by dropping the item from the test or item pool, and that a "debiased" instrument would result. Indeed, some studies have identified item content that is in some way less familiar to members of minority cultures or other subgroups. For example, Breland (1974), Scheuneman (1976), Draba (1977), and Rudner (1978) all cite examples of results that were interpretable in terms of item content. Veale and Foreman (1976) have contended that the source of bias will often be in the content of item foils or distractors that are unusually attractive to members of certain subgroups for cultural reasons; the item content in all of these instances, however, is verbal. In other cases, content is more difficult to defend as an underlying mechanism of bias. Suppose, for example, the subjects are high school students, the content consists of simple geometric forms or letters of the alphabet, and the tasks required are not unlike those in other apparently unbiased items on the same test. Even with verbal content, many investigators have been unable to interpret results in meaningful ways.

180

This chapter is organized into three main sections. The first will focus on sources of high bias indices. I will argue that the major sources of the differences reflected by these indices are, first, flaws in the item or test to which members of different subgroups are differentially sensitive and, second, genuine differences between groups that may or may not be the result of the cultural characteristics of the groups and that may or may not reflect valid differences in the ability being measured. Next, strategies for dealing with the bias results will be discussed. These will include blind screening of items, distractor analyses, and item review. Examples will be provided to show how the interpretation of certain results can also suggest appropriate action. In the last section of the chapter a practical step-by-step procedure will be suggested for conducting a review of those items identified as biased by a statistical procedure.

I will not be presenting experimental data nor results in this chapter. The material is based on my own experience and observations, on the observations and thinking of others as reported in their papers or in personal communications, and on feedback I have received from working with minority reviewers and other groups. The aim is not to provide answers to some knotty problems, but to try to clarify some of the issues and to stimulate thought and discussion concerning this important area of bias research.*

IDENTIFICATION OF ISSUES AND STRATEGIES

Sources of High Bias Indicators

One difficulty in attempting to interpret the results of a bias study is having too narrow a view of the sources of bias in test items. In order to give some sense of the scope and complexity of the problems associated with a statistical bias analysis, I will, in this section, provide examples of why high bias indicators occur and suggest a structure for classifying the sources of these problems. A useful distinction is between those items that are flawed in such a way that they do not reflect equally well the ability of the groups being compared and those items that reflect accurately the results of genuine differences between groups. We tend to think of bias in terms of the former, flawed items that are unfair to one or more subgroups of examinees, but the various procedures will also identify the latter under a number of different circumstances.

Detecting flaws in items and tests. Most of the bias procedures described in the preceding chapters are intended to flag an item as operating in a suspicious manner with regard to different population subgroups, but they

*Sources for the examples cited from my own work are in some cases from unpublished studies. Others are drawn from studies reported in Scheuneman (1976, 1978, 1979a, 1979b, and 1980). Published tests referred to are the *Metropolitan Readiness Tests* (Nurss & McGauvran, 1973, 1976) and *Otis-Lennon School Ability Test* (Otis & Lennon, 1976).

will give us relatively little guidance about what has caused this suspicious outcome. Even the methods designed to isolate distractors that appear to be operating differentially for the groups compared can be reflecting, in the distractor behavior, a fault concealed in another part of the item or in another part of the test. The effect of bias is to reduce the probability of a correct response from what would be expected for a person of a given ability. Two ways in which this can occur are by introducing uncertainty as to the nature of the task required in an item and by the inclusion of cues or other material that make the various options unequally attractive to members of different groups.

Uncertainty can result from failure to provide a sufficient explanation concerning the nature of the task required to successfully complete the item or from the introduction of material into the item stem or options that tends to confuse the respondent. In both cases, ability to guess what is probably required, based on the respondent's own background and experience, becomes part of what is being measured. To conjecture that white examinees may be better able than others to guess what is required in such circumstances does not seem unreasonable.

An example where insufficient explanation of the task may be the source of the high bias indices comes from a study of one subtest from the 1973 item analysis edition of the *Metropolitan Readiness Tests (MRT)*. During the pretest phase, certain experimental tests other than those subsequently included in the published version of the instrument were tried out and later analyzed for bias. One of these, Learning Symbols, was a novel test requiring the child to learn a small number of symbols, each of which was associated with a particular word. The test was divided into three distinct sections. After presentation of the picture-symbol pairs by the teacher, the first series of items directed the pupil to mark, for example, the symbol that stood for a rabbit. After a quick review of the symbols, the second set of items asked the pupils to mark, for example, the symbol that stood for an animal with long ears and a fluffy tail. The third set of items presented a short phrase written in symbols such as "rabbit in box," for which the pupil would select a corresponding illustration. Three such tests were developed, administered, and later analyzed for bias. All items that had significant bias indices appeared as the first item in one of these three sets, or in the case of the symbol phrases, the second item as well as the first. This would be the expected result if the directions for taking this test were less adequate for the black children than for the white children, or were inadequate for both, but whites were better able to surmise what the appropriate behavior was.

The directions that are unclear need not be those given prior to administering the items, however, but may be those provided in the item stem. For example, in the analysis of pretest items for the *Otis-Lennon School Ability Test* (Otis & Lennon, 1976), we found that items requesting opposites were missed more often by black fifth-graders than would be expected on the basis of their scores on other verbal items. Inspection showed that they were more apt than whites to select the synonym, suggesting that the meaning of the stimulus word was known, but that uncertainty existed regarding the word *opposite*. Such differences were not found with older children in junior or senior high school, as would be expected since opposite should not be a difficult concept at the higher level.

A second, similar example occurred with the word *series*. Again in the *Otis-Lennon* pretest, figural series items were missed more frequently by black children than would be expected from their performance on other figural items presented in other formats. The item stem gave little more than an instruction to select the option that should come at the end of a stimulus series. Clearly, if a pupil did not comprehend that a progression was being formed by the series of figural representations, he or she might be at a loss to find the one that would come next.

Confusion also arises from the failure to recognize the correct answer. It is possible that if given only the item stem, an examinee could produce a plausible and defensible response, but that this response would not coincide with any of those provided as options. This is particularly likely to happen with items covering areas with social implications, where the correct answer may actually change for members of different groups. An example is provided by Veale (1975) from a test of career education. A high school girl is concerned about problems with her boyfriend and the item asks who is the best person to speak to about it. However, the most likely confidant may be different for members of different ethnic groups. In such cases, the intended response still may be defensively the best answer and yet not be perceived so by many minority group students.

Confounded with the effects of item ambiguities is a hypothesized tendency of minority groups to omit, rather than to guess, when faced with uncertainty. Frary and Giles (1980) present some evidence to suggest that, at least on more difficult tests, this effect occurs. Omissions that have been treated as incorrect responses may account for a finding of "bias" in some items. Differential effects of speededness may similarly produce high bias indices on items at the end of a test.

Contrasted with those characteristics of items that introduce ambiguity or uncertainty are those characteristics that act to draw respondents to a particular option that is differentially attractive to members of different population subgroups. For example, in one of the pretest versions of the *MRT*, an item in auditory discrimination called for a child to select the picture of an object that had the same beginning consonant sound as a word pronounced by the teacher. In one item, the key word was "heart" and the correct response was "hand." The first option, however, was a large fancy car, which, I was informed, might be called a "hog" in black dialect. Further investigation showed that this option, in fact, had drawn a disproportionate number of black children. Notice that if this interpretation was correct, these children did have the skill necessary to have responded properly to the item.

This particular type of item flaw was analyzed in some depth in a paper by Veale (1978). In this paper, he presented a series of quantitative models that included a parameter representing *overpull*, the attractiveness added to an item distractor by cultural factors. Through these models, he demonstrated how overpull distorts response patterns by comparing the performance of an affected group with that of a group from whom the overpull was assumed not to be functioning. Each distractor of a multiple-choice item has a pull index for a given group that can be expressed as the ratio of the number selecting a distractor to the number getting the item incorrect. In the simplest model, an unbiased item is one in which the pull indices are the same for all groups being compared. (This does not imply that the pull indices are the same for all options of a given item.) Notice that this condition will hold even in cases where the item difficulty is not the same for all groups, since the indices are proportions of the incorrect responses and will sum to one in all cases. When overpull occurs, the proportions will be distorted, with the option to which the overpull is attached drawing a larger proportion of responses and the other options correspondingly fewer. The more complex models also incorporate overpull attached to the correct response, negative overpull (*underpull*), and ability differences between groups.

This effort of Veale's is laudable—the only attempt I know of to model a bias process. However, he explicitly assumed for the purposes of his model that the overpull for the reference group, against which the performance of the other groups is being compared, is zero for all options. This is probably a reasonable assumption for the distractors, so long as both overpull and underpull can occur for the minority groups. For the correct response, however, this orientation obscures what I believe to be an important distinction. Algebraically, there may be little difference between underpull where the correct response fails to be attractive to the minority group members for cultural reasons, as discussed above, and overpull that acts for the majority group, attracting them to the correct response for cultural reasons perhaps combined with knowledge. Conceptually, these alternative explanations of the same result spring from very different causes. We are far too prone to think of bias as including those factors that disadvantage blacks or other minorities rather than those that serve to facilitate the performance of whites. Failure to recognize that both of these effects occur may lead us to overlook those aids we may be inadvertently providing to white examinees when seeking to explain our bias results.

Examples of these facilitative aids would include various of the "testwiseness" cues that can lead a person to successfully eliminate incorrect options without knowing the correct response (see interview technique proposed by

Wildman & Frary, 1981). Further, these can be a "party line" kind of question, where the expected answer can be identified, sometimes without reading the stem, by the values or viewpoints that it expresses. A striking example appeared in a professional certification examination. One of the few items that appeared to be biased against whites was one where the party line cues, which pointed to the correct response in many of the items, were attached to a distractor that appeared much more attractive to whites than to blacks. Surely these cues, to which blacks were shown by this example to be less sensitive, were helping the white examinees on other items on this exam.

Group performance differences. At this point, I want to back away from the term *bias* and talk instead about performance differences between groups beyond those to be expected due to differences in the ability being measured. All of these unexpected performance differences will be identified in at least some cases by the various methodologies discussed in this book, yet I hope to show that most of us would not consider all such differences the results of bias or unfairness in an item.

Unexpected differences in item performance can occur as the result of other real differences that exist between groups. Some of these are related to differences in training or experience resulting from factors that are associated with group membership, but that have no relationship to the cultural or ethnic characteristics of the group. Examples of such factors would be urban-rural distinctions, climatic differences associated with geographic region, or economic advantage or disadvantage. Other differences can occur directly as a result of the cultural characteristics or values of a group. Examples would be the Spanish language heritage of Hispanic groups, the black English dialects, and the interpersonal style and communication modes of different ethnic cultures.

The temptation is strong to declare that all performance differences reflecting these real differences between groups should be considered bias and eliminated if possible, but some of these differences are related to what we want to know as a result of our measurement and some are not. The failure to distinguish between differences that are thus validly reflected in performance and those that are not is probably responsible for much of the heat generated in discussions concerning the value of item bias research.

Table 7.1 illustrates these points. Real differences between groups in any of the four categories defined by this table can result in unexpected performance differences in items that can then be detected by one of several statistical bias procedures. Most of us, however, would not consider items that fell into cells I and II biased. Consider frequently cited examples of bias studies on mathematics tests showing that black children are less apt to be familiar with some specific concept, such as square root, on a standardized achievement test. In such cases we are far more liable to question equality of educational opportunity than the fairness of the item. Examples of items reflecting

TABLE 7.1. Sources of Unexpected Performance Differences between Groups

	Experience & Training	Ethnic Culture or Values
Related to ability measured	I	II
Not related to ability measured	III	IV

real cultural characteristics that are validly related to the skill or ability measured are more difficult to envision. Consider, however, an example from a study of the *MRT* using large samples of minority children tested at the beginning of grade 1 (Scheuneman, 1976). On the Visual Matching tests, children were asked to find, from among four options, the one matching a stimulus set of letters, numbers, or letterlike symbols. Oriental children generally excelled on this task and did particularly well compared to children in the other groups studied, including whites, on those items with letterlike symbols. One might speculate that these children's exposure to the Chinese or Japanese idiograms may have made them attentive to differences in these unfamiliar shapes, which were not required for distinguishing the well-known letter and number shapes of the other stimuli. We might hesitate to call this bias, however, as the Oriental children were genuinely better at the visual matching skill tested with this instrument.

On the other hand, consider several quantitative reasoning items on the *Otis-Lennon*. Written in a form like "story problems," the items show no particular differences between blacks and whites below the high school level beyond those expected from the differences in their respective quantitative scores. At the high-school level, however, half of these items were identified as potentially biased. Inspection shows that these items are very similar to problems in algebra, where pupils are taught how to approach and solve them. These differences are again likely to be real differences in the background and training of the two groups. This time, however, we are measuring, not math achievement, but quantitative reasoning, and the fairness of these items might realistically be questioned.

Another example involved differences in background and training where such differences were directly related to the sex of the pupil. In a number of elementary level items in the *Otis-Lennon* pretest, the task was to judge the approximate height or weight of a number of familiar objects. Most of these items showed little difference between boys and girls, but one item, asking a pupil to identify an object weighing about the same as a pencil, favored boys. Examination of the options showed that girls were less apt than were boys to eliminate a football as an implausible alternative. A reasonable hypothesis is that girls were less liable than boys to have ever handled a football and hence to have a good idea of its weight. Clearly in such a case, real differences in previous exposure to a particular sport are not related to the ability to judge relative weights of objects.

Unfortunately, it is not always so easy to determine whether or not the difference is valid for the purposes of the test. In the *MRT* standardization program, the school language test showed a high proportion of items biased against Mexican-Americans, Puerto Ricans, and/or Orientals. Examination of these items showed that most involved the comprehension of more complex grammatical forms than did the unbiased items. The English grammatical skills of these children, therefore, appeared to be at a lower level than their listening comprehension generally, as measured by their total score on the test. The question then becomes whether in fact it is important for these children to comprehend the more complex syntactic forms in order to perform well in their subsequent schooling. If so, the appropriate action is to work with the children in developing their language skills, not to remove items measuring such skills from the test.

Another example in a different context comes from a current events test that is part of a selection battery for a government job. Women tend to perform more poorly than men on the entire battery so that the score patterns are similar to those obtained between white and minority candidates on many other examinations. In this study, items with the largest differences were contrasted with those with the smallest differences. The items with the largest differences related to particulars of power moves—invasions, coups, manipulation of public officials; the items with the smallest differences concerned religion, agriculture, matters of custom or protocol. The items were based on careful analyses of the job in question and could be demonstrated to be content valid. However, one could question whether those items with large differences reflect material that could reasonably be learned on the job or as part of a training period. If so, they may not be valid items for selection purposes and could be removed from the test. Clearly, such questions of validity cannot be answered solely on the basis of the data available from a bias study.

Strategies for Using Bias Results

Because of the belief that, once the biased items have been isolated, the reason for the bias will be easily discernable and correctable, many studies have been undertaken without due regard to how the results will be implemented in future use of the test. Therefore, the statistical procedure has sometimes become an end in itself. Results are carefully tabulated and reported and nothing further is done. In this section I will first discuss screening items without review and the dangers of doing so. I will then briefly describe some statistical methods of analyzing distractor data to yield additional information and some problems with the use of these procedures. Finally, I will discuss several item review procedures and offer reasons why many researchers have had difficulty explaining their results. I will also cite examples of how such reviews can suggest strategies for correcting some of the problems that have led to the unexpected performance differences.

Screening items without review.   Bias studies are often conducted with pretest data when, if the results are to be used in the construction of the final instrument, the time available for analyzing results is very short. Hence, it is extremely tempting simply to drop from the pool those items that show sufficiently high values of the bias index being used. A number of problems can result from doing this, however. First, the source of bias as discussed in the previous sections may not reside in the item itself. For example, in the Learning Symbols test, where the first item of each type appeared to be biased, putting a new item into that same position without revising the instructions would probably not change the impact of that bias on the test score. Second, the item may be reflecting a valid performance difference that we want to know about, such as the difference in knowledge of square root on the math achievement test. Third, the differences may reflect only peculiarities of the particular samples on whom the analysis was done and would not recur were the item administered to another group. In some sense, the item may have been identified essentially by chance, that is, due to unknown sampling biases, unreliability of the statistic, or other similar factors.

If items are to be screened blindly, this problem of chance selection or "error" becomes important. In such instances, items are dichotomized into biased and unbiased items, and both false positive and false negative errors of classification will be made. The procedure will identify some unbiased items as biased and some biased items as unbiased. We can control the kind of error we make to some extent in our selection of a cutting criterion for forming our dichotomies. We can either set the criterion so that relatively few items are selected, which are thus more likely actually to be biased, but at the cost of missing others that also are biased; or we can set our criterion to select many items, a number of which we know will in fact be unbiased, but with the confidence that we have missed relatively few of the biased items. The cutting criterion should not be set arbitrarily, but judgmentally, taking into account the number of items that can reasonably be removed from the pool, the sample size used, and hence the probable power of the procedure, the purpose of the exam, and the consequences of the two types of screening error. Where items are to be reviewed, many items might be tentatively identified as biased; where items are to be dropped, more certainty would be desirable.

In addition to classification errors, the various procedures will all sometimes yield high indices due to artifacts of the particular method used, and some methods will be insensitive to differences other procedures would detect. For example, unexpectedly large differences may occur in the transformed item difficulty procedure because one item may be more highly discriminating than other items on the test. Given two groups of differing ability, the highly discriminating item will show a larger difference between groups than will an item with low discriminating power. On the other hand, such methods are relatively insensitive to differences in the discrimination of the item for two groups where the difficulty differences are close to the expected values. For example, an item may distinguish poorly between high and low scoring Hispanics because, for one of the reasons described in the previous section, the content is not associated with ability for this group. At the same time, it may be a perfectly acceptable item for the white majority group. If, as is usually the case, the pretest sample is largely made up of white examinees, the overall biserial will probably be in an acceptable range, even though the item is not functioning for a subgroup of the sample. Similar examples could be cited for the other procedures.

Blindly discarding items is not only risky, but may also be impossible if statistical and content specifications for test construction are to be met. Items identified as biased commonly are found to be concentrated in certain content areas and may constitute a higher proportion of difficult than easy items, or vice versa. Two test development models suggest different strategies. The first model is used with tests that will be published and used intact for some time. In this case, the consequences of misusing an item are more serious, but time schedules are often somewhat more flexible. Hence, even a quick review of items may reveal correctable problems. Beyond that, items with high indices can be discarded insofar as possible within the constraints of the test specifications. The second model is used when new forms of a test are assembled relatively frequently from pools of old or pretested items and new, untried ones. The best strategy here may be to retain items in the pool, flagged in some way, and avoid them if suitable replacements are available. Once a new form is administered, the items can be reanalyzed, and those flagged a second time can be discarded and perhaps reviewed outside the assembly cycle to reveal possible sources of the problem. If records can be maintained on a continuing basis, the result over time should be a more accurate removal of items and a larger pool of items for review, making that process easier.

Distractor analysis. Statistical procedures for the analysis of distractor data are presented here as part of a posteriori analyses, but any of the methods mentioned may be utilized independently as a bias procedure. In this section, three methods using distractor information will be presented—a chi-square analysis of incorrect responses proposed by Veale and Foreman, a Rasch model method suggested by Frary and Giles, and a method of my own using the mean scaled scores of the respondents to each option.

The basic analysis in the Veale and Foreman method (1976) is a chi-square test comparing the responses of those who got an item incorrect to each of the item foils or distractors, where the hypothesis tested in that a distractor will be equally attractive to members of different groups in an unbiased item. This approach is illustrated for two items in Table 7.2. The percentage of incorrect responses is shown for each option to facilitate comparison of the groups, but the chi-square tests were performed on the frequencies of selection for the three distractors. A second statistic, Cramer's V,

TABLE 7.2. Examples of Distractor Analysis

Group	A	B	C	D[a]	% Correct
			Option		
Item A: An unbiased item					
			number selecting		
black	7	9	47	52	45.2
white	72	36	437	805	59.6
			% of incorrect responses[b]		
black	11.1	14.1	74.8	—	
white	13.2	6.7	80.1	—	
			scaled scores		
black	11.4	11.6	11.7	14.6	
white	10.0	11.4	11.3	14.2	
Item B: A biased item					
			number selecting		
black	16	47	14	38	33.0
white	159	228	15	948	70.2
			% of incorrect responses[c]		
black	20.8	61.1	18.1	—	
white	39.6	56.7	3.7	—	
			scaled scores		
black	11.0	13.1	11.1	14.1	
white	9.4	11.1	10.5	13.9	

[a]Keyed correct response for both items
[b]$\chi^2 = 4.92$ (n.s.)
[c]$\chi^2 = 28.73$ ($p < .01$)

may also be used to provide a measure of effect size or "degree of cultural variation." An alternative to the chi-square test is also suggested for instances where very small cell frequencies occur. Veale and Foreman chose not to use the information from the correct response, because this is difficult to evaluate without assumptions about the ability of the groups or about the total score or other criteria as measures of ability. Distractor attractiveness, however, is often also a function of the ability of an examinee. Groups differing in ability may thus show differing patterns of distractor attractiveness even in an unbiased item. Veale attempted to deal with differential ability in a later paper (1978), but at the cost of considerably complicating his procedure, and without demonstrating that these efforts have been effective. Moreover, an item where the correct response is differentially attractive to different groups for cultural reasons may show little variation in the attractiveness of the distractors. Therefore, these procedures are probably most effectively used in conjunction with an analysis of correct responses. If accompanied by a careful item review, however, useful information can be gained even when the procedures are used alone. These techniques will point out both potential sources of bias and other item flaws that may be acting to prevent more effective measurement (Veale, 1975.)

The focus of the paper by Frary and Giles (1980) concerns statistics, defined in terms of the Rasch model, with modifications to account for responses to the various distractors of an item as well as to the correct answer. The authors also develop, as a part of this work, an item index that can be used to detect group differences in responses to particular items. In computing this index, the actual response of each person to a given item is compared to the probability of that choice (right or wrong), based on that person's ability estimated according to the Rasch model. Very roughly speaking, these indices are summed across items for each person to yield a person-fit statistic, and summed across people for each item to yield an index of item fit. When the item index is computed separately for two groups defined by their ethnic background, bias might be inferred where differences between indices are large.

Since the authors showed their item index to be similar to the Rasch fit-mean-square statistic (Wright, 1977), the results of such a bias indicator would probably also be similar to those obtained from Durovic's procedure (1975), where the fit-mean-square statistics are compared. If results from these two methods were compared, they would probably be most discrepant on difficult items where the distractor choices might have the most impact. Frary and Giles were able to determine that those items identified using this procedure were contributing to differences between the two groups in mean person-fit, although they were unable to identify reasons to suggest that bias was the source of this agreement. Moreover, items so identified did not appear in general to be important contributions to these person-fit differences. This method is appealing, however, because it uses distractor data and includes ability in evaluating the choices of different groups. On the other hand, this procedure has not yet been shown to produce results that can be meaningfully interpreted, nor has evidence of other kinds validating this index as a bias method yet been presented.

In the distractor technique I devised, scaled scores are produced separately for each group being compared so that the within-group means have the same value on the respective scales (Scheuneman, 1979a). Scores on the scales are determined for each examinee, and the mean score of the persons selecting each option (right or wrong) are obtained for each group. In a good, discriminating item the mean scaled score of those selecting the correct option should be above the mean of the total group, and the mean of those selecting distractors should be below the total mean over a wide range of item difficulties. Further, an implausible option would be expected to have low mean values for those choosing it, and a nearly right response should have values relatively near the mean of the total group. Such patterns should hold in the same way within different groups in an unbiased item. Although other indices might be used for comparison of the two groups, I have used a simple significance test for differences between mean scores for each option.

Examples of this type of analysis are given in Table 7.2, where scores are on a scale with a mean of 13 and a standard deviation of 4. The first item shows a pattern that is appropriate for a discriminating item. For both blacks and whites, the mean scaled score of those selecting the correct option (D) was over 14, while the mean of those selecting the distractors were all below 12. In the second item, the statistics for the white group were similar, showing a properly discriminating item. For the black group, however, a sufficiently large number of the higher scoring examinees selected option B, so that the mean scaled score for that group is slightly above the mean for the total black group. Such results suggest that option B has features that draw relatively high scoring blacks away from the correct response more than is the case for whites. The method of analysis offers, in addition to the explicit incorporation of an ability measure, the advantage of extreme computational ease. Tables of significant values based on different numbers of persons selecting an option can be prepared, and once the scaled means have been obtained, items can be screened very rapidly by hand. Items identified using this procedure agree fairly well with those obtained using the chi-square procedure (Scheuneman, 1979b) and delta-plot method (Angoff & Sharon, 1974). (A discussion of these methods can be found in chapters 5 and 4, respectively.) When a second data set was analyzed on a partially overlapping set of items, the procedure tended to select the same items on both occasions and the results, when reviewed by a committee of subject matter experts, were found to be meaningfully related to subgroup differences.

Distractor analysis is appealing to many researchers as it would seem to identify not only biased items, but the source of bias in these items as well. My experience suggests, however, that performance differences in the distractors of test items are as apt to be a symptom of other problems as to be the source of the difficulty in themselves. In my procedure, for example, when comparing results for the same items administered to different people, a particular item might be identified each time, but the differences between two ethnic groups would be reflected in different distractors. Moreover, notice in Table 7.2 that the two distractor methods have both flagged the second item as potentially biased, yet the procedures focus on different distractors as the presumed source of the problem. Option B, which shows the largest differences in within-group scaled scores, indicates little difference between groups in percentage of incorrect responses. In addition, the number of persons selecting any one distractor is typically less, for easy items much less, than the number selecting the correct response, leading to greater instability of results for distractor data. Hence, the supposed diagnostic value of distractor procedures may be largely illusory, and too great a reliance on distractor data may be misleading. If used alone, the distractor methods should probably be used only where careful item review is to follow, keeping in mind that the distractor information should not be interpreted too literally and being attentive to other possible causes for the differences found.

Item review. One of the obstacles to effective review of items is again too narrow a view of the complexity of the task. Most often, items seem to be extracted from the test and reviewed in isolation. Indeed, some item flaws can be detected by such a review. For example, in the item where the large car might have been seen as a "hog," the source of the problem is, in fact, specific to that item and could be caught by a sufficiently knowledgeable and sensitive reviewer. I believe, however, that only a small proportion of the potential problems in items can be identified in this way.

More often, detecting the reasons for high bias indices will require reviewing groups of items, noting contrasts and similarities, in order to detect patterns that might account for unexpected performance differences. The cumulated weight that comes from selecting large numbers of a specific type of item will suggest problems that might not be evident from the review of any one of these items. For example, of those items with high bias indices in the School Language subtests for the *MRT* pretest study, 6 out of 7 were found to be testing grammatical usage of negatives, although these represented fewer than 20% of the total items on the test. We also knew the use of negatives to be different in black English dialect, which added support to the hypothesis that these items were measuring something different for black and white pupils. Again in the *Otis-Lennon*, where the story-problem items at the high school level were hypothesized to be more difficult for students without algebra, review of any single item would have been unlikely to yield interesting results. However, 5 out of 11 such items were among the most biased items in this section, where only 2 additional items of the remaining 48 items in the pool were so identified. In itself, this is a strongly suggestive finding.

Other differences can best be understood by contrasting items with high and low bias indices or items that appear to be biased in opposite directions. For example, in the current events test mentioned earlier, the generalizations stated concerning sex differences were arrived at only by careful cross-checking against both high and low values as well as against items that fell in neither category. Context may also need to be checked, as in the Learning Symbols test where ordinal position in the test appeared to be important.

The necessity of detecting such patterns is another of the major reasons for failure to find explanations for item bias results. In my study of *MRT* data, 555 items were analyzed; in the *Otis-Lennon*, 720 items were analyzed in the two upper levels; and in the professional certification exam, 300 items. With these pools, sufficient numbers of items of a similar type are present to be able to detect patterns. If the tests analyzed contain 50 to 75 items, which are typical test lengths, and if each test form is analyzed separately from all others, the chance of a sufficient number of items being present to detect the patterns is considerably reduced. In the cases of the negative grammatical forms and the story problems, it was the presence of a fairly large number of such items that made these patterns detectable. With Learning Symbols, the existence of three separate forms with the same structure added considerable weight to the interpretation of an ordinal position effect.

A related consideration concerns format difficulties such as those with the words "opposite" and "series" in the item stem. If format difficulties are to be detected, more than one format to test a particular ability must be used. Otherwise such difficulties are absorbed into the "main effect," that is, they become part of the expected rather than the unexpected differences. In the cases of the series items, at the upper levels of the *Otis-Lennon* two other figural reasoning formats were used, and it is in contrast to these formats that the series items showed the unexpected performance differences. In contrast, the lower-level figural series items were tried out in separate subtests that were later dropped and not included in the final test form. In these cases, the series format was the only one used and few of the items had high bias indices. Comparing scores on this subtest with those earned on the portions of the test, however, confirmed the hypothesis that this test was probably underestimating the ability of the black children.

If review of items is a useful enterprise, one might question why the bias study is necessary. Why can we not train reviewers to do this without the statistical results? I believe that one reason that item reviews, or judgmental item bias methods, and statistical bias results do not more closely agree has to do with the complexity of the bias issue. I have discussed here a large number of different kinds of problem that can yield unexpected performance results. Even if reviewers were aware of all of these problems, reviewing items on more than one or two criteria simultaneously is extremely difficult to do well. Also, what reviewers see—offensive material, stereotypic representation, uneven coverage of content from a minority perspective—is important and should be corrected on moral or ethical grounds, but may not in fact produce performance differences.

Reviewing items for performance differences without statistical evidence and reviewing after statistical bias analysis are approaches to the same problem from opposite directions. In the first case, a reviewer is asked to tell us if something is wrong with an item which might cause performance differences. In the second case, we are saying that certain items have given us unexpected differences and asking the reviewers to tell us if they can detect something wrong with them. This second task is not easy, but it is by far the more manageable one. Item review for offensive or stereotyped material and for sensitivity to minority or women's concerns, as appropriate within the context of the test, is a worthwhile task that should not be abandoned. It cannot, however, serve as a substitute for statistical analysis nor vice versa. (Also see Tittle's arguments on this issue in chapter 2.)

Review following a bias study can give us information to correct some of the faults in items and tests. Where item flaws exist and can be detected, items can be dropped, distractors modified or rewritten, and item stems clarified. In other cases, more specific solutions are suggested. In the *Otis-Lennon*, illustrative examples were added to the test instructions carefully explaining the word *opposite* at the fourth- and fifth-grade levels. Another example on *series* was added at all levels where these items appeared. In cases where differences appear to be due to background differences or cultural characteristics, test content specifications might be reevaluated. The use of the negative grammatical forms was judged to be insufficiently important at the first-grade entry level to justify their inclusion and they were dropped from the final form of the *MRT*. In the case of the professional certification exam, none of the material was deleted, but the weight given to certain topics was shifted somewhat to give minority candidates, who tended to have different professional backgrounds, an opportunity to demonstrate their strengths. These and other possible courses of action, other than simply dropping items, can result only from a critical appraisal and review of the items following the statistical bias analysis.

RECOMMENDATIONS FOR
TEST DEVELOPERS AND TEST USERS

Whenever any statistical procedure is used for the detection of item bias or other unexpected differences between groups, a study should not be considered complete until an attempt has been made to interpret the results. In this chapter, I have hypothesized that the features of items or tests that will produce the performance effects detected by the statistical bias procedures include: (1) flaws that may result from inadequacies or ambiguities of the test instructions, the item stem, the keyed response, or one of the distractors; (2) flaws that cause one or more of the options of an item (correct or incorrect) to be differentially attractive to members of different groups; (3) item features that reflect real differences between groups other than ethnicity; and (4) item features that directly reflect group differences in cultural characteristics or values. All such possible sources of high bias index values should be kept in mind when reviewing the items detected by the statistical procedure.

Reviewing items is a difficult, time-consuming task that should not be approached haphazardly. Careful preparation and a systematic approach to item review will pay off in better information and more inferences as to possible sources of bias. I believe that the best reviewers will be minority people familiar with the subject area for achievement tests, or with measurement in general, in the case of aptitude tests. If a researcher can work with a group of reviewers to help interpret the statistics, the results can be particularly fruitful. Even where minority reviewers are unavailable, however, any person who is sensitive to the problem can usually detect at least some pattern in the results if an adequate number of items have been analyzed.

The following five guidelines are suggested to facilitate the item review process:

1. *Prepare item cards for use in the review process.* Prepare for your review by having items with high bias indices put onto cards—one item per card. Record conventional item statistics, including the number selecting each option, separately for each group of interest on the backs of the cards. Use computer-generated labels if available; these save clerical labor and are apt to be more accurate. Code items to indicate apparent direction of bias (if direction can be determined). The items that were not identified as biased should be readily available for reference, but need not be placed on cards, although it may be more convenient to do so.

2. *Sort all items into relatively broad categories.* Usually, content categories outlined in the test specifications or blueprint will be appropriate, although item formats or some other characteristic believed to be important may be preferred. Tabulate the number of biased and unbiased items in each category (if this was not done previously). If the distribution of biased items into the categories is very similar to what would be expected if the items had been selected at random, the division may be not meaningful and another classification scheme might be tried. If it does not appear to be random, the concentration into specific categories may be the first clue to possible sources of bias or unexpected performance differences.

3. *Group biased item cards by content category.* Carefully review those items identified as biased, working with one classification category at a time. Examine the items, singly or in groups, looking for item flaws and clues suggesting plausible explanations for the differences found and using the conventional item statistics where they may be helpful. Try to find patterns of differences that may support or disprove some of the possible explanations or that may suggest new hypotheses concerning the differences. Do not expect to find an explanation or hypothesis to account for all items. Remember that it is almost certain that some items have been incorrectly classified as biased, and the proportion of such items can be quite high depending on sample size and the decision rule(s) used for selecting biased items.

4. *Verify hypotheses by checking against the set of unbiased items.* Sometimes the similarities seen among the biased items are simply characteristics of the test and will be found among unbiased items as well. If hypotheses suggest differences that might generalize across categories or into new item pools, determine whether such differences have occurred. For example, in the certification exam, items worded negatively ("which of the following is not a true statement"), occurred in the biased item pool more often than would be expected regardless of the content area.

5. *Consider what actions might be taken to correct problems revealed by this*

analysis. If the hypothesis is incorrect and if an action can be taken that should have no adverse impact on scores, such as adding sample items, this can be done without further verification. Otherwise, it may be necessary to involve others in a decision-making process to consider (1) the consequences of making changes if you are wrong versus (2) not making changes if you are right, and (3) the approximate likelihoods of these outcomes. Such discussions may cause a reevaluation of the purposes of the exam, which should be of benefit even if no changes in the test are made as a result.

REFERENCES

Angoff, W. H., & Sharon, A. T. The evaluation of differences in test performance of two or more groups. *Educational and Psychological Measurement*, 1974, *34*, 807-816.

Breland, H. M. *Cross-cultural stability in mental tests*. Paper presented at the annual meeting of the American Psychological Association, New Orleans, September 1974.

Draba, R. E. *The identification and interpretation of item bias* (Research Memorandum No. 26). Chicago: Statistical Laboratory, Department of Education, University of Chicago, 1977.

Durovic, J. J. Test bias: *An objective definition for test items*. Paper presented at the annual meeting of the Northeastern Educational Research Association, Ellenville, N.Y., October 1975. (ERIC Document Reproduction Service No. ED 128 381)

Frary, R. B., & Giles, M. B. *Multiple-choice test bias due to answering strategy variation*. Paper presented at the annual meeting of the American Educational Research Association, Boston, April 1980.

Nurss, J. R., & McGauvran, M. E. *Metropolitan Readiness Tests* (Experimental Edition). New York: Harcourt Brace Jovanovich, 1973.

Nurss, J. R., & McGauvran, M. E. *Metropolitan Readiness Tests*. New York: Harcourt Brace Jovanovich, 1976.

Otis, A. S., & Lennon, R. T. *Otis-Lennon School Ability Test* (Experimental Edition). New York: The Psychological Corporation, 1976.

Rudner, L. M. Using standardized tests with the hearing impaired: The problem of item bias. *Volta Review*, 1978, *80*, 31-40.

Scheuneman, J. D. *Validating a procedure for assessing bias in test items in the absence of an outside criterion*. Paper presented at the annual meeting of the American Educational Research Association, San Francisco, April 1976.

Scheuneman, J. D. Ethnic group bias in intelligence tests. In S. W. Lundsteen (Ed.), *Cultural factors in learning and instruction*. New York: ERIC Clearinghouse on Urban Education, Diversity Series, Number 56, 1978, Pp. 65-77.

Scheuneman, J. D. *Academy of Certified Social Workers: Report of minority performance*. Princeton, N.J.: Educational Testing Service, June 1979.(a)

Scheuneman, J. D. A new method of assessing bias in test items. *Journal of Educational Measurement*, 1979, *16*, 143-152.(b)

Scheuneman, J. D. *Consistency across administrations of certain indices of bias in test items*. Paper presented at the annual meeting of the American Educational Research Association, Boston, April 1980.

Veale, J. R. (Report coordinator). *Development report: Texas career education measurement series*. Iowa City: Westinghouse Learning Corporation/Measurement Research Center, August 1975.

Veale, J. R. A theoretical framework for the cultural variation procedures and a new paradigm for cultural validation. Unpublished manuscript, September 1978. (Available from Dr. J. R. Veale, P.O. Box 4036, Berkeley, Calif. 94704.)

Veale, J. R., & Foreman, D. I. *Cultural variation in criterion-referenced tests: A "global" item analysis*. Paper presented at the annual meeting of the American Educational Research Association, San Francisco, April 1976.

Wildman, T. M., & Frary, R. B. *Minimum competency test bias as reflected by examinee selection of inappropriate answers*. Paper presented at the annual meeting of the National Council on Measurement in Education, Los Angeles, April 1981.

Wright, B. D. Solving measurement problems with the Rasch model. *Journal of Educational Measurement*, 1977, *14*, 97–115.

8 METHODS FOR DETECTING CONSTRUCT AND PREDICTIVE BIAS

CECIL R. REYNOLDS

INTRODUCTION

THE TERM "BIAS" carries many different connotations for the lay public and for professionals in a number of disciplines. To the legal mind, bias denotes illegal discriminatory practices, while to the lay mind it may conjure up notions of prejudicial attitudes. Much of the rancor in psychology and education regarding proper definitions of *test bias* is due to the divergent uses of this term in general, but especially by professionals in the same and related academic fields (also see Shepard, chapter 1). Contrary to certain other opinions that more common or lay usages of the term *bias* should be employed when using the word in definitions or discussions of bias in educational and psychological tests, bias as used in the present chapter will be defined in its widely recognized, distinct statistical sense. Bias denotes *constant* or *systematic error*, as opposed to chance or random error, in the estimation of some value; for our purposes here, this constant or systematic error is usually due to group membership or some other nominal variable, and occurs in the estimation of a score on a psychological or educational test or performance criterion.

Other uses of the term *bias* in research on the differential or cross-group validity of tests are unacceptable from a scientific perspective for two reasons: (1) the imprecise nature of other uses of *bias* makes empirical investigation and rational inquiry exceedingly difficult, and (2) other uses of the term invoke specific moral value systems that are the subject of intense, polemic, emotional debate without a mechanism for rational resolution. The present chapter will proceed by presenting empirically assessable definitions of test bias and discussing the appropriate methodology for researching bias

Parts of this chapter are based on a previous work by the author, titled "The problem of bias in psychological assessment," in C. R. Reynolds and T. B. Gutkin (Eds.), *The handbook of school psychology.* New York: Wiley, 1982. Pp. 178–208.

under the proffered definition. In defining bias in categories of validity, the statistical sense of the term must be preserved. Only two broad categories of validity are to be presented: construct and predictive, or criterion-related, validity. This distinction between types of validity is in many ways artificial since all investigations of test validity assess construct validity. Distinctions between types of test validity are therefore used for simplicity, clarity, and convenience of presentation as well as from a sense of tradition. The discussion will begin by addressing problems of bias in construct validity and then move to questions of predictive bias. The preceding chapters have dealt extensively with item or content bias, and any scientific model of the traditional trinary conceptualization of validity must be hierarchical with content validity prerequisite to construct validity, which should both be prerequisite to predictive validity.

REVIEW OF METHODS FOR INVESTIGATING BIAS IN CONSTRUCT VALIDITY

The construct validity of a test refers to the extent to which the test in question may be said to measure a given psychological or educational construct or trait. Construct validity is easily the most complex of all conceptualizations of test validity and requires greater inference and argument by reason than do other traditionally conceived categories of validity. The defining of bias in construct validity then requires a general, but operational, statement that can be researched from a variety of viewpoints with a broad range of methodology. The following definition has been proffered by Reynolds (1982):

Bias exists in regard to construct validity when a test is shown to measure different hypothetical traits (psychological constructs) for one group than another or to measure the same trait but with differing degrees of accuracy [ital. added]. (p. 194)

The question of bias in construct validity is of substantial concern, not only to practitioners in psychology and education, but to the researcher and theoretician alike. Indeed, if bias in construct validity across groups for males and females, or blacks and whites, or upper and lower SES groups, or other popular nominal groupings of individuals for research purposes occurs with any consistency, then much of the research of differential psychology of the present century must be discarded as confounded and major theories abandoned as primarily artifactual (Reynolds, 1980a; Reynolds & Brown, 1982a). This would present a difficult situation at best since the psychology of individual differences is the basic science underlying much of applied psychology.

As is befitting the complexity of a concept such as construct validity, many methods have been employed to examine existing psychological tests for potential bias in construct validity. We now turn to a direct presentation and examination of many of these techniques.

Factor Analytic Methods

One of the more popular and necessary empirical approaches to investigating construct validity is factor analysis (Anastasi, 1976; Cronbach, 1970). Factor analysis, as a procedure, identifies clusters of test items or clusters of subtests of psychological or educational tests that correlate highly with one another and less so or not at all with other subtests or items. Factor analysis then allows one to determine patterns of interrelationships of performance among groups of individuals. For example, if several subtests of an intelligence scale load highly on (are members of) the same factor, then if a group of individuals scores at a high level on one of these subtests, the group would be expected to score at a high level on other subtests that load highly on that factor. Psychologists attempt to determine through a review of the test content and correlates of performance on the factor in question what psychological trait(s) underlies performance; or, in a more hypothesis testing approach, they will make predictions concerning the pattern of factor loadings. Hilliard (1979), one of the more vocal critics of IQ tests on the basis of cultural bias, has pointed out one of the potential areas of bias dealing with the comparison of the factor analytic results of test studies across race.

If the IQ test is a valid and reliable test of "innate" ability or abilities, then the factors which emerge on a given test should be the same from one population to another, since "intelligence" is asserted to be a set of mental processes. Therefore, while the configuration of scores of a particular group on the factor profile would be expected to differ, logic would dictate that the factors themselves would remain the same. (p. 53)

While not necessarily agreeing that identical factor analyses of an instrument speak to the innateness of the abilities being measured, *consistent factor analytic results across populations do provide strong evidence that whatever is being measured by the instrument is being measured in the same manner and is in fact the same construct within each group.* If factor analytic results (i.e., the interrelationships of the variables comprising the test) are constant across groups then one may have greater confidence that the individuals in each group perceive and interpret the test materials in a similar manner. The information derived from comparative factor analysis across populations then is directly relevant to the use of educational and psychological tests in diagnostic and other decision-making functions. In order to make consistent interpretations of test score data, psychologists must be certain that the test(s) measures the same variable across populations.

Two basic approaches, each with a number of variations, have been employed to compare factor analytic results across populations. The first approach asks how similar the results are for each group; the second, and less popular, approach asks if the results show a statistically significant difference between groups.

Chi-square goodness-of-fit. The most sophisticated approach to the latter question has been the work of Jöreskog (1969, 1971; McGaw & Jöreskog, 1971) in simultaneous factor analysis in several populations. Jöreskog employs the chi-square test for goodness-of-fit across the factor analytic results for several groups to determine whether there is a "fit" or the results differ significantly across groups. A full treatment of Jöreskog's techniques is certainly beyond the scope and intent of the present chapter. The computational procedure is quite complex and the comparison of factors very sensitive. As yet little research has been reported in the bias literature using Jöreskog's method. As computer programs for his analyses become more available, this methodology will almost certainly be employed to compare factor structures in research on internal bias in educational and psychological tests.

A related, but computationally simpler, method for determining the significance of the difference between individual factors for two groups, also employing the chi-square technique, has been presented by Jensen (1980) and has recently been employed by Miele (1979) and Reynolds and Streur (1981). Once corresponding factors have been located, all factor loadings are converted to Fisher z scores. The z scores for corresponding factors are then paired by variable and subtracted. The differences in factor loadings, now expressed as differences between z scores, are squared, summed, and the mean of the squared differences derived. The mean difference must then be divided by the standard error of measurement of the difference between factor loadings, calculated to be the quantity

$$\frac{1}{N_1 - 3} + \frac{1}{N_2 - 3}, \tag{1}$$

where N_1 is the number of subjects in group one and N_2 represents the number of subjects in group two. This division of the mean of the squared differences by the standard error of the difference will be distributed as chi-square with one degree of freedom. Special cases of this test are described in Jensen (1980, chap. 9), though the above general form is applicable in most cases.

Comparing correlation matrices. Factor analysis is typically, though not always, based on a correlation matrix for a set of variables. For this reason, it may be desirable to test for the significance of the difference between two correlation matrices. As Jensen (1980) points out, however, there is no direct test for equivalence of two correlation matrices across samples from different populations, though such a test may be approximated by a form of the above test. To test for the significance of the difference between correlation matrices, correlations in each matrix are transformed to Fisher z's. Corresponding pairs of correlations in each matrix, now expressed as z scores, are then contrasted, the difference squared, and the mean of the squared differences derived. This value then becomes the numerator for the procedure described above. The denominator remains the same (Equation 1). The test statistic thus derived will approximately be distributed as chi-square with one degree of freedom. Since this test is only approximate, Jensen (1980) properly warns that interpretation of differences should proceed cautiously unless $p \leq$ .01. More exact, yet computationally complex, procedures are available for comparing correlation matrices across groups (Timm, 1975).

Significant differences between factor loadings: Conclusion. Methods for determining the significance of the difference in the size and pattern of variable loadings on corresponding factors between samples, while appropriate in certain circumstances, suffer from two major related drawbacks when addressing the more practical problems of test interpretation. With the very large samples necessary for stability of factor analysis results, small, practically negligible differences between factors can easily produce "significant" results. When interpreting test scores across groups, the degree of similarity of factors takes on greater importance for the practitioner; tests for statistically significant differences cannot sufficiently answer questions of similarity. Although psychology and research in most social sciences tend to emphasize differences, similarities may occur in greater frequency and magnitude and deserve close scrutiny and attention. Thus in answering most practical questions of test bias, it becomes more correct to evaluate the degree of similarity of factor structures across groups in evaluating whether test score interpretation may be undertaken without regard for the nominal variable in question.

Determining degree of similarity between factors. A number of methods for determining factorial similarity across groups exists. These methods differ primarily along two lines: whether they allow estimates of shared variance between factors, and the various assumptions underlying their use. With large samples, these various indices of factorial similarity typically produce quite consistent findings (Reynolds & Harding, 1981). In small sample studies, multiple methods of evaluation are necessary to guard against the overinterpretation of what may simply be sampling error.

Katzenmeyer and Stenner (1977) have described a technique for determining the similarity of factors across groups that is based essentially on *factor score comparisons.* A factor score is a composite score derived by summing an individual's weighted scores on each variable that appears on a factor. Weights are derived from the factor analysis procedure and are directly related to the factor loadings of the variables. Katzenmeyer and Stenner propose that factor scores be derived based on a factor analysis of the combined groups of interest. Then, the scores of each group are factor analyzed separately and factor scores again determined. The Pearson product-moment coefficient of correlation between the factor scores based on the total group analysis and the factor scores of the single group analysis is then used as an estimate of the factorial similarity of the test battery across groups. The method is actually somewhat more complex as described by Katzenmeyer and Stenner (1977) and has not been widely employed in the test bias literature, yet it is a practical technique with many utilitarian implications, especially when factor scores are likely to be employed. This method should receive more attention in future work on bias in psychological and educational tests.

The *Pearson correlation* can also be used to directly examine the comparability of factor loadings on a single factor for two groups. The correlation coefficient between pairs of factor loadings for corresponding factors has been used in some previous work; however, in the comparison of factor loadings, assumptions of normality or linearity are likely to be violated. Transforming the factor loadings to Fisher z's prior to computing r helps to correct some of these flaws but is not completely satisfactory. Other technical problems in the use of the Pearson r for determining factorial similarity are detailed by Cattell (1978). Other, more appropriate indices of factorial similarity exist and are no more difficult to determine than the Pearson r in most cases. The use of the Pearson r between factor loadings (or transformations of factor loadings) as a measure of factorial similarity is thus *not* recommended.

One popular index of factorial similarity, which is similar to the Pearson r, based on the relationship between pairs of factor loadings for corresponding factors is the *coefficient of congruence* (r_c). When determining the degree of similarity of two factors, an r_c value of .90 or higher is typically, though arbitrarily, taken to indicate equivalency of the factors in question or factorial invariance across groups (Cattell, 1978; Harman, 1976; Mulaik, 1972). The coefficient of congruence is given by the following equation:

$$r_c = \frac{\sum\limits_{1}^{N} a_1 \cdot a_2}{\sqrt{\sum\limits_{1}^{N} a_1^2 \sum\limits_{1}^{N} a_2^2}}, \tag{2}$$

where a_1 represents the factor loading of a variable for one sample and a_2 represents the factor loading of the same variable for the second sample. Although significance tables are provided for r_c (Cattell, 1978), significance levels can only be approximated for r_c since its distribution will vary as a function of the number of factors in the analysis, the number of variables each factor has in common for each group, and certain other factors. Significance levels are of little importance in the interpretation of r_c in detecting test bias when initial samples for factoring are sufficiently large; the actual magnitude of r_c is of primary concern.

Some concerns have been expressed regarding the use of r_c to compare factors extracted from a correlation matrix when the variances for each variable are not constant across groups. Differences in covariance matrices can result that can alter the distribution of r_c. Some disquietude has also been expressed regarding the comparison of orthogonal factors (Mulaik, 1972). Most of the problems in the calculation and interpretation of r_c work to attenuate its value, so overinterpretation should not be a problem in such cases. However, several corrective or cautionary measures can be undertaken. Covariance matrices can be tested for equality across groups through Box's procedure, yet this is a time-consuming calculation for which there are few available computer programs. If covariance matrices are equivalent, however, fears about the use of r_c should be sufficiently allayed.

If the covariance matrices differ, then the factor analysis should be conducted based on the covariance matrices for each group and r_c calculated on the basis of factor loadings derived from this procedure. Since equality of the covariance matrices may be difficult to assess, use of the covariance matrix for the analyses could be undertaken as a precautionary measure. With large samples, however, the effects on r_c are minimal at best (Gutkin & Reynolds, 1981; Reynolds & Harding, 1981); this procedure is sometimes difficult to interpret and is not common in the test bias literature. Another procedure to consider if using r_c when equivalence of covariance matrices is in doubt, is to supplement the interpretation of r_c with a nonparametric measure of factorial similarity (e.g., Reynolds & Paget, 1981).

Cattell (1978; Cattell & Baggalcy, 1960) has described a useful nonparametric index for factor comparison known as the *salient variable similarity index (s)*. The calculation of s is straightforward with one exception. In the determination of s, one first proceeds by classifying each variable by its factor loading as being salient or nonsalient and as being positive or negative, depending on the sign of the variable's loading. After reviewing several other options, Cattell (1978) recommends a cutoff value of $\pm.10$ to indicate a variable with a salient loading. While this is likely the best choice for analyses of items (or with subscales, in the case of personality scales), this value is probably too liberal when examining subscales of cognitive batteries with high subtest reliabilities and a large general factor, especially given the sensitive nature of questions of potential bias. In the latter case, investigators should consider adopting more conservative values between .15 and .25 for positive salience and $-.15$ to $-.25$ for negative salience. Once the cutoff value has been determined, variable classification should be undertaken and Table 8.1 completed.

Once Table 8.1 has been completed, s is given by the following equation (from Cattell, 1978, p. 260):

$$s = \frac{f_{11} + f_{33} - f_{13} - f_{31}}{f_{11} + f_{33} + f_{13} + f_{31} + \frac{1}{2}(f_{12} + f_{21} + f_{23} + f_{32})} \tag{3}$$

The various f values in the above formula correspond to the frequency of variables in the cells of Table 8.1 for the designated f. The value of s can range

TABLE 8.1. Tabulation Table for Use in Calculating the Salient Variable Similarity Index (s) in Studies of Test Bias

	Factor for Group Two		
Factor for Group One	PS[a]	H[b]	NS[c]
PS[a]	f_{11}^{d}	f_{12}	f_{13}
H[b]	f_{21}	f_{22}	f_{23}
NS[c]	f_{31}	f_{32}	f_{33}

Source: Adapted, with permission, from R. B. Cattell (1978, p. 257).
[a]Positive salient variable
[b]Hyperplane variable (variable with a nonsalient loading)
[c]Negative salient variable
[d]Joint frequency, e.g., the number of variables with positive salient loadings on the factor in both groups. The variables in the analysis must be the same when examining for test bias.

from -1.00 to $+1.00$, with either extreme traditionally taken to indicate perfect agreement between factors since any factor may be reflected 180°, thereby changing the signs of all variables. When examining for test bias, however, a significant negative s must be considered strong evidence of bias, although with very large negative values the appropriate corrective measures become obvious. Additionally, such an occurrence is extremely unlikely with well-developed cognitive scales, when the variables are common across groups and factors are rotated to orthogonal solutions; if a negative s occurs under these conditions, the investigator would be wise to recheck the data to be sure they were all coded correctly and that there were no errors in the mathematical calculations.

The nature of s, as opposed to indices more similar to the Pearson r, requires a significance test of its deviation from zero (when its value $\neq \pm 1.00$). These is no established cutoff value such as with r_c which is accepted as indicating total similarity of factors. Tables for evaluating the significance of an obtained value for s are found in Cattell (1978). When s is significantly different from zero, one may be confident that the two factors in question are indeed constant across groups, especially if r_c has also reached a value of .90 or higher.

Many other methods of determining the similarity of factors exist, and a complete review of these techniques cannot be undertaken here. Configurative matching methods (e.g., Kaiser, Hunka, & Bianchini, 1971) or the use of Cattell's (Cattell, 1978; Cattell, Coulter, & Tsujioka, 1966) coefficient of pattern similarity (r_p) are but two prominent examples. The methods reviewed above, however, will be adequate for the vast majority of cases, especially if analyses can be based on covariance matrices, and are certainly the most common procedures in the test bias literature. Certain other methods of factor matching such as confirmatory factor analysis that attempt to reproduce a factor pattern in one group that has already been located in another group are not directly applicable to questions of bias. When investigating bias in construct validity, especially as it may affect test score interpretation, we are more directly concerned with "naturally occurring" factor solutions and not with whether we can force factors into agreement. Indeed, Mulaik's (1972) many criticisms and cautions regarding factor matching seem to be most applicable to confirmatory types of analysis. When using the above indices of factorial similarity to evaluate overall results of an analysis, not only should individual factors be compared, but the comparison of communalities, unique variances, and specific variances may also be appropriate, especially in the case of diagnostic psychological tests.

Factor extraction and interpreting indices of similarity. Before moving to the next aspect of evaluating construct bias for a test, at least two more issues should be addressed: (1) interpreting indices of factorial similarity (e.g., r_c) in small N studies, and (2) determining the number of factors to rotate in studies of bias. With small sample studies (e.g., the subject:variable ratio is less than 10:1 and/or the N for each group is less than 200), the standard error of the correlation of a variable with a factor can be quite substantial. Thus, when indices of similarity fall below established cutoff or significance levels, a test for the significance of the difference between factor loadings of the two factors that takes this error into account is a necessary supplement prior to concluding that the factors are dissimilar. An r_c value of .80 is typically taken to indicate a lack of factorial similarity or invariance, yet in small sample studies, or studies where the N's are disproportionate across groups, such a finding could easily be attributable to sampling error. Clearly, a method for determining the reliability of such a finding with small N's is a necessary adjunct to the analysis.

Determining the number of factors to extract and rotate is a much debated issue. The most popular methods seem to be the "eigenvalue one" criterion, the scree test, and the "whatever solution most appeals to the investigator's theoretical bent" technique. Regardless of which method is chosen, neither nonjudicious use of rigid cutoffs nor totally subjective methods should be allowed to infiltrate the investigation of test bias. One obvious example of inappropriate conclusions that can be drawn from the use of rigid techniques when analyses are totally separate for each group is the following. An investigator conducts a factor analysis of a popular intelligence scale separately for a group of 6-and-a-half-year-olds and a group of 9-and-a-half-year-olds. Wanting to avoid accusations of subjective influence in the analysis, the investigator adopts a criterion of extracting only factors with eigenvalues of 1.00 or higher. For the younger group, the eigenvalues of the first four factors are 3.12, 2.01, 1.01, and .89. For the older group they are 3.24, 1.96, 0.99, and .87. Since the younger group has three factors with eigenvalues above 1.00 and the older group has only two, the investigator concludes that the factor structure of the test is quite different for the younger and older children since not even the same number of factors results.

Obviously, the difference of .02 in eigenvalues of the third factors can hardly support such a conclusion, yet how can the investigator support comparing the third factor without accusations of biasing the outcome of the study? The use of purely subjective review of factor loadings to determine the proper number of factors boggles the imagination with possibilities for such difficult circumstances. Two methods of avoiding such problems can immediately be applied.

Once having decided on a method for determining the proper number of factors, the investigator can analyze the scores of the major group. The same factor solution can then be applied to the minor group and the two solutions compared, as discussed above. Another, apparently superior, method is available, however. Once having decided on the method for determining the proper number of factors, the investigator can collapse the major and minor groups and derive a factor solution on the combined groups. This factor solution should then be determined separately for each group in the analysis and the resulting solutions compared across groups. The latter method is desirable for a number of reasons, the most notable being the greater sample size available to increase the stability of the solution. The use of this method will also remove the ambiguity of situations such as that described above. Excellent discussions of methods for determining the appropriate number of factors may be found in Cattell (1978), Harman (1976), and Thorndike (1978), as well as in other sources.

Comparing Internal Consistency Estimates

The previously offered definition of bias in construct validity requires equivalency in the "accuracy" of measurements across groups for nonbiased assessment. Essentially, this means that any error due to domain sampling in the choice of items for the test must be constant across groups. The proper test of this condition is the comparison of internal consistency reliability estimates (r_{xx}) or alternate form correlations (r_{ab}) across groups. Different statistical procedures are necessary for the comparison of r_{xx} across groups and the comparison of r_{ab} across groups.

Internal consistency reliability estimates are such coefficients as Cronbach's alpha, Kuder-Richardson 20 (KR_{20}), KR_{21}, odd-even correlations with length corrections, or estimates derived through analysis of variance. Typically, the preferred estimate of r_{xx} is Cronbach's coefficient alpha or KR_{20}, a special case of alpha. Alpha has a variety of advantages; for example, alpha can be shown to be the mean of all possible split-half correlations for a test and is also representative of the predicted correlation between true alternate forms of a test. Feldt (1969) has provided a technique that can be used to determine the *significance of the difference between alpha or KR_{20} reliabilities on a single test for two groups.* Feldt originally devised this method as a test of the hypothesis that alpha or KR_{20} is the same for two tests. The assumptions underlying the test, however, are even more closely met by the use of a single psychological or educational test and two independent samples (Feldt, personal communication, 1980). The test statistic is given by the ratio of $1 -$ alpha for the first group over $1 -$ alpha for the second group as shown in Equation 4:

$$F = \frac{1 - alpha_1}{1 - alpha_2},$$ (4)

where $alpha_1$ is the reliability coefficient of some test x as determined for group 1 and $alpha_2$ is the same reliability coefficient as calculated based on the responses of the second group. KR_{20} reliabilities may be used in Equation 4 as well. The test statistic will be distributed as F with $N_1 - 1$ degrees of freedom in the numerator and $N_2 - 1$ degrees of freedom in the denominator. The quantity $1 - r_{xx}$ represents an error variance term, and the largest variance is always placed over the smallest variance term. The complete development of this technique is described in Feldt. Whenever Equation 4 reveals a statistically significant discrepancy in reliability estimates, the test in question must be considered biased since errors due to domain sampling are different across groups creating disparities in the ability of the test to measure the trait in question for all groups.

Comparisons of correlations between alternate forms of a test across groups may be needed in cases where alpha or KR_{20} is inappropriate or for some reason not available. Alternate form reliability estimates assume that the items on the two scales have been randomly sampled from the same domain of items and that a less than perfect relationship between the two measures represents errors of domain sampling. The Pearson correlation between the two sets of scores then is taken as the "alternate form reliability coefficient" of the test. With two samples, alternate form correlations are calculated separately for each group, producing two independent correlations. Since the standard error of the difference between independent correlations is nonnormal and difficult to estimate precisely, to test for the significance of the difference between correlations for two groups, the correlations must first be transformed to Fisher z's. The standard error of the difference between Fisher z's is normal and is relatively easy to calculate. Equation 5 can be used to produce a Z statistic that is then referred to a table of the normal curve. The numerator of the equation is the difference between the correlations, expressed as Fisher z scores. The denominator is the standard error of the difference between Fisher z scores.

$$Z = \frac{z_1 - z_2}{\sqrt{\dfrac{1}{N_1 - 3} + \dfrac{1}{N_2 - 3}}},$$ (5)

where:

$z_1 =$ correlation for group 1 expressed as a Fisher z;
$z_2 =$ correlation for group 2 expressed as a Fisher z;

N_1 = sample size for group 1; and
N_2 = sample size for group 2.

When a significant difference between alternate form reliability estimates for two groups occurs, several other factors must be considered prior to concluding that bias exists. The tests under consideration must be shown to be in reality alternate forms for at least one of the two groups. Before two tests can be considered alternate forms, they must in fact be sampling items from the same domain. Other methodological problems that apply generally to the investigation of alternate form reliability also will apply. Discussions of alternate form reliability and its investigation can be found in a variety of sources, including Cronbach (1970), Nunnally (1978), and Stanley (1971).

Comparison of test-retest correlations across groups may also be of interest and can be conducted via Equation 5 as well. Whether a test-retest correlation is an appropriate measure of a test's reliability, however, should carefully be evaluated. Unless the trait the test is measuring is assumed to be completely static, test-retest correlations speak more directly to the stability of the trait under consideration than to the accuracy of the measuring device (Reynolds, in press). Certainly there are few psychological traits that would be considered totally unchanging; yet, only under this circumstance can differences in test-retest correlations for two groups be considered as evidence for bias in domain sampling for the two groups.

Rank Order of Item Difficulties

If a test is to be considered nonbiased across groups, the rank order of the item difficulties should be relatively constant across groups. Even though total-test reliability estimates may be similar, the behavior of individual items, while averaging out across items, can be quite different. If the items of a test are being perceived and interpreted in a similar manner across groups, in the case of a unidimensional scale, the difficulty of the items relative to one another should be the same in the two groups.

To evaluate the relative consistency of item difficulties when the test is taken as a whole (evaluating individual items is the principal focus of the other chapters in this work), all test items must first be ranked according to difficulty, separately for each group. A rank-order correlation (i.e., Spearman's rho) should then be calculated between the two sets of ranks. With sufficient sample sizes, a rho of .90 or higher should be taken to indicate relative consistency of item difficulties across groups. Large samples are needed for such an analysis, and, overall, samples of not less than 200 subjects with a subject : item ratio of not less than 10:1 should be used.

A related, generally less acceptable technique requiring even larger samples for stability is the correlation of P decrements between adjacent items. For this analysis, when items arc ordered by difficulty level, as is the case for most aptitude tests, the difference between item difficulties of each pair of adjacent items is calculated separately across groups and a Pearson correlation determined between each pair of "difference scores" (also see Angoff, chapter 4). The poor reliability of difference scores and other factors render the results of this analysis difficult to evaluate. A large correlation, i.e., $\geq .90$, is good evidence of the consistency of the meaning of the total test scores across groups; yet, a lower value is difficult to interpret since many violations of statistical assumptions may be at work producing spuriously low correlations.

Other Methods of Examining for Construct Bias

A variety of other logically derived methods may be determined when examining for bias in construct validity. Indeed, the richness and complexity of construct validation demands ingenuity in research and evaluation of the meaning of psychological test scores. This section will briefly review several methods that have been proposed and one new method; these techniques will generally not have the broader applicability of the above techniques.

Correlations of age with raw scores. A potentially valuable yet seldom employed technique for investigating the construct validity of *aptitude or intelligence tests is the evaluation* of the relationship between raw scores and age. Scores on tests of mental ability during childhood are believed to increase with age in almost all theories of early cognitive development. The original Binet Intelligence Scale, developed by Binet and Simon in France near the turn of the century, relied quite heavily on the relationship between chronological age and the various tasks Binet created to measure intelligence. The location of an item on Binet's scale was determined by the percentage of children passing the item at several age levels. If a test is a valid measure of mental ability, then performance on the test should show a substantial correlation with age when children are sampled across a sufficient range of age levels (provided that relatively stable incremental changes in mental ability are in fact a developmental phenomenon). If a test is measuring some construct of mental ability in a uniform manner across groups with which the test is used (as it must to be free of bias according to the above definition), the correlation of raw scores with chronological age should be constant across groups. The test of this condition is to calculate the correlation of age with raw scores separately for each group under consideration, and then test for the significance of the difference between the two correlations. The method of transforming correlations to Fisher z scores and dividing by the standard error of the difference between z scores should be applied as described above. Examples of the use of this approach with ability tests are available in Jensen (1980) and Reynolds (1980b).

Care must be taken, however, with the interpretation of such analyses. If mean differences in total scores are present, the researcher must be certain that the test has enough floor and ceiling at all ages. A nonsignificant difference also does not "prove" the test is nonbiased; it only adds to other evidence. As with most tests of bias, we cannot prove the null hypothesis, only retain it for further evaluation. Contrary to what will be presented later with regard to a test's predictive validity, differences in slopes of the regression between age and raw score performance indicate only differences in the rate of cognitive development across groups and are unrelated to bias. Jensen (1980) has a number of interesting observations to offer on the interpretation of the relationship between raw scores on ability tests and age when used to evaluate cultural bias. The reader considering the use of this method would do well to review his comments (Jensen, 1980, chap. 9).

Kinship correlations and differences. Jensen (1980) has proposed that "the construct validity of a test in any two population groups is reinforced if the test scores show the same kinship correlations (or absolute differences) in both groups" (p. 427). The evaluation of this test of bias is relatively complex and involves the much debated calculation of heritability estimates across groups. While this method of evaluating test bias is of little utility to the practitioner, it is a valid technique for investigating the construct validity of tests that are purported to be measures of *g*. An in-depth explanation of the necessary methods can be found in Jensen (1973, 1980).

Multitrait-multimethod validation. One of the most convincing techniques for establishing the construct validity of a psychological test is through the use of a multitrait-multimethod validation matrix (Campbell & Fiske, 1959). This technique evaluates both the convergent and divergent validity of a test with multiple methods of assessment; that is, predictions regarding what will correlate with the test score are evaluated along with predictions regarding what the test *will not* correlate with (an equally important facet of validity), using multiple methods of assessment so that the observed relationships are not artifacts of a common assessment method.

A square matrix can be produced which is amenable to evaluation through factor analysis. When evaluating for bias, it is best to put the test reliabilities in the diagonal of the matrix. It would be necessary to establish a multitrait-multimethod matrix for a test separately for each group under consideration. Each matrix could then be factor analyzed and the results of the factor analysis compared using techniques described above. In the evaluation for bias, all methods or tests in the matrix, other than the specific test being evaluated, must be nonbiased, a potential drawback to the use of this technique. This procedure, however, when correctly carried out, has the greatest potential for the ultimate resolution of the question of bias.

Obviously, many techniques for evaluating construct validity can be derived. Research on construct validity is limited only by the investigator's ingenuity and imagination. Any method that can be derived for investigating construct validity can ultimately be applied to the question of bias. (One very common procedure of appraising construct validity, correlation of a test score with an external criterion, will be discussed in a later section on predictive bias.) The search for other methods of investigation should continue.

Many procedures may prove unique to the instrument in question, but should nevertheless be employed.

Two Inappropriate Indicators of Bias: Mean Differences and Equivalent Distributions

Differences in mean levels of performance on cognitive tasks between two groups are mistakenly believed to constitute test bias by a number of writers (e.g., Alley & Foster, 1978; Chinn, 1979; Hilliard, 1979; Jackson, 1975; Wright & Isenstein, 1977). Those who support mean differences as an indication of test bias state correctly that there is no valid a priori scientific reason to believe that intellectual or other cognitive performance levels should differ across race. It is the inference that tests demonstrating such a difference are inherently biased because in reality there can be no difference which is fallacious. Just as there is no a priori basis for deciding that differences exist, there is no a priori basis for deciding that differences do not exist. From the standpoint of the objective methods of science, a priori or premature acceptance of either hypothesis (differences exist vs. differences do not exist) is untenable. As stated by Thorndike (1971), "The presence (or absence) of differences in mean score between groups, or of differences in variability, tells us nothing directly about fairness" (p. 64). According to Jensen (1976), "Score differences per se, whether between individuals, social classes, or racial groups, obviously cannot be a criterion of bias" (p. 341). Some adherents to the mean difference as bias position also require that the *distribution* of test scores in each population or subgroup be identical prior to assuming that the test is nonbiased, regardless of its validity. "Regardless of the purpose of a test *or its validity for that purpose,* a test should result in distributions that are statistically equivalent across the groups tested in order for it to be considered nondiscriminatory for those groups" (Alley & Foster, 1978, p. 2). Portraying a test as biased regardless of its purpose or validity conveys an inadequate understanding of the psychometric construct and issues of bias.

The mean difference and equivalent distribution concepts of test bias have been the most uniformly rejected of all criteria of test bias examined by sophisticated psychometricians involved in investigating the problems of bias in assessment. Ethnic group differences in mental test scores are some of the most well documented phenomena in psychology and persist over time at relatively constant levels (Reynolds & Gutkin, 1981).

Jensen (1980) discusses the mean differences as bias definition in terms of the *egalitarian fallacy.* The egalitarian fallacy contends that all human populations are in fact identical on all mental traits or abilities. Any differences with regard to any aspect of the distribution of mental test scores indicates that something is wrong with the test itself. As Jensen points out, such an assumption is totally, scientifically unwarranted. There are simply too many examples of specific abilities (e.g., Reynolds & Jensen, 1980) and even sensory capacities that have been shown unmistakably to differ across human populations. The result of the egalitarian assumption then is to remove the investigation of population differences in ability from the realm of scientific inquiry, an unacceptable course of action (Reynolds, 1980a). Logically followed, this fallacy leads to other untenable conclusions as well. Torrance (1980, 1982), an adherent to the cultural test bias hypothesis (based principally on the mean difference approach), has pointed out that disadvantaged black children occasionally earn higher scores on creativity tests—and, therefore, have more creative ability—than many white children because their environment has forced them to learn to "make do" with less and with simple objects. The egalitarian assumption would hold that this is not true, but rather the content of the test is biased against white or high-SES children.

The belief of many people in the mean differences as bias definition is quite likely related to the nature-nurture controversy at some level. Certainly data reflecting racial differences on various aptitude measures have been interpreted to indicate support for a hypothesis of genetic differences in intelligence and implicating one race as superior to another. Such interpretations understandably call for a strong emotional response. While IQ and other aptitude test score differences undoubtedly occur, the differences do not indicate deficits or superiority by any race, especially in relation to the personal worth of any individual member of a given race or culture (Dobzhansky, 1973; Torrance, 1975). Many of the studies often cited as supporting genetic or environmental explanations of racial IQ differences have been reviewed by Loehlin, Lindzey, and Spuhler (1975), with the general conclusion being drawn that these data have little to no bearing on genetic (or environmental) variation in IQ between races.

METHODS FOR INVESTIGATING BIAS IN PREDICTIVE AND CRITERION-RELATED VALIDITY

The Illusionary Problem of Definition

The defining of bias with regard to the relationship between a test score and some later level of performance on a criterion measure has produced considerable, as yet unresolved, debate among numerous respected scholars in the fields of measurement and assessment (e.g., Angoff, 1976; Bernal, 1975; Cleary et al. 1975; Cronbach, 1976; Darlington, 1971; Flaugher, 1978; Humphreys, 1973; Linn, 1976; McNemar, 1975; Petersen & Novick, 1976; Reschly, 1982; Reynolds, 1982; Schmidt & Hunter, 1974; Thorndike, 1971). While the resulting debate has generated a number of *selection* models from which to examine bias, selection models focus on the decision-making system and not on the test itself. These selection models are all completely external to the issue of test bias. Each of these models deals solely with value systems and the statistical manipulations necessary to make the test score conform to those values. None of the various *selection* models of "bias" deals with constant error in the estimation of some criterion score (by an aptitude or other predictor test) as a function of group membership. As previously stated in the context of testing, *bias* deals directly with constant or systematic error in the estimation of some true value as a function of group membership. Within the context of predictive validity, bias is concerned with *systematic error in the estimation* (i.e., constant over- or underprediction) *of performance on some criterion measure taken at a later time* (or in the case of establishing concurrent validity, a criterion measure taken at an early point in time).

This is not to minimize the importance of critically evaluating and discussing the most appropriate model for selection in order to meet the goals of society at large. The determination of a selection model that best fits the goals and values of a society is crucial; if tests are to be used in the model, tests without bias, as noted above, are superior to any alternatives. The various selection models that have thus far been proposed are discussed at some length in Hunter and Schmidt (1976), Hunter, Schmidt, and Rauschenberger (1982), Jensen (1980), and Petersen and Novick (1976). The decision-making system chosen, then, must ultimately be a societal decision (especially as regards educational decision making). Prior to choosing a model for test use in selection, decision makers must determine whether the ultimate goal is equality of opportunity, equality of outcome, or representative equality (these concepts are discussed in more detail in Nichols, 1978).

The best way to ensure fair selection under any of these models, however, is to employ tests that are equally reliable and equally valid for all groups concerned. The tests employed should also be the most reliable and most valid for all groups under consideration. The concept of test bias per se then resolves to a question of test validity. How a test is used in a selection model (i.e., fairness) may be defined as biased or nonbiased only by the societal value system; at present, this value system is leaning strongly toward some variant of the representative equality selection model. As noted above, all models are facilitated by using a statistically nonbiased test. That is, a test with equivalent cross-group validities makes for the most parsimonious selection model, greatly simplifying the creation and application of the selection model that has been chosen. *Test bias* refers to systematic error in the estimation of some true value for a group of individuals, while *fairness* in test use in a decision-making system relates to the application of a test in some process designed to achieve a specified set of societally determined goals. Test bias and test fairness are in fact separate issues.

Evaluating bias in predictive validity of educational and psychological tests is less related to the evaluation of group mental test score differences than to the evaluation of individual test scores in a more absolute sense. This is especially true for aptitude (as opposed to diagnostic) tests where the primary purpose of administration is the prediction of some specific future outcome or behavior. Internal analyses of bias (such as in content and construct validity) are less confounded than analyses of bias in predictive validity, however, due to the potential problems of bias in the criterion measure. Predictive validity is also strongly influenced by the reliability of criterion measures, which frequently is poor. The degree of relationship between a predictor and a criterion is restricted as a function of the square root of the product of the reliabilities of the two variables.

Arriving at a consensual definition of bias in predictive validity has seemingly been a difficult task, as has already been discussed. Yet, from the standpoint of the practical applications of aptitude and intelligence tests to decision making, predictive validity is the most crucial form of validity in relation to test bias, and the debate in professional journals concerning bias in predictive validity has centered around models of selection rather than errors of prediction. If one remains concerned with constant or systematic errors of prediction, however, only one definition is logically or statistically permissible. Since the present section is concerned with statistical bias, and not the social or political justifications of any one particular selection model, the Cleary et al. (1975) definition, with only slight restatement, provides a clear, direct statement of test bias with regard to predictive validity, and the problem of definition of bias in prediction is easily seen to be an illusion:

A test is considered biased with respect to predictive validity when the inference drawn from the test score is not made with the smallest feasible random error or if there is constant error in an inference or prediction as a function of membership in a particular group.

Evaluating Bias in Prediction

The evaluation of bias in prediction under the Cleary et al. (1975) definition (the regression definition) is quite straightforward. With simple regressions, predictions take the form of $\hat{Y}_i = aX_i + b$, where a is the regression coefficient and b is some constant. When this equation is graphed (forming a regression line), a represents the slope of the regression line and b the Y intercept. Since our definition of bias in predictive validity requires errors in prediction to be independent of group membership, the regression line formed for any pair of variables must be the same for each group for whom prediction is to be made. Whenever the slope or the intercept differs significantly across groups, there is bias in prediction if one attempts to use a regression equation based on the combined groups. When the regression equations for two (or more) groups are equivalent, prediction is the same for all groups. This condition is referred to as *homogeneity of regression across groups* (or simultaneous regression or nonbiased prediction). This is illustrated in Figure 8.1. In this case, the single regression equation is appropriate with all groups, any errors in prediction being random with respect to group membership (i.e., residuals uncorrelated with group membership). When homogeneity of regression does not occur, separate regression equations must be used for each group for "fairness" in prediction to occur.

FIGURE 8.1. Equal slopes and intercepts results in homogeneity of regression that causes the regression line for group a, group b, and the common regression line derived by combining the two groups to be identical

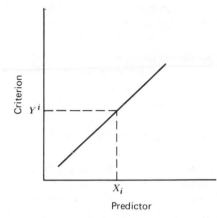

In actual clinical practice, regression equations are seldom generated for the prediction of future performance, though in college admissions and hiring decisions, actuarial prediction is far more common. Rather, some arbitrary, or perhaps statistically derived, cutoff score is determined, below which "failure" is predicted. For school performance, IQs two or more standard deviations below the test mean are used to infer a high probability of failure in the regular classroom if special assistance is not provided for the student in question. Essentially, then, clinicians are establishing mental prediction equations that are assumed to be equivalent across race, sex, and other factors. While these mental equations cannot readily be tested across groups, the actual form of criterion prediction can be compared across groups in several ways. Errors in prediction must be independent of group membership. If regression equations are equal, this condition is met. To test the hypothesis of simultaneous regression, slopes and intercepts must both be compared.

In the evaluation of slope and intercept values, two basic techniques have been most often employed in the research literature. Gulliksen and Wilks (1950) and Kerlinger and Pedhazur (1973) describe methods for separately testing regression coefficients and intercepts for significant differences across groups. Using separate, independent tests for these two values considerably increases the probability of a decision error and unnecessarily complicates the decision-making process. Potthoff (1966) has described a useful technique (to be detailed below) allowing one simultaneously to test the equivalence of regression coefficients and intercepts across K independent groups with a single F ratio. If a significant F results, the researcher may then test the slopes and intercepts separately if he or she desires information concerning which value differs. When homogeneity of regression does not oc-

218   CECIL R. REYNOLDS

cur, three basic conditions can result: (1) intercept constants differ, (2) regression coefficients (slopes) differ, or (3) slopes and intercepts differ. These conditions are depicted in Figures 8.2, 8.3, and 8.4.

Significantly different intercepts.   The regression coefficient is related to the correlation coefficient between the two variables and is one measure of the strength of the relationship between two variables. When intercepts differ and regression coefficients do not, a situation such as that in Figure 8.2 results. Relative accuracy of prediction is the same for the two groups (*a* and *b*), yet the use of a regression equation derived by combining the two groups results in bias that works against the group with the higher mean criterion score. Since the slope of the regression line is the same for all groups, the degree of error in prediction remains constant and does not fluctuate as a function of an individual's score on the independent variable. That is, regardless of group member *b*'s score on the predictor, the degree of under-prediction in performance on the criterion is the same. As illustrated in Figure 8.2, the use of the common regression equation results in the prediction of a criterion score of Y^b for a score of X_i. This score (Y^b) overestimates how well members of group *a* will perform and underestimates the criterion performance of members of group *b*.

Significantly different slopes.   Figure 8.3, nonparallel regression lines, illustrates the case where intercepts are constant across groups but the slope of the line is different for each group. Here, too, the group with the higher mean criterion score is typically underpredicted when a common regression equation is applied. The amount of bias in prediction that results from using the common regression line is not constant in this case, but rather varies as a function of the distance of the score from the mean.

Significantly different slopes and intercepts. Figure 8.4 represents a more difficult, complex case of bias, showing the result of significant differences in slopes and intercepts. Not only does the amount of bias in prediction accru-

FIGURE 8.2. Equal slopes with differing intercepts result in parallel regression lines and a constant bias in prediction

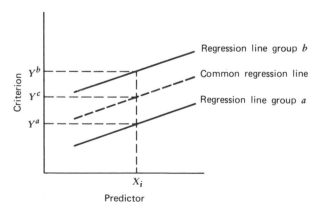

FIGURE 8.3. Equal intercepts and differing slopes result in nonparallel regression lines with the degree of bias dependent on the distance of the score (X_i) from the origin

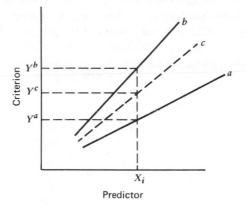

FIGURE 8.4. Differing slopes and intercepts result in the complex condition where the degree and direction of bias is a function of the distance of the score (X_i) from the origin

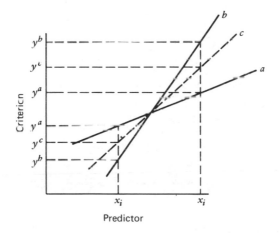

ing from use of a common equation vary in this instance, the actual direction of bias can reverse depending upon the location of the individual's score in the distribution of the independent variable. Only in the case of Figure 8.4 do members of the group with the lower mean criterion score run the risk of having their performance on the criterion variable underpredicted by the application of a common regression equation.

Testing for Cross-group Differences in Single Regression

As noted above, Potthoff (1966) has provided the most efficient method for determining whether the regression equation relating any two variables is constant across groups. Slopes and intercepts are first simultaneously evaluated and then, if a significant difference is revealed, separate tests of these factors may be undertaken if this information is desired. The Potthoff analysis requires the solution of the following equations (6 through 19, from Potthoff, 1966, pp. 18–21, with permission of the author). Potthoff's original notation has been retained to be consistent with other of his computations referred to later; Potthoff's formulas are easily programmable.

$$\bar{Y}_i = \frac{1}{N_i} \sum_{j=1}^{N_i} Y_{ij}, \bar{X}_i = \frac{1}{N_i} \sum_{j=1}^{N_i} X_{ij} \tag{6}$$

$$S_{yyi} = \sum_{j=1}^{N_i} (Y_{ij} - \bar{Y}_i)^2 \tag{7}$$

$$S_{xxi} = \sum_{j=1}^{N_i} (X_{ij} - \bar{X}_i)^2 \tag{8}$$

$$S_{xyi} = \sum_{j=1}^{N_i} (Y_{ij} - \bar{Y}_i)(X_{ij} - \bar{X}_i) \tag{9}$$

$$S_1 = \sum_{i=1}^{g} \left(S_{yyi} - \frac{S_{xyi}^2}{S_{xxi}} \right) \tag{10}$$

$$S_2 = \sum_{i=1}^{g} (S_{yyi}) - \frac{\left(\sum_{i=1}^{g} S_{xyi} \right)^2}{\sum_{i=1}^{g} S_{xxi}} \tag{11}$$

$$N = \sum_{i=1}^{g} N_i, \bar{Y} = \frac{1}{N} \sum_{i=1}^{g} \sum_{j=1}^{N_i} Y_{ij}, \bar{X} = \frac{1}{N} \sum_{i=1}^{g} \sum_{j=1}^{N_i} X_{ij} \tag{12}$$

$$S_{yy} = \sum_{i=1}^{g} \sum_{j=1}^{N_i} (Y_{ij} - \bar{Y})^2 \tag{13}$$

$$S_{xx} = \sum_{i=1}^{g} \sum_{j=1}^{N_i} (X_{ij} - \bar{X})^2 \tag{14}$$

$$S_{xy} = \sum_{i=1}^{g} \sum_{j=1}^{N_i} (Y_{ij} - \bar{Y})(X_{ij} - \bar{X}) \tag{15}$$

$$S_3 = S_{yy} - \frac{S_{xy}^2}{S_{xx}} \tag{16}$$

$$F_1 = \frac{(S_3 - S_1)/(2g - 2)}{S_1/(N - 2g)} \tag{17}$$

$$F_2 = \frac{(S_2 - S_1)/(g - 1)}{S_1/(N - 2g)} \tag{18}$$

$$F_3 = \frac{(S_3 - S_2)/(g - 1)}{S_2/(N - g - 1)} \tag{19}$$

F_1 is the test statistic for the simultaneous test of the hypothesis that regression coefficients and intercept values are constant across groups and is referred to the F distribution with $2g - 2$ and $N - 2g$ degrees of freedom, where g represents the number of groups as in the above formulas. If F_1 reaches the designated level of statistical significance, it is concluded that bias exists. At this point, the investigator may choose to test regression coefficients and intercepts separately to determine which (or if both) differ across groups. If F_1 is not significant, then one may assume that regression equations are constant across groups, and the situation depicted in Figure 8.1 results. Regression coefficients and intercepts should *not* be assessed separately if F_1 is not significant.

F_2, with $g - 1$ and $N - 2g$ degrees of freedom, is used to assess the equivalence of regression coefficients across groups. F_3, with $g - 1$ and $N - g - 1$ degrees of freedom, is used to test the hypothesis of equivalent intercept constants. If F_2, but not F_3, is significant, the situation depicted in Figure 8.3 results. When F_3, but not F_2, reaches significance, the situation shown in Figure 8.2 results. When both F_2 and F_3 reach an acceptable level of significance, the complex problem of bias shown in Figure 8.4 is revealed.

The computations given here are for one independent (predictor) variable and one dependent (criterion) measure only since space is limited and this is typically the question being addressed in specific studies of bias in mental testing. Other situations occur, however, and procedures designed to deal with each have been devised.

The Case of More than One Independent Variable

Potthoff (1966) has provided extensions of the above procedures to account for the situation of more than a single test being used to predict the criterion. The procedure is derived directly from the above technique and will readily be deduced by the statistician. Others who wish to use this approach when more than one test is employed should consult Potthoff (1966).

Potthoff's (1966) extension has some slight difficulties in the estimation of exact probability levels that increase the probability of a Type I error being made by the investigator. Another method that may prove easier and more exact has recently been used by Reynolds (1980c) and involves a direct examination of residual or error terms for each individual by group membership. In this procedure, a multiple regression equation for the prediction of performance on the criterion variable is determined using all independent variables with a single collapsed group of subjects. Using this equation based on the total sample, the investigator predicts criterion scores and calculates a residual score ($\hat{Y}_i - Y_i$) for each individual. Standardized residual scores are then examined by ANOVA with group membership as a main effect to determine if there are any mean differences in errors of prediction as a function of group membership. If there is no constant or systematic error in the prediction of the criterion variable for members of a particular group, the ANOVA will yield nonsignificant results and the mean residual for each group will approach zero. With multiple independent variables, the ANOVA approach has certain advantages, allowing for the examination of interactions and the direct evaluation of variances of each cell. Virtually any ANOVA design can be used with the standardized residuals, and effect sizes are readily determined (e.g., Winkler & Hays, 1975). The direct examination of residuals is also more readily interpretable to nonstatistical audiences.

The Case of More than One Dependent Variable
As Potthoff (1966) has noted, when more than one dependent or criterion variable is being predicted, the test in question may be a nonbiased predictor of one variable but a biased predictor of another variable. Separate tests of bias can be conducted with regard to each dependent variable and alpha levels can be adjusted for the multiple comparison to control Type I error rates. This procedure is probably adequate when only two or three dependent measures are involved. A more exact, appropriate procedure would be a multivariate test for bias simultaneously across all dependent measures. Potthoff (1966, sec. 7) presents the necessary formulas and matrices for carrying out the multivariate test for bias. A multivariate analog of the procedure described in the preceding section of this chapter could also be used. With multiple independent and multiple dependent variables, comparisons of canonical analysis outcomes may prove useful as well.

Testing for Equivalence of Validity Coefficients
The correlation between a test score and a criterion variable, whether measured concurrently or at a future time, is typically referred to as a validity coefficient (r_{xy}) and is a direct measure of the strength and magnitude of the relationship between two variables. Thus, another method for detecting bias in predictive validity is the comparison of validity coefficients across groups. The procedure described in an earlier section of this chapter for comparing alternate form reliabilities may also be used to test the hypothesis that r_{xy} is the same for two groups.

Some researchers, in evaluating validity coefficients across groups, have compared each correlation to zero and, if one correlation deviates significantly from zero and the other does not, have concluded that bias exists. As Humphreys (1973) has explained so eloquently, this is not the correct comparison. To determine whether two correlations are different, they must be compared directly with one another and not separately against hypothetical population values of zero. The many defects in the latter approach are amply explained in Humphreys (1973) and will not be reiterated further here. Other factors must be considered in comparing the correlations directly with one another, however, such as whether to make corrections for unreliability, restriction of range, and other study-specific elements, prior to making the actual comparisons. The particular question involved and whether theory or practice is being assessed will influence the outcome of these deliberations.

Comparing Standard Errors of Estimate

Since the correlation between two variables such as a test and a criterion is almost always less than perfect (± 1.00), there is invariably some error involved in the prediction of the criterion variable; this error has been referred to above as the *residual term*. The standard deviation of the residuals within a sample is known as the *standard error of estimate* (SE_{est}). The SE_{est} is directly related to the size of the correlation between two variables (in conjunction with the standard deviation of the dependent variable), and if the correlations are identical, SE_{est} should also be equal. The SE_{est} can, however, be compared across groups in several ways; the SE_{est} must be equivalent across groups prior to concluding that there is no bias. One method of comparing SE_{est} across groups has already been discussed, which is to compare cell variances for the residuals in the ANOVA procedure; unfortunately, this will not always be convenient. The SE_{est} for a set of predicted scores is given by Equation 20 below,

$$SE_{est} = SD_y \sqrt{(1 - r_{xy}^2)\left(\frac{N-1}{N-2}\right)} \, , \tag{20}$$

where SD_y represents the standard deviation of the scores on Y, r_{xy}^2 represents the squared validity coefficient, and N represents the sample size on which r_{xy} is based. The test for the difference between independent SE_{est} derived from two samples is simply the F ratio formed by the variance errors of estimate, or

$$F = \frac{SE_{est_1}^2}{SE_{est_2}^2} \, , \tag{21}$$

where $SE_{est_1}^2$ represents the square of SE_{est} for group 1 and $SE_{est_2}^2$ represents the square of SE_{est} for group 2. The test statistic is referred to the F distribution with $N_1 - 2$ and $N_2 - 2$ degrees of freedom. This is essentially the F test for homogeneity of variance that would be used to test variances from the

ANOVA referred to above; with multiple groups, some variation such as Hartley's F_{max} may be used.

RECOMMENDATIONS FOR
TEST DEVELOPERS AND TEST USERS

A number of methods for investigating the cross-group validity of psychological tests have been presented in this chapter. Certain methods should almost always be used, while others that are less mandatory retain considerable desirability. The importance of the cultural test bias hypothesis demands thorough investigation.

When assessing construct validity, *equivalent internal consistency reliability estimates* and a *high level of factorial similarity* should be considered mandatory evidence of a lack of bias prior to the use of a test with subsamples of the larger test development population. The other methods for evaluating construct bias presented in this chapter should be viewed as supplementary techniques. Their evidence is highly desirable, however, since the null hypothesis of no differences in validity across groups can never be "proven" at any specific level of confidence.

When evaluating potential bias in predictive validity, *systematic error in the estimation of the criterion score as a function of group membership* becomes the paramount concern. The most appropriate method for determining the existence of such error will vary according to the prediction problem. Construct and predictive validity must both be investigated across groups (Reynolds & Brown, 1982a, 1982b). Neither is typically satisfactory evidence for the use of a test across subsamples of a larger population (or within the larger population itself). Such evidence should be gathered and reported *prior* to the widespread clinical or educational use of a test as well.

This chapter has presented the major techniques currently in use for evaluating bias in mental testing, with the exception of item bias techniques, and has speculated on several other seemingly applicable methods. Under certain circumstances, these methods will not always be appropriate to the investigator's needs. Jensen (1980) and Potthoff (1966) are good sources for other methods and variations on the techniques discussed here, as well as thought-provoking commentary on the statistical issues involved. Other techniques will undoubtedly be developed in the future and the investigator with strong interests in the area of bias in mental testing should watch the literature carefully. Hopefully, the single-source availability of the various methods for detecting test bias presented in this chapter and in the remainder of this volume will hasten the evaluation of existing psychological tests and help spur more in-depth statistical investigations of potential bias by test publishers and authors prior to presenting their instruments for use by the professional public.

REFERENCES

Alley, G., & Foster, C. Nondiscriminatory testing of minority and exceptional children. *Focus on Exceptional Children*, 1978, *9*, 1-14.

Anastasi, A. *Psychological testing* (4th ed.) New York: Macmillan, 1976.

Angoff, W. H. Group membership as a predictor variable: A comment on McNemar. *American Psychologist*, 1976, *31*, 612.

Bernal, E. M. A response to "Educational uses of tests with disadvantaged students." *American Psychologist*, 1975, *30*, 93-95.

Campbell, D. F., & Fiske, D. W. Convergent and discriminant validation by the multitrait-multimethod matrix. *Psychological Bulletin*, 1959, *56*, 81-105.

Cattell, R. B. *The scientific use of factor analysis in behavioral and life sciences*. New York: Plenum, 1978.

Cattell, R. B., & Baggaley, A. R. The salient variable similarity index for factor matching. *British Journal of Statistical Psychology*, 1960, *13*, 33-46.

Cattell, R. B., Coulter, M. A., & Tsujioka, B. The taxonomic recognition of types and functional emergents. In R. B. Cattell (Ed.), *Handbook of Multivariate Experimental Psychology*. Chicago: Rand McNally, 1966. Pp. 288-329.

Chinn, P. C. The exceptional minority child: Issues and some answers. *Exceptional children*, 1979, *46*, 532-536.

Cleary, T. A., Humphreys, L. G., Kendrick, S. A., & Wesman, A. Educational uses of tests with disadvantaged students. *American Psychologist*, 1975, *30*, 15-41.

Cronbach, L. J. *Essentials of psychological testing* (3rd ed.). New York: Harper & Row, 1970.

Cronbach, L. J. Equity in selection: Where psychometrics and political philosophy meet. *Journal of Educational Measurement*, 1976, *13*, 31-41.

Darlington, R. B. Another look at "cultural fairness." *Journal of Educational Measurement*, 1971, *8*, 71-82.

Dobzhansky, T. Differences are not deficits. *Psychology Today*, 1973, *7*, 96-98, 100-101.

Feldt, L. S. A test of the hypothesis that Cronbach's alpha or Kuder-Richardson coefficient twenty is the same for two tests. *Psychometrika*, 1969, *34*, 363-373.

Flaugher, R. L. The many definitions of test bias. *American Psychologist*, 1978, *33*, 671-679.

Gulliksen, H., & Wilks, S. S. Regression tests for several samples. *Psychometrika*, 1950, *15*, 91-114.

Gutkin, T. B., & Reynolds, C. R. Factorial similarity of the WISC-R for white and black children from the standardization sample. *Journal of Educational Psychology*, 1981, *73*, 227-231.

Harman, H. *Modern factor analysis* (2nd ed.) Chicago: University of Chicago Press, 1976.

Hilliard, A. G. Standardization and cultural bias as impediments to the scientific study and validation of "intelligence." *Journal of Research and Development in Education*, 1979, *12*, 47-58.

Humphreys, L. G. Statistical definitions of test validity for minority groups. *Journal of Applied Psychology*, 1973, *58*, 1-4.

Hunter, J. E., Schmidt, F. L., & Rauschenberger, J. Methodological and statistical issues in the study of bias in mental testing. In C. R. Reynolds & R. T. Brown (Eds.), *Perspectives on bias in mental testing.* New York: Plenum, 1982.

Jackson, G. D. Another view from the Association of Black Psychologists. *American Psychologist,* 1975, *30,* 88–93.

Jensen, A. R. *Educability and group differences.* London: Methuen, 1973.

Jensen, A. R. Test bias and construct validity. *Phi Delta Kappan,* 1976, *58,* 340–346.

Jensen, A. R. *Bias in mental testing.* New York: Free Press, 1980.

Jöreskog, K. G. A general approach to confirmatory maximum likelihood factor analysis. *Psychometrika,* 1969, *34,* 183–202.

Jöreskog, K. G. Simultaneous factor analysis in several populations. *Psychometrika,* 1971, *36,* 409–426.

Kaiser, H., Hunka, S., & Bianchini, J. Relating factors between studies based upon different individuals. *Multivariate Behavioral Research,* 1971, *6,* 409–422.

Katzenmeyer, W. G., & Stenner, A. J. Estimation of the invariance of factor structures across race and sex with implications for hypothesis testing. *Educational and Psychological Measurement,* 1977, *37,* 111–119.

Kerlinger, F. N., & Pedhazur, E. J. *Multiple regression in behavioral research.* New York: Holt, Rinehart & Winston, 1973.

Linn, R. L. In search of fair selection procedures. *Journal of Educational Measurement,* 1976, *13,* 53–58.

Loehlin, J., Lindzey, G., & Spuhler, J. N. *Race differences in intelligence.* San Francisco: Freeman, 1975.

McGaw, B., & Jöreskog, K. G. Factorial invariance of ability measures in groups differing in intelligence and socioeconomic status. *British Journal of Mathematical and Statistical Psychology,* 1971, *24,* 154–168.

McNemar, Q. On so-called test bias. *American Psychologist,* 1975, *30,* 848–851.

Miele, F. Cultural bias in the WISC. *Intelligence,* 1979, *3,* 149–164.

Mulaik, S. A. *The foundation of factor analysis.* New York: McGraw-Hill, 1972.

Nichols, R. C. Policy implications of the IQ controversy. In L. S. Shulman (Ed.), *Review of research in education* (Vol. 6). Itasca, Ill.: Peacock, 1978. Pp. 3–46.

Nunnally, J. C. *Psychometric theory.* New York: McGraw-Hill, 1978.

Petersen, N. S., & Novick, M. R. An evaluation of some models for culture-fair selection. *Journal of Educational Measurement,* 1976, *13,* 3–29.

Potthoff, R. F. *Statistical aspects of the problem of biases in psychological tests* (Institute of Statistics Mimeo Series No. 479). Chapel Hill: Department of Statistics, University of North Carolina, 1966.

Reschly, D. J. Assessing mild mental retardation: The influence of adaptive behavior, sociocultural status, and prospects for nonbiased assessment. In C. R. Reynolds & T. B. Gutkin (Eds.), *The handbook of school psychology.* New York: Wiley, 1982. Pp. 209–242.

Reynolds, C. R. In support of "Bias in Mental Testing" and scientific inquiry. *Behavioral and Brain Sciences,* 1980, *3,* 352. (a)

Reynolds, C. R. Differential construct validity of intelligence as popularly measured: Correlations of age with raw scores on the WISC-R for blacks, whites, males, and females. *Intelligence,* 1980, *4,* 371–379. (b)

Reynolds, C. R. An examination for bias in a preschool battery across race and sex. *Journal of Educational Measurement,* 1980, *17,* 137–146. (c)

Reynolds, C. R. The problem of bias in psychological assessment. In C. R. Reynolds

& T. B. Gutkin (Eds.), *The handbook of school psychology*. New York: Wiley, 1982. Pp. 178–208.

Reynolds, C. R. Foundations of measurement in psychology and education. In G. W. Hynd (Ed.), *The school psychologist: Contemporary perspectives*. Syracuse: Syracuse University Press, in press.

Reynolds, C. R., & Brown, R. T. Bias in mental testing: An introduction to the issues. In C. R. Reynolds & R. T. Brown (Eds.), *Perspectives on bias in mental testing*. New York: Plenum, 1982. (a)

Reynolds, C. R., & Brown, R. T. (Eds.) *Perspectives on bias in mental testing*. New York: Plenum, 1982. (b)

Reynolds, C. R., & Gutkin, T. B. A multivariate comparison of the intellectual performance of blacks and whites matched on four demographic variables. *Personality and Individual Differences*, 1981, *2*, 175–181.

Reynolds, C. R., & Harding, R. D. *A comparison of six methods for assessing factorial similarity across groups*. 1981 (Manuscript in review).

Reynolds, C. R., & Jensen, A. R. *Patterns of intellectual ability between blacks and whites matched on "g."* Paper presented at the annual meeting of the American Psychological Association, Montreal, September 1980.

Reynolds, C. R., & Paget, K. D. Factor structure of the revised Children's Manifest Anxiety Scale for blacks, whites, males, and females with a national normative sample. *Journal of Consulting and Clinical Psychology*, 1981, *49*, 352–359.

Reynolds, C. R., & Streur, J. *Factor structure of the WISC-R for emotionally disturbed children*. Paper presented at the annual meeting of the National Association of School Psychologists, Houston, April 1981.

Schmidt, F. L., & Hunter, J. E. Racial and ethnic bias in psychological tests: Divergent implications of two definitions of test bias. *American Psychologist*, 1974, *29*, 1–8.

Stanley, J. C. Reliability. In R. L. Thorndike (Ed.), *Educational measurement* (2nd ed.). Washington, D.C.: American Council on Education, 1971. Pp. 356–442.

Thorndike, R. L. Concepts of culture-fairness. *Journal of Educational Measurement*, 1971, *8*, 63–70.

Thorndike, R. M. *Correlational procedures for research*. New York: Gardner Press, 1978.

Timm, N. H. *Multivariate analysis with applications in education and psychology*. Monterey, Calif.: Brooks/Cole, 1975.

Torrance, E. P. Differences are not deficits. *Teachers College Record*, 1975, *75*, 471–487.

Torrance, E. P. Psychology of gifted children and youth. In W. M. Cruickshank (Ed.), *Psychology of exceptional children and youth*. Englewood Cliffs, N.J.: Prentice-Hall, 1980. Pp. 469–496.

Torrance, E. P. Identifying and capitalizing on the strengths of culturally different children. In C. R. Reynolds & T. B. Gutkin (Eds.), *The handbook of school psychology*. New York: Wiley, 1982. Pp. 481–500.

Winkler, R. L., & Hays, W. L. *Statistics: Probability, inference, and decision*. New York: Holt, Rinehart and Winston, 1975.

Wright, B. J., & Isenstein, V. R. *Psychological tests and minorities* [DHEW Pub. No. (ADM) 78–482]. Rockville, Md.: National Institute of Mental Health, Department of Health, Education and Welfare, 1977 (reprinted 1978).

9 METHODS USED BY TEST PUBLISHERS TO "DEBIAS" STANDARDIZED TESTS

The preceding eight chapters have delineated a variety of judgmental and statistical procedures for detecting test bias. The issues germane to their application and interpretation have also been discussed. The overall intent of this chapter is to demonstrate how the different procedures can be concatenated in actual studies of bias in standardized tests. In all cases, the judgmental review of test items constitutes the initial link in the chain of analyses. Usually, experimental design considerations are second and statistical analysis is third. The types of design and statistics employed vary markedly from publisher to publisher. The choice is often contingent upon theoretical orientation and practical and financial constraints. From the review of statistical item bias methods (chapters 4 through 6), in particular, it appears that along the spectrum of practicability the methods range from the delta-plot or ANOVA to the latent trait models. This factor is clearly reflected in the studies conducted by the publishers.

Another prominent concern in the applications that follow is: When should bias studies be undertaken—during test development or after test use? As the publishers illustrate, it is generally preferable to integrate bias analyses into the test construction process rather than to "debias" the test after it has been used for some time or after charges of bias have been directed at the test. Due in large part to the recency of the research on bias methodology, such early analyses have not always been possible. Furthermore, given the numerous kinds of bias defined and scrutinized in this volume, it seems reasonable to include the judgmental review and item bias studies as integral phases of test development since they address biases that can afflict all tests; however, biases related to specific test score uses (e.g., predictive bias) might better be addressed once those uses have been validated (e.g., predictive validity). Obviously, if there is no evidence to justify the predictive use of a test for any group, it is nonsensical to investigate differential predictive bias among groups.

There are two major purposes to this chapter. First, the presentation is structured to furnish test users with an up-to-date compendium of the judgmental and statistical procedures/studies that have been completed for the majority of standardized achievement and aptitude tests currently used in local and state assessment programs and in college and university admissions. Since methods rather than empirical results are examined, the user is provided with information on what was done as opposed to whether or not a test is biased. The latter decision is a function of both the quality of a study and the interpretation of the findings. At present, the individual test user is in a more appropriate position to reach that decision objectively than either the researchers or the publisher representatives contributing to this book.

The second purpose is to supply test makers and researchers with a methodological and contextual framework for pursuing bias investigations of their own. Certainly any study of test bias must be couched within the context of the judgmental and statistical analyses of a test which have already been conducted. The gulf of need for bias research should thereby be identified, defined, and filled. While replications and cross-validations of previous studies are exigent, it would be pointless to reinvent the "bias study wheel." The avenues for future research suggested by the publisher representatives provide concrete directions for new studies. They deserve the serious attention of professionals involved in criterion-referenced as well as norm-referenced test construction.

Consistent with these purposes, in the remaining pages six test publishers—CTB/McGraw-Hill, Riverside Publishing Company/Houghton Mifflin, The Psychological Corporation, Science Research Associates, The American College Testing Program, and Educational Testing Service—present their official policies on bias, the methods that they have used to "debias" their tests, and the nature of bias research on these tests which is planned for the future. A total of 27 achievement, aptitude, and intelligence tests are examined. They are listed in Table 9.1. The order of the publishers' presentations is arbitrary, except that the first four publishers deal with elementary- and secondary-school level tests and the last two concentrate predominantly on college admissions and professional certification examinations.

CTB/McGRAW-HILL DONALD ROSS GREEN

VIEWS AMONG psychometricians about the nature of bias and what to do about it differ substantially and are changing rapidly. This is true within CTB as well as elsewhere. Nevertheless, I will try to present my view of bias procedures at CTB past, present and future. First, a general position on bias in achievement tests will be stated.* This will be followed by a brief and

---

*Since the overwhelming majority of tests CTB sells are achievement tests and since the issue about bias in aptitude tests is even more complex (Green, 1978), all general statements in this paper are meant to apply to achievement tests only.

TABLE 9.1. Twenty-seven Achievement, Aptitude, and Intelligence Tests Reviewed in This Chapter (listed alphabetically by publisher)

CTB/McGraw-Hill
  California Achievement Tests (CAT)
  Comprehensive Tests of Basic Skills (CTBS)
  Short Form Test of Academic Aptitude (SFTAA)
  Test of Cognitive Skills (TCS)

Riverside Publishing Company/Houghton Mifflin
  Cognitive Abilities Test (CogAT)
  Iowa Test of Basic Skills (ITBS)
  Tests of Achievement and Proficiency (TAP)

The Psychological Corporation
  Metropolitan Achievement Tests
  Metropolitan Readiness Tests (MRT)
  Otis-Lennon School Ability Test
  Stanford Achievement Test
  Wechsler Scales (WPPSI, WISC-R, WAIS)

Science Research Associates
  SRA Achievement Series
  SRA Educational Ability Series

The American College Testing Program
  ACT Assessment

Educational Testing Service
  CIRCUS
  Graduate Management Admission Test (GMAT)
  Graduate Record Examination (GRE) Aptitude Test
  Law School Admission Test (LSAT)
  National Teacher Examinations (NTE)
  *Preliminary Scholastic Aptitude Test/National Merit Scholarship Qualifying Test
    (PSAT/NMSQT)*
  Scholastic Aptitude Test (SAT)
  School and College Ability Tests (SCAT)
  Sequential Tests of Educational Progress (STEP)
  Test of English as a Foreign Language (TOEFL)
  Test of Standard Written English (TSWE)

rather general description of the bias reduction procedures currently used at CTB and their rationale. Next, the specific steps taken for each of the major achievement tests published at CTB/McGraw-Hill to date are described. Essentially, this description constitutes a history of our changing ideas and so, whenever data make it possible, comparisons of the procedures will be given. Finally, a few conclusions, comments, and predictions about the future will be offered.

The position of CTB/McGraw-Hill concerning test bias is based on some general propositions. First, it is held that when students come to school they may differ in their background knowledge, cognitive and academic skills, language, and attitudes and values. To the degree these differences are great, no one curriculum and no one set of instructional materials will be equally suitable for all, and therefore no one test will be appropriate. It is difficult to specify what amount of difference can be called great, and reasonable differences of opinion on this matter exist.

Second, it is the task of schools to increase the amount of knowledge that is common to all, to develop certain basic cognitive skills in all students, to generate proficiency in at least the English language among all students, and to foster certain common attitudes and values in our society. Therefore, there is a need for general tests that measure the knowledge and skills taught in school. Thus, the test publisher's task is to develop tests measuring these common skills and bodies of knowledge, without introducing any extraneous elements into the performances on which the measurement is based. If these tests do require that students have knowledge and skills not taught in school, differences in performance among some students will occur because of differences in school learning, whereas for other students differences in out-of-school learning will matter. Thus the test is measuring different things for different groups and can be called biased (Green, 1975).

The third general proposition is that for some groups,* notably those from families whose language and culture differ sharply from that of "Middle America," no test designed to be used nationally can be completely unbiased. The best one can do is to minimize the role of the extraneous elements, thereby increasing the number of persons for whom the test is appropriate. If care is taken in test construction, however, the influence of these elements can be minimal for most people; but for some groups they will continue to play a substantial role. For example, one simply cannot conclude that students are illiterate if they fail an English test when they speak Spanish, since perhaps they are literate in Spanish. Only when such students have acquired a substantial degree of both facility with the English language and acculturation can one expect our standard tests of basic academic knowledge and skills to elicit performances adequately representative of their academic status.

REVIEW OF BIAS METHODS

Procedures for Reducing Bias

It is probably fair to say that these general propositions approximate the status of opinion at the California Test Bureau even before it became part of McGraw-Hill in 1966. Nevertheless, in 1966 CTB/McGraw-Hill had no explicit policy concerning test bias and no stated procedures for dealing with the matter. Instead, it appears to have been assumed by most of the development staff that careful editorial attention to content validity was the

---

*The groups being discussed are those related to ethnicity and/or race, sex, or other sort of exceptionality. Obviously there are differences within these groups as well as among them with respect to the variables being considered. Nevertheless, at least in part it is because these differences appear to be a function of group membership that claims of bias occur. Hence it is appropriate to refer to groups rather than individuals.

necessary and sufficient step to keep bias in achievement tests to the minimum practicable.

Since 1966 the situation has been changing almost yearly. That does not mean that anyone has abandoned the notion that careful editorial attention to content validity is absolutely necessary, but it does mean that it is no longer deemed sufficient. Content is still considered the first and most essential consideration, and for the foreseeable future no other sort of consideration of validity is likely substantially to supersede it. Careful attention to content validity is the first step in reducing test bias. The reason is simple: lacking content validity, no achievement test can be used for assessing growth or for diagnostic purposes.

The second step is the use of McGraw-Hill guidelines designed to reduce or eliminate bias. Thus item writers are given specifications for their work that include directions to attend to McGraw-Hill's:

1. *Recommended guidelines for multiethnic publishing in McGraw-Hill Book Company publications* (1968, 1974),
2. *Guidelines for equal treatment of the sexes in McGraw-Hill Book Company publications* (1974), and
3. *Guidelines for fair representation of disabled people in McGraw-Hill Book Company publications* (1980).

Editors then review these materials with these specifications in mind. The internal editorial reviews of materials to be used in tryouts are conducted by at least three people: the content editor, who directly supervises the item writers; the project director; and the copy editor, who also checks on this matter. The final version built from the tryout materials is again reviewed by at least three people.

Elaborate as this may seem, additional steps are generally considered advisable or necessary. The third step, like the first two, is editorial in nature; in this case, external reviewers are asked to repeat the review process specifically for bias. They are supplied with the three McGraw-Hill sets of guidelines and are asked to critique the tryout materials for bias, item by item. As a rule these outside reviewers are members of an ethnic minority, and typically there is at least one black and one Hispanic reviewer for each set of materials; other minorities are frequently represented also. These people are usually teachers, curriculum experts, or specialists in the education of minority students. The external reviews help in the selection and/or modification of materials for the final version of the test.

The reasons for taking this third step are:

1. to ensure systematically that all materials are reviewed by people likely to be personally sensitive to racial and sex stereotyping and other stereotyping. Even though the writers and editors are somewhat diverse in group membership, this is not considered in their work assignments, and so the more systematic approach seems desirable.

2. to add to the diversity of views concerning content appropriateness as well as bias. Other content experts are often consulted as well without specific reference to bias.

It is hoped and believed that this procedure improves the quality of the test for the various groups. The evidence to date, however, suggests that expertise in this area is no substitute for data since reviewers are often wrong about what items work to the disadvantage of a group, apparently because some of their ideas about how students react to items are faulty (Jensen, 1980; Sandoval & Miille, 1980). It may be that Scheuneman's recent efforts (see chapter 7) will improve the situation.

In any case, an empirical approach also appears needed as an addition to the editorial procedures. This fourth sort of bias procedure undertaken at CTB depends on doing a separate item tryout for one or more minority groups. To date, this has meant doing tryouts with black, and sometimes Hispanic, students in addition to regular samples of students. CTB has developed the fourth procedure first and foremost because it has been shown that the item quality indices usually used to help select effective items for tests vary by ethnic group often enough to lead to construction of somewhat different tests from the same item pool (Green, 1971; Green & Draper, 1972). Since it does not seem desirable to use items that would have been discarded if the ethnic composition of the tryout group had been different, such items may be labeled "biased." The procedure entails comparing the results of the tryouts for each group and trying to select final forms of the test that are equally good for all without reducing content validity. Note that the items that are therefore deleted (or revised) may or may not have been biased according to the criteria discussed in previous chapters. It should be added that to date no separate analyses of tryout items by sex have been made at CTB/McGraw-Hill and no effort has been made to look at any data for handicapped groups.*

In short, CTB currently uses four types of procedure to deal with the problem of bias, namely,

1. careful attention to content validity,
2. the inclusion of bias considerations and the application of the various McGraw-Hill guidelines in the test specifications used by the writers and editors,
3. bias reviews by both CTB editors and by external experts, and
4. analyses of item tryout data separately by ethnic group in order to find and delete items that appear to be undesirable for one or more groups.

These steps may seem rational to most of us but they are considered inadequate by some (Tyler & White, 1979) and unnecessary by others, as wit-

---

*Clark (1958) did study sex difference in the 1957 edition of the *California Achievement Tests* and found that girls outperformed boys on the language tests, but there were only minimal differences otherwise.

nessed by many tests built by school systems with no attention to the possibility of test bias. In fact, the evidence about the effectiveness of these procedures is so thin that one might well wonder how we got into this. The answer is more political than scientific, as one might suspect given the short time period during which the matter has drawn serious study; technical innovation usually takes longer to be applied. To help understand what has happened, it seems worthwhile to sketch the situation as it was 15 years ago as a context for the description of the bias work done on various CTB tests.

Some Not Very Ancient History

I choose to begin in 1966 both because that was when McGraw-Hill acquired California Test Bureau and because, as far as I know, that marked the first time anyone seriously attacked the problem of bias in achievement tests—Potthoff's (1966) report, in which he outlined some possible procedures for looking at item bias, but reported no data. Actually, other reports on procedures for dealing with item bias appeared in the 1960s (Cardall & Coffman, 1964; Cleary & Hilton, 1968), but the context was aptitude measurement.

As far as I can tell, people simply were not thinking of achievement tests as possibly biased. Intelligence and aptitude tests had been so labeled in some quarters for years. For example, Pintner said it in 1923, and the work of Davis and Eells (see Eells, Davis, Havighurst, Herrick, & Tyler, 1951) after World War II was still well known in the 1960s. Only some psychologists and psychometricians felt the charges were serious, however, and hardly anybody applied them to achievement tests.

In fact, at that time it was more common in education generally to deplore the very idea of ethnic differences, and it was often considered bad taste to acknowledge that mean differences between groups on achievement tests were usually found. This sort of attitude partly explains why so many in education were so much at loss when the furor arose over Jensen's *Harvard Educational Review* article (Jensen, 1969). The article made everybody much more conscious of the problem of test bias and provided those opposed to testing (e.g., National Educational Association) with a weapon, namely the charge of racism. Even so, when a year later a number of publishers were invited to respond to Williams's (1970a) direct attack on achievement tests, several of them dismissed the charges out of hand (Bennett, 1970; Clemans, 1970; Sommer, 1970). Their reasoning was essentially that achievement test validity was a matter of content, and therefore achievement tests could not logically be biased. Instead, they said, the problem was misuse and/or misunderstanding.

Nobody in that series of articles or in another similar series in another journal (see Williams, 1970b) once mentioned studies of item bias. Apparently this was because no one was doing anything. Note that the topic was not discussed at all in the second edition of *Educational measurement*

(Thorndike, 1971) nor in the 1966 version of the *Standards for educational and psychological tests and manuals* (APA/AERA/NCME, 1966).

In short, the empirical work on achievement test bias did not really begin until the 1970s, and test publishers have had little to guide them in their efforts to deal with the now loud accusations of bias.

Procedures Followed for Various Tests

Comprehensive Tests of Basic Skills (CTBS, Forms Q and R).   The first major test battery published by CTB/McGraw-Hill was the *Comprehensive Tests of Basic Skills,* Forms Q and R, which appeared in 1968, two years after McGraw-Hill had acquired California Test Bureau. Of the steps outlined in the previous section, only the first and a portion of the second were taken. The senior editor in charge reviewed the materials for ethnic bias. This assertion is based only on the memory of the survivors of that time, however, since no written record of this step was made and it was not described in any of the associated CTB publications. The only mention of minority groups comes in one statement in the technical report (CTB/McGraw-Hill, 1970), asserting that they must have been adequately represented in the norms because the norms were based on a probability sample.

California Achievement Tests (CAT-70).   About that time, however, McGraw-Hill Book Company employed a resident bias expert, who produced *Recommended guidelines for multiethnic publishing in McGraw-Hill Book Company* (1968). These guidelines were used by the writers and editors when producing the CAT 1970 edition. For this battery all the internal bias reviews described above were done, but without much attention to any minority group other than blacks. Also, McGraw-Hill's adviser on multiethnic publishing served as the sole outside reviewer.

The *Short Form Test of Academic Aptitude (SFTAA),* a derivative of the *California Short Form Test of Mental Maturity,* appeared at the same time and was treated in exactly the same way. The *Test coordinator's handbook* (Sullivan, Clark, & Tiegs, 1971) for the *SFTAA* was the first CTB publication to refer to possible bias and to efforts to eliminate it.

The *CAT*-70 standardization provided the data for the initial studies of bias undertaken at CTB (Green, 1971; Green & Draper, 1972). Since the procedures followed for Forms S and T of *CTBS* and Forms C and D of *CAT* were based on these studies, they will be described briefly.

In these studies various approaches to assessing the quality of items were compared, using data on three ethnic groups in three regions of the country; differences in economic status as well as region were confounded with ethnic identity. The approach was to use the item data to select the best half of the items for that group. Then these best sets of items were compared pairwise among the groups to determine those items best for only one group. Such items were called "biased." Where the central statistic was the point-biserial correlation for the item, the comparison between ethnically different groups produced about 50% more biased items than the comparisons between similar groups.

The conclusion was that standard test development procedures led to tests that probably were biased to some degree and that if one examined items this way, somewhat less biased tests were possible. Accordingly, that step was taken for *CTBS*/S in addition to the three editorial steps.

Comprehensive Tests of Basic Skills (Forms S and T). In fact *CTBS*/S was the first test produced by CTB for which all four steps were taken.* In this case a black tryout sample was added to the standard sample and item analyses were conducted separately for the two groups. The statistic chosen for primary comparison was the point biserial for the items, even though some of the ways of comparing items that were studied by Green and Draper (1972), such as the use of ICC, seemed better theoretically. For one reason or another these alternatives did not appear as practical or simple as the comparison of point biserials, which were already being considered heavily in item selection.

It serves no purpose to detail the procedure described fully in *Comprehensive Test of Basic Skills: Technical bulletin number 2* (1977). It should be noted, however, that the basic concept used was that as much as possible the test constructed should represent the best test one could obtain for each group, given the overriding constraint of content validity. Thus the first step was to eliminate where possible all items that functioned poorly i.e., had point biserials below .20 for either group.

It was shown that this procedure eliminated a number of items on which blacks performed poorly that probably would have been used, lacking the black tryout. Using the distribution of point biserials by group as the criterion, the standardization data showed that in the final test the quality of the items for blacks was considerably closer to that for whites than was the case in the tryout data. The distribution for Spanish-speaking students was similar to that for English-speaking students. As is also reported in the *CTBS Technical bulletin number 2*, it was possible to demonstrate that Form S contained less biased than did Form Q for both blacks and Hispanics in terms of the number of items having point biserials less than .20. Table 9.2 illustrates these points using data for Levels 1, 3, and 5. It is evident that by this criterion the amount of bias in either of these tests is small.

Form T of *CTBS*, published in 1974, one year after Form S, was the first test to which the guidelines concerning sex were applied; in all other respects

---

*At about the same time, however, System Development Corporation "debiased" Levels 2 and 3 of *CAT*-70 by taking steps 3 and 4 listed above. They then deleted the 16 items (of 286) found to exhibit large differences in point biserials for blacks in comparison to whites which were also judged biased by reviewers (Ozenne, Van Gelder, & Cohen, 1974). Their purpose was to use this modified version of *CAT*-70 to evaluate the impact of the Emergency School Aid Act (ESAA).

TABLE 9.2. Proportion of Items with Point Biserials Less than .20 for the Black, Spanish-Speaking, and Other Groups for $CTBS/S$ and $CTBS/Q$ (three grades)

		Black		Spanish		Other	
Level	Grade	$CTBS/S$	$CTBS/Q$	$CTBS/S$	$CTBS/Q$	$CTBS/S$	$CTBS/Q$
1	3	.004	.03	.01	.05	.004	.01
2	5	.02	.05	.04	.06	.003	.01
3	7	.03	.06	.02	.10	.004	.02

it was treated like Form S. A Spanish edition, *CTBS Español,* was published in 1978.

CAT (Forms C and D). The next major test battery produced by CTB was another revision of the *CAT*. Forms C and D were published in 1977. All the bias procedures used with the *CTBS/S* and T were also used. As always, content and editorial considerations were given priority. Three additions to the bias procedures were made, however. First, there was a largely abortive effort to get an adequate Hispanic sample in addition to the samples of blacks and of "others," i.e., nonblacks and non-Hispanics. Although some of the Hispanic data were used, most of it was too thin to be useful. Second, an additional item statistic was considered. In an effort to increase the sensitivity of the test to program effects, the year-to-year growth of items (ΔP) was added to the traditional criteria of appropriate difficulty and adequate point biserials. Some attention to growth has been traditionally part of the item selection process, but for *CAT* it was given major emphasis. Accordingly, this statistic was also examined separately for blacks and if it was unusually low (less than .05), the item was labeled biased. The third change was that differences between groups in the point biserials and in the growth statistics were given more emphasis, even though, as before, the first items cut were those inadequate for any group.

Note that although item difficulty was a major criterion in item selection, differences between groups in difficulty was not considered evidence of bias in itself. Of course, these differences can be involved in comparing point biserials, but again, as before, extremely difficult or easy items were discarded before making bias judgments; so difficulty played a minimal role in the labeling. As was true for *CTBS,* the basis for the inference that these procedures had value is the fact that the differences in the distributions of the statistics between the black and other group were diminished (CTB/McGraw-Hill, 1978). Further support came from the standardization data that demonstrated a further narrowing of between-group differences, especially in the lower and middle levels. At the upper levels only the differences in the point-biserial distributions were improved. For *CAT* C it appears that by grade 8 differences in achievement among ethnic groups are large and fairly stable relative to differences in growth that are neither large nor stable (CTB/McGraw-Hill, 1980).

Comprehensive Tests of Basic Skills (Form U) and *Test of Cognitive Skills (TCS).* The final tests that will be discussed are *CTBS* Form U and *TCS,* which were scheduled to appear in September 1981. *TCS* is an aptitude measure partly derived from *SFTAA.* Once again the specific procedures were changed, this time substantially. Since Form U and *TCS* were built using a three-parameter latent trait model, the obvious procedure is to proceed in the manner recommended by Lord (1980). This procedure consists of comparing the parameter values obtained for the groups (see Ironson, chapter 5, for details). To do this would be consistent with the general concept followed previously since it is these values that were used to describe the statistical quality of the item. In general about 400 cases per item were obtained in the standard tryout sample and an additional 150 to 200 cases of black students (for *TCS* another 200 or so Hispanic students also took the tryout booklets).

Before proceeding with the analyses, grab samples of this size were drawn from the *CAT* C standardization and the consistency of the possible decision rules was checked. It turned out that large differences between groups in item location could be identified reasonably consistently, but that the discrimination parameter differences contributed only noise, either alone or when combined with the location data as Lord suggests. Consequently, it was decided to look at differences in item location only.

Only items whose differences had a high chi-square (over 6.6) were called biased. Items with locations too extreme to be assessed for one group or another were rejected (or revised). It turned out that most of these extreme items would have been rejected anyway if traditional item statistics had been used. All items were given a quality index number based on the bias rating and the parameter values and model fit derived from the pooled tryout groups. As far as bias was concerned, the editors' task was to produce subtests with average bias ratings better than that of the pool of the items eligible for that test. They managed to do that for all the tests at all levels of *TCS* and 90% of the 76 tests in Form U; none of the eight unimproved tests were significantly worse. So it is presumed that all but a few of the tests have been made less biased.

Because this procedure is quite different from that used before, some comparison of the two is desirable. Tables 9.3 and 9.4 show the number of items each approach assigned to the biased category for two levels of the test. Clearly, the approaches are similar, but far from identical, which is of course what one would expect in view of the various studies of this matter (see review by Burrill, chapter 6). The meaning of the two procedures is correspondingly similar, but also far from identical. In one case an item was called biased when its relative location was different for the two groups. In the other case an item was called biased when the relationship between the item score and the total test score differed in strength. In both cases the differences between

TABLE 9.3. Comparison of Number of Items Identified as Biased Using Two Different Criteria for *CTBS*/U Tryout Level G[a]

| | Traditional Rules[b] | | | | Form U Rules | |
Test	N items	N biased items	Proportion same as form U rules	N common biased items	N biased items	Proportion same as traditional rules
Reading Vocabulary	117	29	.38	11	20	.55
Reading Comprehension	130	33	.42	14	20	.70
Mathematics Computation	110	51	.67	34	40	.85
Mathematics Concepts and Applications	135	48	.75	36	44	.82
Spelling	65	3	.67	2	10	.80
Language Mechanics	98	35	.60	21	30	.70
Language Expression	117	5	.40	2	5	.40
TOTAL	772	204	.59	120	169	.71

[a]Black sample. $N = 200$, grades 5,6,7,8.
Other sample: $N \approx 350$, grades 4,5,6,7.
[b]Traditional item statistics, i.e., point biserial and item difficulty.

TABLE 9.4. Comparison of Number of Items Identified as Biased Using Two Different Criteria for *CTBS*/U Tryout Level D[a]

| | Traditional Rules[b] | | | | Form U Rules | |
Test	N items	N biased items	Proportion same as form U rules	N common biased items	N biased items	Proportion same as traditional rules
Reading Vocabulary	66	15	.27	4	7	.57
Reading Comprehension	66	16	.19	3	10	.30
Reading Word Attack	110	48	.29	14	34	.41
Mathematics Computation	61	4	—	0	0	—
Mathematics Concepts and Applications	88	27	.59	16	37	.43
Spelling	55	4	.25	1	3	.33
Language Mechanics	52	14	.29	4	9	.44
Language Expression	68	6	.67	4	8	.50
TOTAL	566	134	.34	46	108	.43

[a]Black sample: $N \approx 200$, grades 2,3,4.
Other sample: $N \approx 350$, grades 1,2,3.
[b]Traditional item statistics, i.e., point biserial and item difficulty.

the groups are being measured, but it does not seem likely that the differences are the same in nature. Of course, no one item bias approach can claim greater validity than another with any confidence, since the relationship to test bias may not be linear and may not be uniform across kinds of sample and kinds of test.

FUTURE RESEARCH ON BIAS

The relative youth of the enterprise of trying to improve tests by finding biased items is illustrated by the many changes in procedures that have occurred over the past 15 years. It has been easy to think of new and hopefully better ways to proceed, but it is hard to demonstrate that the effort has produced substantially better tests. To be sure, every approach CTB has used has improved the tests for minorities somewhat by the criteria used; and since these criteria have involved traditional indices of item quality, that improvement must be worth something. The improvement has probably not been large because the amount of bias in the test does not appear to have been large to start with.

It seems to me that what we are doing is useful and beneficial and that it is reasonable to say that current standardized tests are more fair and appropriate for diverse groups than they used to be. Nonetheless, certainly no millennium has been reached. Lacking external criteria of validity for achievement tests, we do not really have a good idea of how much bias is in the tests and how much we have done to alleviate it. After all, this is still a "bootstrap operation," as Angoff (1975) has characterized it. The need for adequate measures of test bias and external validity criteria continues (Green, 1975).

Although the use of latent trait approaches seems to be a step forward, it does not change this problem. I do believe that as work in item response theory progresses and as more and more people make use of it—a trend I predict—perceptions of the bias issues will change. The assumption of unidimensionality and the issue of bias are obviously closely related. It is from work on the dimensionality issue that the next steps forward are likely to come in the efforts of the profession to deal with bias.

RIVERSIDE PUBLISHING COMPANY/HOUGHTON MIFFLIN
WILLIAM E. COFFMAN

THE PURPOSE OF this paper is to describe the steps that are being taken by Riverside Publishing Company, the subsidiary of Houghton Mifflin Company that publishes and distributes a number of widely used aptitude and achievement tests, to insure that its tests are as unbiased as possible. Needless to say, Riverside Publishing Company is dedicated to the proposition that all of its tests shall be as fair as it is possible to make them. This means not only that there is concern about the fairness of the content of the published test copy, but also that the manuals accompanying the tests carry information to inform the user of what interpretations are and are not fair. It is unlikely that we will ever be able to provide tests whose scores interpret themselves. A major aim of research on test bias is to provide information not only to test developers about how to minimize bias at the test construction stage, but also to test users about factors that need to be weighed when interpreting test scores for particular subgroups of the population.

A statement in the *Preliminary technical summary, second edition, K-12 Basic Skills Assessment Program* (Houghton Mifflin, 1979) offered by Riverside Publishing Company expresses the ultimate goal of the company's policy. It notes that the tests "have been designed both to minimize the possibility of systematic error for three very important subgroups—extremely high or low achievers, cultural or racial minorities, and female students—and at the same time to keep the test relevant and useful for their counterparts, average-achieving, majority-group, and male students" (p. 17). Ideally, a test should measure with equal accuracy at all points on the scale of reported scores for members of readily identified subgroups of the population.

Of course, this is a statement of a goal to be worked toward rather than of a standard to be claimed, at least at present. As anybody with experience in comparing samples soon learns, anytime one has other than random samples, systematic differences are likely to be observed. For example, distributions of mean scores of groups of pupils from different schools will be found to spread out more than mean scores from random samples of the same size. It is difficult to think of any two differently defined groups that would not differ systematically on any meaningful measure one might dream up. The issue of fairness, then, is not one of insuring that there are no systematic differences between groups in test scores, but rather that when differences are observed, the factors contributing to those differences are relevant to the ability one is measuring or that, if irrelevant factors are present, they are clearly understood and taken into consideration by users of the tests.

REVIEW OF BIAS METHODS

The approach to insuring test fairness that characterizes the activities of the Riverside Publishing Company at present has been outlined in some detail in Part 4 of the *Preliminary technical summary* cited previously (pp. 17-25). This account is directly concerned with the three test batteries that constitute the *K-12 Basic Skills Assessment Program*: the *Cognitive Abilities Test,* the *Iowa Tests of Basic Skills,* and the *Tests of Achievement and Profi-*

ciency. The approach might be characterized as an eclectic one, designed to provide as much data as possible using methods recommended by various authorities while at the same time encouraging systematic studies leading to a resolution of ambiguities of interpretation and a refinement of method. The approach consists of five stages: (1) applications of careful professional judgments at the item writing stage, (2) systematic reviews by representative panels of test users at the test assembly stage, (3) statistical analyses based on a variety of bias models, (4) comparisons among the results of stages 2 and 3, and (5) special follow-up studies designed to seek answers raised by the comparisons at stage 4. In the remainder of the paper the experiences in applying this approach will be explicated in detail.

Professional Judgments

The question of bias in tests is not of recent origin. As early as 1905 Binet and Simon (1916) were concerned that their test of general ability be as independent as possible of items that required a background of schooling. Over the years, studies of the performance of different groups have resulted in a wide literature available to people who write questions for tests. The influence of a variety of cultural factors on test performance have been documented (Anastasi, 1950, 1973; Charters, 1963; Coffman, 1965). Test developers can draw on such published studies for insights into possible sources of bias as they construct test specifications and write test questions. To a considerable extent, the fairness of the tests published by the Riverside Publishing Company rests on the knowledge of test authors, who have access to this literature. As the *Preliminary technical summary* (Houghton Mifflin, 1979) states,

It is . . . clear that schools do differ in emphasis and quality from place to place, language differences by region and cultural group clearly exist, and the common culture is supplemented by many rich and unique cultural varieties. The implications of this diversity for national tests are at least threefold: (1) national tests must focus primarily on what is common to the experiences of students in this country; (2) in focusing on the common, special efforts must be made to avoid content unfamiliar to the experiences of special groups or at least to use content balanced in familiarity to the various major cultures of the country; and (3) the interpretation of test scores can be made best at the local level so that the unique circumstances of local youth can be considered in conjunction with the test scores. (p. 18)

Since any one author's knowledge is necessarily limited, it is common practice to have each test question reviewed by several individuals other than the original item writer before the item is placed in the pool of items to be pretested. Such reviews, and the discussions that ensue, contribute to increasing the sensitivity of writers to the multiplicity of factors that might contribute to unfairness.

Systematic Review

There is little doubt that the informal give-and-take that accompanies the process of item writing and review results in the elimination of many potential sources of bias. Backgrounds of experience for making judgments, however, are limited in any case, and particularly with respect to factors that have received limited research attention, such as the effects of Hispanic or Native American background on test performance. Furthermore, it is all but impossible to carry out systematic studies on the basis of such informal interactions. To supplement the informal efforts at the item writing and review stage, provisions were made to have all of the items in the recently developed forms of the *Iowa Tests of Basic Skills* and the *Tests of Achievement and Proficiency* reviewed by panels of educators working directly in the kinds of settings in which the tests would be used and representing both sexes and a variety of racial backgrounds. (Background characteristics of the reviewers are presented in Table 9.5.)

Reviewers were convened in central locations where they could devote concentrated efforts to making the desired judgments without interruption. Each was provided with general background concerning the tests to be reviewed. The specific instructions provided are reproduced in Figure 9.1 and the general format of the response forms is represented in Figure 9.2. It should be noted that each reviewer was to make judgments from a broad frame of reference, not simply from the viewpoint of a particular racial background.

Many of the comments made by the reviewers were like those we had come to expect from reviewers within our own staff. Reflected in the comments were not only concerns about racial and cultural factors that might influence pupil responses; the reviewers also expressed reservations about the appropriateness of content for a particular grade level, or about the possibility of more than one right answer, or about whether a particular wording might be misunderstood by an individual student who otherwise understood the concept being tested. On the other hand, it is fair to say that, in general, the points noted by one reviewer were not the same as those noted by others. More details on this point will be given later.

In summary, the systematic reviews of draft tests by panels representing a

TABLE 9.5. Summary of Racial and Sex Characteristics of the Reviewers

	Race				
Sex	Black	White	Hispanic	Native	Asian
Female	4	2	2	2	2
Male	5	3	3	1	—
TOTAL	9	5	5	3	2

FIGURE 9.1. Directions to review panels judging *ITBS* items

```
                              Houghton Mifflin Company

                           IOWA TESTS OF BASIC SKILLS
                              Cultural Factors Study


    Test Form _____       Name of Judge _____

    Subtest _____      Date _____


    DIRECTIONS:  The purpose of the Iowa Tests of Basic Skills is to measure the de-
    velopmental level of school children in the background knowledge and intellectual
    skills they are expected to learn during the elementary school years.  It is ex-
    pected that these concepts and skills can be developed through experiences with a
    variety of content, both in school and out of school, and that maximum learning
    can occur when instruction is adjusted to the developmental level of the child.
    The results of the Iowa Tests of Basic Skills provide the teacher with information
    useful in planning the instructional program and in evaluating the results of in-
    struction.

              In constructing the tests, every effort is made to select questions
    that require the student to apply basic knowledge and skill, not simply to specif-
    ic answers that have been memorized.  Each question is stated as directly as pos-
    sible so that failure to answer correctly means that the underlying knowledge or
    skill is missing and that a correct answer is evidence of mastery, not the result
    of getting the right answer for the wrong reason.  This means that in writing
    questions we try to avoid using words that have specialized meanings in any par-
    ticular subculture and to avoid question format that may confuse children from a
    particular subculture more than children in general.

              To help us judge whether or not our attempt to construct a test that
    is "fair" in this sense has been successful, will you please do the following:

              a)  Fill in the blanks at the top of this page showing the test form
                  and subtest you are asked to judge, your name, and today's date.

              b)  Examine each question independently, i.e. without conferring with
                  other judges, and place a check mark in the appropriate column
                  to indicate your judgment that:

                  1)  the item appears to be "fair," i.e. there's nothing to sug-
                      gest that children from some subculture will get the item
                      right or wrong for the wrong reason;

                  2)  the item is possibly "unfair," i.e. there may be a possibil-
                      ity misunderstanding the question because of irrelevant cul-
                      tural factors; or

                  3)  the item is probably "unfair," i.e. the format or wording
                      may present relatively greater problems for children from
                      some backgrounds than for others.

              c)  If you check in either column 2 or 3, explain your judgment using
                  the space in column 4.
```

broad range of potential users of the tests turned up observations that had not been noted previously by those responsible for reviewing draft items and assembling the experimental test forms. Since there was considerable disagreement among the judges, at this point most of the data collected must be viewed as a source of hypotheses about possible sources of bias rather than as definitive evidence supporting specific conclusions. On the other hand,

FIGURE 9.2. Response forms for recording bias judgments

Item No.	(1) probably "fair"	(2) possibly "unfair"	(3) probably "unfair"	(4) comments
1	( )	( )	( )	
2	( )	( )	( )	
3	( )	( )	( )	
4	( )	( )	( )	
5	( )	( )	( )	
6	( )	( )	( )	
7	( )	( )	( )	
8	( )	( )	( )	
9	( )	( )	( )	
10	( )	( )	( )	
11	( )	( )	( )	
12	( )	( )	( )	
13	( )	( )	( )	
14	( )	( )	( )	
15	( )	( )	( )	
16	( )	( )	( )	
17	( )	( )	( )	
18	( )	( )	( )	
19	( )	( )	( )	
20	( )	( )	( )	
21	( )	( )	( )	
22	( )	( )	( )	
23	( )	( )	( )	
24	( )	( )	( )	
25	( )	( )	( )	
26	( )	( )	( )	
27	( )	( )	( )	
28	( )	( )	( )	
29	( )	( )	( )	
30	( )	( )	( )	
31	( )	( )	( )	
32	( )	( )	( )	
33	( )	( )	( )	
34	( )	( )	( )	
35	( )	( )	( )	
36	( )	( )	( )	
37	( )	( )	( )	
38	( )	( )	( )	
39	( )	( )	( )	
40	( )	( )	( )	

there is no doubt that the procedure will be repeated in the future. There appears to be much to learn from the reactions of panels of educators with varied cultural backgrounds.

Statistical Analyses

Given the judgments of test writers and reviewers that items in a test may or may not be biased, one would like to be able to support such evaluations by referring to actual responses of representative samples of the subgroups to which the judgments refer. Such evidence is particularly relevant when different judges report different judgments.

The approaches used in collecting evidence with respect to the three tests that constitute the *K-12 Basic Skills Assessment Program* have been based on procedures that have been described in previous chapters. Since no one methodology has proved to be clearly superior and since there are problems with each, we have decided to collect data using various methods, to introduce refinements in the methods, and to conduct special studies to explore relationships among the methods to the end that it may be possible to evolve better methods. This effort is moving forward with the able assistance of a number of graduate students in measurement and statistics at the University of Iowa, and already we are beginning to see improvements in our understanding of the problems involved and of possible directions to take in future work.

Iowa Tests of Basic Skills (ITBS).   Four studies have involved data from the *ITBS*. In all four studies, particular attention has been given to defining the groups to be compared in such a way as to avoid a confounding of various sample characteristics, a practice that has not characterized many studies of bias. Specifically, we have identified various potential sources of variance (for example, race, sex, school attended, level of achievement) and have then sampled from the several strata in order to balance those sources that are not the subject of the particular investigation.

In order to answer the question, Are raw scores for children at different grade levels that take the same level of the *ITBS* really comparable?, Plake (1977) studied children at five different grade levels who had taken the same level of the *ITBS*. Three subtests of the *ITBS* were selected because of their varying degrees of curriculum dependency: Vocabulary, Reading, and Mathematics Concepts. Each of four different "out-of-level" groups was compared with an "in-level" group, samples consisting of pairs of students matched on raw scores.

The inputs to the analysis were the arcsin transformed values corresponding to the percentage of each group responding correctly to each item. (See Angoff, chapter 4, for further details on the arcsin transformation.) The method of analysis was a three-factor ANOVA, and the arcsin transformation was required because the original p values did not satisfy the assumption that the input to the ANOVA represents samples from populations where sampling errors are homogeneous. The factors were school system, groups, and items, with items treated as a repeated measure. School system was considered a random effect while the other two factors were considered as fixed effects. Since individuals were matched across groups within systems, group effects and group-by-system effects were essentially zero and were of no interest.

If the item-by-group effect was significant in any of the several analyses, one for every out-of-level group in comparison with the matched in-level group for each of the three subtests, the interaction contrast for each item was obtained to identify items contributing to the significant effect. In order to maintain the experimentwise alpha level at .05, a Bonferonni technique was used, that is, the alpha level for each comparison was taken as equal to $1 - (1 - \alpha)^{1/q}$ where q is the number of comparisons to be made.

When all four of the comparisons across grades for one of the three subtests yielded item-by-group interaction terms that were significant, two further procedures were performed. First, three judges were asked to indicate which items, if any, might be expected to operate differently for each of the out-of-level groups from the way it would operate for the in-level group. Items on which at least two judges agreed were designated as "biased" by this procedure and were then compared to the items selected by the ANOVA procedure. The second procedure consisted of regrouping the student pairs by score level, ignoring school system and carrying out another three-factor ANOVA treating groups and items as fixed factors and score level as a random effect. For this design, the hypothesis of interest was that there was no item-by-group-by-score levels interaction. Since the design had only one observation per cell, there was no direct error term available for testing the triple interaction of interest. The quantity used for this purpose was $1/\tilde{N}$, where $\tilde{N}$ was the harmonic mean for the five score levels.

Loyd (1980) studied samples of Anglo and Hispanic responses to items in four of the subtests of the *ITBS*: Vocabulary, Reading, Mathematics Problems Solving, and Mathematics Computation. The data were obtained from 16 school systems that reported results for both Hispanic and Anglo seventh-grade students on the 1977 *ITBS* national standardization, equal numbers of Anglo and Hispanic students being drawn from each system. The total number of students in each of the two samples was 270. A three-factor ANOVA design was used, the three factors being items, ethnic groups, and school systems. The first two factors were considered fixed, the third random. The primary hypothesis of interest was: "There is no interaction between items and groups." The triple interaction provided an estimate of error for testing this hypothesis. The procedure for interpreting a significant interaction was the same as that followed by Plake.

Coffman (1978) conducted an exploratory study of differences between the performance of blacks and whites in grades 6, 7, 8, and 9 on the items in the *ITBS*, Form 5. He argued that the assumption of unidimensionality and local independence that underlies most methods of conducting bias studies was probably an inappropriate assumption and that, therefore, it was not sufficient to concentrate attention on identifying outliers from an overall central tendency. Rather, one should explore the nature of the total set of observations in an effort to understand what might be its characteristics. For example, one finding might be that the items actually fell into two clusters with different mean differences and that outliers on one side belonged in one cluster, while outliers on the other side belonged in the other cluster.

For this exploratory effort, rather than carrying out an ANOVA, Coffman examined the distribution of differences between the arcsin transformations of the p values of individual items in each subtest. The samples consisted of equal numbers of blacks and whites from each of a number of different schools within a single school system. If independent samples were drawn at random from populations of items where the arcsin differences between the two populations being compared were always the same, the distribution of arcsin differences would be expected to fall around a mean, approximately equal to the population mean difference with a standard deviation of the distribution of differences equal to the square root of $1/N_1 + 1/N_2$, where N_1 and N_2 are the numbers of cases in the two samples being compared. This is what one would expect if the items in the test met the assumptions of unidimensionality and local independence. To the extent that there is dependence, as in the case where item intercorrelations are positive rather than zero (as in the case where all item differences were estimated from the same two samples), one would expect the sampling variance of the differences to be somewhat less than $1/N_1 + 1/N_2$.

A computer program to carry out this analysis of arcsin differences for comparing the performance of two samples from different populations has been prepared at the University of Iowa and can be obtained by writing the Iowa Testing Programs, University of Iowa. It has been used in further studies of group differences in performances on items in the *ITBS*, Forms 7 and 8. The output of the computer program is illustrated in Figure 9.3. Here the samples being compared are samples of males (B) and females (W) who took Form 7 of the *ITBS* Reading Comprehension subtest, Level 9·(grade 3) as part of the 1978 *ITBS* national norms administration. The sample consisted of 400 males and 400 females drawn in equal numbers from each of a number of different schools. With samples of this size, if each difference were based on an independent pair of samples, one would expect the standard deviation of the obtained difference to be that shown under the indicators of sample size, i.e., SQR (1/NB + 1/NW) = 0.07071.

The computer program calculates the actual mean and standard deviation of the distribution of arcsin differences. In Figure 9.3 the mean arcsin difference is -0.15280, indicating that a smaller percentage of the male sample on the average answered items correctly than of the female sample, and the standard deviation of the differences is 0.10407, a quantity larger than the expected value for independent random samples. A large standard deviation of differences indicates that there is probably a significant item-by-group interaction.

The computer program also prints a histogram showing the location of each item by item number in the distribution, and, using the actual standard deviation as the measure of deviation, lists outliers in terms of four criteria—outside the 95% confidence band, between the 90 and 95% bands, between the 80 and 90% bands, and between the 50 and 80% bands. For ex-

FIGURE 9.3. Computer printout for analysis of arcsin differences (Coffman, 1978)

```
APRIL-1978 ITBS  NATIONAL NORMS SAMPLE  FORM 07              10/12/78              PAGE   1

TEST   RC READING COMPREHENSION
GRADE  03
LEVEL  09
                                                MALE     N  =   400      ITEMS   =    44
                                                FEMALE   N  =   400      MEAN    =-0.15280
                                                SQR(1/NB+1/NW) = 0.07071  STD DEV = 0.10407
       INTERVAL FOR    COUNT      HISTOGRAM OF ITEMS
       DIFFERENCE

       BELOW -.70        0

       -.70 TO -.65      0

       -.65 TO -.60      0

       -.60 TO -.55      0

       -.55 TO -.50      0

       -.50 TO -.45      0

       -.45 TO -.40      0

       -.40 TO -.35      2       6   17

       -.35 TO -.30      4       4   10  11  19

       -.30 TO -.25      2      16   28

       -.25 TO -.20      5       7   13  22  23  38

       -.20 TO -.15      7       2   14  15  24  30  32  39

       -.15 TO -.10      8       1    3   5  18  26  31  36  41

       -.10 TO -.05      8      12   20  25  27  33  34  40  42

       -.05 TO 0.00      5       8    9  21  29  35

       0.00 TO 0.05      3      37   43  44

       0.05 TO 0.10      0

       0.10 TO 0.15      0

       0.15 TO 0.20      0

       0.20 & ABOVE      0

       CONFIDENCE INTERVAL         ITEMS IN FAVOR OF MALE              ITEMS IN FAVOR OF FEMALE

       95%= -0.0142 TO -0.2914    29  37  43  44                    4    6  10  11  17  19
       90%= -0.0369 TO -0.2688     9                               16
       80%= -0.0623 TO -0.2433     8  21  35                       28
       50%= -0.1051 TO -0.2005    12  20  25  27  33  34  40  42    7  13  22  23  38
```

ample, in Figure 9.3, items 29, 37, 43, and 44 are outliers that favor males, and items 4, 6, 10, 11, 17, and 19 are outliers that favor females when the 95% confidence interval is used.

Interpretation involves comparing the observed standard deviation of differences with the theoretical standard deviation and examining the content characteristics of the items relatively easier for one or the other of the groups being compared. From such exploratory data analyses, hypotheses may be generated that can be explored further using more rigorous procedures.

Laksana (Laksana, 1979; Laksana & Coffman, 1980) compared two methods of studying item bias in the vocabulary and the mathematics problem solving subtests of the *ITBS*, Form 7. The two methods were the ANOVA method originally proposed by Cardall & Coffman (1964) (see Angoff, chapter 4) and the three-parameter logistic model (see Ironson, chapter 5). The samples consisted of equal numbers of black males, black females, white males, and white females drawn from each of a number of different schools participating in the 1978 national norms study. The detailed study was carried out on samples of 800 students each that took levels 9, 11, and 13 of the Vocabulary and the Mathematics Problem Solving subtests, but the analyses were also carried out for all of the other subtests.

For the ANOVA, each of the four subsamples of 200 cases each was divided into four random subsamples of 50 cases each. Each of these subgroups represented the units of observation. The design consisted of three factors—race, sex, and items—all being considered fixed effects. The inputs to the cells of the design were the arcsin transformations of the p values for each of the four subsamples. The index of bias was the presence of a significant item-by-race or item-by-sex interaction.

For the three-parameter ICC method, the item parameters were estimated using the LOGIST program (Wood, Wingersky, & Lord, 1976). The parameters were transformed to a common scale using the technique suggested by Marco (1977), and two ICCs on each item for the two groups under comparison were estimated on the same axis. Two estimates of aberrance were generated for each item: absolute-aberrance (ABS.ABER.), in which the area between the two curves was calculated without regard to the directionality of the differences, and signed-aberrance (SIGN.ABER.), in which the directionality of the differences was considered. Both measures of aberrance were considered in arriving at a rule-of-thumb criterion of bias. The criterion was ABS. ABER. $\geq$ .30 and SIGN. ABER. $\geq$ .20.

To compare the results from the two analyses, two kinds of indicators were used: (1) the consistency of the two measures in identifying biased items, and (2) the magnitude of the Spearman rank difference correlation.

Tests of Achievement and Proficiency (TAP).   Haebara (1979) used data from samples of blacks and whites balanced by schools to illustrate a method for investigating item bias using Birnbaum's three-parameter logistic model. The samples were 400 black and 400 white ninth-graders drawn from the national norms group that had taken the reading comprehension subtest of the *TAP,* Form 7, Level 15.

Haebara argued that it was not sufficient simply to apply a method of analysis and to accept a previously adopted level of significance for defining bias. He wrote:

In trying to solve bias problems in the absence of an external criterion, the greatest emphasis ought to be placed on the examination of content validity and the continuous accumulation of relevant evidence of construct validity, rather than any single-shot statistical analysis. And once the agreement has been obtained that a test is reasonably unbiased as a whole, the test constructors' efforts are turned to detecting biased items and to improve further the fairness of the test either by eliminating those items or by revising them. Those item bias studies are useful not only for improving the particular test in which the items are contained but also for obtaining general ideas on what factors are tending to make items biased. (p. 4)

Haebara's approach differs in certain ways from those of Láksana (1979), Lord (1977), and Rudner (1977). In particular, Haebara questioned the appropriateness of assuming that the c_g parameter be the same for both samples or of estimating the value of the c_g parameter using the higher ability group. Haebara outlines his proposed method thus:

1. Using LOGIST, the parameters a_g, b_g, and c_g of each item and θ of each examinee are estimated for each subgroup separately.
2. Approximate values of asymptotic standard errors of the estimates of c_g are computed.
3. Asymptotic significance tests are performed for each item to see whether the values of c_g estimated from the two subgroups are significantly different. Those items which show a statistically significant difference between the two estimates of c_g are considered to be biased with respect to the pseudo-chance level of correctly answering the item.
4. For each of those items that were not considered to be biased with respect to c_g in Step 3, a single value of c_g is assigned to the ICCs for both groups (equating of c_g). This can be done either (a) by reestimating c_g by LOGIST, using the total combined group of examinees and only those items that are not rejected in Step 3; (b) by taking a weighted average of the estimates obtained from the two subgroups, weighted by their respective relative precision; or (c) by using the estimates obtained from the lower performance subgroup.
5. Using the values of c_g obtained in Step 4 as conditioning values, the parameters a_g and b_g are reestimated for each subgroup. If in Step 4, the first procedure was employed for determining the common values of c_g, the ability parameters obtained in that process are also used as conditioning values.
6. The parameters a_g and b_g estimated in Step 5 are equated.
7. Steps 2 and 3 are repeated for a_g and b_g. The rejected items are considered to be biased with respect to the item discrimination or with respect to the item difficulty.
8. Final decisions on item bias are made on the basis of the results obtained above, visual inspection of the forms of the ICCs, and examination of the format and content of items. (pp. 14–15)

Cognitive Abilities Test (CogAT). Rusinah (1980) compared the performance of blacks and whites and of males and females on the items of the *CogAT,* Form 3, using as the basic method of analysis the examination of the distributions of arcsin differences proposed by Coffman (1978). Separate samples of 1,200 each were drawn from the students in grades 3, 5, 7, and 10 in the October 1977 national norms sample, and a sample of 1,000 was drawn from the grade 12 group. Equal numbers of black males, black females, white males, and white females comprised each sample. Equal numbers in every subgroup were drawn for each school to insure that any differences observed among the subgroups would not be attributable to school effects. The distributions of arcsin differences between blacks and whites and between males and females were obtained in the form illustrated in Figure 9.3. Altogether there were 30 such figures, one for the black-white comparisons and one for the male-female comparisons for each of the three *CogAT* tests (Verbal, Quantitative, and Nonverbal) at each of the five levels (Levels A, C, E, G, and H). These were the procedures for reducing these data:

1. The mean differences and the standard deviations of differences in arcsin values for each of the three tests (Verbal, Quantitative, and Nonverbal) and for each of the 10 subtests were tabulated separately for the black-white comparisons and for the male-female comparisons. These data were examined for trends across grades and across subtests.
2. Items falling outside of the 90 percent band were considered as outliers, and they were classified by subtest and by content characteristics. For example, the outlier items for the verbal tests were classified according to the four subtests—Vocabulary, Sentence Completion, Verbal Classification, and Verbal Analogies. They were also classified as (1) very hard, (2) literary, domestic, or artistic, (3) scientific, mechanical, or sports, (4) about people, (5) about things, and (6) other. The numbers of outliers falling in each category that favored blacks were compared with the numbers favoring whites, and the numbers favoring males were compared with the numbers favoring females.
3. Finally, because it appeared that one factor producing outliers was the overall difficulty of items, all items in each subtest were classified as having mean difficulty greater than chance or having mean difficulty equal to or less than chance, and the mean arcsin differences for the several groups were compared.

Comparisons among Methods

As has been indicated in earlier chapters, particularly Burrill's (chapter 6), the several methods of identifying item bias do not produce comparable results. The *Preliminary Technical Summary* (Houghton Mifflin, 1979) cited previously reports comparisons of items identified as biased by judges and items identified as biased by the arcsin difference procedure. There appears to be little agreement across the two methods, and agreement among judges is slight. Laksana (1979) concludes that

under the assumptions and approaches of the ANOVA and ICC methods, sets of possibly biased items were identified with few common items and moderate rank correlations between these two methods. These results support the conclusion that different assumptions and approaches lead to different items being identified as possibly biased. (pp. 78–79)

Haebara (1979) complains that there is too much sampling error involved in the estimates of the parameters for the three-parameter logistic analysis with samples of the size that are typically available, and that for satisfactory results "when applying the procedure proposed in the present study, it seems desirable to have a sample of two or three thousand since the sampling distributions have been derived for 'genuine' ML estimators that are free from such adjustments as assigning the median value to some estimates of c_g" (p. 43). Thus it is difficult to replicate results with new samples of the sizes usually available or to apply the method at the preassembly stage.

In view of these problems, it seems desirable to explore further the nature of the differences among the several methods in an effort to determine what the differences imply and what approach or combination of approaches is likely to increase our insights into bias issues.

Special Follow-up Studies

To throw additional light on the nature of the several analytical methods, graduate students at the University of Iowa have conducted special studies using data from the foregoing studies. Haebara (1980) reasoned that one problem with the results of the three-parameter logistic analysis might be that the equating of item parameters across groups might be less precise than desirable. Therefore, he proposed a general procedure for equating logistic ability scales that involves the use of a loss function and formulated an optimization process. As one of the optimum estimation procedures, he proposed a weighted least squares method and applied it to the items in the first subtest of the *CogAT* Verbal Battery, Test 1, Form 3, Level E, using the black seventh-grade sample (600 examinees) and the white seventh-grade sample (600 examinees) originally drawn for Rusinah's study. He also applied the method to the sample used in the study previously reported (Haebara, 1979). An advantage of the method over the other proposed procedures is that highly discriminating items tend to affect equating more strongly than less discriminating items.

Qualls (1980) reasoned that there was little agreement among judges regarding the presence of bias in test items because most of the biased items tended to be eliminated during the test assembly process. Perhaps judges familiar with minority pupils, i.e., teachers working directly with pupils, could identify really biased items.

To explore this possibility, Qualls asked 41 white and 51 black teachers in Chicago schools to rate each of 38 items on a five-point scale: (1) definitely favors whites, (2) probably favors whites, (3) favors neither group, (4) probably favors blacks, and (5) definitely favors blacks. Thirty of the items had appeared as extreme outliers in the ANOVA analyses performed by Laksana (1979), six each from the Vocabulary, the Spelling, the Capitalization, the Punctuation, and the Usage subtests of the *ITBS*, Form 7. Eight additional items—two vocabulary, three capitalization, one punctuation, and two usage—were written by the author. The intent was to write appropriate items that obviously appeared to favor either black or white children. These were treated as a sixth subtest identified in her report as "Intentional Favoritism."

The resulting ratings were analyzed using a three-factor ANOVA design with repeated measures on two factors. The three factors were: (1) teacher race, (2) item type—statistical indices favoring blacks or favoring whites, and (3) subtest—Vocabulary, Spelling, Capitalization, Punctuation, Usage, and Intentional Favoritism. All were treated as fixed factors in an ANOVA. A summary of the ANOVA design is shown in Table 9.6.

If a significant item type-by-subtest interaction was found, Qualls carried out a follow-up two-way analysis in order to determine the interaction effects for each subtest separately. The follow-up investigation also permitted the revelation of any pertinent information regarding teacher race interactions and main effects that could easily be masked in a three-dimensional design.

To determine the extent of the relationship between teacher ratings and the statistical indices (the arcsin differences) used to classify the items into the two types, product moment correlations between the average of the ratings for each item and the arcsin difference were computed and tested for significance using a t-test. Qualls also calculated from the original data point-biserial correlations, differences in point biserials for the two groups, and correlations between the average ratings and the differences in point biserials. Finally, correlations of these two sorts were calculated separately with the average ratings for black teachers and for white teachers. The hypothesis that there is no difference in the correlations of black and white teacher ratings with item difficulties or item discriminations was tested using a Z-test (Qualls, 1980, p. 30).

FUTURE RESEARCH ON BIAS

The studies of the *ITBS,* the *TAP,* and the *CogAT* conducted to date suggest that there is still much to learn about the nature of the tests themselves, about the performance characteristics of various subgroups of the total population of test takers for each test battery, and about the several models being used for assessing bias. Obviously, additional studies will be required to understand these matters. Meanwhile, the methods 'described in this paper are being applied in the development of other tests published by Riverside. For example, minority panels are reviewing the items being pretested for a new form of the *Stanford-Binet,* and as data are collected, plans call for statistical analyses designed to minimize bias in the final published test.

It seems clear that methods based on indices of difficulty alone, such as the ANOVA and the one-parameter logistic model, provide different information from that provided by indices based on additional parameters, such as the three-parameter logistic model. We need many additional studies, carefully designed to check out hypotheses generated from the data already collected and analyzed. Some such studies are now underway and others will be designed and carried out as resources permit.

TABLE 9.6. Summary of Analysis of Variance

Source of Variation	df
Between subjects	$n_1 + n_2 - 1$
A (Teacher race)	$p - 1$
Subjects within groups (error between)	$(n_1 + n_2 - 2)$
Within subjects	$(n_1 + n_2)(qr - 1)$
B (item type)	$q - 1$
AB (teacher race $\times$ item type)	$(p - 1)(q - 1)$
B $\times$ subjects within groups	$(n_1 + n_2)(q - 1)$
C (subtest)	$r - 1$
AC (teacher race $\times$ subtest)	$(p - 1)(r - 1)$
C $\times$ subjects within groups	$(n_1 + n_2 - 2)(r - 1)$
BC (item type $\times$ subtest)	$(q - 1)(r - 1)$
ABC (teacher race $\times$ item type $\times$ subtest)	$(p - 1)(q - 1)(r - 1)$
BC $\times$ subjects within groups	$(n_1 + n_2 - 2)(q - 1)(r - 1)$

Source: Qualls, 1980.

Haebara and Coffman have initiated a study of the comparability of results from the one-parameter logistic model and results from the analysis of arcsin differences using the same samples as those used by Rusinah. Preliminary results strongly suggest that the two approaches give essentially the same results, provided responses of subjects to items are treated in exactly the same manner. They are also exploring the usefulness of factor analysis to provide information about the appropriateness of the assumption of unidimensionality that underlies all of the methods. Preliminary results indicate that, at least for the *CogAT*, the factor structure is highly complex. It may turn out that the results of a factor analysis could provide an identification of a core of homogeneous items to use as the basic input to one of the other approaches. Such research, however, is far from simple and routine. Rather, it calls for careful design at the outset and for creative insight at the point of interpretation of results. This means that it is unreasonable to expect results on a rapid schedule. As results accumulate, we expect to report them promptly so that they may have an impact on the ongoing test development activities and on the interpretations generated by test users.

THE PSYCHOLOGICAL CORPORATION JOANNE M. LENKE

THE ISSUE OF potential bias in standardized tests is of concern to test publishers as well as to test users. Throughout the 1960s and 1970s, national attention focused on the protection of an individual's civil rights, one aspect of which was the "fairness" of ability, aptitude, and achievement tests for all students in the nation's schools. The fairness issue is most often discussed in relation to "bias" of one kind or another. Unfortunately, no one has yet been able to come up with a definition of bias that is either universally acceptable or universally applicable to all types of test or in all types of situation (see Shepard, chapter 1). Until we can all agree on a definition of bias that can be applied in a meaningful way to the examination of test content and to the interpretation of test performance, there will be no such thing as a "bias-free" test.

Therefore, the discussion of bias methods in this paper will focus on methods used by The Psychological Corporation to evaluate the appropriateness of test content for all students, regardless of ethnic-group membership, sex, or habitat; specific methods used to ensure the appropriateness of test norms will not be addressed. Most test publishers, including The Psychological Corporation, take great pains to ensure that their norming samples reflect the performance of the nation as a whole by including students representing all ethnic groups, socioeconomic levels, and geographic regions in approximately the same proportions as the national population. It is also its policy to provide guidelines for the proper interpretation and use of test results through its test manuals and accessory materials (Burrill & Wilson, 1980).

In the discussion that follows, two types of bias analysis as they relate to the development of test content will be addressed: facial bias and item bias. *Facial bias* refers to situations in which a test item, or a group of test items, *appears* to reflect some prejudice, stereotype, derogatory or offensive association, over- or underemphasis of the worth of particular ethnic or sex groups, and over- or underrepresentation of particular types of environmental settings (see Tittle, chapter 2, for further details). *Item bias* refers to situations in which a test item *functions* differently in some systematic way for different groups. While several methods exist for the detection of item bias, it is not yet clear which method, or combination of methods, is most appropriate for the identification of "unfair" items. For this reason The Psychological Corporation views statistical item bias detection procedures as helpful in evaluating the performance of individual items; however, such procedures are not used in the absence of sound, professional judgment.

REVIEW OF BIAS METHODS

Until five or six years ago, the concern for bias in tests or test items was limited to issues of facial bias. It has only been since the mid-1970s that attention has been focused on ways of determining whether or not a particular item is statistically biased. It is for this reason that tests published prior to 1976, though examined for facial bias, were not routinely subjected to item bias procedures during their development; the state of the art was simply not as developed as it is today. It will become clear in the subsequent description of the procedures used by The Psychological Corporation that the more recent the test, the more specific and well defined the procedures become. Today, such procedures are an integral part of the test development process.

Stanford Achievement Test (1973 Edition)

All items included in the 1971 National Item Analysis program were reviewed by a panel of minority-group educators for curriculum appropriateness, ethnic and racial bias, quality of items for the greatest number of students, adequacy of content coverage, and clarity of item presentation. Since more than twice as many items than are usually needed for the final forms of the test were reviewed, nearly all of the items that were considered to have some facial defect were eliminated; other items were altered slightly to eliminate judgmental criticisms. The name of each reviewer, his or her position, and type of review (content, ethnic or sex bias, etc.) are listed in the *Stanford Achievement Test* Technical Data Report (Madden, Gardner, Rudman, Karlsen, & Merwin, 1974).

Metropolitan Readiness Test (*MRT,* 1976 Edition)

All items in the *MRT* were critically reviewed by teachers and parents representing various minority groups prior to the first experimental tryout program in the fall of 1972. Items considered to be inappropriate were either eliminated or revised. Data obtained from this 1972 research program included both score distributions and item characteristics for the total group tested and for different sex and ethnic groups. After careful consideration of these data, decisions were made about the structuring of the tests, i.e., the specific skills to be retained and the items that, for one reason or another, had to be discarded. On the basis of this information, the 1973 tryout editions were developed. In addition to the traditional data gathered for the tryout tests, item data were obtained for bilingual groups of Puerto Rican and Mexican-American children and for groups in which the majority of children spoke dialects other than standard American English. From these groups of children item bias information was obtained using Scheuneman's (1975) chi-square procedure (see Ironson, chapter 5) for the subtests selected for inclusion in the final test forms. Items were also scrutinized again by black and Spanish reviewers.

Performance of each item by sex was examined at this phase in the test's development as well. When an item displayed a significant difference between the performance of boys and girls, a careful study of that item was made—its *specific* task, the situation or characters involved, the experience required for answering the item correctly, and the drawings constituting the response options. If for any one of these reasons the item did not appear to be equally appropriate for both sexes, a change in the context of the item was considered. The final test forms were constructed to yield a sex balance of characters, names, and activities; similar balance was also sought in regard to urban/suburban/rural and racial/ethnic contexts.

Metropolitan Achievement Tests (1978 Edition)

In developing the 1978 edition of the Metropolitan, the authors and publisher developed a series of steps in an attempt to eliminate sex and ethnic bias. Sex bias in this context was defined as: (1) the over- or underrepresentation of one or the other sex group in the test materials—artwork, dictated or printed test items, directions or interpretive materials; (2) the portrayal of either sex in restricted or stereotypic roles; and (3) the over- or underrepresentation of a sex group in either a primary or a secondary role. Given the limitations that are necessarily involved in the test development process, limitations with respect to vocabulary control (e.g., mailman vs. mail carrier) and curricular "bias" (e.g., the great majority of historical figures referred to in history courses are males), sets of guidelines were developed for item content and artwork and for supportive materials. Both quantitative and qualitative analyses of the Metropolitan series for sex bias were conducted. The quantitative method employed was a variation of the one used by Faggen-Steckler, McCarthy, and Tittle (1974). The qualitative analysis involved the coding of test items according to active or passive roles and traditional or nontraditional occupations and activities; artwork was coded along the same dimensions, plus traditional or nontraditional clothing and physical stature. The number of children and adults in mixed-sex or same-sex groups was also tallied. The results of these analyses are presented in Jensen and Beck (1979) and in *Metropolitan Achievement Tests,* Special Report Number 15 (The Psychological Corporation, 1978a).

Ethnic bias concerns were addressed using both subjective and objective rating procedures. The subjective raters were members of an advisory panel of minority educators, selected on the basis of their sensitivity to minority-group concerns and their active involvement in education. The role of the panel members was to provide needed input to each of the five major stages in the development of a major test series: blueprinting, content development, item analysis, standardization, and publication. At each of these stages, panel members were asked to review the materials for potential problems in content, such as irrelevance or insensitivity to minority students, and unclear or potentially biased artwork.

The objective rating procedures involved the use of three statistical methods: (1) Angoff's (chapter 4) delta-plot procedure; (2) Green and Draper's (1972) procedure (see Angoff, chapter 4); and (3) Veale and Foreman's (1976) procedure (see Scheuneman, chapter 7). The two samples used for the statistical detection of possible item bias were the total Metropolitan item analysis sample and a special "large city" sample, which was comprised of students in schools in New York, Los Angeles, Chicago, St. Louis, and Hartford enrolling 80% or more minority students. Each item in the item analysis pool was subjected to all three statistical procedures, and approximately 40% of the items were identified as potentially biased through one of the three procedures. There was minimal overlap, however, among the items identified by more than one procedure—for only 3% of the total item pool did at least two procedures detect the same items, and for only .5% of the pool did all three procedures detect the same items. A complete discussion of the results of both the subjective and objective methods used to detect biased items in the Metropolitan pool can be found in Beck and Sklar (1978) and in *Metropolitan Achievement Tests*, Special Report Number 16 (The Psychological Corporation, 1978b).

Otis-Lennon School Ability Test (1978 Edition)

As part of the process in developing the 1978 edition of the *Otis-Lennon*, all items were reviewed by a panel of minority-group advisors for possible ethnic bias. In addition, items comprising the item-analysis editions of the Intermediate and Advanced levels were subjected to Scheuneman's (1975, 1976) chi-square technique for the purpose of detecting biased items. Data were obtained from schools participating in the Item Analysis Program which had 15% or more minority-group representation within the community. Two additional sites with more than 50% minority populations were specially selected for the bias study. The results of the study, which are reported in Scheuneman's (1978) chapter, were used to build the final forms of the test. Specifically, items that appeared to be statistically biased were not used wherever possible, and sample items were added to clarify the test-taking task for the letter series and figural series items.

A statistical item bias study of the final test form was also conducted as part of the 1977 Standardization Program for Form R of the *Otis-Lennon*. The performance of black, Spanish, and white children was examined to determine (1) whether bias exists in this final form and (2) if so, which item types appear to be biased. Scheuneman's technique (1975, 1976) identified only 7% of the items in the total item pool across all levels of the test, with a proportionately greater number detected at the primary levels. The analysis revealed that items of all types—Verbal Comprehension, Quantitative, and Following Verbal Directions—were identified at the primary levels, while more Verbal Comprehension and Verbal Reasoning items than Figural Reasoning and Quantitative items were identified at the upper levels of the test.

Wechsler Scales

Due to the individual nature of the various Wechsler scales—*WPPSI, WISC-R, WAIS*—follows procedures that are somewhat different from those used for group measures. As a first step, new items are prepared and/or existing items are reviewed for a planned revision. An attempt is made to tap material that is generally familiar, or equally unfamiliar, to those living in what might be called "Western civilization"; material associated with a highly cultivated life style, requiring obscure or academic knowledge, or strongly associated with either sex is avoided. A first tryout form of the new scale, usually longer than that planned for the final instrument, is then administered to 30 to 60 individuals representing various sex and ethnic groups by perhaps 5 to 10 examiners who react to the directions and items for clarity and the test materials for usability and practicality. The results of the item analysis at this stage help to identify items that correlate poorly with total scores and to sequence the items in approximate order of difficulty. A second tryout may be conducted on a larger sample, if necessary, or may focus on a small number of troublesome tests.

Following adjustments in item content and/or directions for administration, the standardization edition of the scale is prepared, also somewhat longer than the final edition is to be, and is reviewed by minority-group psychologists. As part of the standardization research, item difficulty values for Wechsler test items are computed separately for males and females and for whites and nonwhites. The data are inspected for items that are systematically more difficult for one sex or ethnic group than another; items that are valid for one group and not for the other are deleted.

It is worthwhile to note here that, in general, sex differences on ability tests tend to be small. They are negligible for summary scores (IQs), but may be significant for some of the individual tests that contribute to the IQ. While test content has been selected so that items favoring females are approximately balanced by other items favoring males, males do tend to perform better on all Wechsler Mazes, for example; and females tend to outperform males on all Digit Symbol tasks.

Ethnic-group differences present different problems, since they are found to exist across all, or nearly all, types of tasks on the Wechsler scales. Nevertheless, items that are much more difficult for nonwhites than for whites are generally discarded, and items for which difficulty differences are small or in the opposite direction are retained.

A number of studies of bias in the *WISC-R* exist (see, for example, Cotter and Berk, 1981; Gutkin and Reynolds, 1980; Reschly and Reschly, 1979; Reynolds and Hartlage, 1979; Sandoval, 1979; and Sandoval and Miille 1980).

FUTURE RESEARCH ON BIAS

As the body of knowledge as to what constitutes a "biased" test item continues to grow, test publishers will continue to pursue ways of developing tests that will be perceived as "fair" to all examinees. The Psychological Corporation will continue to obtain both subjective and objective ratings of test items that are in experimental forms. For example, all tryout items prepared for the revision of *Stanford Achievement Test,* which is currently underway, have been reviewed by two members of a 10-member advisory panel, comprised of individuals representing various ethnic groups. Their comments are being given the same weight in the item selection process as the tryout data itself. The application of latent trait theory in the identification of biased items is also being explored for use with this revision of *Stanford,* as are other techniques in current use.

SCIENCE RESEARCH ASSOCIATES   NAMBURY S. RAJU

IN THIS PART of the chapter, the specific judgmental and statistical procedures used by Science Research Associates to detect sex and racial bias in the development of the 1978 *SRA Achievement Series* and *Educational Ability Series* will be described. SRA's commitment to the development of bias-free materials will be addressed first. Since this commitment is described in a publication entitled in *Fairness in educational materials* (SRA, 1976), only a brief summary of that commitment will be presented here.

We, at Science Research Associates, are concerned with human dignity and are determined to honor it as best we can in everything we publish.
Our publications have always been designed with a deep concern for their effectiveness as learning aids, but our concern does not stop there. School learning materials must also be consonant with the spirit of respect for human variety that America at its best seeks to instill in the young.
Neither by commission nor omission should any instructional aid suggest that the worthiness or human potential of individuals abides in their racial and ethnic backgrounds, their choice of occupation, or in any other circumstances that we know to be peripheral to the central issues of character and ability.
Whatever the omissions or insensitivities of the past may have been we are determined to offer materials that are not merely free of overt bias but that actually encourage, whenever possible, a belief in the equal worthiness of all people. To make this determination a reality, we must be continually conscious of the problem in our daily work. (p.1)

An explanation follows of how this commitment was translated into specific guidelines for use by editorial personnel and psychometricians at SRA and also how it was actually implemented in the development of the 1978 *SRA Achievement Series* and the *Educational Ability Series*. A major portion of this paper will be devoted to this aspect of test development at SRA. Since the same procedures were used with both the *Achievement Series* and the *Educational Ability Series*, only the procedures employed with the former will be described.

REVIEW OF BIAS METHODS

The work on the 1978 *SRA Achievement Series* started in 1976. The new edition (hereafter referred to as the *Achievement Series*) is available in two forms, with each form containing eight overlapping levels (Levels A-H) spanning kindergarten to grade 12. Reading, Language Arts, and Mathematics are measured in lower grades (Levels A-D), and these same areas plus Social Studies, Science and Reference Materials are measured in the upper grades

(Levels E-H). Multiple-choice format is used with all items, with four or five alternatives per item. Since the test development procedures employed with the *Achievement Series* are not unlike those used by other test publishers, only the two important aspects of the development process that are relevant to the thrust of this book will be presented. For the sake of simplicity, these two aspects will be referred to as *editorial bias analysis* and *statistical bias analysis,* and they will be described separately.

Editorial Bias Analysis

All items in the *Achievement Series* were analyzed for editorial bias at several stages of the test development phase. Probably the most significant event that no doubt contributed to a lessening of bias in an editorial sense took place at the time of the development of detailed specifications for item writers. These specifications, in addition to describing the desired content and format of test items, were written so as to make the item writers sensitive to the issues as well as to SRA's commitment to the development of bias-free materials. The sensitization of item writers to the issues of editorial bias is an important first step in the development of bias-free materials.

All item writers were given copies of SRA guidelines for preparing bias-free materials. They were instructed to avoid moralizing, artificial enthusiasm, topics that might become dated, and topics that were emotionally loaded and might place students under stress. More specifically, the item writers were instructed to pay special attention to the following major features concerning bias-free materials:

1. Use of unbiased language
2. Work roles/life styles
3. Numerical representation

Regarding the first feature, the item writers were asked to use sexually neutral terminology and phrasing, whenever it was consistent with clarity of expression and with accepted principles of grammar, style, and usage. Item writers were also told to avoid patronizing phrases (such as "the little woman," "the fair sex"). In addition, they were asked to avoid such things as diminutive and feminine forms (for example, to use the word *author* in place of *authoress,* or *lawyer* in place of *woman lawyer*); to avoid job designations that end in *man* (for example, to use the word *police officer* in place of *policeman,* or *fire fighter* in place of *fireman*); and to avoid the use of *man, men,* and *mankind* as collective terms for the human race, but rather to use such terms as *humanity, people, men and women,* and so on.

In implementing the second feature, work roles/life styles, the item writers were asked to ensure that women and minorities be highly visible and positively portrayed in a wide range of traditional and nontraditional roles. If professional or executive roles, or vocations, trades, or other gainful occupations are portrayed, whites and minorities—both female and male—should be adequately presented. Although no specific proportions were recommended for various groups, the item writers were told to avoid "tokenism." Item writers were also asked to avoid stereotypes, especially those with negative connotations—such as the Chinese launderer and the black porter. Moreover, merely avoiding those portrayals that were weak, negative, or patronizing would not accomplish the task of avoiding the stereotypes. Positive stereotypes (for example, a woman as loving mother) should be balanced by a sufficient number of nontraditional portrayals. In other words, women and minorities should occur in as many different varieties and fulfill as many different roles as do white males in test materials.

The instructions to item writers regarding numerical representation included the recommendation that when there is room for editorial discretion in including people of any race or group, it is important that black Americans, Latin Americans, Native Americans, and ethnic minorities be represented *at least* in proportion to their incidence in the general population. It is also SRA's position that women should appear in the test materials no less often than men.

The test materials were evaluated to see how well they met the guidelines at two crucial stages during the test development period. The first evaluation was done prior to pretesting and the second at the time of the selection of items for the final test forms. In addition, all test materials were reviewed by educators, curriculum and test experts and, more importantly, representatives of various minority groups and women. The reviews were conducted not only prior to pretesting, but also during the selection of items for the final test forms. For the final test product, detailed tallies were made of all proper names, ethnic groups, activities (active, passive, neutral), roles (traditional, nontraditional, neutral), adult role models (worker, parent), character development (major, minor, incidental), and settings (city, suburban, rural, neutral). Separate tallies were also made by subtest for artwork and test material. The content was then adjusted to achieve a balance of male and female references and fair representation of ethnic groups. Table 9.7 shows the kind of data tallies available on each subtest in the *Achievement Series*.

Data in this table, along with a review of items in the final tests, provide an indication of the degree to which the final product reflected the major tenets of SRA's guidelines for developing bias-free materials.

Statistical Bias Analysis

The items in the *Achievement Series* were also statistically analyzed for bias. The delta method (see Angoff, chapter 4) was employed in the development of the *Achievement Series* as part of both the pretest analysis and post-standardization analysis. The pretest analysis will be described first and, for ease of presentation, the delta method will be described in terms of its use with Level E of the *Achievement Series*. The same pretest procedures were followed with the other seven levels of the *Achievement Series* and all levels of

TABLE 9.7. An Example of Tallies for Level E of the *SRA Achievement Series*

Project Title ___Level E, Form 1___

$\% = \dfrac{\text{Total number in ethnic group}}{\text{Character total}}$

GROUP	Female	Male	Total	%
Asian American	3	2	5	5%
Black	0	3	3	3%
Native American	0	1	1	1%
Spanish American	3	6	9	9%
White	3	4	7	7%
Not identified	43	29	72	70%
Ethnic (Other)	3	3	6	6%
Character Total	55	48	103	

PERCENTAGE	53%	47%

Female*

GROUP	ACTIVITY Active	ACTIVITY Passive	ACTIVITY Neutral	ROLE Traditional	ROLE Nontraditional	ROLE Neutral	ADULT ROLE Worker	ADULT ROLE Parent	SETTING City	SETTING Suburban	SETTING Rural	SETTING Neutral
Asian American	2	—	1	—	2	1	—	—	—	—	—	3
Black	0											
Native American	0											
Spanish American	1	—	2	—	1	2	—	—	—	—	—	3
White	—	—	3	—	—	3	3	—	—	—	—	3
Not identified	27	—	16	—	12	31	5	3	—	—	—	43
Ethnic (Other)	2	—	1	1	—	2	—	—	—	—	—	3
Character Total	32	—	23	1	15	39	8	3	—	—	—	55

Male*

GROUP	ACTIVITY Active	ACTIVITY Passive	ACTIVITY Neutral	ROLE Traditional	ROLE Nontraditional	ROLE Neutral	ADULT ROLE Worker	ADULT ROLE Parent	SETTING City	SETTING Suburban	SETTING Rural	SETTING Neutral
Asian American	2	2	—	—	1	1	—	—	—	—	—	2
Black	2	—	1	—	1	2	3	—	—	—	—	3
Native American	—	—	1	—	—	1	—	—	—	—	—	1
Spanish American	2	—	4	—	—	6	1	—	—	—	—	6
White	2	—	2	2	—	2	4	—	—	—	—	4
Not identified	18	1	10	4	4	21	6	3	—	—	—	29
Ethnic (Other)	1	—	2	1	—	2	1	—	—	—	—	3
Character Total	27	1	20	7	6	35	15	3	—	—	—	48

*Do not combine major and minor character development on the same summary form.

Source: Developed by Science Research Associates, Inc. Reprinted by special permission.

the *Educational Ability Series.* For detailed information concerning these analyses, the reader should consult the technical bulletins published by SRA (1978, 1979, 1980).

Level E of the *Achievement Series* is designed for assessing achievement in grades 3, 4, and 5. All pretest items for Level E were tried out in all three grades simultaneously in the Spring of 1977. As part of this tryout, pretest items were also administered to samples that consisted of predominantly black Americans, Hispanic Americans, and Native Americans. A total of 2,064 students took the pretest items in grade 3; 4,771 students in grade 4; and 2,573 students in grade 5. The fourth-grade sample included a black sample of 644 students, a Hispanic sample of 522 students, and a Native American sample of 101 students.

Initially, p values and point-biserial correlations were obtained for all items, for each of the three grades. Items that did not meet the traditional psychometric criteria were excluded from subsequent analysis. The remaining items were then analyzed for sex and racial bias. Four separate analyses were conducted: female versus male, black versus white, Hispanic versus white, and Native American versus white. To perform each bias analysis, the item p values for the two groups were transformed to deltas (see Angoff, chapter 4) and then plotted in a two-dimensional space. Figure 9.4 shows the female/male delta plot for the Reading Comprehension (pretest) items, whereas Figure 9.5 shows the delta plot for the black/white comparison for the same test.

An ellipse was drawn around the item plots in such way as to include the greatest number of items within the narrowest possible ellipse. Outliers were labeled as biased because, according to the delta procedure, they measured something different from the other items in a given set. (In Level H, in addition to plotting the deltas, for each comparison the major axis was drawn through the plot and the perpendicular distance between the major axis and item plot was calculated [d_i] for each item.). The actual location of an item in relation to the handdrawn ellipse was used to identify biased items. The same procedure was followed for all other subtests in Level E and the remaining seven levels of the *Achievement Series* and all levels of the *Educational Ability Series.* In addition to the female/male and black/white comparisons, the Hispanic/white and Native American/white comparisons were made whenever adequate samples of subjects were available. For this presentation, d_i values were computed for Reading Comprehension and are summarized in Table 9.8.

The table shows the percentages of items with d_i values at or above .75, 1.00, and 2.00. This information is given separately for the two comparisons female/male and black/white. The data given in Figures 9.4 and 9.5 and Table 9.8 are also typical of the data obtained for the other content areas.

As previously indicated, the final set of items in each content area was selected after a careful analysis of the delta plots and content requirements of

FIGURE 9.4 Plot of *pretest* delta values for Reading Comprehension female/male comparison

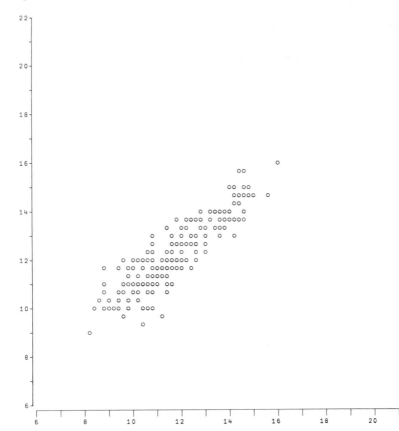

each subtest. The bias analysis, however, did not stop there. All subtests in their final form were again analyzed for bias following the standardization, using nationally representative samples. The results from the poststandardization analysis are given in Tables 9.9 and 9.10 and Figures 9.6 and 9.7.

As in the case of pretest items, the information in these figures and tables also centers on female/male and black/white comparisons with respect to Reading Comprehension. Table 9.9 shows the summary statistics for various groups. Table 9.10 shows the item p values by group and also the d_i values for the two comparisons. It should be noted that all absolute d_i values are less than .75. The low figures of all d_i values can also be inferred from the two plots given in Figures 9.6 and 9.7.

A comparison of Figures 9.4 and 9.5 with Figures 9.6 and 9.7 will indicate the degree to which SRA succeeded in eliminating statistically biased items from the final forms of the *Achievement Series*.

FIGURE 9.5. Plot of *pretest* delta values for Reading Comprehension black/white comparison

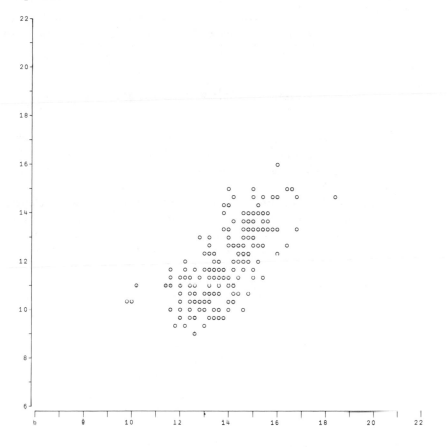

TABLE 9.8. Percentage of Absolute d_i Values ($|d_i|$) at Three Selected Points Based on Reading Comprehension Pretest Data

	Reading Comprehension		
Comparison	$|d_i| \geq .75$	$|d_i| \geq 1.00$	$|d_i| \geq 2.00$
Female/male	12.3	4.1	0.0
Black/white	36.6	20.4	1.6

TABLE 9.9. Reading Comprehension Test Raw Score Means and Standard Deviations for Four Groups Used in the Item Bias Analysis Based on the Standardization Samples

Group	Sample Size	Number of Items	M	SD
Female	1279	50	33.3	10.4
Male	1220	50	30.9	11.4
Black	418	50	26.2	10.2
White	1897	50	33.8	10.7

The preceding examples are reasonably representative of what is encountered in the development of the *Achievement Series*. Whatever may be the pros and cons of the use of the delta method (see Angoff's assessment, chapter 4), the results obtained in the studies with the *Achievement Series* have been most encouraging. A couple of practical matters that all test developers should be aware of in applying the item bias technology also deserve attention. First, no matter how hard one tries to build a totally unbiased test, in practice, one is generally forced to accept a few so-called biased items for the final test. Given the psychometric and content requirements, it is almost impossible to avoid such a possibility even when one has an extremely large pool of items. (A large pool of pretest items will no doubt reduce the magnitude of the problem but is unlikely to eradicate it completely.) Also, the inclusion of a few biased items is much more likely to happen in Reading subtests rather than in Math subtests. One way to minimize this is to start with more pretest items than is normally considered sufficient. Even if one has totally unbiased items (based on the pretest data), there is no guarantee that they will remain unbiased when they are reanalyzed using the standardization data. These problems, however, should not discourage test developers from carrying out item bias studies and seeking to develop bias-free tests.

The second point is the extreme difficulty associated with determining why a particular item is biased. This currently appears to be one of our blind spots. Even a careful analysis of distractor data will not generally help solve this problem. Irrespective of whether the problem lies in the definitions of item bias or somewhere else, the test developers, at least in the foreseeable future, will be forced to discard items as biased even though they may not have the faintest idea as to why they are biased. It may not appear serious to some test developers, but for those of us who have to work closely with editorial personnel in the development of new tests, the problem is indeed very serious. Individuals who spend a great deal of time writing and editing items tend to treat edited items, especially the good ones, as their personal friends and, therefore, find it difficult to dispose of items without a good reason for doing it.

In recent work in the development of the *Achievement Series*, psychometricians had to tell editors to discard certain otherwise good items, which met

TABLE 9.10. Reading Comprehension Test p Values and d_i Values for the Female/Male and Black/White Comparisons Based on the Standardization Data

Item	Female/Male			Black/White		
	p_f	p_m	d_i	p_b	p_w	d_i
1	.86	.84	.527	.77	.87	.011
2	.88	.83	.151	.78	.88	.046
3	.68	.59	−.302	.56	.67	−.363
4	.76	.71	.108	.66	.76	−.324
5	.78	.72	.023	.61	.78	.264
6	.40	.37	−.204	.33	.40	−.737
7	.57	.57	.280	.44	.61	.000
8	.86	.81	.158	.75	.86	.032
9	.81	.74	−.045	.74	.79	−.669
10	.74	.70	.168	.66	.75	−.411
11	.73	.67	−.034	.59	.72	−.149
12	.63	.58	−.039	.44	.65	.319
13	.58	.59	.384	.44	.63	.145
14	.50	.54	.490	.36	.56	.202
15	.81	.71	−.323	.60	.80	.522
16	.80	.73	−.062	.68	.78	−.259
17	.62	.59	.104	.50	.63	−.268
18	.70	.65	.040	.55	.71	.040
19	.66	.64	.227	.47	.69	.417
20	.85	.78	−.050	.71	.84	.130
21	.79	.73	.040	.66	.79	−.035
22	.84	.76	−.165	.70	.83	.097
23	.82	.74	−.147	.67	.81	.113
24	.63	.59	.054	.53	.63	−.406
25	.70	.60	−.362	.53	.69	.004
26	.44	.48	.407	.37	.48	−.460
27	.76	.71	.108	.63	.77	.011
28	.71	.66	.057	.55	.73	.214
29	.60	.56	−.016	.45	.61	−.083
30	.56	.58	.418	.49	.60	−.416
31	.48	.54	.617	.37	.55	.062
32	.51	.51	.197	.35	.56	.257
33	.81	.72	−.231	.66	.79	−.035
34	.80	.73	−.062	.66	.79	−.035
35	.71	.67	.119	.55	.73	.214
36	.74	.70	.168	.58	.75	.195
37	.68	.59	−.302	.53	.67	−.170
38	.64	.58	−.115	.48	.65	.043
39	.66	.57	−.330	.52	.65	−.232
40	.53	.49	−.084	.36	.54	.057
41	.72	.63	−.297	.50	.72	.485
42	.64	.57	−.177	.44	.65	.319
43	.65	.58	−.192	.43	.67	.519
44	.52	.46	−.255	.36	.53	−.001
45	.35	.39	.281	.23	.41	.148
46	.57	.47	−.493	.36	.57	.289
47	.61	.54	−.221	.45	.61	−.083
48	.47	.42	−.260	.31	.49	.068
49	.53	.45	−.393	.36	.53	−.001
50	.57	.54	.033	.43	.59	−.090

FIGURE 9.6. Plot of *standardization* delta values for Reading Comprehension female/male comparison

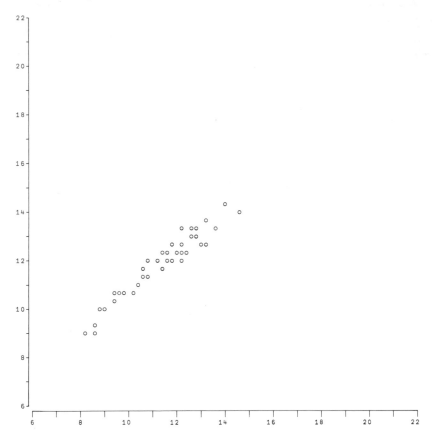

all the editorial criteria for fairness, as biased simply because they fell outside an ellipse or they were too far removed from the rest of the items. The failure to explain why these items were biased against certain groups in terms of the content of the items almost ruined what was otherwise a very warm and friendly relationship with the editorial personnel.

There are a few lessons to be learned from our experience that is certainly not unique to people at SRA. First, more effort should be spent on understanding why certain items behave in an unpredictable manner in certain groups and less effort on assessing the commonality of various bias methods. Such redirection should contribute significantly to our understanding of the nature and meaning of item bias. In fact, the issue of item bias may be redirected to an issue of the unpredictability of a (or any) student's response to an item. That is, only a small percentage of either the majority or minority group may be contributing to the unpredictability of an item rather than

FIGURE 9.7. Plot of *standardization* delta values for Reading Comprehension black/white comparison

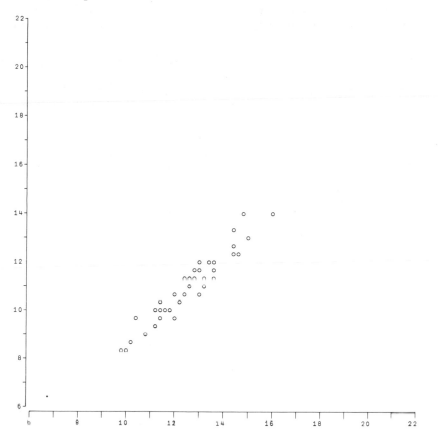

acting as though the item is biased against an entire group. Second, when you have to tell a test editor that a particular item is biased and, therefore, should be discarded, tell the editor that there is a lot that you do not know about the item bias methodology. Such a confession is not only good for your psychometric soul, it may induce your editorial colleagues to treat you as a human being.

FUTURE RESEARCH ON BIAS

The topic of item bias will continue to receive special attention at SRA. The SRA guidelines for developing bias-free materials are constantly under review and will continue to serve as the standard against which all SRA developed test materials will be evaluated.

Concerning the psychometric techniques for detecting item bias, a study sponsored by SRA to assess the relationship between various statistical methods of bias detection was recently completed. This study, conducted by Devine (1980), compared the delta method, point-biserial method, chi-square method, and the three-parameter ICC method with one another using Level F of the *Achievement Series*. The results from Devine's study are not unlike those obtained in the studies reviewed by Burrill (see chapter 6).

Since future development plans will probably call for the use of latent trait models, it is likely that the same methodology will be used in the study of sex and racial bias in test items. The importance of the practical problems associated with. implementing the latent trait models, however, should not be minimized, especially concerning the three-parameter model on such a large scale as the development of a multilevel achievement series. Fortunately, work is currently underway to address and hopefully to solve some of these problems. The future appears bright as well as challenging for the item bias detection procedures.

THE AMERICAN COLLEGE TESTING PROGRAM

FANNIE A. HANDRICK AND BRENDA H. LOYD

THE BIAS PREVENTION procedures used by the American College Testing (ACT) Program are based on the firm belief that test developers have a responsibility to produce assessment instruments that are as free from racial, ethnic, and sex bias as possible. Within measurement contexts, various definitions of bias have been proposed. One of the most generally applicable definitions describes bias as "differential validity." A test can be differentially valid for two groups of examinees if it measures different constructs or traits for the two groups or if it measures the same construct with differing degrees of accuracy.

One way to reduce the possibility of differential validity of a test or minimize its effects is to maximize the overall validity of the test. Ensuring that the purposes of the test are clearly delineated, that the methods for fulfilling such purposes are specifically prescribed, and that the appropriate uses of test results are precisely defined are the procedures that will have the greatest impact on the reduction of bias in an educational assessment battery.

In addition, out of that sense of responsibility to society, ACT responds to minorities by (1) reflecting within the test the cultural diversity of the examinee population, (2) employing judgmental procedures to detect potentially unfair material, and (3) using statistical and experimental procedures to identify the variables that may influence test performance of sex and minority groups.

The following sections describe the procedures employed by ACT during test development to detect and prevent bias in the ability tests of the ACT Assessment Program. A brief summary of that program is presented here to orient the reader to the context in which these procedures are applied.

The ACT Assessment Program is a comprehensive evaluative, guidance, and placement service for students involved in the transition from high school to postsecondary education. It is based on the *ACT Assessment*, which consists of four ability tests, the *Student Profile Section*, and the *ACT Interest Inventory*.

The four tests of the *ACT Assessment* measure abilities in the subject areas traditionally identified with college and high school programs: English, mathematics, social studies, and natural sciences. The English Usage Test measures understanding of the conventions of standard written English and the use of the basic elements of effective expository writing. The Mathematics Usage Test measures mathematical reasoning and problem-solving ability. The Social Studies Reading Test measures comprehension, analytical and evaluative reasoning, and problem-solving skills required in the social studies. The Natural Sciences Reading Test measures interpretation, analysis, evaluation, critical reasoning, and problem-solving skills required in the natural sciences. The arithmetic average of the scores on these four tests is the ACT Composite Score, which is often used as a measure of overall developed academic ability.

REVIEW OF BIAS METHODS

Detection of Bias during Test Development

Procedures for maximizing validity and for detecting potential bias in the tests of the *ACT Assessment* are employed at each of the following stages of test development:

1. Development of tables of specification
2. Recruitment and training of item writers
3. Editing of test materials
4. Pretesting of test materials
5. Assembly and review of final forms
6. Analysis of the results of final form administration

Development of tables of specifications. The tests of the *ACT Assessment* are designed to measure the developed academic abilities of the examinees. To ensure the maximum validity of each test for that purpose, a table of specifications is developed; it identifies the item and test format to be used, the specific type of skill to be measured, the subject matter context for measuring those skills, and the technical psychometric considerations to be heeded.

Because curriculum or content bias is one important source of potential bias that may have a profound effect on test performance, the ACT specifications include a continual review of each content area. Three methods are used to accomplish this task: (1) literature in each subject area is monitored for possible changes in over-all emphasis, (2) national subject matter conferences are attended by ACT staff members, and (3) curriculum conferences are periodically convened by ACT to determine the status of the curriculum and the potential for change. As the results of these reviews indicate the need for change, test specifications are updated to reflect national trends in the curriculum.

Adherence to the tables of specifications during the development of the forms of the tests ensures that they measure the knowledge and skills helpful in predicting success in postsecondary education. To the extent that this emphasis on test specifications maximizes the content validity and predictive validity of the tests, the differential or potential bias of the tests is minimized.

Recruitment and training of item writers. The initial stage in the construction of the *ACT Assessment* test forms involves recruitment of item writers. During each test development cycle, approximately 200 educators are invited to write test materials in the four major content areas. The items contributed by approximately 125 of these educators are then included in the pretest units that form the basis for three test forms.

As a group, the writers represent a wide variety of background. All writers invited to work with ACT are chosen for their content expertise, item-writing ability, and teaching experience. In addition, there is a concentrated effort to involve individuals of both sexes who are located at educational institutions in all the geographic regions of the United States, who reflect a variety of racial and ethnic backgrounds, and who represent different educational philosophies due to their training and professional experiences.

Although skills and contexts for each content area are clearly outlined in the test specifications, and thus passages of minority-related material appear routinely in the English and social studies tests of the battery, the specific topic that forms the basis of an item or set of items varies widely with the interest and creativity of the item writer. This variability further ensures that the *ACT Assessment* includes items based on topics of interest and relevance to minority groups.

As regards bias, the training of item writers consists of two strategies: ensuring fairness to minorities and avoiding unfairness to minorities. To ensure fairness, item writers are encouraged to represent majority and minority groups in a balanced way; that is, to present majority and minority group members in a variety of roles and occupations and to refer to them in the same way with respect to the use of first names or titles.

To reduce potential unfairness, item writers are instructed to avoid stereotypic depictions or unfair characterizations of sex or minority groups and to avoid sexist or racist language. In addition, materials presenting controversial or inflammatory issues with respect to any minority, sex, or religious or ethnic constituency are avoided.

Editing of test materials. Materials submitted by item writers are edited by ACT staff to ensure content and grammatical accuracy and to eliminate ambiguities, thereby maximizing content validity. ACT staff employ a number of criteria to avoid biased or stereotypic material or language in the test material. For example, sex groups and minority groups are represented equally in references to occupations, occupational titles, and active or passive participation in activities. When gender is not pertinent to the context, masculine or feminine references are rephrased.

Pretesting of test materials. After the test materials have been edited by the staff, they are pretested by administering them to a sample of students representative of the national sample. In addition to these general administrations, some pretests are given in selected regions of the country to provide clearer information about the performance of minority groups on items and pretests. The pretest item analyses are examined for sex group, minority group, and regional differences in performance, as well as for general item statistics. Although all items have been evaluated and judged acceptable by editors and consultants, any item or set of items identified by these statistical procedures as being potentially unfair is removed from consideration for current tests. When possible, these materials are revised and pretested again. All items meeting the content and statistical specifications, as well as the fairness criteria, become part of the item pool. Final test forms are constructed by drawing items from the pool

Assembly and review of final forms. After acceptable items have been identified on the basis of the pretesting results, the assembly of the test forms begins. The tables of specifications, in the form of skills-by-content classification matrices, once more provide guidelines to ensure content validity and continuity from form to form in the test assembly process.

During the assembly phase, special steps are taken to achieve balance and fairness in the forms. Within the various content areas, a variety of topics is presented to ensure adequate sampling of the content domain and to avoid specific curriculum bias. Within each form, there is an effort to maintain balance in the use of male and female names and pronouns, in the inclusion of both sexes in active and passive activities, in the representation of both sexes in all occupations, and in the portrayal of both sexes in traditional and nontraditional roles. During this phase, the representation of majority and minority groups is balanced, and names representing different minority or ethnic groups are included in the tests.

After the test forms are assembled, and prior to any administration, they are sent to consultants for review. Reviewers are selected for their content knowledge and for their sensitivity to minority- and sex-related issues and language. These experts examine the test forms to ensure that emotional or inflammatory content is excluded. All consultant judgments and opinions are taken seriously; any item or stimulus material that cannot be corrected or revised to the satisfaction of the reviewer is replaced.

Analysis of the results of final form administration. Quality control and concern for maintaining validity continue after the final forms of the tests have been assembled. Immediately after the first administration of the test forms, a sample of examinees is selected and the mean scores for each test are examined by sex group and minority group. This provides a general check of overall effectiveness of the test forms.

Additional Procedures for Detection of Bias

The procedures just described are routinely implemented in the process of test development and administration. Additional procedures are employed periodically, including the use of statistical techniques and experimental studies.

Statistical analysis. The effectiveness of these routine bias detection procedures is checked periodically by selecting a complete test form for more extensive statistical analyses. The techniques employed in these analyses involve the use of ANOVA and chi-square.

In the ANOVA model, significant first-order interactions may be considered to indicate potential bias. The interactions involving items and each of the other experimental factors, such as race or sex, are the foci of attention. When interaction effects are found, follow-up interaction contrasts are analyzed to pinpoint the specific item or items contributing to the relevant interaction.

In the application of the chi-square technique, subgroups of examinees are randomly selected, and each examinee is placed in an ability level interval on the basis of test scores. For each item on the test and within each ability level, it is assumed that the proportion of individuals answering the item correctly (and incorrectly) should be similar for each subgroup (race or sex). The assumption is tested with a chi-square statistic. Items that show significantly different proportions across ability levels are identified as potentially biased.

Any items identified by these or other statistical procedures as potentially biased are then evaluated for content, format, and style in an attempt to find a plausible reason for differential performance on that item. This information then serves as the basis for the definition of future studies to examine potential causes of bias. When the results of such studies suggest changes, test development procedures and specification guidelines are revised or refined accordingly.

Experimental studies. Special studies, which deal with specific issues affecting the test development process, are also conducted. For example, the effects of item-writing practices on test performance were recently examined.

Huntley and Plake (1980) investigated the effects of grammatical cues in the stem and foils of multiple-choice items. In these items, relevant grammatical agreement cues (such as singular/plural and vowel/consonant agreements) in the stem led to one of the alternative responses. The examinee who followed these cues could have been directed to either the correct response or the incorrect response. The effects of such cue types were analyzed by comparing the response patterns of sex and racial subgroups. Results of the investigation indicate some differences in sensitivity of males and females to these kinds of cuing and suggest that phrasing items in neutral, yet grammatically correct, language can eliminate the effects of this sensitivity.

Other experimental studies have investigated the effects of specific content areas, culture-related materials, and skill domains on the test performance of racial groups (Schmeiser, 1980; Schmeiser & Ferguson, 1978). For example, Schmeiser and Ferguson used test materials especially developed to reflect both black and white cultures to study the effect of test content on the performance of black and white examinees. Two major subject matter areas were involved: English and social studies. Although the results supported the findings of other studies that white examinees tend to outscore black examinees, no differential effect of test content on examinee performance by race was demonstrated. The results of studies such as these help to determine whether or not such test material will appear in the final form of the test.

Summary and Review of Procedures

ACT employs many procedures to detect possible bias and to actively ensure fairness within the tests. These procedures are based on the professional judgment of content and test development experts and on statistical and experimental methodology.

Judgmental methods of bias detection are employed through the test development process from the development of tables of specifications to the determination of possible sources of bias in the items identified by statistical techniques. Reviews and analyses of item stimulus materials and individual items for sex and minority bias are conducted by item writers, editors, consultants, and measurement specialists. Items, as well as entire test forms, are inspected for appropriateness of content and format; special attention is devoted to the reduction or elimination of ambiguities, stereotypic representations, and inaccurate or emotionally charged material.

Judgmental and statistical methods for identifying bias complement each other extremely well. Conscientiously applied in accordance with ACT's guidelines, these methods substantially reduce the likelihood of the occurrence of bias in ACT's tests. That likelihood continues to diminish as the results of carefully designed research are used to modify existing test specifications and bias detection procedures.

FUTURE RESEARCH ON BIAS

As the definition of bias and the methodology for its detection evolve, continued research in this area remains imperative. ACT's research plans for the future will focus on three general areas:

1. A variety of judgmental and statistical methods for detecting bias will be examined to determine the internal consistency of the different methods for detecting bias, to establish how consistent the statistical and judgmental techniques are with one another, and to verify these techniques on the basis of criteria external to the techniques.

2. The influence of various test construction practices and types of test content on the performance of subgroups of examinees will be investigated.

3. Characteristics of the testing situation that may lead subgroups of the examinee population to perform differentially on the ACT tests will be examined experimentally. Plans include investigations of the effects on sex or minority group performance of such characteristics as detail of prior knowledge of the nature of the tests (for example, sample questions vs. complete test copy), test-taking strategies, and modifications of time limits for each of the tests.

These are the general directions that future research in the area of bias will take. If the results of such studies indicate a need for change, modifications will be made in test development procedures, in test content, and in testing situations, with the constant goal of increasing test validity and thereby decreasing the potential for bias.

EDUCATIONAL TESTING SERVICE
SYDELL T. CARLTON AND GARY L. MARCO

EDUCATIONAL TESTING SERVICE (ETS) has a longstanding commitment to producing tests that acknowledge the multicultural nature of our society, to avoiding language or content that is offensive to or demeaning of any group within the population, and to attempting to understand and use information about the performance of different groups on test items. This commitment most recently became codified in a 1977 document (revised in 1979) entitled *Principles, policies, and procedural guidelines regarding ETS products and services* (1979).

Among the several relevant guidelines in that document are the following:

Specifications for tests should require material reflecting the cultural background and contributions of women, minorities, and other subgroups. (p. 24)

Individual test items, and the test as a whole, should be reviewed to eliminate language, symbols or content which are generally considered potentially offensive, inappropriate for major subgroups of the test-taking population or serving to perpetuate any negative attitude which may be conveyed toward these subgroups. No item in any

---

Authorship listing is alphabetical. Carlton was responsible for the parts of the paper related to test and item distortion, and Marco was responsible for the parts related to differential item performance.

test should include words, phrases or description that is generally regarded as biased, sexist or racist (e.g., demeaning modifiers and stereotypes). (p. 25)

[ETS should engage in] studies to determine the sources of significant differential performance of sex, ethnic, handicapped, and other relevant subgroups on ETS tests. (p. 17)

Studies relating item performance to subgroups should be carried out for new or substantially revised tests when there are adequate data concerning sufficient samples of large subgroups whose education and experience may be different from the majority of examinees. (p. 26)

The next section describes the procedures for ensuring that these guidelines are met, along with the precedents of the procedures. The first part of the section describes methods for detecting and eliminating distortion in the content of tests and test items, that is, for ensuring that items are not offensive to any group in the population and that groups of diverse backgrounds are represented in test content. The second part describes methods that have been used for detecting differential item performance. The final section outlines some of the problems and information needs that still remain and presents other steps and other options that would go even further toward fulfilling ETS's commitment to equity in tests and test items.

REVIEW OF BIAS METHODS

Methods for Detecting and Eliminating Distortion in the Content of Tests and Test Items

Unless otherwise specified, it should be assumed that the methods for detecting and eliminating item and test distortion described here apply to all tests developed by ETS. Where exceptions are noted, they represent, not exemptions from, but rather additions to, the methods prescribed by ETS. That is, some programs, acting on decisions made by the policy boards who contract with ETS for the development of tests and testing programs, have implemented procedures over and above those required by ETS.

Past practices.   Before describing the current mechanism for eliminating offensive items and ensuring representation of diverse groups in ETS tests, it would be useful to outline procedures followed in the past. The chief reason for this, other than the information it provides about the evolutionary nature of the current system, is that the current process, although incorporating many procedures that were already in place for some testing programs, is relatively new, having been developed in 1979 and 1980 and implemented only recently. Since most, if not all, of the tests familiar to the public were developed prior to the new system, they do not yet reflect all of the fruits of the process.

In the early years of the last decade, ETS, along with other test publishers and the public at large, recognized the need to pay particular attention to several segments of the population with a long history of neglect, if not actual oppression, particularly women, black Americans, Hispanic Americans, Native Americans, and Asian Americans.* It became corporate policy, transmitted in the form of directions to the test development staffs, that these groups were to be represented in the test passages and items and, furthermore, were to be represented in a manner free of offensiveness or negative stereotyping. Accordingly, specifications for the content of tests were revised to mandate that test passages and items include the accomplishments and concerns of these groups. Similarly, test developers were informed of the need—both in writing items and in reviewing items—for sensitivity with regard to the language used to describe these groups. Further, a conscious effort was made to include women and members of minority groups on the committees external to ETS that were assembled to work on various aspects of the tests. The *ETS guidelines for testing of minority groups* (1973), developed and monitored by a Review Committee on the Testing of Minorities, sets forth many of these specifications. In addition, the ETS Committee on Women in Education developed the *ETS guidelines for sex fairness in tests and testing programs* (1975), and several individual programs issued guidelines to ensure fairness to ethnic groups (see, for example, the *Position statement of the SAT Minority Review Committee on guidelines,* 1975).

In the mid-1970s, the process became more intensified and more formalized. The "workfolder" for each test—containing all the materials generated in the development of the test—had a specific sign-off box for minority review. To fulfill this purpose, minority staff members were asked to review tests specifically for their adherence to guidelines for fairness and to include written documentation. This represented a separate and additional review, carried out after all of the other reviews had been completed. Any problems that came to light during the review were discussed by the minority reviewer and the test developer, and the reviewer's written comments became part of the documentation for each test.

Although this reviewing procedure represented a vast improvement over early practices, its use over a few years revealed a need for further development. First, there were no complete and universally applied written and specific criteria that reviewers could use in making their judgments, either about adequate representation or about adequate descriptions of groups; each reviewer applied his or her own opinions. Further, reviewers were not trained. Most important, in cases of disagreements between reviewers and test developers, test developers had the final word. Reviewers had no formal mechanism for recourse.

---

*Editorial policy of Educational Testing Service dictates that the *B* in *Black* and the *W* in *White* be uppercase letters in this context. These letters appear in lowercase here and in the remainder of this chapter because of the editorial policy of The Johns Hopkins University Press.

Current Procedures. The current system of sensitivity reviews at ETS, although incorporating many past practices that already existed in several testing programs, represents a major step forward in that it seeks to remedy the shortcomings cited above and, moreover, to do so by using a formal procedure that is applied to all ETS tests. In the spring of 1979, Ronald V. Hunter and Carole D. Slaughter, working with other staff members, drafted the procedure that, after intensive review, was implemented in the spring of 1980 by E. Belvin Williams, senior vice-president for the Programs Area at ETS. The salient features of the current procedure include: (1) a group of reviewers who undergo training; (2) a set of training materials; (3) a list of specific criteria for sensitivity reviews; (4) a list of words, phrases, and concepts that may signal offensiveness; (5) adjudicators to make decisions in instances of intractable disagreement between reviewers and test developers; and (6) a steering committee to oversee the entire process.

Sensitivity reviewers are selected from a pool of volunteers. While volunteers can come from any part of ETS most reviewers are members of the test development staffs, since knowledge of the subject-matter areas of the tests is required. Some reviewers are also members of minority groups, many reviewers are women, and all major ethnic groups are represented in the reviewer pool. As stated in the *ETS Test Sensitivity Review Process,* however, *"It should be stressed* that minority group membership is not a mandatory prerequisite to performing sensitivity reviews and serious consideration [is] given to *all* interested ... staff who volunteer" (Hunter & Slaughter, 1980, p. 8). The same document sets forth the criteria for the selection of sensitivity reviewers: "A. Ability to perceive offensive material. B. Ability to review tests from multiple perspectives, not simply from the viewpoint of one group, or social/political perspective. C. Coverage within the reviewer pool of key subject areas such as humanities and social sciences is desirable" (Hunter & Slaughter, 1980, p. 8.).

Reviewers are trained for one-and-a-half days, during which the process is explained, criteria are discussed, and examples of acceptable and unacceptable practices are worked on. The training materials are drawn from or adapted from items and passages in past tests. Part of the training process includes discussions of how to revise unacceptable material into acceptable material.

The test evaluation criteria are designed to ensure that the tests reflect the diverse cultures of American society, through the inclusion of both *representational items* and *substantive items.* The former group of items include "those in which references are made to minorities and women, but where the subject matter content of the test is intended to measure factors unrelated to such groups" (Hunter & Slaughter, 1980, p. 8). Items can often be revised to become representational. An example of such a revision is given in Table 9.11.

Substantive items are those that directly measure knowledge about a group. Examples here would include items or groups of items dealing with

TABLE 9.11. Example of Item Revision to Include Representational Reference (Skill: identification of error in grammar)

Original Item

The *newly enacted* legislation requires that all countries *with* large rural populations *to provide*
      (A)   (B)   (C)

transportation to the polls and absentee *ballots*.
                                         (D)

No error
  (E)

Revised Item

The *newly enacted* legislation requires that all countries *with* Spanish-speaking populations
      (A)   (B)

to provide bilingual registration and election *materials*.
  (C)   (D)

No error
  (E)

Source: Hunter, R. V., and Slaughter, C. D. *ETS test sensitivity review process.* Princeton, N.J.: Educational Testing Service, 1980. P. 9. Reproduced by permission of Educational Testing Service, the copyright owner.

the emergence of ethnic studies programs, the migration of black from rural to urban communities, changing enrollment figures for women in science, and changes in employment patterns of Chicanos in the United States.

Each item is evaluated from two perspectives: the *cognitive dimension,* which deals with the factual accuracy of an item, and the *affective dimension,* which deals with the feelings an item may evoke in group members. Needless to say, items that are factually wrong are rejected. More to the point, an item can be factually correct but still be rejected because it is judged to evoke negative feelings on the part of group members. Examples of the latter would include items that focus on the high birth rate in Third World nations or on the high suicide rate among Native Americans.

Further, the guidelines state that highly controversial issues (e.g., hypotheses regarding genetic inferiority) may not be included in a test unles these issues are "both relevant and essential to effective measurement" (Hunter & Slaughter, 1980, p. 13). When both the test developer and the sensitivity reviewer agree that such issues are both relevant and essential, items must be worded in such a way as to make it clear that ETS does not subscribe to the position stated.

Another explicit criterion is that items referring to groups should be reviewed from the perspective of the test taker, who does not have access to the correct answer when he or she is working on the item. What this comes down to is that *no* part of the item, including the incorrect options, can contain material that might be offensive.

Other criteria state that no test item may contain material that reinforces offensive stereotypes, nor may it include underlying assumptions about a group that reflect an individual's ethnocentric beliefs. Examples of the latter would include items that imply an inferiority or deficiency on the part of one or more groups. A list of unacceptable stereotypes for each group is given in the appendix of the test sensitivity document. Examples of such stereotypes would include statements or implications that a particular group is deserving of a particular fate or that a group is by nature dependent on the majority culture.

Another portion of the test sensitivity document lists "caution words and phrases," words and phrases that are usually legitimate and unoffensive but that experience has taught often accompany sensitive material. Reviewers are provided with this list and are taught to pay particular attention to the context in which the words and phrases occur because of their potential for offensiveness. Examples of such words are *lower class, housewife, backlash*, and *ignorant*. The appendix of the test sensitivity document lists caution words and phrases for all groups, as well as caution words and phrases for each particular group. In each list, some words and phrases are designated as "generally unacceptable" despite the context. Examples of these would include *Chinaman, colored people, redman*, and *better half*. An additional section of the appendix gives special review criteria for women's concerns, listing principles along with generally unacceptable terms and ways of revising these terms to make them acceptable.

A final set of criteria, labeled "context considerations," presents judgmental guidelines for reviewing material that may be considered sensitive by some groups but that may be necessary in testing. The four areas in which this occurs with some frequency are presented below.

Historical Domain: When testing one's knowledge of history, it is sometimes desirable to draw from material written during earlier periods when social values were markedly different from present values. Thus, material that was not considered offensive at the time has become potentially offensive when judged by present standards. For example, a passage describing the condition of Southern Blacks during the reconstruction period may include the term "colored people" or "Negro." While it may be desirable to avoid the use of such material where possible, the sensitiveness of the item must be judged in the overall context in which it is presented.

Literary Domain: Tests of literature or use of literary passages may encounter a similar problem. For example, many passages from material written before the 1970s may include constant use of the generic "he," a style that was considered editorially correct until recently. Again, the sensitivity of such items must be reviewed carefully.

Legal Domain: It is frequently desirable and sometimes necessary to test one's knowledge of sensitive material in areas strongly influenced by legal concerns. For example, real estate tests may contain references to federal, state, or local laws governing discrimination in the mortgage rights of EEO classes.

Psychological Domain: Like the legal domain, certain examinations in the health areas may require knowledge of information that may be considered sensitive in other contexts. For example, nursing tests may find it necessary to test one's knowledge of the predominance of sickle-cell anemia among Black people or Tay-Sachs syndrome among the Jewish populations. It is expected that the test assembler, when preparing the test, will exercise prudent judgment relative to the inclusion of such materials. It is also expected that reviewers will exercise similar judgment and review such material relative to the context of the entire test. *In some cases where the reviewer feels the contextual justification is not sufficient to support inclusion, a recommendation will be made to modify or delete the reference.* (Hunter & Slaughter, 1980, pp. 15–16)

The entire sensitivity review process is conducted late enough in the test production cycle to ensure that the reviewer sees the test in its entirety, but early enough to allow time for changes that the review may necessitate. An added feature of the procedure enables the test developer, at his or her option, to request a sensitivity review earlier in the process. This is not a substitute for the final sensitivity review, which is conducted for all tests, but rather an additional review conducted early so that the test developer can be alerted to possible problems before the final review. It should be emphasized that this final sensitivity review is applied to all tests in all programs administered by ETS.

After the review is completed, the test is returned to the developer (or test assembler), who then acts on the reviewer's comments. If, after discussion, agreement between the two cannot be reached, a meeting is arranged between the developer, the reviewer, and the test development area director. If this meeting does not resolve differences to the satisfaction of both developer and reviewer, third-party adjudication follows. From a pool of five arbiters, who represent black Americans, Hispanic Americans, and women, three are called upon to resolve stubborn differences of opinion. The arguments of both sides are presented in writing. In such cases, a simple majority rules. The vote of the arbiters is binding.

At all steps along the way, written documentation is required. This documentation stays with all test materials for each test. The instructions pertaining to each step in the process and a sample report form for the sensitivity review, and suggested summary data to be collected and retained in order to audit the process are provided in Appendixes A and B, respectively.

The steering committee oversees the entire procedure, assigns arbiters when they are needed, and monitors the system and makes suggestions for revision as appropriate. Reviews of the process are also sought from other ETS staff, the client boards who contract with ETS for the development of tests, and external groups. The process is reviewed at regular intervals and modifications are made as needed.

Test distortion and the testing programs. As mentioned earlier, all ETS tests must be subjected to the procedure just described. No exemptions have been granted. It should be borne in mind, however, that since the procedure is relatively new, not all tests now available to the public reflect the rigor of the procedure. On the other hand, several of the testing programs have mechanisms additional to the ETS-wide one to ensure the detection and elimination of test and item distortion. These will be described briefly below.

Sequential Tests of Educational Progress (STEP). STEP III, copyrighted by ETS in 1979 and published and distributed by the Addison-Wesley Publishing Company, contains 10 levels—from preschool through high school—and measures development in the areas of reading, vocabulary, writing skills, mathematics, science, social studies, study skills, and listening. In the development of *STEP III,* the test committees for each field, which were responsible for establishing test specifications, consisted of representatives of various levels of teaching and curriculum development as well as of all geographical regions of the United States, both urban and rural schools, both sexes, and ethnic minorities. These various interests are thus represented in the tests. The norming sample for *STEP III* consisted of similar representation. Further, in addition to the subject-matter committees, four minority review committees were established (one for reading, writing skills, study skills, and listening; one for mathematics; one for social studies; and one for science), containing a total of 13 people representing both sexes and different ethnic groups. These minority review committees reviewed each test in the *STEP III* battery.

Test of English as a Foreign Language (TOEFL). Because of the nature of the test, foreign, rather than domestic, students make up the test-taking population of *TOEFL.* Since the students come from all parts of the world and represent every culture, the need for cultural sensitivity in the test takes on an even broader range. To meet this need, in the fall of 1979, a formal and unique procedure of sensitivity review was initiated, which is carried out in addition to the ETS-wide review described earlier. A group of eight reviewers was assembled, each of whom had had a minimum of 10 years of living and working abroad and among whom were represented all of the major population areas of test takers. Among the eight were cultural anthropologists, art historians, and area studies specialists, all of whom underwent training sessions at the inception of the review procedure. Each form of *TOEFL* is examined by two of these reviewers. Principles of cultural sensitivity have been established and undergo periodic review and revision. These principles are reflected in a checklist, which each reviewer fills out, to ensure that cultural groups are satisfactorily and positively represented in *TOEFL.*

Other major ETS testing programs. Many of the other major testing programs administered by ETS have test committees that set test specifications, review test specifications, write test items, and/or review tests before publication. Although these committees are not charged solely with the responsibility for reviewing tests from the standpoint of sensitivity, committee make-up is designed so as to include women as well as men, along with representatives of different geographical regions and of different ethnic groups. Specifications for the establishment of the committees require such a balance. Major testing programs in this category include, along with *STEP* and

TOEFL discussed previously: the *Scholastic Aptitude Test (SAT)*, the *Achievement Tests*, the *Advanced Placement (AP) Tests*, and the *College-Level Examination Program (CLEP) Tests* of the College Board; the *Graduate Management Admission Test (GMAT)* of the Graduate Management Admission Council; the *GRE Advanced Tests* of the Graduate Record Examinations Board; and the *National Teacher Examinations (NTE)*.

Further, all of the above tests, in addition to the *GRE Aptitude Test*, the *Law School Admission Test (LSAT)*, and other tests prepared by ETS, contain varying proportions of test items written by "outside item writers," i.e., by persons not part of the permanent staff of ETS. Manuals and directions for outside item writers contain guidelines and instructions both about the need to represent the interests, concerns, and accomplishments of women and ethnic minorities and about the need to represent these groups in a manner free of stereotypes, unfavorable assumptions, and offensiveness. Needless to say, the same principles and instructions govern the work of all permanently employed item writers and inform the work of reviewers at every stage *before* each test undergoes the ETS test sensitivity review.

Methods for Detecting Differential Item Performance

This part of the paper focuses on the empirical methods used to detect differential item performance for major testing programs administered by ETS. The purpose of this discussion is to point out the methodological aspects of testing program studies relevant to the topic of item bias. These aspects include the tests, samples, procedures, and cutoff criteria for identifying deviant items used in the studies. Readers interested in the substantive findings will need to refer to the original reports. Studies in progress as well as completed studies are covered in the review. While all or nearly all of the studies conducted by the major ETS programs are included, no claim is made that the review is exhaustive, particularly since many testing programs conduct informal analyses that never appear in written documents. Also, other testing programs administered at ETS have conducted studies of differential item performance that are not covered in this review.

In this review the terms *differential item performance* and *deviant item* have been used instead of *item bias* or *biased item*. This is deliberate. Unfortunately, use of the latter terms in reports has led readers to conclude that differential item performance implies bias. Statistical procedures can identify items that are deviant, that is, items that seem to behave differently for different groups. However, the content of an item must be taken into consideration in determining whether an item is biased. Differential item performance may be an artifact of the analysis method; it might be due to unequal exposure to content; it might be due to cultural differences. Bias cannot be inferred without considering the reasons why an item is deviant.

The testing programs administered at ETS for the various clients do not have an established way of treating item data from different groups. In the

1960s a few item-by-group interaction studies using ANOVA were conducted at ETS. The Cardall and Coffman (1964) study of a 1963 *SAT* form was the earliest of these. Even then, the need to use more than one sample from a particular group was recognized. In the 1970s the delta-plot method as refined by Angoff was commonly used. The Angoff and Ford (1973) study of a 1970 form of the *PSAT* and Sinnott's (1980) study of a 1978 form of the *Graduate Management Admission Test (GMAT)* are excellent examples of the application of the delta-plot method. Angoff and Ford were the first to use samples matched on an external variable to adjust for differences in performance between samples. Sinnott used an iterative procedure to eliminate from the criterion those items showing relatively large differences in performance. She also described a generalized delta-plot method that can be applied to data from more than two groups.

Recently, other methods have been studied. Lord (1977) showed how latent trait theory (referred to as "Item Response Theory" by Lord) could be used by investigating differential item performance on the *SAT;* Alderman and Holland (1981) applied log-linear analysis to item data from a form of *TOEFL*, and Stricker (1981) used *GRE Aptitude Test* data to compare a partial correlation index with several other commonly used indices of differential item performance. Although the analysis of wrong answers *(distractors)* has not received much attention at ETS in studies of differential item performance, distractor analysis was mentioned in two studies of the *NTE* (Humphry, 1979; Spencer, 1972).

To date, most ETS testing programs have analyzed item data from final forms rather than from pretests. The purpose of most of these studies was to discover whether a test was in general an appropriate measuring instrument for selected groups and to identify possible factors that might explain any large differences in item performance. Before the methods can be applied generally to pretest items, guidelines on how to use the data produced by the various methods must be developed.

Many of the studies reviewed here used the delta-plot method. This method, which utilizes transformed item difficulties (deltas) and distance measures, is described by Angoff in chapter 4 and thus is not described in any detail in the reviews. Brief descriptions of other methods referred to in the studies are provided as appropriate. The studies are reviewed testing program by testing program.

GMAT. In a recent study, Sinnott (1980) analyzed *GMAT* item response data to isolate factors that make some items unexpectedly easy or difficult for minority groups. Sinnott's study is important from a methodological point of view in that it represents the first real refinement in delta-plot methodology since the early 1970s. The form of *GMAT* used in the study was administered in January 1978. It contained five operational sections: Reading Comprehension, Problem Solving, Practical Business Judgment, Data Sufficiency, and Usage. Analyses focused on these sociological dimensions: (1) sex (males and females); (2) race (Caucasian, Oriental, Hispanic, and black); (3) race and sex (Caucasian males, Caucasian females, Oriental males, black males, and black females); (4) age (less than 20, 20–22, 23–25, 26–29, 30–34, 35–39, and 40–65); and (5) language fluency (U.S. citizens, Chinese, English, French, Indo-Iranian, Japanese, and Spanish). Only U.S. citizens were included in the first four analyses. The Hispanic sample, which consisted of all 309 Hispanics who took the test, was the only one that failed to reach the desired sample size of 400.

For each of the five analyses, the item performance of each minority group was compared to the item performance of a designated "majority" group. Deltas were calculated for each item for each group, a line of best fit was computed for the scatterplot of minority versus majority deltas, perpendicular distances were calculated from the line of best fit, and deviant items were identified. The line of best fit was the usual major axis of the ellipse formed by the delta plot (see Angoff, chapter 4). Sinnott introduced the refinement of the use of a "purified" criterion, so that the major axis line was fitted to the plot of those items whose distances were within a fixed cutoff of the major axis. Another refinement was the use of random groups of Caucasians to determine what results must be expected from sample-to-sample variation, so that reasonable cutoffs could be established on the distance measures. Distances were computed for sample 2 versus sample 1 and sample 3 versus sample 1. The distributions of distances were examined and cutoffs established such that all or almost all of the items would not be identified as deviant for the homogeneous samples. A cutoff of .7 was used for the first four analyses, and a cutoff of 1.0 for the fifth analysis. Considerable discussion in the report was devoted to a content analysis of the deviant items. One other contribution of note in Sinnott's report is an extension of the delta-plot methodology to more than two groups at a time. Although this extension was not used in the study, it is described in one of the appendixes and should be useful in future investigations.

GRE Aptitude Test.   Donlon, Hicks, and Wallmark (1980) conducted a study of sex differences in item responses on a form of the *GRE Aptitude Test* administered in December 1974. This form consisted of three separately timed sections. The first contained Vocabulary items: antonyms, analogies, and sentence completions; the second section contained Reading Comprehension items; and the third, Regular Mathematics and Data Interpretation items. The sample consisted of 1,720 white males and 1,735 white females randomly selected from the total population of December 1974 test takers. Separate item analyses were performed for the two groups. Delta-plot methodology was then used to obtain the major axis lines and the perpendicular distance measures for each of the three sections. Outliers were arbitrarily defined as those items whose distances were at least 1.5 standard deviations from the mean. Correlations of the deltas from the two samples were computed. The authors examined the average distance for the various item types and the content of the outliers to suggest what kind of item tended to favor males or females.

Because of the methodological problems associated with studies of differential item performance, Stricker (1981) undertook a comparative study of three indices of differential item performance for the *GRE* board: distances as computed by delta-plot methodology, a chi-square index of differences in the *a* and *b* parameters of the item response curves associated with the three-parameter logistic model of Item Response Theory, and the partial correlation of item score and group membership with total score held constant. Stricker examined the consistency of the various methods in identifying items that showed statistically significant differential item performance. Operational items from a form of the *GRE Aptitude Test* administered in October 1977 and January 1978 were used. Parallel analyses were carried out by race (black, white) and sex. The basic samples consisted of white males (1,122 examinees), white females (1,471 examinees), black males (284 examinees), and black females (626 examinees). In addition, matched samples of black and white females and of white males and females were obtained for Verbal, Quantitative, and Analytical (a new part of the test introduced in October 1977) sections. The samples were matched on frequencies of estimated true scores on the odd items in each of the three sections. The matched female samples consisted of 437 to 487 examinees; the matched male and female samples consisted of 1,064 to 1,122 examinees. Random samples of white males and white females of the same sizes as the corresponding black samples were also drawn for use in the analyses by sex. The data were analyzed separately for males and females in the race analyses and separately for blacks and whites in the sex analyses. The partial correlation was computed in the analyses for all three parts of the test; the other two indices were computed only for the Verbal part. Each of the three indices was tested for statistical significance (.05 level), and the numbers of items identified as significant were tabulated for Verbal, Quantitative, and Analytical as well as for various item classifications based on item type and content. The kappa coefficient and chi-square were used to assess the correspondence among the items identified by the three indices.

LSAT. The first study of the *LSAT* for possible differential item performance was completed by Angoff and Herring (1976) in 1971. They attempted to discover whether the *LSAT* contained items that were "not quite as appropriate" for Canadian students as for American students. Items from all five sections of the test were included in the study: Reading Comprehension, Data Interpretation, Reading Recall, Principles and Cases, and Figure Classification. Two samples of Americans were used: one of 900 candidates selected randomly from the total group of 19,467 candidates who took the *LSAT* form introduced in November 1967, and another of 995 candidates selected randomly from the 13,749 candidates who took the same November 1967 form in April 1970. The Canadian sample of 500 students took the

LSAT in a special Canadian administration in May 1970. (Centers with the possibility of significant numbers of French-speaking applicants were eliminated from the study.) The authors noted that the three samples were similar in ability, with the section means for the Canadian sample generally between the means for the American samples.

Item analyses were conducted for each of the three samples. Delta-plot methodology was applied for each of the three pairs of samples (American vs. American, etc.). Items from the five sections of the test were also examined separately. The delta plot for the two American samples provided a baseline for the other two plots. Cross-national correlations were compared with the within-national correlations, and outliers in the cross-national plots were identified. (Outliers were those outside of a 95% band drawn about the major axis of the correlation ellipse for the two delta plots of Americans vs. Canadians.) The outliers from one of the plots were not found to be outliers on the other plot.

In a 1972 study, Cowell and Swineford (1976) compared the performance of white males with that of white females on *LSAT* items. They treated each section separately. All sections of the test were studied: Reading Comprehension, Data Interpretation, Reading Recall, Principles and Cases, Error Recognition, and Sentence Correction. Their study was based on data from 1,165 white females and 1,150 white males (selected from 6,887) who took the form introduced in October 1971. The male and female samples were divided at random into two 575-case and two 580-case groups, respectively, to provide a guide for assessing between-sex differences. The correlations of the deltas for each part were examined in relation to the correlations for the half samples of the same sex. Plots of the deltas were prepared for men versus women for each of the six sections of the test and examined for deviant items.

In another study completed in 1972, Swineford (1976) conducted test analyses for several ethnic groups of candidates who took the December 1971 form of the *LSAT*. Items from all sections of the test were studied. The groups included in the study were black males (two samples), black females, Chicano males, white males, and white females. The sample sizes ranged from about 400 to about 600 cases. For the purpose of obtaining a standard for identifying items that were relatively easy or hard for a particular group, the black male sample of 1,190 cases was divided randomly into two groups of equal size. The item performance of each of the black and Chicano groups was compared with that of the white group of the same sex. For each section of the test, Swineford examined the extent to which the differences between item difficulties followed the average difference between the groups, and identified items that appeared to be deviate from the overall trend.

The most recent study of the *LSAT* to assess group differences in relative item difficulty was completed by Wightman (1977) in 1976. This study essentially repeated the earlier Angoff and Herring (1976) study for a revised format of the *LSAT* introduced in December 1975. The sections studied were

Logical Reasoning, Practical Judgment, Data Interpretation (part A), Data Interpretation (part B), Principles and Cases, Error Recognition, and Sentence Correction. The samples consisted of 2,085 individuals who took the *LSAT* in Canadian test centers outside the province of Quebec, and a spaced sample of 2,055 individuals took the *LSAT* in non-Canadian (primarily United States) centers. The item deltas for the two groups were correlated section by section, deltas were plotted, and the plots were examined for outliers.

NTE. The *NTE Common Examinations,* that portion of the *NTE* consisting of a professional education test and three general education tests, has been investigated several times to assess differential item performance. Medley and Quirk (1972) conducted a study to find out the effects of changing the content of the general education items to reflect the contributions of black and "modern" cultures. Their study, however, dealt with group-by-item-type interactions and was not really a study of differential item performance because the analysis was not at the item level.

Spencer (1972) investigated the possibility of cultural bias in the *NTE Common Examinations*. In one part of the study she compared response patterns across racial groups, and it is in this regard that her study is relevant to the topic of item bias methodology. Spencer used item response data from individuals who took the *NTE* in January 1971. Items on the four subtests of the *Common Examinations* were analyzed: Professional Education; Written English Expression; Social Studies, Literature, and the Fine Arts; and Science and Mathematics. For the analyses of item responses, high- and low-scoring candidates from selected black and white private and public colleges in the South were used—eight groups in all. High-scoring candidates were the 250 candidates in each of the four types of Southern institutions who obtained the highest scores on the examination. Low-scoring candidates were similarly defined. The analysis of item responses was limited to the items judged to be biased on the basis of content. The analyses were intended to discover whether the apparent content bias would be reflected in performance data. For each of the four types of institutions, chi-squares were computed using the frequencies for the high- and low-scoring samples associated with each response option (A, B, C, D, E, omit). The incorrect options that seemed to contribute most to the chi-square were noted, and Spencer then made comparisons across the samples for the four types of institutions.

Another study of the *NTE Common Examinations* was conducted by Humphry (1979). Her study used the more common delta-plot method. The sample consisted of 626 black examinees who took the *NTE Common Examinations* at a recent administration, and a general sample of 1,905 examinees selected systematically from the total population of examinees. Delta plots were prepared for the six parts of the test making up the four subtests: Professional Education; Written English Expression; Social Studies, Literature and the Fine Arts; Science and Mathematics. Outlying items were those falling relatively far from the major axis line. Humphry also looked at those items for which the black examinees tended to select a particular wrong answer almost as often or more often than the correct answer for the purpose of identifying possible misconceptions among the test takers. In addition, she examined omit patterns.

The Spencer and Humphry studies are noteworthy in that both investigated incorrect response options and omits. The investigators paid attention to data that could be very useful from a diagnostic point of view.

In addition to studies like these, special item analyses are conducted routinely on the *NTE Common Examinations*, but the results are not available in summary form. The item analysis results are shared with faculty members of predominantly minority institutions for the purpose of helping them identify possible strengths and weaknesses in their teacher-education programs. One of the analyses shared with institutions compares item percentages correct to the national average. Another reports items on which 50% or more of the candidates got the right answer, items on which 33% or more of the candidates tended to select a single distractor, and items that 33% or more of the candidates omitted. Sharing these types of reports holds the promise of getting important information off the shelf and into the classroom. Of course, the kind of information that is shared and the way it is shared are very important for ensuring its proper use.

Preliminary Scholastic Aptitude Test (PSAT), SAT, and Test of Standard Written English (TSWE).   The *PSAT* and *SAT,* tests offered by the College Board, are treated together because they use the same item pool. In fact, the *PSAT,* an easier test than the *SAT,* is constructed primarily from retired forms of the *SAT.* Beginning in 1971, the *PSAT* was used in the selection of scholars for programs of the National Merit Scholarship Corporation and since then has been referred to as the *Preliminary Scholastic Aptitude Test/ National Merit Scholarship Qualifying Test (PSAT/NMSQT). TSWE* is included here because it has been administered with the SAT since its introduction in 1974.

The first study of differential item performance in which either the *PSAT* or *SAT* is mentioned is that of Cardall and Coffman (1964). Although their article is primarily a description of a method of comparing the item performance of different groups, they illustrated the method by applying it to the May 1963 form of the *SAT.* Forty verbal items from one section of the test and 25 mathematical items from another section were analyzed. Ethnic and regional differences were evident in the groups they studied: those who took the test in rural centers in Illinois and Indiana, those who took the test in the Bronx in New York City (excluding independent and specialized schools), and blacks tested in the Southeast. Three samples of 300 cases each were drawn, so that within-group variation could be estimated. Cardall and Coffman transformed the item percentages correct to arcsin values to satisfy the assumption of homogeneity of variance in ANOVA (see Angoff, chapter 4).

A two-way repeated measures ANOVA was then used to investigate item-by-group interactions in each of the two sections of the test. In order to assess if the statistically significant differences were of practical significance, Cardall and Coffman examined the within-group and between-group correlations of item difficulties. Two of the three samples for each group were used to obtain the within-group correlations. The other sample, coupled with one from each of the other groups, was used to obtain the between-group correlations. The authors pointed out that any interactions of items with groups may point to either cultural bias or to deficiencies in developed abilities and that it is important to make this distinction in deciding whether or not to delete certain items from the test. They also called attention to the need to examine the content of items and to assess whether the differential item performance is in one direction or balanced.

Cleary and Hilton (1978) investigated the differential performance of racial and SES groups on *PSAT* items. Both *PSAT*-Verbal and *PSAT*-Mathematical were studied. The sample for the study consisted of twelfth-graders in seven schools from three metropolitan areas. These students had taken the October 1960 form of the *PSAT* in 1961 (636 students) or the October 1962 form in 1963 (774 students) as part of a longitudinal study of academic growth. All black students and an equal number of white students randomly selected from the larger population were used. Each group was further divided into three SES subgroups of equal size. (Different cutting scores were applied for each group to determine SES level.) Thus, each of the six 1961 groups had 106 students, and each of the six 1963 groups had 129 students.

For *PSAT*-Verbal and *PSAT*-Mathematical separately, the data from a given form were subjected to a three-factor repeated measures ANOVA. The factors were race, SES, and item. In contrast to many studies, the items were scored in a way consistent with how the total score was derived. One point was given for a correct response, zero for no response, and minus one-fourth for an incorrect response. Cleary and Hilton tested the various interactions for significance, estimated variance components, and calculated the percentage contribution of each effect. The sums of the item scores associated with each of the two forms and each part of the *PSAT* were plotted for blacks versus whites, and the plots were examined for deviant items. The Cleary and Hilton study is important in that it introduced an analysis that is particularly appropriate for scores corrected for guessing (formula scores). The Cardall and Coffman analysis had used a transformation of the percentage correct.

Angoff and Ford (1973) also investigated item-by-race interactions on the *PSAT*, using data from Georgia high-school students who took the test in October 1970. The investigators identified race on the basis of responses to an optional question on a pilot form of the Student Descriptive Questionnaire (SDQ), now given routinely with the *SAT*. Ten samples were drawn: two random samples of Atlanta blacks, one sample each of blacks and whites matched frequency for frequency on *PSAT*-Verbal, one sample each of blacks and whites matched frequency for frequency on *PSAT*-Mathematical, two random samples of Atlanta whites, a random sample of Savannah blacks, and a random sample of nonurban blacks. The samples matched on *PSAT*-Verbal were used to study performance on *PSAT*-Mathematical items. Similarly, the samples matched on *PSAT*-Mathematical were used to study the performance on *PSAT*-Verbal items. Sample sizes ranged from 125 to 340 test takers. Angoff and Ford analyzed item responses for each sample, transformed resulting percentages correct on the items to deltas, plotted deltas for various pairs of samples, and calculated distances from the major axes. Correlations of deltas were also computed. Angoff and Ford examined particular items that deviated most extremely from the major axes of the plots. A key feature of this study was the use of samples matched on a related external variable to reduce overall sample differences and diminish the confounding of differences in overall test performance with the item-by-group interactions.

Donlon (1973) studied the differential item performance of males and females on the May 1964 form of the *SAT*. The entire population of some 56,000 males and 47,000 females was used. Donlon used the percentage of candidates reaching the item who answered it correctly as the index of item difficulty. He identified as deviant items those that had large differences in percentages correct between males and females. Donlon then examined the item classifications of those items to suggest possible factors explaining the differential item performance. He also summarized average differences in percentages correct by item type.

Strassberg-Rosenberg and Donlon (1975) continued the investigation of the differential item performance of males and females, using the April 1974 form of the *SAT*. They drew male and female samples of 1,000 cases each. The delta-plot method was used, yielding distance measures based on the delta plots of Verbal, Regular Mathematics, and Data Sufficiency items. Deviant items for a particular plot were those with distance measures more than 1.5 standard deviations above or below the mean. The authors examined various content dimensions of the deviant items and suggested explanations for the differences. For this purpose they also used the mean distances for various item classifications.

Lord (1977) reported on Marco and Lord's use of Item Response Theory procedures to investigate differential item performance on *SAT*-Verbal. Item response data from 2,250 blacks and 2,250 whites who took the April 1975 form of the *SAT* were analyzed. The computer program LOGIST was used to estimate the ability of each examinee and the a (discrimination), b (difficulty), and c ("pseudo-guessing") parameters associated with each item (see Ironson, chapter 5, for details). The items were calibrated for blacks and whites separately. Item parameters were placed on the same scale by using the first principal axis of the plot of b parameters. Asymptotic significance tests using approximate standard errors were carried out to test the hypothesis that the black and the white item response curves are identical. (For this test the c parameter for an item was required to be the same for both groups.) To ensure that ability estimates were based on "unbiased" items, items showing significant differences beyond the 15 percent level were eliminated. This process is sometimes called "purifying the criterion." The groups were combined and the item and ability parameters re-estimated on the remaining 32 items. The resulting ability estimates were then fixed and item parameters estimated for each group separately. Approximate asymptotic significance tests were again carried out. The entire statistical analysis was then repeated on two 2,250-case random samples from the combined group of blacks and whites. The results showed that the significance test used was a good approximation. Since the study had a methodological focus, no attempt was made to study the item response curves to identify differences that were of practical significance, nor was there any attempt to figure out why particular item response curves were different.

Beginning in 1973, differential item performance of various groups has been monitored on several forms of the *SAT* and its companion test, the *TSWE*. The purposes of this monitoring arc (1) to ensure that over time the *SAT* and *TSWE* remain appropriate for major groups of the candidate population, and (2) to identify possible content factors related to differential item performance that would help the test developer in constructing an unbiased test. Item data from six forms of the *SAT* and five forms of the *TSWE* have been analyzed. Summaries of these analyses were prepared for internal ETS and College Board use, but formal technical reports have not been written. The delta-plot method was used in all of the studies, but was supplemented by other analyses in some cases.

In 1974 Stern (unpublished; see Table 9.12) summarized the results of a pilot study of the December 1973 form of the *SAT*. Separate 1,000-case samples of blacks and whites were used. For *SAT*-Verbal and *SAT*-Mathematical, Stern plotted deltas corresponding to the item percentages correct, determined the major axes, and calculated perpendicular distances. Correlations of the deltas were computed for Vocabulary, Reading Comprehension, Regular Mathematics, and Data Sufficiency items as well as for *SAT*-Verbal and *SAT*-Mathematical. Frequency distributions of the distance measures were also given. Items were considered deviant if their distance measures were at least 1.25 standard deviations above or below the mean. The content of the 16 deviant verbal items and the 16 deviant mathematical items was examined and related to the direction of the differential performance.

In 1975 Stern (unpublished; see Table 9.12) summarized the results of a study of forms of the *SAT* and *TSWE* introduced in November 1974. In these and succeeding *SAT* forms, Regular Mathematics and Quantitative Comparison items were used in the Mathematical part instead of Regular

Mathematics and Data Sufficiency items. *TSWE* contained Usage and Sentence Correction items. Again, black and white samples of 1,000 cases each were drawn. The methodology used was identical to the one employed in the previous study; but, in addition to the usual results, mean distances were reported for items classified by type and content.

Also in 1975, Cook and Stern (unpublished; see Table 9.12) presented findings from a study of the *SAT* and *TSWE* forms introduced in December 1974. The methodology was identical to that of Stern's previous 1975 study. However, not only were mean distances given, but they were tested for statistical significance.

Stern's next analysis (unpublished; see Table 9.12), summarized in 1978, was broader in scope. The April 1975 forms of the *SAT* and *TSWE* were studied. Because of the concern expressed that the results of the previous studies might have been due at least in part to the large ability differences between the samples, matched samples were used. A sample of 1,000 black males was drawn. Then samples of 1,000 black females, 1,000 white males, and 1,000 white females were drawn by selecting those test takers whose scores on a short verbal test (administered with the other tests) closely matched the scores of the black males. For use in determining the cutoffs for deviant items, a second white male sample matched with the black sample was obtained. Item-by-sex as well as item-by-race interactions were investigated. For *SAT*-Verbal, *SAT*-Mathematical, and *TSWE*, item deltas for the following pairs of samples were plotted: black males versus white males, black females versus white females, black males versus black females, and white males versus white females. Mean distances were reported for detailed content classifications as well as for item types, and tested for statistical significance. The cutoff for determining deviant items was set at 3.0 standard deviations above or below the mean based on the distance measures derived from the deltas of the two white male samples.

The next analysis, conducted by Blew and Ishizuka (unpublished; see Table 9.12) on the November 1975 forms of the *SAT* and *TSWE* and summarized in 1978, reverted to the use of the procedures for unmatched samples. Samples of 1,000 blacks and 1,000 whites were used. Delta plots and correlations were presented. Also, mean distances were calculated for various item classifications and tested for statistical significance. Blew and Ishizuka introduced two changes in the procedures: (1) comparisons were made of distances before and after dropping difficult items (those with deltas greater than 16 for the white sample); and (2) score-level information was used for items identified as deviant on the distance measures (at least 1.25 standard deviations above or below the mean), and chi-square statistical tests were made. The score levels used were 200–290, 300–390, 400–490, 500–590, and 600–690 (20–29, 30–39, 40–49, 50–59, and 60+ for *TSWE*). The difference between the numbers of blacks and whites responding correctly and incorrectly to an item was tested for significance at each score level. Descriptive data by score level were also given.

One other summary of *SAT* and *TSWE* forms has been completed. In 1979 Blew and Stern (unpublished; see Table 9.12) reported the results for the December 1975 forms of the *SAT* and *TSWE*. Unmatched black and white samples of 1,000 test takers each were used. Mean distances by item classification were reported, and score level information was used. As in the previous study, deviant items were those whose distance measures were at least 1.25 standard deviations above or below the mean of the distance measures, and chi-squares for the deviant items were calculated by score level.

STEP, including CIRCUS and School and College Ability Tests (SCAT). No formal empirical studies of differential item performance by sex, ethnic background, or other factors have been conducted at ETS on *CIRCUS*, *STEP*, or *SCAT* tests. However, the *CIRCUS* technical manual for Levels A, B, C, and D notes that "all *CIRCUS* tests and items were analyzed separately for children of different races and sexes to minimize any bias in measurement" (*CIRCUS*, 1979, p. 12). Percentages correct and item-total biserial correlations were examined for these groups. On the basis of these data a few items that showed marked differences in percentages correct were not included in the final test forms.

TOEFL. As part of a larger study, Angoff and Sharon (1971) examined the performance on *TOEFL* items of 71 American students (college freshmen) and 495 foreign candidates. Both groups had taken the same form of *TOEFL*—the Americans at a special February 1969 administration at a Western state university and the foreign candidates at a regular *TOEFL* administration. Items from all five parts of *TOEFL* were studied: Listening Comprehension, English Structure, Vocabulary, Reading Comprehension, and Writing Ability. A total of 140 of the 270 *TOEFL* items were dropped from the analysis because they were too easy for the American students (percentages correct greater than .95). Item deltas for the two groups were plotted for each of the five parts of *TOEFL*, and the deltas were correlated.

In a later study Angoff and Sharon (1972, 1974) investigated differential patterns of linguistic ability among six language groups: German, Spanish, Arabic, Chinese, Japanese, and Gujarati. Members of these groups took *TOEFL* in October 1969. Items from all five sections of *TOEFL* were studied. The sample sizes ranged from 116 (for the German sample) to 2,853 (for the Chinese sample). In addition, to provide a general baseline, a general sample of 1,000 cases was selected at random from the 14,045 candidates tested in October 1969. The item data for each section were subjected to a two-way repeated measures ANOVA, with groups and items being the two main factors, and the item-by-group interactions were tested for statistical significance. Perpendicular distances from the major axis of the elliptical plot of item deltas (language group vs. general group) were calculated for each language group for each section. Frequency distributions of the distances were reported, but the authors' interpretations were based primarily on the correlations of the deltas rather than the standard deviations of the distances. No attempt was made to identify deviant items.

In another *TOEFL* study, Alderman and Holland (1981) examined the *TOEFL* forms administered internationally in November 1976 and November 1979 in an attempt to identify regularities in discrepant performance among language groups. Seven language groups were included in this study: Germanic, Spanish, African, Chinese I, Chinese II, Japanese, and Arabic. The sample sizes ranged from about 500 to about 1,000 examinees. The two samples of Chinese (the group with the greatest number of test takers) were used to help establish guidelines in evaluating results. Alderman and Holland's procedures were different from the usual delta-plot methodology, although they also applied that methodology to check on the results and help with the interpretation. Their study is the first application at ETS of log-linear analysis (see Bishop, Fienberg, & Holland, 1975) to item response data from different groups.

For each language group, responses to a given item were tabulated by score level on the appropriate section of the test. (Nine score levels were used in the analysis.) By means of log-linear analysis, various models were fitted to the data to assess the dependence of the probability of a correct response to an item on score level and language group, simultaneously. Chi-square tests were used to test the fit of these models. One model assumed only an overall score-level effect and a separate-group effect. Another model assumed that there was, in addition, a group-by-score-level interaction. Indirect standardization techniques borrowed from epidemiology were used to calculate for each item and for each language group a descriptive index of differential item performance. On one of the *TOEFL* forms, items with the highest chi-squares in each section were identified as deviant items to be scrutinized by language experts. On the basis of this content analysis, judgments were made about which items in the second *TOEFL* form should be deviant and subjected to a confirmatory analysis. Although procedures for using the interaction chi-squares still need to be developed, this study is noteworthy in that log-linear statistical methods were used and score-level adjustments were incorporated into the analysis.

Summary.   The various studies that have been reviewed here are summarized in Table 9.12. Included in the table for each of the tests are references to the studies that have been completed or are in progress and indications of the test forms, groups, and methods that were used. A *?* in the table denotes that the information could not be determined from the report or summary referenced in the table. All of the studies referred to in the table except those for the *SAT/TSWE* are included in the list of references at the end of the paper. The *SAT/TSWE* summaries were prepared as a part of ongoing program operations and have not been documented in published reports.

FUTURE RESEARCH ON BIAS

Test and Item Distortion

Any system that is relatively new and still developing will not be perfect by any means. This section will indicate the various directions in which the procedure could be expanded and the various questions that still need to be answered.

Population groups. Although all of the principles and most of the criteria in the ETS test sensitivity review process are applicable to any group of the population, the process specifically addresses only five groups: Asian Americans, black Americans, Hispanic Americans, Native Americans, and women. Clearly, the focus could be broadened to include the specific concerns of other groups of the population, e.g., Polish Americans, Italian Americans, Irish Americans, Jewish Americans. Criteria could be established for representing these and other groups in test items; unacceptable terms, stereotypes, assumptions could be specified for other groups, whether or not they are part of the American population. While flagrant examples of offensiveness and stereotyping would certainly be detected and eliminated by the current procedure (e.g., a statement about the "stinginess of the Scottish"), more specific and more rigorous guidelines could be established. Questions here include: How many groups, if any, should be specifically added? Which ones? How would they be chosen?

Number of reviewers. Although the current procedure involves a large number of staff members in the review process (reviewers, coordinators, trainers, arbiters, steering committee members), any one test is initially reviewed by one trained person. If no disagreements arise between the test developer and the reviewer, there is no need for arbitration, and only the one sensitivity reviewer has reviewed the test for fairness. This has obvious advantages in terms of time and cost. It has equally obvious disadvantages in other terms: limited coverage, limited perspective, the assumption that one person can adequately represent several groups, and so on.

Options for the future include consideration of expanding the mandatory number of reviewers for each test. Two, three, or more reviewers could be required. Further, after an internal sensitivity review, each test could be sent to an external individual or outside group, as long as each person involved possessed an adequate degree of subject-matter knowledge. All of these are clear possibilities, contingent on time and cost, as well as on the results of the first year's experience with the current procedure. Questions here include: What incremental benefit accrues from the addition of each additional reviewer? If the number of reviewers is increased, who would they be? Should

TABLE 9.12. Studies of Differential Item Performance Conducted for Testing Programs Administered by ETS

Test	Study	Test Form(s) or Level(s) Studied	Groups Studied[a]	Method(s) Used
GMAT	Sinnott (1980)	Jan. 1978	Sex (2), race (4), age (7), language (7)	Delta plot
GRE Aptitude Test	Donlon, Hicks, & Wallmark (1980)	Dec. 1974	Sex (2)	Delta plot
	Stricker (1981)	Oct. 1977/ Jan. 1978	Sex (2)[b], race (2)[b]	Delta plot, item response theory, partial correlation
LSAT	Angoff & Herring (1976)	Nov. 1967/ April 1970	Country (2)	Delta plot
	Cowell & Swineford (1976)	Oct. 1971	Sex (2)	Delta plot
	Swineford (1976)	Dec. 1971	Sex (2), race (3)	?
	Wightman (1977)	Dec. 1975	Country (2)	Delta plot
NTE Common Examinations	Spencer (1972)	Jan. 1971	Race (2), type of college (2), ability level (2)	Chi-square
	Humphry (1979)	?	Race (2)	Delta plot
PSAT	Cleary & Hilton (1968)	Oct. 1960 (1961 Spec. Admin.), Oct. 1962 (1963 Spec. Admin.)	Race (2), socioeconomic status (3)	ANOVA
	Angoff & Ford (1973)	Oct. 1970	Race (2)[b], location (3)	Delta plot

SAT	Cardall & Coffman (1964)	May 1963	Race (2), region (3)	ANOVA
	Donlon (1973)	May 1964	Sex (2)	Delta plot
	Stern (1974)[c]	Dec. 1973	Race (2)	Delta plot
	Strassberg-Rosenberg & Donlon (1975)	April 1974	Sex (2)	Delta plot
	Lord (1977)	April 1975	Race (2)	Item response theory
SAT/TSWE	Stern (1975)[c]	Nov. 1974	Race (2)	Delta plot
	Cook & Stern (1975)[c]	Dec. 1974	Race (2)	Delta plot
	Stern (1978)[c]	April 1975	Race (2), sex (2)	Delta plot
	Blew & Ishikura (1979)[c]	Nov. 1975	Race (2), ability level (5)	Delta plot, chi-square
	Blew & Stern (1979)[c]	Dec. 1975	Race (2), ability level (5)	Delta plot, chi-square
CIRCUS	CIRCUS Manual and Technical Report (1979)	Levels A, B C, & D	Race (2), sex (2)	?
TOEFL	Angoff & Sharon (1971)	Feb. 1969 Spec. Admin.	Language (2)	Delta plot
	Angoff & Sharon (1972, 1974)	Oct. 1969	Language (6)	ANOVA, delta plot
	Alderman & Holland (1981)	Nov. 1976/Nov. 1979	Language (7), ability level (9)	Log-linear analysis

[a]The number of groups is given in parentheses.
[b]Matched samples were used.
[c]Unpublished summary unavailable from ETS.

the number of mandatory reviewers be expanded for all tests or for only some tests?

Criteria for offensiveness.   While few people would disagree about most, if not all, of the criteria for offensiveness and the need for positive representation of women and ethnic groups, it should be remembered that the guidelines adhered to in the sensitivity review were codified internally. They were subjected to intensive and extensive staff review and, moreover, incorporate some of the guidelines issued by other publishers. The fact remains, however, that they are not based on empirical data relating to what students or other groups regard as either offensive or positively representational. The guidelines could be modified on the basis of how test takers feel about them, how clients feel about them, and how external groups feel about them. These would seem to be clear information needs. Information could be obtained through face-to-face interviews and/or through questionnaires. Data on the degree of consensus about the guidelines, along with group views of their appropriateness and completeness, would contribute to a stronger base from which to operate.

Stimulus materials for tests.   As mentioned earlier, there are many instances in which whether or not to include controversial material becomes a difficult decision. For example, a reading comprehension passage dealing with the causes of the high suicide rate of Native Americans might be viewed as legitimate for inclusion, or even as performing a positive social function. The other side of the coin is that such a passage, while indicting, not the Native Americans, but rather the majority culture, might be viewed as reinforcing a stereotype or in other ways evoking negative feelings on the part of some test takers. Similarly, does one include a passage dealing with the lower-than-average educational attainments of blacks or with the lower-than-male mathematical achievements of women? To what extent should a test be a vehicle for social change, if in the process of being such a vehicle the test might disrupt the test-taking behavior of substantial numbers of students?

As of now, the test sensitivity review guidelines acknowledge this general problem, but caution only that careful judgment be exercised. Here again, information needs exist. Attempts could be made to ascertain the extent to which materials of varying degrees of sensitivity disrupt more than help. Input from students and other groups, as well as empirical studies, might be used in setting tighter and more specific guidelines in this area.

A different problem, but one also related to test stimulus materials, involves the relative paucity of materials that represent women and ethnic groups in a favorable light. Given the recency of concern in this area, relevant material more than 5 or 10 years old is often very difficult to find. The problem is exacerbated by the fact that ETS, in an effort not to provide an undue advantage to members of the test-taking population, generally avoids using very recent material (which might be familiar to some, but not most, test takers) unless it can be sure that the recent material has had very limited circulation.

A further step in the test sensitivity review process would entail the compilation of a list of resource materials for test developers to use, a list long enough to preclude prior study by advantaged test takers and recent enough to provide a broad range of positively representational materials. The list of resource materials would have to take into account that, without the perspective of time, it is difficult to determine what will remain and what will change or disappear. Since today's hero can be next year's forgotten and therefore usually irrelevant figure, materials that are both current and relevant are relatively rare. Providing help to test developers in this area would be an important next step.

Performance effects. Although it is not within the province of this part of the discussion to deal with differential item performance among groups, it is important to point out that the criteria of test sensitivity reviews could have a large impact on test performance and on how test takers feel about the tests and about themselves. This would seem to be fairly obvious. Perhaps not so obvious, and yet legitimately in this area, is the issue of how the language, format, general topics, physical layout, etc., of tests—that is, elements of the item contexts—might differentially affect different groups. ETS tests, for example, adhere relatively strictly to standard written English, which means, among many other things, that contractions and colloquialisms are not used unless they are necessary. If it were found that the use of contractions and colloquialisms in tests improved the scores of some groups of the population—or that other "informalities" that did not affect overall test quality or overall test difficulty level had similar effects—this could have profound implications for test development. Once again, systematic empirical studies as well as interviews and questionnaires would be needed to answer these questions. Once answers were available, informed discussions could take place concerning, for example, the relationship between differential group performance and test validity. Contingent on ETS and client policy with regard to what is to be tested and how, test sensitivity review guidelines might be modified to reflect information concerning performance effects.

Final note. The foregoing discussion of some limitations and information needs of the test sensitivity review process is entirely in keeping with the principle with which the procedure was implemented. A process was set into place that represented a leap forward relative to what had gone before. At the same time, it was recognized that improvements could and would be made, and the procedure is being monitored accordingly. Some of the "limitations" outlined in this section indicate the ways in which growth can occur. As the review process continues to evolve, it is incumbent on everyone involved to think in terms of the ideal future and to take the steps necessary to approach that ideal.

Differential Item Performance

This review of testing program studies of differential item performance has pointed to a number of refinements that have occurred in methodology in the last decade. In the future, further development and refinement are needed. For example, Sinnott's (1980) extension of the delta-plot method to more than two groups at a time needs to be tried out and refined, and the use of within-group samples to establish empirical sampling errors when groups differ initially in ability needs study.

The Admissions Testing Program (College Board), the *TOEFL* program, and the *GRE* program have initiated investigations of new methods, such as latent trait methods (Lord, 1977) and log-linear analysis (Alderman & Holland, 1981), for studying differential item performance. The *GRE* program is investigating a simple index of differential item performance that might be useful to test developers (see Stricker, 1981). Such investigations need to be continued, particularly in the wake of recent criticisms directed at the delta-plot method.

Validity studies of the various methods, both old and new, are also needed. Most of the studies reviewed here have been on final test forms, which would not be expected to contain many biased items. New empirical studies, including simulation studies, should be aimed at investigating how well the various methods identify biased items embedded experimentally into a test. Such research is likely to be more productive than research on final forms.

Statistical methodology, however, is not the only area that requires further research and development. There is a desperate need for test development studies to complement the methodological investigations. Identifying factors that explain why items are biased should be one major goal of test development research. In this regard, it is particularly important to assess the effects of different item contexts. This kind of research will probably have greater payoff if conducted on experimental forms created especially to represent the variations that require study, not on final forms.

Discovering when differential item performance and statistical significance really indicate item bias should be another major goal of test development research. Unfortunately, in many studies an item has been considered to be biased when statistically significant differential item performance has been observed. Differential item performance might be due to an artifact of the analysis method or to unequal exposure to content, however, rather than to group differences. Moreover, when samples are large, small differences of little practical importance can be statistically significant. Bias simply cannot be inferred without considering how large a difference is important from a practical point of view and why the differential item performance occurred. Such test development research will lead to guidelines for using the results of studies of differential item performance, guidelines that will facilitate the use of such information in screening items prior to test assembly or in balancing items showing relative advantages and disadvantages for particular groups.

In addition to methodological and test development research, operational development is needed if the results of studies of differential item performance are to be used. Operational systems that are flexible and allow options for testing programs must be built. The storage and retrieval of item information and the input, processing, and output specifications for the statistical methods must be considered in developing such a system. Only when "user friendly" systems exist will testing programs make full use of the options available.

APPENDIX A: Test Sensitivity Review Report Form

Instructions

Step 1.   Test sensitivity reviewer completes items 1a, 1b, 2a, 2b, and 3a.
Step 2.   Test sensitivity reviewer signs and dates the form (item 4a), retains a copy, and forwards the original to the test assembler.
Step 3.   Test assembler completes items 1c, 2c, and 3b.
Step 4.   Test assembler signs and dates the form (item 4b) and returns it to the sensitivity reviewer.
Step 5.   Sensitivity reviewer completes item 5 and, if necessary, item 6.
Step 6.   Sensitivity reviewer signs and dates the form (item 5), and returns it to the test assembler.
Step 7.   If all actions are approved, the assembler files the report in the workfolder.
Step 8.   If all actions are not approved, the reviewer will arrange a meeting with the test development area director and the test assembler to attempt to resolve all differences. If all differences cannot be resolved to the mutual satisfaction of both the reviewer and the assembler, the form will be forwarded to an arbitration panel.
Step 9.   The arbiters document their decision and, where appropriate, the rationale, complete item 7, sign and date the form (item 8), and return the workfolder and the form to the test assembler for action. A copy of the arbiters' report will be sent to the sensitivity reviewer.

APPENDIX B: Test Sensitivity Review Process Audit

Suggested Summary Data

It is suggested that the following data be collected and summarized separately by test development area and across the entire corporation:

• Number of test forms reviewed
• Number of items reviewed (total number of all items on reviewed test forms)

TEST SENSITIVITY REVIEW REPORT FORM

Test Name:	Test Form:	Program:

Test Assembler:	Sensitivity Reviewer:

1. TEST SPECIFICATIONS 1a Test specifications require the inclusion of multicultural material.   Yes ☐   No ☐

1b Reviewer's Comments and Recommendations	**1c** Assembler's Response

2. SUBGROUP REFERENCE ITEMS

2a Representational Items		Substantive Items NA ☐		Population Subgroup
Item #'s	No. of Items	Item #'s	No. of Items	
				Women
				Black Americans
				Hispanic Americans
				Native Americans
				Asian Americans
				Other Subgroups

Total Representational Items = ☐   Total Substantive Items = ☐   Total Number of Items in Test = ☐

2b Reviewer's Comments and Recommendations	**2c** Assembler's Response

3. ITEM REVIEW

3a Reviewer's Recommendations and Comments	**3b** Test Assembler's Response

3a Continued Reviewer's Recommendations and Comments	3b Continued Test Assembler's Response
4a Reviewer's Signature Date	**4b** Test Assembler's Signature Date

5 Reviewer Signoff: ☐ I have reviewed and discussed this report with the test assembler and I concur with all planned actions as stated on this document.

☐ I have reviewed and discussed this report with the test assembler and I do not concur with all planned actions as documented below.

Reviewer's Signature	Date

6 Reviewer's Objections	7 Arbiter's Decisions and Rationale
	8 Arbiter's Signature Date

Note: Reproduced by permission of Educational Testing Service, the copyright owner.

- Number and percent of items found to be deficient with respect to sensitivity criteria
- Number of test forms where specifications required the inclusion of multicultural material
- Number and percent of tests containing multicultural items
- Number and percent of items with multicultural references
- Number and percent of representational items
- Number and percent of substantive items
- Number and percent of tests to arbitration
- Number of issues to arbitration
- Number and percent of issues where arbiters concurred with sensitivity reviewer
- Number and percent of issues where arbiters concurred with test assembler
- Number and percent of issues where arbiters negotiated compromise between assembler and reviewer
- Number of complaints received for reviewed test forms

Note: Reproduced by permission of Educational Testing Service, the copyright owner.

REFERENCES

Alderman, D. L., & Holland, P. W. *Item performance across native language groups on the Test of English as a Foreign Language* (TOEFL Research Reports, Report 9; ETS Research Report 81-16). Princeton, N.J.: Educational Testing Service, 1981.

Anastasi, A. Some implications of cultural factors for test construction. In *Proceedings of the 1949 Invitational Conference on Testing Problems*. Princeton, N.J.: Educational Testing Service, 1950. Pp. 13-17.

Anastasi, A. (Ed.). *Assessment in a pluralistic society*. Princeton, N.J.: Educational Testing Service, 1973.

Angoff, W. H. *The investigation of test bias in the absence of an outside criterion*. Paper presented at the National Institute of Education Conference on Test Bias, Annapolis, Md., December 1975.

Angoff, W. H., & Ford, S. F. Item-race interaction on a test of scholastic aptitude. *Journal of Educational Measurement*, 1973, *10*, 95-105.

Angoff, W. H., & Herring, C. L. Study of the appropriateness of the Law School Admission Test for Canadian and American students (Report No. LSAC-71-1). In Law School Admission Council, *Reports of LSAC sponsored research: Volume II, 1970-1974*. Princeton, N.J.: Law School Admission Council, 1976.

Angoff, W. H., & Sharon, A. T. A comparison of scores earned on the Test of English as a Foreign Language by Native American college students and foreign applicants to U.S. colleges. *TESOL Quarterly*, 1971, *5*, 129-136.

Angoff, W. H., & Sharon, A. T. *Patterns of test and item difficulty for six foreign language groups on the Test of English as a Foreign Language* (ETS Research Bulletin 72-2). Princeton, N.J.: Educational Testing Service, 1972.

Angoff, W. H., & Sharon, A. T. The evaluation of differences in test performance of two or more groups. *Educational and Psychological Measurement*, 1974, *34*, 807-816.

APA/AERA/NCME Committee. *Standards for educational and psychological tests and manuals.* Washington, D. C.: American Psychological Association, 1966.

Beck, M. D., & Sklar, J. *An assessment of item "bias" in the 1978 Metropolitan Achievement Tests.* Paper presented at the annual meeting of the Eastern Educational Research Association, Williamsburg, Va., March 1978.

Bennett, G. K. Response to R. L. Williams. *Counseling Psychologist,* 1970, *2*, 88–99.

Binet, A., & Simon, T. *The development of intelligence in children (The Binet Scale).* (E. S. Kite, trans.). Baltimore: Williams & Wilkins, 1916.

Bishop, Y.M.M., Fienberg, S. E., & Holland, P. W. *Discrete multivariate analysis.* Boston: MIT Press, 1975.

Burrill, L. E., & Wilson, R. *Fairness and the matter of bias* (Test Service Notebook 36). New York: The Psychological Corporation, 1980.

Cardall, C., & Coffman, W. E. *A method for comparing the performance of different groups on the items in a test* (College Entrance Examination Board Research and Development Report 64-5, No. 9; ETS Research Bulletin 64-61). Princeton, N.J.: Educational Testing Service, November 1964.

Charters, Jr., W. W. Social class and intelligence tests. In W. W. Charters, Jr., & N. L. Gage (Eds.), *Readings in the social psychology of education.* Boston: Allyn & Bacon, 1963. Pp. 12–21.

CIRCUS manual and technical report. Reading, Mass.: Addison-Wesley, 1979.

Clark, W. W. *Research findings on mental sex differences and their implications for education: An analysis of sex differences found in mental ability and achievement test results.* Paper presented at the annual meeting of the American Association of School Administrators, Cleveland, March 1958.

Cleary, T. A., & Hilton, T. L. An investigation of item bias. *Educational and Psychological Measurement,* 1968, *28*, 61–75.

Clemans, W. V. Response to R. L. Williams. *Counseling Psychologist,* 1970, *2*, 90–91.

Coffman, W. E. Principles of developing tests for the culturally different. In *Proceedings of the 1964 Invitational Conference on Testing Problems.* Princeton, N.J.: Educational Testing Service, 1965. Pp. 82–92.

Coffman, W. E. *An exploratory study of group differences in performance of pupils in grades 6, 7, 8, and 9 on the items in the Iowa Tests of Basic Skills.* Iowa City: Iowa Testing Programs, University of Iowa, 1978. (ERIC Document Reproduction Service No. ED 156 713)

Cotter, D. E., & Berk, R. A. *Item bias in the WISC-R using black, white, and Hispanic learning disabled children.* Paper presented at the annual meeting of the American Educational Research Association, Los Angeles, April 1981.

Cowell, W., & Swineford, F. Comparisons of test analysis data for white male candidates with white female candidates (Report No. LSAC-72-2). In Law School Admission Council, *Reports of LSAC sponsored research: Volume II, 1970–1974.* Princeton, N.J.: Law School Admission Council, 1976.

CTB/McGraw-Hill. *Comprehensive Test of Basic Skills, Forms Q and R: Technical report.* Monterey, Calif.: Author, 1970.

CTB/McGraw-Hill. *California Achievement Tests, 1970 edition: Technical report.* Monterey, Calif.: Author, 1974.

CTB/McGraw-Hill. *Comprehensive Test of Basic Skills: Technical bulletin number 2.* Monterey, Calif.: Author, 1977.

CTB/McGraw-Hill. *California Achievement Tests, Forms C and D: Technical bulletin 1.* Monterey, Calif.: Author, 1978.

CTB/McGraw-Hill. *California Achievement Tests, Forms C and D: Technical bulletin 2.* Monterey, Calif.: Author, 1980.

Devine, P. J. An investigation of the degree of correspondence among four methods of item bias. Unpublished doctoral dissertation, Illinois Institute of Technology, 1980.

Donlon, T. F. *Content factors in sex differences on test questions* (ETS Research Memorandum 73-28). Princeton, N.J.: Educational Testing Service, 1973.

Donlon, T. F., Hicks, M. M., & Wallmark, M. M. Sex differences in item responses on the Graduate Record Examination. *Applied Psychological Measurement,* 1980, *4,* 9–20.

Educational Testing Service, *ETS guidelines for testing of minority groups.* Princeton, N.J.: Author, 1973.

Educational Testing Service. *ETS guidelines for sex fairness in tests and testing programs.* Princeton, N.J.: Author, 1975.

Educational Testing Service. *Position statement of the SAT Minority Review Committee on guidelines.* Princeton, N.J.: Author, 1975.

Educational Testing Service. *Principles, policies, and procedural guidelines regarding ETS products and services.* Princeton, N.J.: Author, 1979.

Eells, K., Davis, A., Havighurst, R. J., Herrick, V. E., & Tyler, R. W. *Intelligence and cultural differences.* Chicago: University of Chicago Press, 1951.

Faggen-Steckler, J., McCarthy, K. A., & Tittle, C. K. A quantitative method for measuring sex "bias" in standardized tests. *Journal of Educational Measurement,* 1974, *11,* 151–161.

Green, D. R. *Racial and ethnic bias in test construction.* Monterey, Calif.: CTB/McGraw-Hill, 1971.

Green, D. R. What does it mean to say a test is biased? *Education and Urban Society,* 1975, *8,* 33–52.

Green, D. R. Problems of achievement tests in program evaluation. In M. J. Wargo & D. R. Green (Eds.), *Achievement testing of disadvantaged and minority students for educational program evaluation.* Monterey, Calif.: CTB/McGraw-Hill, 1978.

Green, D. R., & Draper, J. F. *Exploratory studies of bias in achievement tests.* Paper presented at the annual meeting of the American Psychological Association, Honolulu, September 1972. (ERIC Document Reproduction Service No. ED 070 794)

Gutkin, T. B. & Reynolds, C. R. Factorial similarity of the WISC-R for Anglos and Chicanos referred for psychological services. *Journal of School Psychology,* 1980, *18,* 34–39.

Haebara, T. *A method for investigating item bias using Birnbaum's three-parameter logistic model* (Iowa Testing Programs Occasional Papers, Number 25). Iowa City: Iowa Testing Programs, University of Iowa, December 1979.

Haebara, T. *Equating logistic ability scales by a weighted least square method* (Iowa Testing Programs Occasional Papers, Number 27). Iowa City: Iowa Testing Programs, University of Iowa, August 1980.

Houghton Mifflin. *Preliminary technical summary, second edition. K–12 Basic Skills Assessment Program.* Iowa City: Author, Spring 1979.

Humphry, B. J. *A review of data based on the performance of a sample of black students from southern colleges on the NTE Common Examinations.* Paper presented to the Consortium of Black Colleges, Houston, April 1979.

Hunter, R. V., & Slaughter, C. D. *ETS test sensitivity review process.* Princeton, N.J.: Educational Testing Service, 1980.

Huntley, R. M., & Plake, B. S. *Effect of selected item-writing practices on test performance: Can relevant grammatical cues result in flawed items?* Paper presented at the annual meeting of the American Educational Research Association, Boston, April 1980.

Jensen, A. R. How much can we boost IQ and scholastic achievement? *Harvard Educational Review,* 1969, *39,* 1–123.

Jensen, A. R. *Bias in mental testing.* New York: Free Press, 1980.

Jensen, M., & Beck, M. D. Gender balance analysis of the Metropolitan Achievement Tests, 1978 edition. *Measurement and Evaluation in Guidance,* 1979, *12,* 25–34.

Laksana, S. Application of analysis of variance approach and item characteristic curve approach for assessing item bias in the ITBS Form 7. (Doctoral dissertation, University of Iowa, 1979). *Dissertation Abstracts International,* 1979, *40,* 2615A. (University Microfilms No. 79-24, 495)

Laksana, S., & Coffman, W. E. *A comparison of an ANOVA approach and an ICC approach to assessing item bias in an achievement test* (Iowa Testing Programs Occasional Papers, Number 29). Iowa City, Iowa: Iowa Testing Programs, University of Iowa, September 1980.

Lord, F. M. A study of item bias, using item characteristic curve theory. In Y. H. Poortinga (Ed.), *Basic problems in cross-cultural psychology.* Amsterdam: Swets and Zeitlinger, 1977. Pp. 19–29.

Lord, F. M. *Applications of item response theory to practical testing problems.* Hillsdale, N.J.: Lawrence Erlbaum Associates, 1980.

Loyd, B. H. *An investigation of differential item performance by Anglo and Hispanic pupils.* Paper presented at the annual meeting of the American Educational Research Association, Boston, April 1980.

Madden, R., Gardner, E. F., Rudman, H. C., Karlsen, B., & Merwin, J. *Stanford Achievement Test* (Technical Data Report). New York: The Psychological Corporation, 1974.

Marco, G. L. Item characteristic curve solutions to three intractable testing problems. *Journal of Educational Measurement,* 1977, *14,* 139–160.

McGraw-Hill. *Recommended guidelines for multiethnic publishing in McGraw-Hill Book Company publications.* New York: Author, 1968.

McGraw-Hill. *Guidelines for equal treatment of the sexes in McGraw-Hill Book Company publications.* New York: Author, 1974.

McGraw-Hill. *Recommended guidelines for multiethnic publishing in McGraw-Hill Book Company publications.* New York: Author, 1974.

McGraw-Hill. *Guidelines for fair representation of disabled people in McGraw-Hill Book Company publications.* New York: Author, 1980.

Medley, D. M., & Quirk, T. J. *Race and subject matter influences on performance on general education items of the National Teacher Examinations* (ETS Research Bulletin 72-43). Princeton, N.J.: Educational Testing Service, 1972.

Ozenne, D. G., Van Gelder, N. C., & Cohen, A. J. *Achievement test restandardization: Emergency School Aid Act National Evaluation.* Santa Monica, Calif.: System

Development Corporation, 1974. (ERIC Document Reproduction Service No. ED 101 017)

Pintner, R. *Intelligence testing.* New York: Holt, 1923.

Plake, B. S. The comparability of equal raw scores for children at different grade levels: An issue in "out-of-level" testing. (Doctoral dissertation, University of Iowa, 1976). *Dissertation Abstracts International,* 1977, *37,* 7709A. (University Microfilms No. 77-13, 125)

Potthoff, R. F. *Statistical aspects of the problem of biases in psychological tests* (Institute of Statistics Mimeo Series No. 479). Chapel Hill, N.C.: Department of Statistics, University of North Carolina, 1966.

Qualls, A. L. Black and white teacher ratings of elementary achievement test items for potential race favoritism. Unpublished master's thesis, University of Iowa, 1980.

Reschly, D. L., & Reschly, J. E. Validity of WISC-R factor scores in predicting achievement and attention for four sociocultural groups. *Journal of School Psychology,* 1979, *17,* 355–361.

Reynolds, C. R., & Hartlage, L. Comparison of WISC and WISC-R regression lines for academic prediction with black and with white referred children. *Journal of Consulting and Clinical Psychology,* 1979, *47,* 589–591.

Rudner, L. M. *An approach to biased item identification using latent trait measurement theory.* Paper presented at the annual meeting of the American Educational Research Association, New York, April 1977.

Rusinah bt. Joned. A comparison of the performance of blacks and whites and of males and females on the items of the Cognitive Abilities Test, Form 3. Unpublished master's thesis, University of Iowa, 1980.

Sandoval, J. The WISC-R and internal evidence of test bias with minority groups. *Journal of Consulting and Clinical Psychology,* 1979, *47,* 919–927.

Sandoval, J., & Miille, M.P.W. Accuracy of judgments of WISC-R item difficulty for minority groups. *Journal of Consulting and Clinical Psychology,* 1980, *48,* 249–253.

Scheuneman, J. D. *A new method of assessing bias in test items.* Paper presented at the annual meeting of the American Educational Research Association, Washington, D.C., April 1975. (ERIC Document Reproduction Service No. ED 106 359)

Scheuneman, J. D. *Validating a procedure for assessing bias in test items in the absence of an outside criterion.* Paper presented at the annual meeting of the American Educational Research Association, San Francisco, April 1976.

Scheuneman, J. D. Ethnic group bias in intelligence tests. In S. W. Lundsteen (Ed.), *Cultural factors in learning and instruction.* New York: ERIC Clearinghouse on Urban Education, Diversity Series, Number 56, 1978. Pp. 65–77.

Schmeiser, C. B. *Analysis of the impact of skill category on the performance of black and white examinees on black and white English test content.* Paper presented at the annual meeting of the American Educational Research Association, Boston, April 1980.

Schmeiser, C. B., & Ferguson, R. L. Performance of black and white students on test materials containing content based on black and white cultures. *Journal of Educational Measurement,* 1978, *15,* 201–211.

Science Research Associates. *Fairness in educational materials: Exploring the issues.* Chicago: Author, 1976.

Science Research Associates. *Technical report #1: SRA Achievement Series* (1978 edition). Chicago: Author, 1978.

Science Research Associates. *Technical report #1: Addendum for fall 1978 standardization: SRA Achievement Series* (1978 edition). Chicago: Author, 1979.

Science Research Associates. *Technical report #3: SRA Achievement Series* (1978 edition). Chicago: Author, 1980.

Sinnott, L. T. *Differences in item performance across groups* (ETS Research Report 80-19). Princeton, N.J.: Educational Testing Service, 1980.

Sommer, J. Response to R. L. Williams. *Counseling Psychologist,* 1970, *2,* 92.

Spencer, T. L. An investigation of the National Teacher Examinations for bias with respect to black candidates. Unpublished doctoral dissertation, University of Colorado, 1972.

Strassberg-Rosenberg, B., & Donlon, T. F. *Content influences on sex differences in performance on aptitude tests.* Paper presented at the annual meeting of the National Council on Measurement in Education, Washington, D.C., April 1975.

Stricker, L. J. *A new index of differential subgroup performance: Application to the GRE Aptitude Test* (GRE Board Professional Report GREB No. 78-7P; ETS Research Report 81-13). Princeton, N.J.: Educational Testing Service, 1981.

Sullivan, E. T., Clark, W. W. & Tiegs, E. W. *Short Form Test of Academic Aptitude: Test coordinator's handbook and guide to interpretation.* Monterey, Calif.: CTB/McGraw Hill, 1971.

Swineford, F. Comparisons of black candidates and Chicano candidates with white candidates (Report No. LSAC-72-6). In Law School Admission Council, *Reports of LSAC sponsored research: Volume II, 1970-1974.* Princeton, N.J.: Law School Admission Council, 1976.

The Psychological Corporation. *Metropolitan Achievement Tests* (Special Report Number 15). New York: Author, 1978. (a)

The Psychological Corporation. *Metropolitan Achievement Tests* (Special Report Number 16). New York: Author, 1978. (b)

Thorndike, R. L. (Ed.). *Educational measurement* (2nd ed.). Washington, D.C.: American Council on Education, 1971.

Tyler, R. W., & White, S. H. *Testing, teaching and learning* (Report of Conference on Testing). Washington, D.C.: National Institute of Education, 1979.

Veale, J. R., & Foreman, D. I. *Cultural variation in criterion referenced tests: A global item analysis.* Paper presented at the annual meeting of the American Educational Research Association, San Francisco, April 1976.

Wightman, L. E. Law School Admission Test: Comparisons of Canadian candidates with non-Canadian candidates (Report No. LSAC-76-5). In Law School Admission Council, *Reports of LSAC sponsored research: Volume III, 1975-1977.* Princeton, N.J.: Law School Admission Council, 1977.

Williams, R. L. Black pride, academic relevance and individual achievement. *Counseling Psychologist,* 1970, *2,* 18-22. (a)

Williams, R. L. Danger: Testing and dehumanizing Black children. *Clinical Child Psychology Newsletter,* 1970, *9,* 5-6. (b)

Wood, RL, Wingersky, M. S., & Lord, F. M. *LOGIST: A computer program for estimating examinee ability and item characteristic curve parameters* (ETS Research Memorandum 76-6). Princeton, N.J.: Educational Testing Service, 1976.

BIOGRAPHICAL NOTES

WILLIAM H. ANGOFF is Distinguished Research Scientist and Executive Director for Technical Development at Educational Testing Service in Princeton, New Jersey. He received his Ph.D. degree from Purdue University in 1948. Since then, he has served in a variety of positions at ETS in the Statistical Analysis Division, Division of Analytical Studies and Services, College Board Division, and Developmental Research Division. Dr. Angoff is a Fellow of the American Psychological Association, American Educational Research Association, and American Association for the Advancement of Science. His research on test score equating and test standardization generally, test bias, cultural differences, and examinee cheating has appeared in numerous journals, books, and monographs.

RONALD A. BERK is Associate Professor of Education and Director of the Johns Hopkins University National Symposium on Educational Research (NSER). He received his Ph.D. degree from the University of Maryland in 1973. Prior to assuming a teaching position at Johns Hopkins, he taught elementary school in the District of Columbia (1968–72) and served as an evaluator in the Montgomery County (Md.) School System (1973–76). Dr. Berk has developed over 60 tests and scales and has published more than 40 articles in psychometrics, evaluation, and computer applications. He has edited two state-of-the-art books that were based on the first two NSERs and has also been a reviewer for several journals and publishing companies.

LOIS E. BURRILL is Manager of Information and Advisory Services at The Psychological Corporation. She received her Ph.D. degree from Fordham University in 1981. Previously, she taught social studies and served as registrar and testing coordinator at the Barnard School for Girls in New York (1959-63), and was Professional Assistant for Educational Relations at Educational Testing Service (1964-65). Since then, Dr. Burrill has held the positions of Test Editor (1965-71), Staff Associate (1971-73), and Assistant Manager of Information and Advisory Services (1973-77) in the Test Department, Harcourt Brace Jovanovich, reorganized as The Psychological Corporation beginning in 1976. She was also associated with the Division of Urban Education at Harcourt (1970-71). Her research interests include item writing procedures, criterion-referenced measurement, item bias, and latent trait theory. She was also chairperson of the 1976 annual convention of the National Council on Measurement in Education in San Francisco.

SYDELL T. CARLTON is Staff Associate in the Office of Program Planning at Educational Testing Service. She received her M.A. degree from Indiana University in 1959.

Previously, she was Examiner in Test Development, Higher Education and Career Programs Division (1972–80), and Test Development Coordinator for the Law School Admission Test (1973–80) at ETS. Ms. Carlton has also taught English at Indiana University and Rider College (1974–present). She has coauthored a variety of technical manuals, reports, and textbooks published by ETS and Harcourt Brace Jovanovich.

WILLIAM E. COFFMAN is E. F. Lindquist Emeritus Professor of Education and former Director of the Iowa Testing Programs at the University of Iowa. He received his Ed.D. degree from Teachers College, Columbia University in 1949. Prior to joining the faculty of the University of Iowa in 1969, Dr. Coffman taught junior and senior high school English, mathematics, and science in West Virginia (1934–37), was an elementary–junior high school principal (1937–44), and served in a variety of positions at ETS (1952–69), beginning as Assistant Director of Test Development and ending as Research Advisor for the Developmental Research Division. He has also taught at Oklahoma State University, Rutgers University, and Syracuse University. Dr. Coffman is a past president of the National Council on Measurement in Education (1972) and a Fellow of the American Psychological Association (Divisions 5 and 15). His more than 60 journal articles, chapters, book reviews, and test reviews have dealt with numerous aspects of standardized testing and psychometric theory, including cultural factors, sex differences, and test bias.

DONALD ROSS GREEN is Director of Research and Senior Research Psychologist at CTB/McGraw-Hill in Monterey, California. He received his Ph.D. degree from the University of California at Berkeley in 1958. Prior to joining CTB/McGraw-Hill in 1967, Dr. Green was an instructor in mathematics in Pennsylvania (1948–50), a statistician for the Cancer Research Institute at the University of California Medical School (1953–56), and an Associate Professor of Education and Psychology at Emory University (1957–67). He has authored numerous articles, book chapters, books, and CTB technical bulletins on test bias, and recently coedited the volume *Achievement Testing of Disadvantaged and Minority Students for Educational Program Evaluation* (1978), published by CTB/McGraw-Hill.

FANNIE A. HANDRICK is Director of the Test Development Department, Assessment Programs Area, at The American College Testing Program in Iowa City. She received her Ed.D. degree from Harvard University in 1967. Before joining ACT in 1976, Dr. Handrick held a variety of positions including Research Assistant and Consultant for the School and University Program for Research and Development at Harvard University (1958–68), Editor and Program Director at ETS (1968–75), and staff member of the Planning, Research, and Evaluation Division of the Delaware Department of Public Instruction (1975–76). She has also authored or coauthored several articles in journals such as the *Journal of Experimental Psychology* and *American Psychologist*.

GAIL H. IRONSON is Assistant Professor of Psychology at the University of South Florida. She received her Ph.D. degree from the University of Wisconsin in 1977. Dr. Ironson has been an industrial consultant for a variety of organizations (1978–present) and a measurement/statistical consultant for the Laboratory of Experimental Design, University of Wisconsin (1973–75), and Testing and Evaluation Services in Madison, Wisconsin (1977), and for numerous legal firms in the area of employment discrimination in Georgia and Florida (1979–present). Most of her journal articles have dealt with item bias, selection bias, and latent trait theory. She has also been a reviewer for several research, measurement, and statistics journals, conducted a workshop on latent trait theory at the 1979 American Psychological Association Convention, and serves as a member of the American Psychological Association Committee on Psychological Tests and Assessment.

JOANNE M. LENKE is Assistant Director of the Measurement Division at The Psychological Corporation. She received her Ph.D. degree from Syracuse University in 1968. Prior to joining The Psychological Corporation in 1967, Dr. Lenke taught mathematics in the Evanston, Illinois, School System (1960–63) and was Research Assistant for the Syracuse Board of Education (1964–65). Her publications and recent research have concentrated on the predictive validity of particular tests and applications of the Rasch model to test development. She also has served as advisory editor of the *Journal of Educational Measurement*.

BRENDA H. LOYD is Assistant Director of Resident Programs, Research and Development Division, at The American College Testing Program. She received her Ph.D. degree from the University of Iowa in 1980. Dr. Loyd was an elementary and junior high school mathematics teacher in White Deer, Texas, (1975–76) and Special Research Assistant for the Iowa Testing Program (1976–80). She has also taught measurement at the University of Iowa. Her publications have focused on test score equating, sex bias, sex differences, and latent trait theory. Dr. Loyd was also a contributing author to the early primary and primary levels of the *Iowa Tests of Basic Skills* (1978 and 1979).

GARY L. MARCO is Director of Statistical Analysis of the College Board Programs Division at Educational Testing Service. He received his Ph.D. degree from the University of Illinois in 1966. Prior to joining ETS in 1964, he was a junior and senior high school teacher in the Cedar Bluffs and Arlington, Nebraska, Public School Systems (1959–61). Dr. Marco has also been Project Director for the Chicago Title I evaluation (1967–71), the Day Care Policy Research Study (1972–73), and the multilevel *SAT*-M field testing (1974–76), and a member of a development project team responsible for designing alternative approaches for ETS testing programs to deal with test disclosure. Many of his numerous articles and research reports have focused on test score equating and latent trait models.

NAMBURY S. RAJU is Assistant Professor of Psychology at the Illinois Institute of Technology. He received his Ph.D. degree from the Institute in 1974. Prior to his current teaching position, he served in a variety of positions at Science Research Associates (1961–78) including Manager of the Research and Statistical Analysis Department, Senior Project Director of "Mastery: An Evaluation Tool," and Manager of the Educational Assessment Lab. Dr. Raju's publications in journals such as *Psychometrika* and *Educational and Psychological Measurement* have dealt with different issues in norm-referenced and criterion-referenced test reliability and multiple matrix sampling. He is also advisory editor of *Educational and Psychological Measurement*.

CECIL R. REYNOLDS is Associate Professor of Educational Psychology at Texas A & M University. He received his Ph.D. degree from the University of Georgia in 1978. Previously, Dr. Reynolds was Associate Director of the Buros Institute of Mental

Measurements and Associate Professor of Educational Psychology at the University of Nebraska (1978-81). He has authored or coauthored more than 65 journal articles, book chapters, and reviews on test bias, individual assessment, neuropsychology, and childhood emotional disturbance, and has coedited three books, including *Perspectives on Bias in Mental Testing* (Plenum, 1982). Dr. Reynolds is book review editor of *Clinical Neuropsychology* and serves on the editorial boards of *Journal of School Psychology*, *Psychology in the Schools*, *School Psychology Review*, *Educational and Psychological Measurement*, and *Special Education Assessment Matrix*.

JANICE DOWD SCHEUNEMAN is Director, Statistical Analysis, Elementary and Secondary School Programs at Educational Testing Service. She is also the current first vice president of the Eastern Educational Research Association. She received her Ph.D. degree from Indiana University in 1973. Prior to joining ETS, Dr. Scheuneman was Senior Research Associate at The Psychological Corporation (1976-78). She has published numerous articles and book chapters on item bias, sex differences, and latent trait theory and has served as a reviewer for several measurement and statistics journals.

CYNTHIA BOARD SCHMEISER is Assistant Vice President of Test Development, Research and Development Division, at The American College Testing Program. She received her Ph.D. degree from the University of Iowa in 1982. Before joining the ACT Program in 1973, she consulted for several nursing colleges in Iowa and served as Research Assistant for Evaluation and Examination Service at the University of Iowa. Dr. Schmeiser's recent publications in journals such as *Applied Psychological Measurement* and *Journal of Educational Measurement* have focused on the validity of the *ACT Assessment* Program and experimental approaches to determining racially biased test content.

LORRIE A. SHEPARD is Associate Professor of Education and Chairperson of the Evaluation Methodology Division at the University of Colorado at Boulder. She is also the current president of the National Council on Measurement in Education. She received her Ph.D. degree from the University in 1972. Previously, she was Research and Evaluation Specialist in the California State Department of Education (1972-74). Dr. Shepard has authored numerous articles and book chapters on criterion-referenced testing and, most recently, on item bias. She has also served as editor of *Journal of Educational Measurement* (1977-80) and as a frequent reviewer for several other journals.

CAROL KEHR TITTLE is Professor of Education at the University of North Carolina at Greensboro. She received her Ph.D. degree from The University of Chicago in 1956. Prior to her present teaching position, Dr. Tittle was Project Director at Science Research Associates (1965) and Associate Director of the Assessment and Research Centre in London (1968). She has also taught at Hunter College, Queens College, University of Georgia, and City University of New York. Dr. Tittle has published 10 books/monographs and more than 50 articles, chapters, reviews, and reports, especially on the topic of sex bias. She has also been a reviewer for half a dozen research and measurement journals and has been a member of the editorial board of *Sex Roles: A Journal of Research* since 1977.

INDEX